THE
KNIGHTS
TEMPLAR
ON TRIAL

THE KNIGHTS TEMPLAR ON TRIAL

The Trial of the Templars in the British Isles

1308-1311

HELEN J. NICHOLSON

First published 2009

The History Press
The Mill, Brimscombe Port
Stroud, Gloucestershire, GL5 2QG
www.thehistorypress.co.uk

British Library Cataloguing in Publication Data.
A catalogue record for this book is available from the British Library.

ISBN 978 0 7509 4681 0

Printed in Great Britain

Contents

Abbreviations

CCR	*Calendar of the Close Rolls preserved in the Public Record Office*
CDRI	*Calendar of Documents relating to Ireland, preserved in Her Majesty's Public Record Office*, ed. H.S. Sweetman *et al.*, 5 vols (London, 1875-86)
CPR	*Calendar of the Patent Rolls preserved in the Public Record Office*
Easson	D.E. Easson, *Medieval Religious Houses in Scotland, with an Appendix on the Houses in the Isle of Man* (London, 1957)
Gooder	Eileen Gooder, *Temple Balsall: the Warwickshire preceptory of the Templars and their fate* (Chichester, 1995)
G&H	Aubrey Gwynn and R.N. Hadcock, *Medieval Religious Houses in Ireland* (London, 1970)
IEP	*Irish Exchequer Payments, 1270–1446*, ed. Philomena Connolly (Dublin, 1998)
K&H	David Knowles and R. Neville Hadcock, *Medieval Religious Houses: England and Wales*, 2nd edn (Harlow, 1971)
Lees	Beatrice Lees, *Records of the Templars in England in the Twelfth Century: The Inquest of 1185 with illustrative Charters and Documents* (London, 1935)
L&K	*The Knights Hospitallers in England: Being the Report of Prior Philip de Thame to the Grand Master Elyan de Villanova for A.D. 1338*, ed. Lambert B. Larking, introduction by John Mitchell Kemble, Camden Society First Series, 65 (1867)

Lord	Evelyn Lord, *The Knights Templar in Britain* (London, 2002)
MacNiocaill	G. MacNiocaill, 'Documents relating to the Suppression of the Templars in Ireland', in *Analecta hibernica*, 24 (1967), pp. 183-226
MS A	Oxford, Bodleian Library, Bodley MS 454
MS B	London, British Library, Cotton MS Julius B xii
MS C	Vatican, Archivio Segreto Vaticano, MS Armarium XXXV 147
MS D	London, British Library, Cotton MS Otho B iii collated to British Library, Additional Manuscripts MS 5444
ODNB	*Oxford Dictionary of National Biography* (Oxford, 2004; online edn, May 2005)
Pevsner	Nikolaus Pevsner, general ed., *The Buildings of England* (Harmondsworth, 1951-)
Schottmüller	*Der Untergang des Templerordens mit urkundlichen und kritischen Beiträgen*, ed. Konrad Schottmüller, 2 vols (Berlin, 1887, repr. Vaduz, Liechtenstein, 1991), vol. 2
TNA:PRO	The National Archives of the UK: Public Record Office, at Kew, London.
VCH	*The Victoria History of the Counties of England*, ed. William Page, *et al.* (London, 1901–)
Wilkins	*Concilia Magnae Britanniae et Hiberniae*, ed. David Wilkins (London, 1737), vol. 2
Wood	Herbert Wood, 'The Templars in Ireland', in *Proceedings of the Royal Irish Academy*, section C, 25 (1906-1907), pp. 363-75

List of Illustrations

People
1. The tomb of King Edward II of England at Gloucester cathedral.
2. The tomb of the Templar Gioberto, now in Barletta museum.
3. The tomb of the Templar Simone di Quincy, now in Barletta museum.
4. The tomb of the Templar Gerard de Villers, at Villers-le-Temple, in Flanders.
5. A Templar altarpiece showing images of St Bernard, abbot of Clairvaux.

The Templars in the Holy Land
6. Athlit or Castle Pilgrim, from inland.
7. Ruad (Arwad) island, looking across the sea the short distance to Tortosa.
8. The site of the fortress of Maraclea, viewed from the shore.

The Templars in France
9. The Templars' tower at Paris.
10. The memorial to Jacques de Molay in Paris.

Templar property in the British Isles
11. The Templars' chapel at Balantrodoch (now Temple).
12. The chapel at Temple Balsall.
13. Bisham today, by the River Thames opposite Marlow.
14. The chapel at Temple Bruer.
15. Eagle, Lincolnshire.
16. Faxfleet farm, view from the sea wall.
17. The exterior of the modern farm at Foulbridge.
18. Garway church.
19. The exterior of New Temple Church, London.
20. The interior of the small room in Temple Church, London.
21. View of the small room from the chancel of Temple Church, London.

Maps

Preface

This book is based on my new edition of the trial proceedings against the Templars in the British Isles, which has been produced with the assistance of a British Academy/ Leverhulme Trust Senior Research Fellowship in 2003–4, and will be published in two volumes.

I have included here two appendices based on unpublished medieval records. The first is a list of all the Templars who were in the British Isles at the time of the arrests at the beginning of 1308. It is based on the information in the manuscripts of the trial proceedings, the records which the royal sheriffs made of the arrests, the accounts kept by the custodians of the Templars' lands, and information recorded in the bishops' registers. The second, based on the same sources, lists all the Templars' properties in the British Isles that were mentioned during the course of the trial proceedings, giving their location and explaining what happened to these properties after the Templars were dissolved: whether they passed to the Hospitallers, as the pope had ordered, or fell into other hands. Because many of these sources have not yet been published, much of this information will be completely new to most readers. I have included full references, so that readers may check the information here to the original documents. Unless otherwise stated in the notes, all translations from Latin and Old French are my own, and should not be used by other writers without acknowledgement.

I have incurred many debts in the research and writing of this study. My greatest debts are to the staff of the Bodleian Library, Oxford; the British Library, London; the Archivio Segreto Vaticano (Vatican Secret Archives); and The

National Archives: Public Record Office, London, for their assistance during my research. I am grateful to the following for permission to use unpublished material: Archivio Segreto Vaticano for permission to cite my transcription of MS Armarium XXXV 147; the librarian of Trinity College, Dublin, for permission to cite: 'The Memoranda Roll of the Irish Exchequer for 3 Edward II', 2 vols, ed. David Victor Craig, unpublished Ph.D thesis, University of Dublin, 1984, and Niav Gallagher, 'The mendicant orders and the wars of Ireland, Scotland and Wales, 1230–1415', unpublished Ph.D thesis, University of Dublin, 2005; Seymour Phillips of University College, Dublin, for allowing me to see Martin Messinger's unpublished M.Phil. thesis, 'The Trial of the Knights Templar in Ireland', University College Dublin, 1988; Maeve B. Callan for allowing me to use her unpublished Ph.D thesis, '"No such art in this land": Heresy and Witchcraft in Ireland, 1310–1360', Northwestern University, Evanston IL (2002); Simon Phillips for allowing me to refer to his unpublished Ph.D thesis, 'The Role of the Prior of St John in Late Medieval England, *c.* 1300–1540', University College Winchester (2005) and Clive Porro for allowing me to cite his unpublished paper on the trial of the Templars in Portugal.

I am also very grateful to the following for their assistance (in alphabetical order): Richard Armitage, Malcolm Barber, Jochen Burgtorf, Richard Copsey O. Carm., Paul Crawford, Alain Demurger, Peter Edbury, Alan Forey, Robin Frame, Beth Hartland, Balázs Major, Elizabeth Matthew, Colmán Ó Clabaigh OSB, José María Pérez de las Heras, Denys Pringle, John Walker and Jack Wallace. Many others who have given assistance on specific points are mentioned in the notes at the appropriate place. I offer my heartfelt thanks to the staff of the museums, archives, libraries and other institutions which supplied many of the pictures for this book and/or gave permission for them to be used here; a full list can be found in the list of plates. In addition, I thank the individuals who have allowed me to use their photographs: Jochen Burgtorf, Paul Crawford, Gawain and Nigel Nicholson and Denys Pringle. Regretfully, recent changes at the publishing company led to a late change in contractual terms which has meant that I have not been able to use all the pictures I initially hoped to use. The maps were produced by Nigel Nicholson, based on my own sketches.

My thanks are due to everyone who has given support to my project on the trial of the Templars in the British Isles over the last eight years. In particular, I thank Nigel and Gawain for their patience in seeing this book to publication.

Introduction

The trial of the Templars in France (1307–12) is notorious for cruel tortures which forced confessions, and the burning at the stake of those Templars who retracted their confessions. The Templars' trial in the British Isles was a much smaller-scale affair. There were only 144 Templars in the whole of the British Isles at the time of the arrests in early 1308, and rather fewer by July 1311 when the Order in Britain was dissolved. The confessions were unimpressive – only three Templars confessed to personal involvement in the most serious accusations: denial of Christ and spitting on the cross. No Templars were burned at the stake and there were no Templar curses. Several Templars went missing, most of whom later reappeared – two returned from Ireland, where they had been living openly and collecting government pensions alongside the Irish Templars. In 1311 the Templars were sent to monasteries to perform their penance and live on a small pension.

King Edward II of England (plate 1) was clearly unconvinced by the charges. Throughout the trial, he remained at a distance from proceedings. When the trial began in London in October 1309 he was in York, and he did not return to Westminster until the start of December, when the bulk of the initial investigations was complete. He left London again on 26 July 1310 and headed north for Scotland, which he reached in September, and remained in Scotland or on the Anglo-Scottish border until the beginning of August 1311, after the Templars in Britain had been disbanded.[1]

Past studies of the Templars' trial in the British Isles have been brief; there have been no in-depth analyses as have been produced on the trial in France, Aragon or Cyprus.[2] Yet the trial in the British Isles is as important in the Templars' history as the more spectacular and tragic events elsewhere. The Templars' testimonies from the British Isles show the distrust felt by the Templars in England towards Templars from France and the regional differences between those in different parts of England. The records also display the Scots' suspicion of anyone of English origin, and the dislike held by the Anglo-Irish in Ireland towards anyone from 'the other side of the sea' – that is, the Irish Sea.

The Templars in the British Isles did not produce much scandalous material, but non-Templars did. While some of these tales may contain a germ of truth, the main message that they carry is that Templar houses in the British Isles were not closed to outsiders and Templars were familiar travellers on the roads, guests at banquets and hosts to their varied friends. This is important, as it shows that the accusations of Templar secrecy were baseless.

This trial also gives us the opportunity to read in bulk the (admittedly, edited) views of people in the early fourteenth century who were not members of the high aristocracy or of the clergy. In the course of the trial, around 935 Templars,[3] most of them not of the knightly classes, were asked for details of their religious beliefs and their sex lives. While the Templars' testimonies from France are of dubious value because they were given as a result of torture or under fear of torture, those from the British Isles were, for the most part, given freely and offer some evidence of what these men saw as important in their religious faith. Interestingly, when questioned on their sex lives, the Templars in the British Isles all insisted that they avoided all sexual activity.

The trial in the British Isles also sheds valuable light on the value of the Templars' depositions in France. The government and leading churchmen in the British Isles quickly realised the political necessity of co-operating with the papacy to obtain a conviction. The Templars were repeatedly interrogated in an attempt to get some definite evidence for the Church Council that the pope had summoned to Vienne, in what is now southern France, to decide the case. The official transcript of the trial states that every effort was made to encourage, threaten, persuade or bully them into confessing.[4] The Templars had plenty of opportunity to explain themselves and to give a rational account for the charges against them, if there was a rational explanation – such as the so-called abuses in the admission ceremony being an obedience test, as some historians have suggested. Yet they did not. Until June 1311, when torture finally had some effect, the Templars in the British Isles refused to confess to any of the major charges. The obvious conclusion to draw is that there was no rational explanation for the charges against them, because the charges were false.

Finally, the trial of the Templars was the first large-scale heresy trial in the British Isles. Unlike other parts of western Europe, there had been very few charges of heresy in these islands in the twelfth and thirteenth centuries. Cathars who had come to England in the mid-twelfth century had been outlawed and perished in the winter cold; heretics who drew attention to themselves were arrested by the sheriff alongside other evildoers.[5] The papal inquisitors who arrived in Britain in autumn 1309 found that the kingdoms of England and Scotland lacked the machinery required to investigate heresy. Generally in Catholic Christian Europe heresy was wholly a matter for the Church, and torture was routinely used to extract confessions from suspects. In England, the sheriff was responsible for the arrest and custody of suspected heretics, and torture was not used as a means of interrogation. The inquisitors sent by the pope to conduct the trial in the British Isles were shocked by these differences in procedure, and suspected a plot by the king and his cronies to foil their efforts. It was largely because they could not find anyone prepared to torture the Templars in the British Isles that they were unable to get any substantial evidence against them. Not until the end of June 1311, after torture had been used, did three brothers in England produce confessions which allowed the Provincial Church Council at London to conclude the case.

Evidence for the Trial of the Templars in the British Isles

A great deal of evidence survives for the trial of the Templars in the British Isles, but much of it has not yet been published.

There are four manuscripts recording the trial proceedings against them. Two give a full version of the testimonies. One of these two is now in the Bodleian Library, Oxford (referred to in the notes to this book as MS A), while the other is a fragment in the British Library, London (MS B).[6] The other two manuscripts are summaries, of which one survives in the Vatican Archives (MS C), while the other was copied into a set of fourteenth-century annals about the city of London (MS D).[7] A summary of MS A was published by the Prussian historian David Wilkins in 1737,[8] but he left out a great deal of valuable material. The two summaries were published in the late nineteenth century.[9] I am currently completing a new, complete edition of all four manuscripts.[10]

The majority of studies on the trial of the Templars in the British Isles from the nineteenth century onwards have relied on David Wilkins' summarised edition. Only the American scholar Clarence Perkins, writing in the first decade of the twentieth century, used all the original manuscripts for his study of the trial in the British Isles; and he never published his findings in full.[11] As this book is based on the original manuscripts, even readers who are already familiar with the Templars' trial in the British Isles will find plenty of information which is new to them.

In addition to the records of the trial proceedings, the English government produced many documents relating to the trial, now preserved in the United Kingdom's National Archives at the Public Record Office in Kew, London. The correspondence between King Edward II and his officials regarding the Templars in individual counties, including the instructions to arrest the Templars, the sheriffs' inventories of the Templars' property at the time of the arrests, and royal grants of Templar lands to individuals, form a collection of small bundles of parchments of various size, filed with the exchequer records (E) under '142' – 'extents, investigations and valuations of lands forfeited to the Crown'. The royal keepers' accounts for the Templars' lands, as presented at the English exchequer at Easter and Michaelmas each year, are recorded in three large rolls of parchment, filed under E/358 – 'miscellaneous exchequer documents'.[12] Other government records for the years 1308–11 also contain a great deal of information about the Templars' lands and their produce.[13] Very little of this material has been published, although Eileen Gooder's study of Temple Balsall indicates where some material can be found, while Evelyn Lord has produced a summary of the Templar records in the Public Record Office.[14]

The Hospitallers, who inherited most of the Templars' lands in the British Isles, went to enormous lengths to recover all the former Templar property and rights. To help them in their struggle they kept detailed records. The cartulary (charter-collection) of the English Hospitallers is preserved in London in the British Library, MS Cotton Nero E vi.[15]

Many English episcopal registers from this period survive and have been published, although the register from the diocese of Lincoln has not.[16] There are also a number of contemporary or near-contemporary chronicles that refer to the trial in the British Isles.[17] The most useful of these, written by a contemporary of events, is in the continuation of the chronicle of Walter of Guisborough (formerly known as Walter of Hemingburgh). Walter stopped writing in 1305; this later section was possibly written by a monk at Durham.[18]

The material for Ireland is sparser than that for England. Many of the medieval records of the Anglo-Irish administration in Ireland were destroyed in 1922 in an explosion at the Four Courts building in Dublin. However, some of the contemporary or post-trial evidence relating to the Templars' properties in Ireland had been published by Herbert Wood in 1906–7,[19] and some material survived outside Ireland. In 1967 G. MacNiocaill published some records of Templars' property in Ireland, which had been sent to King Edward II of England and are now in the Public Record Office at Kew.[20] Some of the exchequer documents produced by the Anglo-Irish government in Dublin have survived and are now being published.[21]

The evidence for Scotland is even sparser than for Ireland: as the Anglo-Scottish war was in progress, no Scottish government records relating to the trial of the Templars survive, and neither apparently do any relevant bishops' registers. The best guide to the Templars' properties in 1308 is the Hospitallers' rental of 1539–40, which includes many properties called 'Temple lands' but in some cases this may simply mean that they had 'Temple rights' of tenure and privileges of not paying certain dues.[22] It is clear that, although sources for the Templars' trial in the British Isles are abundant, much research remains to be done.

Notes

1 *The Itinerary of Edward II and his Household, 1307–1328*, ed. Elizabeth Hallam, List and Index Society 211 (London, 1984), pp. 52–4, 62–76.

2 The most important are: Clarence Perkins, 'The Trial of the Knights Templars in England', *English Historical Review*, 24 (1909), pp. 432–47; Anne Gilmour-Bryson, 'The London Templar Trial Testimony: "Truth", Myth or Fable?', in *A World Explored: Essays in Honour of Laurie Gardiner*, ed. Anne Gilmour-Bryson (Melbourne, Australia, 1993), pp. 44–61; Eileen Gooder, *Temple Balsall: The Warwickshire Preceptory of the Templars and their Fate* (Chichester, 1995; henceforth cited as 'Gooder'), pp. 87–129; J.S. Hamilton, 'Apocalypse Not: Edward II and the Suppression of the Templars', *Medieval Perspectives*, 12 (1997), pp. 90–100; Evelyn Lord, *The Knights Templar in Britain* (Harlow, 2002; henceforth cited as 'Lord'), pp. 191–203; Eileen Gooder, 'South Witham and the Templars. The Documentary Evidence', in *Excavations at a Templar Preceptory: South Witham, Lincolnshire, 1965–67*, ed. Philip Mayes (Leeds, 2002), pp. 80–95; Alan J. Forey, 'Ex-Templars in England', *Journal of Ecclesiastical History*, 53 (2002), pp. 18–37. For France, see: Malcolm Barber, *The Trial of the Templars*, 2nd edn (Cambridge, 2006); for Aragon, see: Alan Forey, *The Fall of the Templars in the Crown of Aragon* (Aldershot, 2001); for Cyprus, see: Anne Gilmour-Bryson, *The Trial of the Templars in Cyprus: A Complete English Edition* (Leiden, 1998).

3 Gilmour-Bryson, *Trial of the Templars in Cyprus*, p. 9.

4 Oxford, Bodleian Library, MS Bodley 454 (henceforth cited as MS A), folio 170r (published in *Concilia Magnae Britanniae et Hiberniae*, ed. David Wilkins, vol. 2 (London,

1737), p. 393; henceforth cited as 'Wilkins'); Clarence Perkins, 'The Trial of the Knights Templars in England', *English Historical Review*, 24 (1909), pp. 432–47: here p. 443.

5 *Heresies of the High Middle Ages: Selected Sources Translated and Annotated*, ed. Walter L. Wakefield and Austin P. Evans (New York, 1991), pp. 245–7; see also Matthew Paris, *Historia Anglorum*, ed. Frederic Madden, Rolls Series 44, 3 vols (London, 1866–9), vol. 2, p. 194; Frederick Pollock and Frederic William Maitland, *The History of English Law before the time of Edward I*, 2nd edn, vol. 2 (Cambridge, 1923), pp. 547–9.

6 London, British Library Cotton MS Julius B xii.

7 Vatican, Archivio Segreto Vaticano, MS Armarium XXXV 147; London, British Library, Cotton MS Otho B iii. This last was virtually destroyed in the Cotton fire of 1731; a copy survives in the British Library, Additional Manuscripts MS 5444.

8 Wilkins, pp. 329–93.

9 MS C by Konrad Schottmüller, *Der Untergang des Templerordens mit urkundlichen und kritischen Beiträgen*, 2 vols (Berlin, 1887, repr. Vaduz, Liechtenstein, 1991), vol. 2 (henceforth cited as 'Schottmüller'), pp. 78–102; MS D by William Stubbs, as *Chronicles of the Reigns of Edward I and Edward II, vol. 1: Annales Londonienses and Annales Paulini*, ed. William Stubbs, Rolls Series 76 (London, 1882), pp. 180–98.

10 *The Trial of the Templars in the British Isles, 1308–1311*, 2 vols (Aldershot, Hants., and Burlington, VT: Ashgate Publishing, forthcoming).

11 Perkins, 'Trial of the Knights Templars in England', based on his unpublished Ph.D. thesis, 'The history of the Knights Templars in England', Harvard University, 1908.

12 The National Archives: Public Record Office (TNA:PRO) E142/10–18 and 89–118, totalling 358 membranes; the keepers' accounts are at TNA:PRO E358/18–20, totalling 130 rolls.

13 For example, TNA:PRO E368/78 and E368/79 are the lord treasurer's remembrancer: memoranda rolls for Michaelmas 1307 to Trinity 1309. Some material from the government records was published in: *Foedera, conventiones, literæ, et cujuscunque generis acta publica, inter reges Angliæ*, ed. Thomas Rymer (London, 1704–1717), revised by Robert Sanderson, Adam Clarke and Frederic Holbrooke, 4 vols in 7 (London, 1816–69), vol. 2, pt 1; some material has been summarised in: *Calendar of the Close Rolls preserved in the Public Record Office, prepared under the Superintendence of the Deputy Keeper of the Records* (henceforth cited as CCR) *Edward II, AD 1307–1313* (London, 1892); *Calendar of the Patent Rolls preserved in the Public Record Office, prepared under the Superintendence of the Deputy Keeper of the Records* (henceforth cited as CPR) *Edward II, AD 1307–1313* (London, 1894).

14 Gooder, pp. 147–50, 156–61; Lord, pp. 238–9. Material for some specific areas has been published, for example, P.M. Ryan, 'Cressing Temple: its History from Documentary Sources', in *Cressing Temple: A Templar and Hospitaller Manor in Essex*, ed. D.D. Andrews (Chelmsford, 1993), pp. 11–24; *Victoria County History* (henceforth cited as VCH), *Leicester*, ed. W. Page, W.G. Hoskins *et al*, vol. 2, pp. 32, 172–3; *VCH, Cambridge and the Isle of Ely*, ed. L.F. Salzman *et al.*, vol. 10, p. 308. Selections have been published in, for example, 'Original Documents Relating to the Knights Templars', in *The Gentleman's Magazine and Historical Review*, new series 3 (1857), pp. 273–80, 519–26; and 'Inventory seized by the Sheriffs of London of Templars and their goods seized in the Temple Church and Temple, London', in T.H. Baylis, *The Temple Church and Chapel of St. Ann, etc., An Historical Record and Guide* (London, 1893), pp. 131–46.

15 Michael Gervers has published the records relating to Essex: Michael Gervers, *The Hospitaller Cartulary in the British Library (Cotton MS Nero E vi)* (Toronto, 1981); *The Cartulary of the Knights of St. John of Jerusalem in England. Secunda Camera: Essex*, ed. Michael

Gervers (Oxford, 1982), pp. 52–6, nos 83–5 (London, British Library, Cotton MS Nero
E vi, fols 302v–304); *The Cartulary of the Knights of St. John of Jerusalem in England, part 2.
Prima Camera: Essex*, ed. Michael Gervers (Oxford, 1996), pp. 39–42, no. 30 (Cotton MS
Nero E vi, fols 105–106); see also *Records of the Templars in England in the Twelfth Century: the
Inquest of 1185 with Illustrative Charters and Documents*, ed. Beatrice A. Lees (London, 1935;
henceforth cited as 'Lees'), pp. lxxxix, 171–2 (Cotton MS Nero E vi, fols 56v–57r).

16 *Calendar of the Register of John de Drokensford, Bishop of Bath and Wells (A.D. 1309–1329)*, ed.
E. Hobhouse, Somerset Record Society, 1 (1887); *Registrum Ricardi de Swinfield, episcopi
Herefordensis, A.D. MCCLXXXIII–MCCCXVII*, ed. W.W. Capes, Canterbury and York
Society, 6 (London, 1909); *Registrum Radulphi Baldock, Gilberti Segrave, Ricardi Newport et
Stephani Gravesend, episcoporum Londoniensium, A.D. MCCCIV–MCCCXXXVIII*, ed. R.C.
Fowler, Canterbury and York Society, 7 (London, 1911); *The Register of John de Halton,
Bishop of Carlisle, A.D. 1292–1324*, ed. W.N. Thompson, Canterbury and York Society,
12–13 (London, 1913); *The Register of Walter Reynolds, Bishop of Worcester, 1308–1313*, ed.
R.A. Wilson, Dugdale Society, 9 (London, 1928); *The Register of William Greenfield, Lord
Archbishop of York, 1306–1315*, ed. W. Brown and A.H. Thompson, Surtees Society, 145, 149,
151, 152, 153 (1931–40); *Registrum Simonis de Gandavo diocesis Saresbiriensis, A.D. 1297–1315*,
ed. C.T. Flower and M.C.B. Dawes, Canterbury and York Society, 40–41 (Oxford, 1934);
Registrum Henrici Woodlock, diocesis Wintoniensis AD 1305–1316, ed. Arthur Worthington
Goodman, Canterbury and York Society, 43 (London, 1940); *Registrum Roberti Winchelsey,
Cantuariensis Archepiscopi*, ed. Rose Graham, Canterbury and York Society, 51, 52 (Oxford,
1952–6); *Records of Antony Bek, Bishop and Patriarch, 1283–1311*, ed. C.M. Fraser, Surtees
Society, 162 (1957); *The Register of Walter Langton, Bishop of Coventry and Lichfield, 1296–
1321*, ed. J.B. Hughes, Canterbury and York Society, 91, 97 (Woodbridge, 2001–7).

17 *The Chronicle of Walter of Guisborough, previously edited as the Chronicle of Walter of
Hemingford or Hemingburgh*, ed. H. Rothwell, Camden Society, 3rd series, 89 (London,
1957); *Flores Historiarum*, ed. Henry Richards Luard, Rolls Series 95 (London, 1890),
vol. 3, pp. 143, 144–48 (Westminster manuscript); pp. 331–4 (Tintern manuscript); *Vita
Edwardi Secundi*, re-edited text with new introduction, new historical notes, and revised
translation based on that of N. Denholm-Young by Wendy R. Childs (Oxford, 2005),
pp. 80–1; *Continuatio Chronicarum Adæ Murimuth*, ed. Edward Maunde Thompson,
Rolls Series, 93 (London, 1889), pp. 13–17; *Chronicon Galfridi le Baker de Swynebroke*, ed.
Edward Maunde Thompson (Oxford, 1889), pp. 5–6.

18 John Taylor, 'Guisborough, Walter of (*fl. c.*1290–*c.*1305)', *Oxford Dictionary of National
Biography* (Oxford, 2004; henceforth cited as *ODNB*), vol. 24, pp. 316–17.

19 Herbert Wood, 'The Templars in Ireland', *Proceedings of the Royal Irish Academy*, section
C, 25 (1906–1907); henceforth cited as 'Wood', pp. 363–75.

20 G. MacNiocaill, 'Documents relating to the Suppression of the Templars in Ireland',
Analecta hibernica, 24 (1967); henceforth cited as 'MacNiocaill', pp. 183–226.

21 'The Memoranda Roll of the Irish Exchequer for 3 Edward II', 2 vols, ed. David Victor
Craig, unpublished Ph.D. thesis, University of Dublin, 1984; *Irish Exchequer Payments,
1270–1446*, ed. Philomena Connolly (Dublin, 1998; henceforth cited as *IEP*); Maeve
B. Callan, '"No such art in this land": Heresy and Witchcraft in Ireland, 1310–1360',
unpublished Ph.D. thesis, Northwestern University, Evanston IL (2002), p. 55 n. 133, cites
Philomena Connolly's forthcoming edition of the justiciary roll for 6–7 Edward II.

22 *The Knights of St. John of Jerusalem in Scotland*, ed. Ian B. Cowan, P.H.R. Mackay and
Alan Macquarrie, Scottish History Society 4th series, 19 (Edinburgh, 1983), pp. 11, 12,
14, 17–20, 25–6, 28–31, 35.

1

The Beginning of the
Trial of the Templars

The Order of the Temple was a religious–military institution originally
founded by a group of warriors in Jerusalem in the decades following the
First Crusade.[1] The function of this group was approved both by the king of
Jerusalem and by the patriarch (head of the Christian Church in the kingdom) at a Church Council at Nablūs in 1120. It was to protect Christian
pilgrims on the roads to the pilgrimage sites around Jerusalem, while its
members also helped to defend the territories that the crusaders had conquered. In January 1129, at a Church Council at Troyes in Champagne, in
what is now north-eastern France, the Templars were given papal approval
and acknowledgement as a formal religious Order, with an official uniform
or 'habit', and a rule of life. As members of a religious Order, the members
of the Order made three vows: to obey their superior officer, to avoid sexual
activity and to have no personal property. They became known as 'Templars'
after their headquarters in Jerusalem, which westerners believed had been
King Solomon's Temple but in fact was the Aqsa mosque, constructed from
the seventh century AD onwards.[2]

Western European Christians gave the Templars extensive gifts of land
and money and privileges (such as tax concessions and legal rights) to help
them in their work of fighting on behalf of Christendom, and the members
of the Order also traded and acted as government officials for the rulers
of western Christendom. On the frontier between Christian and Muslim
rulers in the Iberian Peninsula they conducted military operations, but elsewhere in Europe they lived a peaceful life, very similar to members of other

religious orders. For nearly two centuries the Templars were an everyday sight; they farmed their lands, lodged travellers in their houses and looked after the valuables of merchants and rulers. Their estates in Europe were divided into provinces, each administered by a grand commander, while the individual houses in each province were grouped into commander-ies, each under a commander (in Latin, a *preceptor*). Each province had an annual general meeting of commanders, known as a 'chapter meeting' – the traditional monastic term for house management meetings – at which their incomes were collected together to be forwarded to the East, business was discussed and problems resolved. The grand commanders were summoned less frequently to a general chapter meeting, which was generally held at the Order's headquarters in the Levant.

But although in the Iberian Peninsula their military operations alongside the Christian kings of the Peninsula were largely successful, in the Middle East – where they were facing increasingly well-organised, militarily effi-cient opponents – it became clear by the second half of the thirteenth century that even the military skills of the Templars and their sister military orders the Hospitallers and the Teutonic Knights could not protect the crusader states forever. The Latin (Catholic) Christians finally lost con-trol of Jerusalem in 1244, and the new capital of the kingdom, Acre, was conquered by al-Ashraf Khalīl, Mamluk sultan of Egypt, in May 1291. The Templars and the Hospitallers who survived the heroic final defence of Acre moved their headquarters to Cyprus and set about trying to organise a new crusade. They were still involved in fighting the Turks of Anatolia and the Mamluks in Syria, as well as the Muslim rulers of the kingdom of Granada in the south of the Iberian Peninsula. But various factors conspired to prevent their launching a new expedition to recover the territories in the Middle East.

Nearly two decades later, during the trial of the Templars in France, John Cenaudi, sergeant-brother and commander of Chalons-sur-Saône in the diocese of Clermont in the Auvergne, France, stated that he had taken part in a general chapter meeting which had taken place at Nicosia in Cyprus in the year which Acre fell, with 400 brothers present.[3] As there were not as many as 400 brothers on Cyprus, this must have included brothers from overseas. The obvious reason for assembling such a large meeting would be planning for a new crusade. Shortly after this meeting, the newly-elected Templar grand master Jacques de Molay travelled to the West to see the leader of Catholic Christendom, Pope Boniface VIII (1294–1303), and discuss the possibilities for a new crusade. Encouraged by the pope's support, he then went on to visit the kings of France (Philip IV) and England (Edward I). Edward I had begun his reign when he was on crusade to the East in 1271–2; Philip IV came from a long line of crusading kings. But as these two kings were currently at war against each other in Aquitaine they were not able to promise any military aid.

Jacques de Molay was in England between late 1293 and early summer 1294, where he presided over a provincial chapter meeting. He then moved on to the kingdom of Aragon, which he reached by the end of August 1294. He eventually returned to the East with promises and privileges, but no actual military aid.[4]

The Templars were still active in military affairs in the East, but on a small scale. At the start of the fourteenth century they maintained a garrison on the island of Arwad, called Ruad by the Franks, which is just off the coastal city of Tortosa (plate 7). But the island is too small to be defensible, and in October 1302 the naval forces of the Mamluk sultan of Egypt sacked the island and took the Templars there prisoner or killed them.[5] The scandal of this defeat clearly had a serious impact on the Order, as the grand commander of Ireland, Henry Danet, referred to it during the trial of the Templars in Ireland.[6]

Although no new crusade materialised, Jacques de Molay continued his planning. The Templars' operations continued as usual, with the grand commanders of the Order's provinces in western Europe being summoned to consult with the grand master and convent, while the official known as 'the visitor' travelled around the western provinces checking that high standards of discipline were being maintained. According to Brother William Middleton – one of the two Templars in Scotland in 1308 – Brother Hugh Peraud, the visitor, came to England when Brother William de la More, the grand commander of England, was out of the country meeting the grand master Jacques de Molay. Hugh Peraud removed some commanders from their posts and substituted others. This would have been in 1304.[7] As well as reorganising the management of the Order in England, Hugh Peraud apparently collected money in large quantities. During the trial of the Templars in Ireland, Brother Ralph of Bradley was asked about the duties of the visitor. He replied: 'that he has never seen the visitor, but he has heard tell from a great many brothers that he sells grain and timber and having accumulated money he transports it to overseas parts; and he does nothing else, as far as he has heard.'[8]

Pope Boniface VIII died in October 1303 after a serious dispute with King Philip IV of France, which saw the pope arrested by King Philip's leading minister Guillaume de Nogaret and members of the Colonna family, the pope's political enemies. The next pope, Benedict XI, died within a year. His successor was selected because he was acceptable both to the king of France and to his opponents. Bertrand de Got, who took the name Clement V, had been born in France; but he was not a direct subject of the king of France because he was from Gascony, which was the king of England's hereditary fief. Clement V was crowned pope at Lyon in what is now southern France on 14 November 1305. Preferring to avoid the factional disputes in Rome, Clement never went to the traditional papal home, but remained within what is now France.[9]

King Edward I of England died on 7 July 1307. Renowned across Europe for his military skills and courage and a patron of chivalry, he had long been a friend of the military religious Orders of the Temple and the Hospital. While he lived, the Templars could hope that he would sponsor a new crusade to the east; but Edward died en route to another military expedition to Scotland, with his latest crusading vow unfulfilled. King Philip IV of France might talk of crusades, but he had no money to launch one. Clearly no other European monarch was about to embark on such an enterprise.

The Beginning of the Trial of the Templars

Instead, by the summer of 1307, some monarchs of western Europe had decided that the Templars' property could be put to better use. Clive Porro has recently shown that on 18 August 1307 King Dinis of Portugal initiated legal proceedings against the Templars in his kingdom. He claimed from them certain lands which had been given to them by his ancestors, but (he said) the lands had been granted only temporarily because the Templars were in the king's service. Now he wanted those lands back.[10] In France, King Philip IV took far more drastic measures. On 13 October 1307 all the Templars within the kingdom of France were arrested on charges of heresy, and their property confiscated. The Templars were imprisoned and interrogated. They were told that witnesses had already told the pope and king about the heretical practices at the Templars' reception ceremonies, and that unless they confessed they would be killed. Philip's instructions to his officials were that torture should be used if necessary to obtain confessions.[11] If the Templars were found guilty of heresy, then the king could legally keep their property.

Philip needed money. His financial problems had already led to riots – notably in Paris in 1306, where the king himself had had to hide from the rioters in the Templars' tower (plate 9). But he could not simply take the money he needed from his subjects, because he had to abide by the law and precedent. The machinery of the heresy trial offered him a means of bypassing the law. He could show his subjects that he was an effective Christian ruler while at the same time resolving his financial problems.[12]

The success of the king's plan relied on the use of torture to extract confessions. Since 1252 the papacy had allowed torture to be used in the interrogation of heretics in order to obtain confessions, and it had become normal procedure when suspects refused to confess.[13] The most common form of torture used at this time was the *strappado*: the accused's hands were tied behind his or her back and attached to a rope which was thrown over a beam; the accused was hauled into the air and allowed to hang there, then lowered to the ground, then hauled into the air again. The rack was also used: this was a triangular frame on which the accused was tied, the ropes holding the accused were attached to a windlass, the windlass was turned and the ropes tightened until the accused's joints were dislocated. Lesser tortures included tying the accused's hands tightly to cut off the circulation of the blood, preventing the accused from sleeping, or simply starving the accused by keeping him or her on a diet of bread and water for several weeks.[14]

There were strict rules about the use of torture: it should not cause death or permanent injury, a medical expert should be present, and a notary had to keep a record of what was done.[15] Yet the Templars of France claimed that these procedures were not always followed during the trial of their Order. When the papal investigation into the Templars' affair in France got under way in 1309, the papal commissioners heard many cases of the misuse of torture. Bernard of Vado, a priest from Albi, told the papal commissioners that his feet had been rubbed with fat and then held in front of a fire, so that the skin of his toes burned, and a few days later two bones fell out of his feet.[16] John of Cormeilles, serving-brother, had lost four teeth through being tortured during his interrogation at Paris.[17] Other Templars had not suffered permanent physical injury, but had lied because of the torture.[18]

Against this background of torture and intimidation it is not surprising that out of 138 Templar testimonies which survive from the interrogations in Paris in October–November 1307, only four Templars did not immediately confess to the charges. Of ninety-four Templar testimonies which survive from other provinces of France in this period, the majority confessed to the charges.[19] However, a contemporary writer pointed out that thirty-six Templars in the Parisian house alone had died under torture rather than confess to the charges.[20] Apparently, the interrogators in France did not always record the testimonies of those who refused to confess.

King Philip IV had been successful in obtaining confessions, but he had stepped outside his own jurisdiction. The prosecution of heresy was not the responsibility of a secular ruler but a spiritual matter, and so the business of the Church. In August 1307, Pope Clement V had written to the king that when he first became pope in November 1305 he had heard rumours about heresy within the Order of the Temple, which he had been inclined to dismiss; but he had at last decided to launch an investigation. Now Clement was furious that Philip had gone ahead with his own enquiry without his authority or permission. However, the Templars in France had confessed to the charges of heresy, and even though those confessions had been obtained by force they could not simply be set aside. Again, as Clement was then staying near Poitiers, within the kingdom of France, his freedom to act against the French king was limited. Accepting Philip's actions as a fait accompli, on 22 November 1307 he sent out letters to the kings of Catholic Christendom, telling them to arrest and interrogate the Templars.[21]

King Edward II of England had already told his father-in-law-to-be what he thought about the charges against the Templars. Philip had sent Bernard Pelet, one of the original denouncers of the Templars, to England with details of the appalling heresies of which the Templars were accused. But Edward had replied that he was not prepared to believe the accusations, for the Templars had always faithfully served his ancestors and protected the Holy Land.[22] On 4 December 1307 he wrote on the same lines to the pope, to his allies King James II of Aragon and King Dinis of Portugal, and to his relatives, King Ferdinand of Castile and King Charles II of Naples.[23] Yet Edward did undertake to investigate the affair, and on 16 November 1307 he wrote to William de Dene, royal seneschal in Agen (the general area where the charges had originated), instructing him to come to Boulogne at Christmas to brief him about the Templars' case.[24]

In the long run Edward could not oppose the pope's commands, because in England his position was unstable. He owed vast sums of money, debts left to him from the wars of his father, King Edward I;[25] he was unpopular with his nobles, who despised his friendship with Piers Gaveston, a knight from Gascony,[26] and who believed that the gifts, favour and influence the young king gave to his friend would be better given to themselves; he was losing the war in Scotland against Robert Bruce, whom the pope had excommunicated, and he wanted to retain papal support on that front; and also he was due to marry King Philip IV of France's daughter Isabelle, a ceremony which took place at Boulogne in what is now northern France on 25 January 1308.[27]

King James II of Aragon and Albert of Habsburg, emperor-elect of Germany and Italy, were also sceptical,[28] but like Edward II they could not withstand events. But while these rulers set about organising the arrest of the Templars within their realms, Pope Clement V demanded that the French trial be put into the hands of the Church. Jacques de Molay and the other high dignitaries of the Templars in France then withdrew their confessions, claiming that they had confessed only out of fear of being tortured. In February 1308 Clement V called a halt to the trial.[29]

As he had done against Pope Boniface VIII, King Philip IV attempted to muster the support of the French Church and people behind him, attacking the pope's reputation and arguing that it had been his duty as a good Christian monarch to arrest the Templars. In early May 1308, Philip called representatives of the 'three estates' of his kingdom – the clergy, nobles and townspeople – to a meeting at Tours. Representatives went with the king to the pope at Poitiers to urge him to continue the trial.[30]

In June 1308 Clement V decided to hear the Templars' testimonies for himself. Seventy-two Templars were sent to Poitiers by King Philip IV, and the pope listened as they repeated the confessions that they had made to the king's interrogators.[31] After further discussion with King Philip, Clement agreed that the investigations against the Templars should continue, but that the bishops – who had always held primary responsibility for investigating heresy in their dioceses – should lead the investigations. Each bishop should be assisted by two canons (priests) of his cathedral church, two Dominican friars and two Franciscan friars.[32]

In August the pope sent three of his cardinals to Chinon to hear the confessions of the leading Templars then in France. The details of these confessions are now well known. A manuscript in the Vatican Archive containing a summary of them was published by Heinrich Finke in 1907, while in 2003 Barbara Frale published a more detailed record, known as 'the Chinon Parchment'. A facsimile version of that manuscript was published in 2007 in commemoration of the 700th anniversary of the trial of the Order.[33]

The Confessions at Chinon:
Testimonies, Torture and Truth

In August 1308 Pope Clement V sent out a series of papal bulls. One, which began with the words *Regnans in coelis* (reigning in Heaven), summoned a Church Council for 1 October 1310 to discuss the Templars' case. This council was to meet at Vienne, in the Rhône valley south of Lyon. A second bull, beginning *Deus, ulcionum dominus* (God, Lord of punishments), assigned the Templars' properties to the care of the Church authorities. The revenues were to be kept for the Holy Land. In a third, which began with the words *Faciens misericordiam* (acting mercifully), Pope Clement explained that the leading officials of the Temple in France – the grand master, the visitor and the grand commanders of Outremer (the Holy Land), Normandy and Aquitaine – had confessed to the charges against them, recanted and been absolved. The date on the bull is 12 August, but as the interrogations described were not actually completed until 20 August, the true date was probably over a week later.[34]

The pope did not actually set out the details of these testimonies in *Faciens misericordiam*, but the records of the proceedings published by Finke and by Frale show that the confessions were not as complete as *Faciens misericordiam* implies. None of these leading Templars confessed to all of the charges against their Order, and they claimed that if they had committed any of the alleged errors during their admission into the Order, they had done so in words only, not from the heart. None of them expressed any support for the alleged errors. Two claimed that they had already confessed their actions and had been absolved and given penance.[35] Apparently, the pope exaggerated the strength of the confessions to make the Templars appear to be worse heretics than these French brothers had admitted.

All the witnesses denied being threatened with torture and, when their confessions were read back to them, confirmed that they were correct. It was normal procedure in heretical investigations, when heretics confessed and abjured heresy, that they should state that their confession had been made freely and without coercion.[36] This was because, under Romano-canon law, a confession made under torture was not enough on its own to secure a conviction.[37] Some contemporaries of the trial of the Templars expressed doubts over the use of torture as a means of revealing the truth. In particular, the commentators who cast doubt on the confessions extracted during the trial of the Templars in the French king's dominions emphasised the fact that those confessions had been extracted through torture.[38] Professor Malcolm Barber has argued that in fact all the leading Templars mentioned in *Faciens misericordiam* had either been physically tortured or subjected to 'other methods of a less crude kind to wear down any resistance'.[39]

But did the use of torture during the French interrogations really invalidate the French Templars' confessions, or can torture do what its supporters claim: force the accused to tell the truth? Historians of the trial of the Templars do not agree. The majority of historians of the Templars and their trial – such as Malcolm Barber, Marian Melville, Norman Cohn, Peter Partner and Elena Bellomo – believe that confessions extracted under torture are not good legal evidence. But the eminent crusade historian Jonathan Riley-Smith has recently argued that the Templars were guilty as charged – while admitting 'torture seems to have been applied quite often' during the Templars' trial – basing his argument almost entirely on evidence acquired under torture or the threat of torture. In his recent revised history of the Templars, the French historian Alain Demurger has offered a more nuanced discussion, concluding that the charges represented an 'initiation test' of new recruits, but not that the Templars were heretics. Similar arguments have been advanced by Arnaud de la Croix and Barbara Frale. But if the 'confessions' were not true, these theories collapse.[40]

As Pope Clement V in *Faciens misericordiam* specifically stated that the Templar trial was dealing with heresies,[41] it would be reasonable to consider this trial in the context of other medieval heresy trials. John Arnold has argued that inquisitorial records from medieval heresy trials are a 'discourse of power', which cannot be regarded as objectively true; these records show the 'truth' which the inquisitors wished to impose on those under interrogation, not what those under interrogation actually believed.[42] In this case, the testimonies from the Templar trial tell us what the inquisitors believed about them, not what the Templars themselves believed. Again, James Given, considering the work of the inquisitors in the Languedoc area of southern France, summed up the trial of the Templars in France as 'the most famous example of the inquisitorial ability to bend truth to its needs ... the medieval inquisitors had perfected techniques by which the very fabric of reality could be altered.'[43] If the inquisitors were altering reality, the Templars' testimonies from France tell us nothing about the real Order.

Another aspect of the problem which modern historians of the Templars' trial could consider is the opinion of legal experts. Some argue that torture does sometimes gain useful information: 'it is hard to believe that it is always and everywhere ineffectual: if it were, we would not have to spend so much time debating it.'[44] According to this viewpoint, torture is justified in emergency situations. The counter-argument is that even if torture does produce information, it is impossible to know whether that information is reliable.[45] In a judgement published on 9 December 2005, the UK Law Lords ruled that evidence obtained by torture is inadmissible in UK courts. They stated that the common law rejects the use of torture, due to 'the inherent unreliability of the confessions or evidence so procured'.[46] In April 2008, the British courts refused to allow the deportation of terrorist suspects to countries in which evidence against them may have been extracted by torture, as they could not then receive a fair trial.[47]

If torture produces inherently unreliable information, the French Templars' recorded confessions cannot be relied on as a source of information about the internal life and organisation of the Templars in the early fourteenth century. These confessions contain much circumstantial detail which apparently offers additional insights into the Order,[48] and some Templars held to their confessions even when the papal commissioners gave them the opportunity of retracting them. Yet modern scientific research has revealed that these are characteristics of false, as well as true, confessions.

In the UK, the Runciman Report of 1993 considered the problem of false confessions which had 'led or contributed to serious miscarriages of justice'. The report referred to 'four distinct categories of false confession'. These have been summarised as:

'fantasy confessions' made by people suffering from severe mental problems which prevent them from distinguishing fact from reality; what may be termed 'diversionary confessions' made in the attempt to protect someone else from interrogation and prosecution; 'coerced-compliant confessions' made by those who desperately want to escape the stress caused by police interviews; and 'coerced-internalized confessions' made by the highly suggestible who, though entirely innocent and sometimes even physically incapable of having done what is alleged, nevertheless [come to believe that they have committed the crime].[49]

It would be an interesting exercise to attempt to allocate the confessions made by the French Templars to each of these categories.

The Runciman Report referred to the scientific research of Gisli H. Gudjonsson, a clinical psychologist, who worked alongside the late Dr Jim MacKeith, forensic psychiatrist, on the cases of the Guildford Four and the Birmingham Six – ten individuals convicted through false, forced confessions whose convictions were eventually quashed. Considering the problem of false confessions, Gudjonsson set out to discover how it could come about that 'suggestible innocent people may be led to believe that they are in fact guilty', and showed that even in modern western democracies legal interrogations can produce false confessions. In fact, in a significant minority of confessions which were later found to be false, the confessor actually confessed to a crime which had not taken place.[50] The fact that a great deal of circumstantial detail is included in the confession does not mean that it is more likely to be true. All the examples of false confessions discussed by Gudjonsson contained considerable circumstantial detail and were sufficient to lead to a conviction, yet turned out to be miscarriages of justice.[51] Gudjonsson also noted that a 'strong tendency to comply with people in authority, and language problems' could 'contribute in varying degrees' to an accused's ability to cope with interrogation.[52] Both these factors would have affected the Templars' ability to cope with interrogation, as they were trained to obey those in authority, while the charges against them and the record of their testimony were written in Latin, a language very few of them knew.[53]

Gudjonsson discussed how interrogators could quite unintentionally influence the responses given by those under interrogation. Simply by asking certain questions, interrogators shape the form of the response they expect from the accused.[54] In the same way, the fact that the French Templar confessions form 'a broad pattern' or that 'certain themes run through' the confessions[55] does not demonstrate that there was any truth to them, because the inquisitors worked together. From the 1240s, those involved in the investigation of heresy had kept registers of testimonies and compared notes with each other.[56] During the trial of the Templars, the inquisitors in England obtained from their French colleagues evidence from French Templar confessions, which they presented to the English Templars in an attempt to make them confess to similar things.[57] It is very likely that the inquisitors in France followed the same procedure, presenting Templars who were under interrogation in France with the confessions of their fellow-Templars and urging them to make similar confessions. The purpose of the interrogation was to obtain confirmation of the charges, rather than to obtain the truth; in effect, interrogators were directing those under interrogation to create a 'guilty' identity for themselves, even if that identity had little connection with actuality.[58]

A 'devil's advocate' might suggest that the Templars who confessed in France and elsewhere had not necessarily been tortured, for many of the French Templars told the papal commissioners that they had not. Yet some of these later admitted that they had in fact been tortured,[59] while at least one brother admitted that he had confessed at the simple threat of torture and without it actually having been applied.[60] Moreover, the definition of torture was not always clear: a Templar who did not confess during torture or immediately after but only after three weeks in prison on bread and water was recorded as having confessed 'of spontaneous free will without any force'.[61]

There were also other reasons why those who confessed as a result of torture might deny that torture had been the cause of their confession. As under Roman Law torture should normally be applied only to slaves and persons of low birth,[62] it was deeply demeaning for free men and especially for knights to have to admit to having been tortured, still more to admit to having been forced under torture to give false testimony.[63] As if in a desperate attempt to defend their self-esteem, some Templars told the papal commissioners at Poitiers that although they had confessed under torture, it was not the torture which had caused them to confess.[64]

All in all, because torture was permitted as a means of interrogation in the dominions of the king of France, no modern scholar can be confident that any Templar's confession in those dominions was voluntary and accurate – even if he himself claimed that it was. Modern scholarly study of inquisitorial procedure in other medieval heresy trials, set alongside modern expert legal opinion and rigorous scientific psychological studies, indicate that the French Templars' confessions do not prove their guilt. As these confessions formed the pope's justification for ordering the trial of the Templars in the

British Isles and throughout Europe, the whole basis of the trial was funda-
mentally flawed.

When they had confessed and abjured or 'sworn off' all heresy, the leading Templars in France were reconciled to the Church. They would then
have been given penance to perform. The fact that the pope absolved the
Templars does not mean that he thought that they were innocent of heresy,
or that their sins were insignificant.[65] In fact, absolution was normal procedure in heresy cases, but only after the accused had confessed, repented and
sworn to abandon all heresy.[66] A person accused of heresy who insisted on
maintaining his or her innocence could not be absolved; the accused had to
admit guilt before the Church could give absolution.

Faciens misericordiam shows that the pope regarded the Templars' confessed
crimes as extremely serious. The crimes, he said, were disgusting and shame-
ful, *orribilia et inhonesta*. He said nothing to support the modern theory that
the crimes were an initiation test. On the contrary, he stated that they were
a terrible offence which had to be fully investigated and eradicated, and
he gave instructions for investigations to proceed throughout the rest of
Christendom. He specified which bishops were to be involved in the trial,
which clergy he was sending to help them, and ordered that a Provincial
Council should assess the evidence and either absolve or condemn the
Templars. The *inquisitores pravitatis heretice* (investigators of heretical depravity) he sent to conduct the trial in England, Scotland, Ireland and Scandinavia
were Dieudonné, abbot of Lagny in the diocese of Paris, and Sicard de Vaur,
canon of Narbonne and papal chaplain. He also drew up a list of English
clergy who should act as judges, and stated that he had appointed separate
inquisitors to investigate the grand commander in England.[67] But although
the pope made these decisions in August 1308, his inquisitors did not arrive
in England until September 1309.

The Charges Against the Templars in the British Isles

The interrogations in the British Isles were based on a short list of around
eighty-eight charges against the Templars, which the pope devised for use
in episcopal inquiries, and which was also used in Aragon and Castile. A
longer list, comprising some 127 charges, was used in France by the papal

commissioners, in the Papal States, in Brindisi and in Cyprus.[68] The short list used in England contained the following charges:

1–4   When they were received into the Order, they were ordered by the receiving officer to deny Christ, and sometimes to deny the Blessed Virgin and all the saints.

5–8   The receivers told those who were being received that Christ is not true God, did not suffer to redeem the human race but for His crimes; and no one has any hope of finding salvation through Him.

9–13   The receivers made those whom they received spit on the cross and trample it with their feet. The Templars also urinated on the cross, and often did this on Good Friday.

14–15   To insult Christ and the Catholic Christian religion, they adored a cat.

16–19   They did not believe in the Eucharist, nor in the other sacraments of the Church.

20–23   As instructed by the receivers, the priests of the Order did not say the words of consecration of the body of Christ during the canon of the mass.

24–29   They believed that the grand master of the Order could absolve them from their sins, as could the other officers of the Order, many of whom were laymen. The grand master openly confessed that he himself had done this.

30–33   When brothers were received into the Order, the receiver and the one being received kissed on the mouth, the navel, the anus or at the base of the spine, and sometimes on the penis.

34   The receivers made those being received swear that they would not leave the Order.

35   New entrants into the Order were immediately regarded as fully professed.

36–37   The receptions of their brothers took place in secret; only other Templars were present.

38–39   Great suspicion had been developing generally for a long time against the Templars.

40–45   The receivers said to the brothers whom they were receiving that they could have sexual relations with each other. They themselves or many of them did this.

46–57	The Templars in each province had idols, which were heads, some with three faces, some one, and some had a human skull. They venerated these as if they were God.
58–61	They wound around or touched these idol heads with the cords that they tied around themselves over their shirt or skin. These cords were given to each of the brothers at his reception, and they were instructed to wear the cord as a belt at all times.
62–65	The Templars were habitually received like this. They did this devotedly, everywhere.
66–69	Those who did not wish to do the aforesaid things were killed or put in prison.
70–74	They had to swear not to reveal these things, nor discuss the method of their reception, even among themselves. Anyone who did so would be punished with death or prison.
75	They were told not to confess their sins to anyone except to other Templars.
76–77	The Templars failed to correct these errors, did not stop observing them, and did not leave the Order, although they could easily have done so.
78–79	The Templars swore to win advantage and gain for the Order by whatever means they could, lawful and unlawful. They did not regard this as a sin.
80–81	All and each of these things were well known among the Templars, and there was public talk, general opinion and rumour both among the Templars and outside the Order.
82–85	Many Templars, knights and priests and others, confessed on oath to these errors in the presence of the pope and the cardinals.
86–88	The inquisitors should ask each Templar the details of his reception: who received him, where, when, how, and who was present; whether he knew how or when these abuses began and why; whether he knew the whereabouts of the said heads or idols, and how they were transported; and anything else relevant.

The author has commented elsewhere on the charges against the Templars,[69] but some additional remarks and summary are useful here.

Charges 1–4: effectively stated that when the Templars joined the Order of the Temple they ceased to be Christians. The accusation of denying Christ was a standard one against heretics, as Malcolm Barber has shown.[70] Although some modern writers have suggested that this alleged procedure was intended to prepare new recruits for what would happen to them if they were captured by the Muslims, this explanation was not put forward by the leaders of the Templars during the trial. If this were the true explanation, why did none of them assert this in their defence? Instead, the Templars who confessed to this alleged denial all said that they denied with mouth only, not from the heart; and many said that they had later confessed the sin and had been absolved. This indicates that they did not regard such a deed as a simple matter of training, but that in their opinion it was a deeply offensive act. The fact that there was no official justification for such a procedure within the Order indicates that no such procedure existed.

Charges 5–8: the claim that Christ is a false prophet was not – as is sometimes argued – drawn from Muslim belief. Muslims regard Christ as a true prophet, who will return at the end of the world. Jews, on the other hand, condemned Christ as a false prophet who was executed for his sins, as is stated in the *Talmud*.[71] The early-fourteenth-century author of the Westminster continuation of Matthew Paris's *Flores Historiarum* ('highlights of history') stated that the Templars were accused of a mixture of 'pagan' (i.e. Muslim) and Jewish rites.[72] The Jews had been persecuted by King Philip IV of France, who levied heavy taxes on them in 1284, 1292 and 1303, and in 1306 had expelled them from his kingdom, seizing their property. He also pressured King Edward II of England to expel the Jews from Gascony.[73] So it is not surprising that the charges he brought against the Templars included accusing them of Jewish beliefs.

Charges 9–13: the charge of dishonouring Christ's cross was another standard accusation against enemies of the Christian faith, and so also against heretics. In the epic literature of the period and chronicles of the crusades the Muslims appeared spitting or urinating on the cross, or dragging it through the streets.[74] The Cathar heretics refused to venerate the cross because they did not believe that Christ had a physical body.[75]

Charges 14–15: 'adore' was the word used to describe a pious Christian's veneration of religious relics or an image of a saint. Since at least the early eleventh century, the accusation of worshipping a cat had been regularly brought against those accused of heresy in western Europe. In the inquisitor Bernard Gui's handbook about the investigation of heresy, written shortly after the trial of the Templars, he accused the Waldensian heretics of southern France and Italy of worshipping a cat.[76] The Waldensian's actual crime against the Church was that they insisted on preaching without an official licence from their bishop.

Charges 16–23: the charges of not believing in the sacraments of the Church, and not performing those sacraments correctly, were further accusations that the Templars were not true Catholic Christians. These charges not only attacked the Templars' own piety, but also destroyed one of their major sources of income. Many people had given money or land to the Order so that its priests would perform mass for their souls and the souls of their families; but if the Templars did not believe in the sacraments, these gifts had been for nothing. Malcolm Barber has also pointed out that as popular belief held that the devil could not look at the consecrated host, which became Christ's body during the service of the mass, then if the Templars would not look at it they must be in league with the devil. Certainly, two of the outside witnesses during the trial in Ireland alleged that the Templars would not look at the consecrated host, but kept their eyes downcast.[77]

Charges 24–29: indicated that laymen within the Order of the Temple had taken over the role of priests. In fact, the trial in the British Isles revealed that many of the Templars were not fully aware of the difference between sins on the one hand, which were committed against God, and faults on the other, which were committed against the Rule of the Order. But whereas the charge indicated that the Templars were deliberately flouting the distinction between priests and laymen, and making a mockery of the Church's sacraments, the evidence from the British Isles indicates that the problem was simply ignorance.

Charges 30–33: again concerned alleged abuses during the reception ceremony. This ceremony was never called 'an initiation', as many modern writers have named it; in the contemporary manuscripts it was always simply a *receptio*, a reception. Here the Templars were accused of sexual abuses, another standard charge against heretics – indeed, it had been a standard charge against religious deviants under the Roman Empire, although at that time those accused of sexual deviancy had been the early Christians and the Gnostic heretics.[78]

Charges 34–37: sought to explain how these abuses had remained unknown until now. Charge 34 stemmed from the fact that from their earliest days, the Templars – like other military religious orders – had had regulations preventing members from leaving without gaining formal permission from their superior.[79] Apart from the obvious military necessity of discouraging desertions, this was in fact a normal rule in a monastic Order. Sometimes monks and canons were allowed to leave their Order for a stricter Order if they obtained papal permission.[80] The problem for the Military Orders was that early on in their existence they had given up the monastic tradition of the novitiate.[81] The novitiate gave new members of a religious Order a year's trial period during which they could decide to leave the Order. If this probationary period were omitted, effectively they had no means of escape if they found that the Order was not suitable for them.[82] This in itself was an abuse, but the Church authorities were well aware of it, and so far had done nothing about it; and it was hardly a reason for closing down the Order. Charges 36 and 37 claimed that receptions took place in secret. These were the only charges which seem to have held some truth and for which the Templars were unable to supply a reasoned explanation.

Charges 38–9: claimed that there was public rumour about the alleged abuses, for it was admissible to use public reputation (*fama*) as evidence in a heresy trial if no better evidence was available.[83]

Charges 40–45: were further charges of sexual deviancy, which were standard charges against heretics or other religious deviants. The accusation was based on truth, but was a misrepresentation of the Order's real practices. Templars were actually told that if there was a shortage of beds – for example, when they were travelling – they would have to sleep two to a bed.[84]

Charges 46–57: were charges of idolatry. The Templars' alleged beliefs regarding their alleged idol or idols are those which Catholic Christians of this period habitually held regarding saints' relics, and, as the Templars did indeed possess the relics of various saints, it is possible that these charges were a distortion of their veneration of saints.[85] In the early fourteenth century the many-faced spiritual being was a relatively common image of horror or awe. The Holy Trinity could be depicted as a three-faced or three-headed man. Dante Alighieri described Lucifer as having three faces on his head, like a sort of 'Unholy Trinity', in Canto 34 of the Inferno in his *Divine Comedy*, which he was writing at the time of the trial of the Templars. Similarly, the Cathar heretics were accused of believing in a demon with four faces: a man, a bird, a fish and an animal.[86] The imagery of the four-faced spiritual being also appears in the Old Testament, with the four-winged, four-faced creatures or cherubim of the Book of Ezekiel, ch. 1 v. 5–10, whose faces (human, lion, ox, eagle) were interpreted in the Middle Ages as representing the four gospel writers of the New Testament.

Perhaps the original idea for the alleged idol was inspired by such a picture. Yet the Templars themselves could not agree over what the charge referred to,[87] and none of the Templars in the British Isles had seen any idol.

Charges 58–61: continued the theme of idolatry. The Cathar heretics were also accused of wearing cords, in their case as a sign of having received the *consolamentum*.[88] This group of charges also foreshadowed the later witchcraft trials: during the Kilkenny witchcraft trial in Ireland in the 1320s, William Outlaw in the diocese of Ossory was accused of wearing the devil's girdle.[89] Like the previous group of charges, this group was a misinterpretation of the truth. In accordance with their Rule, the Templars at all times wore a woollen cord around their waists, over their shirts, which was intended to keep their underclothes in place and ensure that their bodies were decently covered even when in bed, hence reminding them of their vow of chastity.[90] Some of the Templars testified during the course of the trial proceedings that they had touched their cords to certain holy objects, perhaps believing that the saintly power thus absorbed would help them to keep their vow of chastity.[91] Yet this religious devotion was not heretical. The practice was entirely in line with Catholic Christian practice of the time.

Charges 62–5: originally stated that these things took place at night (*de nocte*), but the scribe who copied the list of charges used in the English trial made a mistake, so the Templars were asked whether they did these things devotedly (*de vocte*). Again, heretics were normally depicted performing their evil deeds at night, when no one could see them.[92]

Charges 66–74: stated that the Templars were forbidden to discuss their reception ceremony with anyone, including other brothers of their Order, on pain of imprisonment or death. This was not in their rule, but remarks by some brothers in Ireland and Yorkshire indicate that in some areas the prohibition on discussing chapter business with anyone who had not been present also applied to reception ceremonies, which took place as part of a chapter meeting.[93] The accusation that some men had been murdered after joining the Order may have reflected resentment among friends and family of Templars who had gone to the East and simply disappeared, because they had died in battle or been captured by the Muslims. One English cleric developed this charge, stating that Templars were not buried like Christians.[94]

Charge 75: stated that they should not confess their sins to anyone except a priest of the Order. This was true, but the Templars' rule added 'if one is available'.[95] As the Order had relatively few priests, usually no priest would be available. A possible reason for the shortage of brother-priests was offered by the brother-priest William of Kilros, in Ireland: priests admitted to the Order remained at the rank they held when they were admitted, and could not be promoted.[96]

Charges 76–7: stated that the Templars had been aware of the abuses but had not attempted to correct them and had not left the Order to escape them. The list of charges used in Ireland, Castile and Aragon added that they had not informed holy Mother Church. If the allegations were true, this failure to act would prove that they had been willingly involved in the abuses.

Charges 78–9: accusing the Templars of acquiring property illegally, reflected criticism of the Order's vast accumulation of wealth in the west, and the inevitable legal claims by outsiders against some of their acquisitions.

Charges 80–1: returned to the allegation of public reputation as evidence of guilt.

Charges 82–5: referred to the confessions of the leading Templars in France in August 1308, as described in the so-called 'Chinon Parchment' and in the papal bull *Faciens misericordiam*.

Charges 86–8: asked for additional details about each Templar's reception into the Order (if this had not been covered under the first eight charges) and asked whether the Templars had any information about the supposed idols or the origin of the alleged abuses.

These were the charges on which the Templars in the British Isles were to be investigated. When the trial at last began – twenty months after the arrests, and two years after the initial interrogations in Paris – the interrogators collected evidence from 108 Templars in the British Isles. It is debateable what use modern scholars may make of this evidence. Although torture was not apparently used in Britain until June 1311, the interrogators stated that throughout the trial they used every possible means to obtain confessions,[97] indicating that the Templars' testimonies were made under pressure even if they were not extracted through the use of physical force. In addition, given the differences between the two versions of the testimonies preserved in MS A and B, and the fact that the notaries omitted anything which they did not consider relevant,[98] the records of the testimonies are clearly not a word-for-word record of what the Templars said.

That said, until torture was used, the Templars in the British Isles apparently resisted the inquisitors' urgings to produce an account of themselves which would fit the accusations against them. The inquisitors accused the

Templars of colluding to deny the charges. When they produced a summary of the Templars' testimonies which indicated that they were guilty on some charges, the Templars objected strenuously and declared their innocence.[99] Given that the Templars maintained their resistance to the inquisitors until tortured, the majority of the testimonies in the trial in the British Isles taken before that date probably did reflect what the Templars actually believed – although not necessarily official procedure, or the actual situation in the Order.

Notes

1 The standard history of the Order of the Temple in English is Malcolm Barber, *The New Knighthood. A History of the Order of the Temple* (Cambridge, 1994). See also Alain Demurger, *Les Templiers. Une chevalerie chrétienne au moyen âge* (Paris, 2005); Alan J. Forey, *The Military Orders. From the Twelfth to the Fourteenth Centuries* (Basingstoke, 1992); Helen J. Nicholson, *The Knights Templar: A New History* (Stroud, 2001).

2 On the Aqsa mosque in the Middle Ages, see Denys Pringle, *The Churches of the Crusader Kingdom of Jerusalem: a Corpus*, vol. 3, *The City of Jerusalem* (Cambridge, 2007), pp. 417-34.

3 Jules Michelet, *Le Procès des Templiers*, 2 vols (Paris, 1841-51), vol. 2, p. 139. On John Cenaudi's career in the Order of the Temple, see *Le Procès des Templiers d'Auvergne*, ed. Roger Sève and Anne-Marie Chagny-Sève (Paris, 1986), p. 278.

4 Marie Luise Bulst-Thiele, *Sacrae domus militiae Templi Hierosolimitani magistri: Untersuchungen zur Geschichte des Templerordrens 1118/9–1314* (Göttingen, 1974), p. 306 and notes 51, 52; Malcolm Barber, 'James of Molay, the Last Grand Master of the Temple', *Studia Monastica*, 14 (1972), pp. 91-124, here pp. 95-6, reprinted in his *Crusaders and Heretics, 12th–14th Centuries* (Aldershot, 1995), II; Barber, *New Knighthood*, pp. 290-95; Alain Demurger, *Jacques de Molay: le crépuscule des templiers* (Paris, 2002), p. 364; translated by Antonia Nevill as *The Last Templar: the Tragedy of Jacques de Molay, Last Grand Master of the Temple* (London, 2005).

5 See Paul Crawford, *The 'Templar of Tyre': Part III of the 'Deeds of the Cypriots'* (Aldershot, Hants and Burlington, VT, 2003), pp. 160-61, sections 635-38; *The Memoirs of a Syrian prince: Abu'l-Fidā, Sultan of Hamāh (672–732/1273–1331)*, trans. Peter M. Holt (Wiesbaden, 1983), pp. 12-17; or 'Resumé de l'histoire des croisades tiré des annales d'Abou 'l-Feda', in *Recueil des historiens des Croisades: historiens orientaux*, vol. 1 (Paris, 1872), p. 165.

6 MS A, fol. 139v; summarised at MS A, fol. 91r-v (Wilkins, p. 358).

7 MS A, fol. 157r (Wilkins, p. 381); *CCR, 1302–1307*, p. 208.

8 MS A, fols 144v-145r (Wilkins omits).

9 Barber, *Trial of the Templars*, 2nd edn, pp. 32-3; Sophia Menache, *Clement V* (Cambridge, 1998), pp. 11-30.

10 As explained by Clive Porro in his paper 'Reassessing the dissolution of the Templars: King Dinis and their suppression in Portugal', presented at the International Medieval Congresses at Kalamazoo, MI and at Leeds, England, in May and July 2007. I am very grateful to Clive Porro for allowing me to cite his unpublished research.

11 Barber, *Trial of the Templars*, 2nd edn, p. 68.

12 For the argument that Philip used the accusation of heresy against the Templars because it enabled him to escape the normal legal constraints on his actions, see James Given, 'Chasing Phantoms: Philip IV and the Fantastic', in *Heresy and the Persecuting Society in the Middle Ages: Essays on the Work of R.I. Moore*, ed. Michael Frassetto (Leiden, 2006), pp. 271–89.

13 Edward Peters, *Torture* (Oxford, 1985), pp. 50, 57-8, 65-6; Andrew P. Roach, *The Devil's World: Heresy and Society, 1100–1300* (Harlow, 2005), pp. 148-9; Barber, *Trial of the Templars*, 2nd edn, pp. 28-9; see also pp. 133-4. Roach points out that interrogators apparently used psychological torture more than physical torture. See also Robert Bartlett, *Trial by Fire and Water: The Medieval Judicial Ordeal* (Oxford, 1986), pp. 139-43, who argues that: 'it is reasonably clear that in the period 1200-1700 judicial torture fulfilled the same function as ordeals had done in the period 800-1200' (p. 142).

14 Barber, *Trial of the Templars*, 2nd edn, p. 71; Peters, *Torture*, p. 68.

15 Peters, *Torture*, p. 57.

16 Barber, *Trial of the Templars*, 2nd edn, p. 71; Michelet, *Procès*, vol. 1, p. 75.

17 Michelet, *Procès*, vol. 1, p. 521.

18 Michelet, *Procès*, vol. 2, pp. 13-14, 15, 19, 210. On the Templars' treatment, see also Jean Dunbabin, *Captivity and Imprisonment in Medieval Europe, 1000–1300* (Basingstoke, 2002), pp. 127-8.

19 Figures from Barber, *Trial of the Templars*, 2nd edn, p. 69.

20 'Lamentacio quedam pro Templariis', in C.R. Cheney, 'The Downfall of the Templars and a Letter in their Defence', in C.R. Cheney, *Medieval Texts and Studies* (Oxford, 1973), pp. 314-27: here p. 323.

21 For Pope Clement V and the trial of the Templars, see Sophia Menache, *Clement V* (Cambridge, 1998), pp. 205-46; here pp. 207, 208, 216; Barber, *Trial of the Templars*, 2nd edn, pp. 88-90.

22 Barber, *Trial of the Templars*, 2nd edn, pp. 65, 217-18 and p. 343 notes 1-5; Menache, *Clement V*, p. 212; MS A, fols 15v, 19v, 49r, 57r.

23 *Foedera*, ed. Rymer, vol. 2, pt 1, pp. 19-20.

24 *Gascon Rolls Preserved in the Public Record Office, 1307–1317*, ed. Yves Renouard under the supervision of Robert Fawtier (London, 1962), pp. xxv, 25-6, no. 3; Hamilton, 'Apocalypse Not', p. 93; Barber, *Trial of the Templars*, 2nd edn, p. 217.

25 Michael Prestwich estimates the debt at £200,000: 'Edward I (1239–1307)', *ODNB*, vol. 17, p. 817.

26 J.S. Hamilton, *Piers Gaveston, Earl of Cornwall 1307–1312: Politics and Patronage in the Reign of Edward II* (Detroit, MI and London, 1988), pp. 19-20, argues that far from being the son of a penniless common knight, Piers Gaveston's father was one of the '"leading barons" of Béarn' (quotation p. 19).

27 J.R.S. Phillips, 'Edward II (1284–1327)', *ODNB*, vol. 17, pp. 824-37; J.S. Hamilton, 'Gaveston, Piers, earl of Cornwall (d. 1312)', *ODNB*, vol. 21, pp. 654-6; on the pope's view of Robert Bruce, see Menache, *Clement V*, pp. 269-75; for Isabelle see John Carmi Parsons, 'Isabella (1295–1358)', in *ODNB*, vol. 29, pp. 419-23.

28 Menache, *Clement V*, p. 212.

29 Menache, *Clement V*, pp. 217-18; Barber, *Trial of the Templars*, 2nd edn, pp. 91-95.

30 Barber, *Trial of the Templars*, 2nd edn, pp. 95-116; Menache, *Clement V*, pp. 219-224; Sophia Menache, 'Contemporary Attitudes Concerning the Templars' Affair: Propaganda's Fiasco?', *Journal of Medieval History*, 8 (1982), pp. 135-47.

31 Barber, *Trial of the Templars*, 2nd edn, pp. 116-22; Menache, *Clement V*, pp. 224-5.

32 Barber, *Trial of the Templars*, 2nd edn, pp. 122-4. I am grateful to Dale R. Streeter for drawing this point to my attention.

33 Heinrich Finke, *Papsttum und Untergang des Templerordens*, 2 vols (Münster, 1907), vol. 2, pp. 324-9, no. 154; Barbara Frale, *Il Papato e il processo ai Templari* (Rome, 2003), pp. 198-219; the commemorative facsimile of these documents, *Processus contra Templarios*, was published by the Vatican's own publishers, Scrinium, on 25 October 2007.

34 Barber, *Trial of the Templars*, 2nd edn, pp. 125-6, 332, n. 34. For *Faciens misericordiam* itself see *Register of William Greenfield*, part 4, pp. 287-92; MS A, fols 1r-7r (Wilkins, pp. 329-331).

35 Finke, *Papsttum und Untergang*, vol. 2, pp. 324-9, no. 154; Frale, *Il Papato*, pp. 198-219.

36 See, for example, John H. Arnold, *Inquisition and Power: Catharism and the Confessing Subject in Medieval Languedoc* (Philadelphia, 2001), pp. 74, 94, 99.

37 Peters, *Torture*, p. 57.

38 Barber, *Trial of the Templars*, 2nd edn, pp. 92-4. The majority of the brothers in England stated that if Templars overseas had confessed, they had lied; some singled out confessions in France as unreliable: MS A, fols 73r, 75v; some specified that this was because torture had been used on them to force them to confess: MS A, fols 73v, 126v, 129r (twice), 131r, 133r. For an example of a heresy trial of 1299-1300 in which contemporaries doubted confessions obtained by torture, see James Given, 'Social Stress, Social Strain, and the Inquisitors of Medieval Langedoc', in *Christendom and its Discontents: Exclusion, Persecution and Rebellion, 1000–1500*, ed. Scott L. Waugh and Peter D. Diehl (Cambridge, 1996), pp. 67-85: here p. 80.

39 Barber, *Trial of the Templars*, 2nd edn, pp. 80-84: quotation from p. 80; see also Menache, *Clement V*, p. 215.

40 Barber, *Trial of the Templars*, 2nd edn, pp. 68, 69-72, 120, 133-7, 143-7, 150-1, 155, 160-1, 184, 192-6, 283; pp. 296-304, especially p. 304; Elena Bellomo, *The Templar Order in North-west Italy (1142–c. 1330)* (Leiden, 2008), p. 201; Jonathan Riley-Smith, 'Were the Templars Guilty?' in *The Medieval Crusade*, ed. Susan J. Ridyard (Woodbridge, 2004), pp. 107-24, quotation at p. 111: discussed by Barber, *Trial of the Templars*, 2nd edn, pp. 307-8. Riley-Smith, 'The Structures of the orders of the Temple and Hospital in *c.* 1291', in *Medieval Crusade*, ed. Ridyard, pp. 125-43, is also based almost entirely on evidence acquired under torture or the threat of torture. Alain Demurger, *Les Templiers*, pp. 489-94; Arnaud de la Croix, *L'Ordre du Temple et le reniement du Christ* (Paris, 2004); Barbara Frale, 'The Chinon Chart: Papal absolution to the last Templar, Master Jacques de Molay', *Journal of Medieval History*, 30 (2004), pp. 109-34.

41 'Hereses varias': MS A, fol. 4v; Wilkins, p. 329.

42 See Roach, *Devil's World*, p. 250; Arnold, *Inquisition and Power*, pp. 7-15, 76-8, etc.

43 James Given, 'The Inquisitors of Languedoc and the Medieval Technology of Power', *American Historical Review*, 94 (1989), pp. 336-59, here pp. 351-2. The matter is also discussed by Barber, *Trial of the Templars*, 2nd edn, pp. 308-9.

44 Richard A. Posner, 'Torture, Terrorism and Interrogation', in *Torture: A Collection*, ed. Sanford Levinson (Oxford, 2004), pp. 291-8, here p. 294; although he admits that torture is 'clumsy and inefficient' and has 'frequent inefficacy'.

45 Richard H. Weisberg, 'Loose Professionalism, or Why Lawyers take the Lead on Torture', in *Torture*, ed. Levinson, pp. 299-305; Andrew Sullivan, 'The Abolition of Torture', in ibid., pp. 317-27.

46 Decision of the UK House of Lords of 8 December 2005, published in *The Times* (London), p. 81, Friday 9 December 2005. The House of Lords is the final court of appeal within the UK.

47 'Osama bin Laden's "right-hand man" Abu Qatada wins deportation fight', *The Times*, 10 April 2008.

48 Riley-Smith, 'Were the Templars Guilty?', p. 118: 'I have been struck by … comments from witnesses which sound so circumstantial that they could hardly have been invented.'

49 Viscount Runciman of Doxford (chair), *Report on the Royal Commission on Criminal Justice*, Cm.2263 (London, 1993), p. 57, paras 31-2; for the summary of the four categories, see Steven Greer, 'Towards a Sociological Model of the Police Informant', *The British Journal of Sociology*, 46 (1995), pp. 509-27, here p. 524.

50 Gisli H. Gudjonsson, *The Psychology of Interrogations, Confessions and Testimony* (New York, 1992), esp. pp. 205-59, here pp. 208, 211; see the review by Peter N. Naish in *Journal of Psychophysiology*, 13 (2) (1999), pp. 126-7; see also the Obituary for Dr Jim MacKeith in *The Times*, Friday 10 August 2007, p. 57. See also *Forensic Psychology: A Guide to Practice*, ed. G.H. Gudjonsson and L.R.C. Haward (London, 1998), pp. 175-8.

51 Gudjonsson, *Psychology of Interrogations*, pp. 234-73.

52 Ibid., p. 259.

53 Obedience to authority was central to the Templars' discipline and effectiveness in their vocation: *La Règle du Temple*, ed. Henri de Curzon (Paris, 1886), sections 1, 39, 41, 92, 98, 233, 274-5, 313, 382, 661, 664, 667, 675; translated by J.M. Upton-Ward as *The Rule of the Templars: The French Text of the Rule of the Order of the Knights Templar* (Woodbridge, 1992), pp. 19, 29, 42, 44, 74, 81, 88, 104, 169-71. On the Templars' lack of education, see Alan Forey, 'Literary and Learning in the Military Orders during the Twelfth and Thirteenth Centuries', in *The Military Orders*, vol. 2: *Welfare and Warfare*, ed. Helen Nicholson (Aldershot, 1998), pp. 185-206.

54 For the Confait case, in which three youths were convicted of murder and then freed on appeal, see Gudjonsson, *Psychology of Interrogations*, pp. 239-40; see also p. 259 on information 'unwittingly communicated' to suspects by interrogators.

55 Riley-Smith, 'Were the Templars Guilty?', pp. 116, 118.

56 Roach, *The Devil's World*, pp. 139, 145.

57 See discussion below, chapter four.

58 Barber, *Trial of the Templars*, 2nd edn, p. 29; Arnold, *Inquisition and Power*, for example, pp. 11-12, 76-7, 93-98, 196-7, 213-4, 224-5.

59 See Barber, *Trial of the Templars*, 2nd edn, particularly pp. 69-72.

60 Schottmüller, p. 49.

61 Ibid., p. 65 and n. 4.

62 S.P. Scott, *The Civil Law*, vol. 15: *The Code of Justinian*, 2nd edn (Cincinnati, 1932, repr. New York, 1973), Bk 9, title 41 (pp. 66-70); Clyde Pharr, *The Theodosian Code and Novels and the Sirmondian Constitutions* (Princeton, 1952), Bk 9, ch. 35 (pp. 250-1).

63 Schottmüller, pp. 48, 49, 52.

64 Ibid., pp. 68, 69.

65 This is implied by Frale, 'The Chinon Chart'; and see her edition of the manuscript, *Il Papato*, pp. 198-219.

66 Bernard Hamilton, *The Albigensian Crusade*, Historical Association leaflet G. 85 (London, 1974), pp. 25-6; and see Bernard Gui's *Practica Inquisitionis Heretice Pravitatis*, ed. C. Douais (Paris, 1886), translated as *The Inquisitor's Guide: A Medieval Manual on Heretics*, trans. Janet Shirley (Welwyn Garden City, 2006), here pp. 153-73.

67 MS A, fol. 6v (Wilkins omits).

68 The short list of charges appears in MS A, fols 7r-8v (Wilkins, pp. 331-3); see also Alan Forey, *The Fall of the Templars in the Crown of Aragon* (Aldershot, 2001), pp. 79, 106-107 note 30; Gonzalo Martinez Diez, *Los Templarios en la Corona de Castilla* (Burgos, 1993), pp. 204-8 (my thanks to José María Pérez de las Heras for sending me a copy of this text). For the long list of 127 charges see Schottmüller, pp. 119-124; for discussion, see Barber, *Trial of the Templars*, 2nd edn, pp. 125-6, 133-5.

69 Nicholson, *Knights Templar: A New History*, pp. 207-17.

70 Barber, *Trial of the Templars*, 2nd edn, pp. 204-6.

71 *The Babylonian Talmud, Seder Nezikīin*, ed. I. Epstein: *Sanhedrin*, trans. Jacob Shachter and H. Freedman, vol. 1 (London, 1935), 43a, pp. 281-2.

72 *Flores Historiarum*, ed. Henry Richards Luard, Rolls Series 95 (London, 1890), vol. 3, p. 145.

73 Elizabeth M. Hallam and Judith Everard, *Capetian France, 987–1328*, 2nd edn (Harlow, 2001), pp. 378, 387.

74 See, for example, the incident in Albert of Aachen, *Historia Ierosolimitana: History of the Journey to Jerusalem*, ed. and trans. Susan Edgington (Oxford, 2007), Bk 6, ch. 8, pp. 414-15; *Itinerarium peregrinorum et gesta regis Ricardi*, ed. William Stubbs, vol. 1 of his *Chronicles and Memorials of the Reign of Richard I*, Rolls Series 38 (London, 1864), Bk 1, chs 10, 56; see also *Das Itinerarium peregrinorum. Eine zeitgenössische englische Chronik zum dritten Kreuzzug in ursprünglicher Gestatt*, ed. Hans E. Mayer, Schriften der Monumenta Germaniae Historica 18 (Stuttgart, 1962); translated as *Chronicle of the Third Crusade*, trans. Helen Nicholson (Aldershot, 1997), pp. 39, 110; *L'estoire de la guerre sainte: histoire en vers de la troisième croisade (1190–1192) par Ambroise*, ed. Gaston Paris (Paris, 1897), lines 3701-30; *The history of the Holy War: Ambroise's Estoire de la guerre sainte*, ed. Marianne Ailes and Malcolm Barber, 2 vols (Woodbridge, 2003), vol. 1, lines 3700-24; vol. 2, p. 84. See also Barber, *Trial of the Templars*, 2nd edn, p. 209; John Tolan, 'Muslims as Pagan Idolators in Chronicles of the First Crusade', in *Western Attitudes towards Islam*, ed. Michael Frassetto and David Blanks (New York, 1998); C. Meredith Jones, 'The Conventional Saracen of the *Chanson de Geste*', *Speculum*, 17 (1942), pp. 201-25; Matthew Bennet, 'First Crusaders' Images of Muslims: the Influence of Vernacular Poetry?' *Forum for Modern Language Studies*, 22.2 (1986), pp. 101-22.

75 Barber, *Trial of the Templars*, 2nd edn, p. 209.

76 Ibid., pp. 204-5; see Bernard Gui, *The Inquisitor's Guide*, p. 57.

77 Barber, *Trial of the Templars*, 2nd edn, p. 214; MS A, fols 151r, 153r (Wilkins, pp. 378, 379).

78 Barber, *Trial of the Templars*, 2nd edn, pp. 204-5; citing J.B. Russell, *Witchcraft in the Middle Ages* (Ithaca, NY, 1972), pp. 88-93.

79 Alan J. Forey, 'Desertions and Transfers from Military Orders (Twelfth to Early Fourteenth Centuries)', *Traditio*, 60 (2005), pp. 143-200: here pp. 143-5.

80 *Corpus Iuris Canonici, Pars Secunda: Decretalium Collectiones. Decretales Gregorii P. IX. Liber Sextus Decretalium*, ed. Emil Ludwig Richter and Emil Friedberg (Leipzig, 1881), Liber III, Titulus XXXI: de Regularibus and Transeuntibus ad religionem, cap. xviii, pp. 575-6. I am very grateful to Jennifer Halliday for this reference.

81 Alan J. Forey, 'Novitiate and Instruction in the Military Orders during the Twelfth and Thirteenth Centuries', *Speculum*, 61 (1986), pp. 1-17.

82 See *Decretales Gregorii IX*, Lib. III tit. XXXI de Regularibus, caps viii-ix, xvi, pp. 572-5. I am very grateful to Jennifer Halliday for this reference.

83 Paul Hyams, 'Due Process versus the Maintenance of Order in European Law: The Contribution of the *ius commune*', in *The Moral World of the Law*, ed. Peter Coss (Cambridge, 2000), here p. 82.

84 Anne Gilmour-Bryson, 'Sodomy and the Knights Templar', *Journal of the History of Sexuality*, 7 (1996), pp. 151-83, here pp. 179, 180; Michelet, *Procès*, vol. 1, pp. 242, 250, 317, 333, 345-6, 354, 567, vol. 2, p. 178.

85 Barber, *Trial of the Templars*, 2nd edn, pp. 209-13; Malcolm Barber, 'The Templars and the Turin Shroud', *Catholic Historical Review*, 68 (1982), pp. 206-25. For the cult of saints in western Europe in the Middle Ages see, for example, Patrick J. Geary, *Furta Sacra: Thefts of Relics in the Central Middle Ages* (Princeton, 1978); Patrick J. Geary, *Living with the Dead in the Middle Ages* (Ithaca, NY, 1994); Bernard Hamilton, *Religion in the Medieval West* (London, 1986), pp. 126-8; *The Cult of Saints in late antiquity and the Middle Ages: Essays on the Contribution of Peter Brown*, ed. James Howard-Johnston and Paul Antony Hayward (Oxford and New York, 1999); Kathleen Kamerick, *Popular Piety and Art in the late Middle Ages: Image Worship and Idolatry in England, 1350–1500* (New York, 2002).

86 David Williams, *Deformed Discourse: The Function of the Monster in Mediaeval Thought and Literature* (Exeter, 1996), pp. 132–4; Dante Alighieri, *The Divine Comedy 1: Inferno*, trans. Robin Kirkpatrick (London, 2006), Canto 34, lines 38-69, pp. 307-8, 445; 'De heresi catharorum in Lombardia', translation in Edward Peters, *Heresy and Authority in Medieval Europe: Documents in Translation* (London, 1980), no. 22A, p. 134; from Jeffrey Burton Russell, *Religious Dissent in the Middle Ages* (New York, 1971), pp. 72-3; original text ed. Antoine Dondaine, 'La hiérarchie cathare en italie', *Archivum Fratrum Praedicatorum*, 19 (1949), pp. 280-312.

87 Barber, *Trial of the Templars*, 2nd edn, pp. 76, 77, 185, 189-90, 209-10.

88 Ibid., p. 213.

89 Eithne Massey, *Prior Roger of Kilmainham, 1314–1341* (Dublin, 2000), p. 39.

90 *Règle*, p. 347, section 680, see also p. 110, section 138; trans. Upton-Ward, pp. 53, 173; *Procès*, ed. Michelet, vol. 1, pp. 326, 615-6, vol. 2, p. 98; *Papsttum und Untergang*, ed. Finke, vol. 2, p. 314; *Procès des Templiers d'Auvergne*, ed. Sève and Chagny-Sève, p. 253.

91 *Procès*, ed. Michelet, vol. 1, p. 419; Schottmüller, pp. 65, 93; MS C, fols 8r-v; MS D, fol. 189r (*Annales Londonienses*, ed. Stubbs, p. 195); MS A, fols 106r, 135r, 139r (Wilkins, pp. 366, 375, omits last example).

92 Barber, *Trial of the Templars*, 2nd edn, pp. 204-5.

93 On this, see below, chapter seven.

94 Richard Berards, MS A, fol. 94v (Wilkins omits).

95 *Règle*, section 354; trans. Upton-Ward, p. 98.

96 MS A, fol. 149v (Wilkins, p. 377).

97 MS A, fol. 170r.

98 See the notaries' comments on the testimony of Brother William de Scotho, MS A, fol. 18v.

99 MS A, fols 92v, 101v-102v (Wilkins, pp. 359, 364-5); the summary of the testimonies is probably that in MS A, fol. 91r (Wilkins, p. 358).

2

The Arrests in the British Isles

When King Edward II of England initially received the papal instructions to arrest the Templars, he protested that he was not prepared to give credit to malicious rumours. The Templars, he wrote, had always been constant in the purity of the Catholic faith, and he and the people of his kingdom had often commended their actions and their practices. 'We cannot believe suspicions of this sort, until we are given more evidence of them.'[1] He continued to deal with the Templars as normal. On 15 December 1307 he approved the request of the grand commander of the Temple in England, Brother William de la More, to set up attorneys for legal cases. On 18 December he asked William de la More to lend him three carts to help carry his household equipment to Dover, preparatory for his voyage to Boulogne to marry Isabelle, daughter of Philip IV – which, incidentally, would take him out of the country while the Templars were arrested.[2]

Nevertheless, although he protested to Pope Clement V and to his own allies and relatives, Edward II knew that he had little room to manoeuvre. His dependence on the papacy for political support, the antagonism of his own nobles and the fact he was soon to marry the king of France's daughter, all convinced him to go along with papal orders. On 20 December 1307 he sent instructions to all the sheriffs in England, his justiciars (chief government officials) in Scotland, North and West Wales and Chester, and to John Wogan, his justiciar in Ireland, to arrest the Templars, make an inventory of their possessions, and keep the Templars in custody but not under harsh conditions until such time as he should order otherwise. He then wrote to Pope Clement V confirming that he had given the order for the Templars' arrest. The Templars in England were arrested between 9 and 11 January 1308.[3]

The arrests were administered as follows. Each individual sheriff in England received a writ from the king – a slip of parchment on the front of which were written his instructions – instructing him on the procedure for arresting the Templars. On the due day each sheriff went to arrest the Templars who lived within his county. The sheriff, or his representatives, made an inventory of the property of the Templars' house in the presence of the commander of the house. The Templars were escorted to the nearest royal castle, where they were housed 'under safe guard' – not in a locked prison cell – with their possessions.

The fact that the inventories of the Templars' houses do not mention any beds indicates that they were allowed to take their beds with them – but these were simply a bedroll with a blanket, not a wooden bedstead.[4] On the other hand, for the most part luxuries such as silver spoons and tablecloths were left behind.[5]

When the arrests were complete, the sheriff wrote a report of what he had done – usually on the back of the original writ – and sent this back to the king. The endorsed writs were retained by the king's exchequer officials for future reference.[6]

The grand commander of England, William de la More, was arrested at Temple Ewell in Kent, with Imbert or Himbert Blanc, grand commander of the Auvergne, Ralph of Barton, prior (chief chaplain) of New Temple in London, Ralph of Malton, commander of Temple Ewell, Robert of Sautre, also stationed at Ewell, and Thomas of Loudham, who had been received at Ewell eleven days before the arrests. Presumably William de la More, Himbert Blanc and Ralph of Barton had come to Ewell to perform the reception ceremony for Thomas of Loudham and had stayed there over the Christmas period. They were all taken to Canterbury castle, a magnificent Norman structure which was not only secure but also contained good quality accommodation, suitable for high-status guests (plate 28).[7] The four Templars who were at Sandford (Oxfordshire) and one from Bisham (Berkshire) were taken to Oxford Castle (plate 27), while those of Dinsley (Hertfordshire) and Cressing (Essex) were taken to Hertford Castle (plate 29) and to Colchester Castle. The four Templars arrested at Temple Thornton in Northumberland were taken to Newcastle upon Tyne, and

Map of locations in the British Isles mentioned in the text.

Map of locations in England and east Wales mentioned in the text.

those in Lincolnshire were taken to Lincoln Castle (plate 30).[8] But not all of these castles had facilities for the long-term custody of prisoners. Normally criminals were locked up only for a short time to await trial, not to live in prison for months. What was more, the king had given instructions that the Templars were to be well cared-for, and in some cases this simply was not possible, because of the poor state of the accommodation.

The Templars in Yorkshire, for example, were initially sent to York Castle, but had to be released and sent to private houses because the tower was unfit to house prisoners.[9] The commander of Yorkshire, William of Grafton, was allowed to live in his Order's house at Whitley and have use of his horses.[10]

The Order's officials did not keep written lists of their members, so modern historians can only estimate how many Templars there were in the British Isles at the beginning of 1308 by comparing the sheriffs' records of whom they arrested, the inquisitors' complaints about who was missing, the sheriffs' records of which Templars were receiving upkeep and which had died, and the Templars mentioned in the trial proceedings. Some Templars' names could be spelt in more than one way, and sometimes one brother was known by two different surnames: for example, John of Stoke, commander of the Templars' house at Sutton in Essex, was also called John of Sutton,[11] while in Yorkshire Ivo of Hoghton, commander of Temple Hirst, was also called Ivo of Etton.[12] This means that it is all too easy to count one man twice. Eileen Gooder reckoned that there were around 153 Templars in the British Isles at the time of the arrests, but the American scholar Clarence Perkins, working from all the surviving evidence, reached a total of 144.[13] Neither of them gave a complete list of the Templars in question (Gooder's lists do not total 153). The sheriffs' records of the arrests, the trial testimonies and inquisitors' lists of missing brothers indicate that there were 144 Templars in the British Isles, including those who escaped and those who died before interrogation (see Appendix 1).

King Edward's initial instructions to his sheriffs indicated that he was not absolutely certain where all the Templars were. When the sheriffs arrived at a Templar house, they did not necessarily know whom they would find. For example, despite Edward's instructions to his justiciars in Wales, there were no Templars in Wales at the start of January 1308.[14] Temple Sowerby in Cumberland was deserted in January 1308, and to judge from the sparseness of the inventory later taken there, the area had recently been sacked by the Scots.[15] Eileen Gooder argued that no Templars were arrested at Sutton in

Essex; yet the full record of the trial proceedings records Brother John of Sutton at that house – presumably he was away from the house on the day of the arrest.[16] According to Henry of Halton, who was one of the brothers stationed at Lydley in Shropshire, there were normally three brothers resident there, and so the sheriff who arrived at Lydley probably expected to find all three.[17] But in fact he did not find the commander, Stephen of Stapelbrugge. An Austin friar, Adam of Smeton, later informed the bishop of Hereford that Brother Stephen had been at the Templars' manor at Hopesay that day and had fled at dawn, no one knew where.[18]

Yet not many Templars disappeared. In November 1309 the inquisitors in London noted that Templars Michael of Baskerville and John of Stoke were missing, 'having thrown off their habits', and had not yet appeared to be questioned. However, neither of these had in fact run away; they had been appointed by William de la More as his attorneys or representatives, and were going about his business. In due course they appeared before the inquisitors to be cross-examined.[19] Brothers William of Hereford or Hertford and Walter of Rockley also failed to appear before 17 November 1309 – both appeared eventually, although on 18 February 1310 King Edward II had to send specific instructions to the constable of Marlborough Castle to bring Walter of Rockley from Wiltshire to the Tower of London. Brother Walter was eventually interrogated on 18 March 1310.[20]

One individual who did run away was Roger of Stowe, a priest who had formerly been a Templar, but – he said – left the Order with the grand commander's formal permission just before the arrests in January 1308. The bishop of Lincoln's register told another story: when Roger heard of the forthcoming arrests he had thrown off his habit and fled. Having given evidence on 8 November 1309, he was instructed to return for further questioning on 25 November, but there is no indication in the trial proceedings that he did.[21]

Other brothers were mentioned by their peers as having disappeared. The most frequently mentioned was Stephen of Stapelbrugge or Stapelbrigge (now Stalbridge in Dorset).[22] In fact, he and his colleague Thomas of Lindsey, and possibly Walter the Rebel, were in Ireland, living off a government pension like the other Templars there.[23]

After Stephen of Stapelbrugge, the most notorious escapee was Thomas of Thoraldby, alias Thomas Totty. He fled before the arrests, but was recaptured and interrogated at Lincoln on 10 April 1310, escaped again after giving testimony and then gave himself up and was interrogated at

London, 25–29 June 1311.[24] 'Thoraldby' is probably now Thoralby, in the North Riding of Yorkshire. Although the Scottish brothers both mentioned Brother Thomas as one of the escapees,[25] there is no evidence that he was ever actually stationed in Scotland. A contemporary Cistercian monk based at Tintern Abbey in Monmouthshire stated that Brother Thomas was 'called master and commander of Garway near Grosmont' in Herefordshire.[26] As Tintern Abbey is relatively close to Garway (eighteen miles, almost due south), this Cistercian monk was in a position to know this. Perhaps there had been some dispute between the Templars and the Cistercians while Brother Thomas was commander at Garway, which could help explain why this particular Cistercian monk was happy to record the accusations against the Templars without questioning them. By January 1308 Philip de Meux was commander of Garway. Thomas may have been one of those whom Brother Hugh Peraud, the visitor, had removed from office in 1304.[27]

The other fugitives attracted less attention. John of Ebreston was mentioned by one Templar as having fled, but gave himself up voluntarily and was interrogated at York on 4 May 1310.[28] Richard Engayn was arrested before the end of 1311 and sent to a monastery.[29] William of Grafton junior, presumably a younger relative of William of Grafton the commander of Yorkshire, gave himself up before 1313.[30] Thomas of Hagworthingham also returned and in 1313 was doing penance in Winchester diocese.[31] Only five Templars who were in the British Isles at the start of January 1308 were never traced: Thomas of Frouby, who fled before the arrests;[32] John of Usflete or Husflet, an English brother who had been commander of Balantrodoch in Scotland before Walter of Clifton (who was commander in 1308) and was mentioned by three brothers as having fled;[33] Edmund Latimer or Barville;[34] John of Poynton and Ralph of Bulford.[35]

Were these really all? Late in 1309 the Archbishop Robert Winchelsey of Canterbury sent out an edict to all the bishops, listing the Christian names only of the Templars who had so far failed to appear before the inquisitors – a total of fourteen. All these names match those of Templars who were recorded elsewhere as missing. The list is as follows, with probable surnames in brackets: 'Brothers Michael [of Baskerville], John [of Stoke], William [of Hereford], Roger [of Stowe], Thomas [of Lindsey, Thoraldby, Frouby or Hagworthingham], William [of Grafton junior], John [of Usflete], John [of Ebreston], Edmund [Latimer/Barville], John [of Poynton], Richard [Engayn], Ralph [of Bulford], Stephen [of Stapelbrugge] and Walter [le

Rebel, or of Rockley].[36] In fact, there were at least four Thomases and two Walters missing at the end of 1309, but only one of each is mentioned in this list.

In sum, only five Templars from the British Isles were never traced. There certainly is no evidence to support the popular modern suggestion that vast numbers of Templars fled from Britain to Scotland and formed an army which in 1314 defeated the English at the battle of Bannockburn.[37] Five would hardly be enough to form a raiding party.

The imprisonment of the more prestigious officials of the Templars was something of an embarrassment for the English government. These were men who had been exercising considerable responsibility on the king's behalf, then were suddenly deprived of their freedom on the basis of accusations which the king and his leading officials did not believe. On 25 June 1308 King Edward II gave Lord Henry de Percy permission to take charge of William of Grafton, on condition that he bring him back for trial when requested, in the same state as he left prison. Brother William was also granted support for himself (six pence per day) and a servant.[38] Henry Percy, a leading baron with property in the north of England and Scotland, was then a trusted friend of the king, although he later joined the opposition.[39] But Henry Percy did not look after Brother William for long – when Bishop John of Chichester, chancellor of England, wrote in September 1309 to Henry Percy instructing him to bring William of Grafton for trial, Henry Percy replied that William of Grafton was no longer in his hands and had not been for a long time.[40] On 27 November 1308 the king had commanded the sheriffs of London and Middlesex to have all the Templars within their area of authority arrested and confined to the Tower of London; probably it was at this time that William of Grafton was confined to the Tower of London.[41] He was still there in early 1310,[42] but subsequently he was transferred to York, where he was interrogated in late April.[43]

Further south, on 18 March 1308, William de la More, then imprisoned in Canterbury Castle, was allowed to go out and about with two companion-brothers during daylight hours, provided he had a guard. They could also have their own beds, clothes and silver plate.[44] The grand commander had initially been granted a pension of two shillings per day, while the two brothers with him received four pence each; on 14 March this was increased to a pension of two shillings and sixpence per day for the grand commander, while the two brothers with him would receive sixpence each; other Templars received four pence per day.[45] On 23 May 1308, Edward wrote to the sheriff of Kent instructing him to hand over the grand commander to Antony Bek, patriarch of Jerusalem and bishop of Durham, who would go bail for him.[46] On 23 July the king assigned the revenues from several Templar manors to William de la More, to provide direct support for him and his two companion-brothers, and the six brothers of the Order who were imprisoned in Hertford castle.[47] Brothers Michael de Baskerville (commander of the New Temple, London) and John of Stoke (priest, and treasurer of the New Temple) were released on 26 July and handed over to Brother William de la More, with their horses and equipment.[48] The grand commander again had an entourage worthy of his rank, and incomes to support them. At Michaelmas 1308, the sheriffs of London recorded that they had handed over to Brother William de la More the contents of his wardrobe in the New Temple, London. This included a gold clasp, lengths of Birmingham cloth, coverlets, a flasket or wicker container, and a crossbow without a bolt.[49]

Even when he was locked up with other Templars in the Tower of London at the end of November 1308, William de la More – or, to give him his English name, William atte More – was still regarded with special respect. He was not examined on the eighty-eight charges listed by the pope – at least, no record of his interrogation has survived. As a result, there is no record of when or where he was received into the Order. A throwaway remark by one of the brothers in Scotland, Walter de Clifton, informs us that he was born in Yorkshire. Brother Richard of Burthesham, one of the Templars in Ireland, mentioned that Brother William was one of those present when he was received into the Order at Pentecost 1286 at Tripoli in Syria; so he had spent time in the East.[50] He had been commander of Ewell in Kent in 1294, and had succeeded Brother Brian le Jay as grand commander in England after the latter's death at the Battle of Falkirk in 1298.[51]

William de la More was not subjected to questioning until 4 February 1310.[52] In the same way, William de Warenne, grand commander in Ireland until the beginning of 1308, was not interrogated at all, although a pension was being paid to him with the other Templars until at least 1312. Possibly these two officials were excluded from the shame of interrogation because of their status: William de la More as a faithful servant of the king and of the king's father,[53] and Warenne because of his noble blood – he was related to the powerful Botiller family.[54]

Another Templar who was of high status, but not spared interrogation, was the grand commander of the Auvergne, variously called Himbert, Imbert, or Humbert Blanc, arrested at Temple Ewell in Kent.[55] It is not clear why Himbert Blanc was in England in January 1308, some three months after all the French Templars had been arrested.[56] The French scholar Alain Demurger has drawn attention to a letter of Pope Clement V of 13 June 1306, in which he commends Himbert Blanc and Pierre de Langres, citizen of Marseilles and 'admiral of the galleys dispatched to aid the Holy Land' to the kings, princes, bishops and clergy. The pope wrote that as Brother Himbert and Pierre de Langres had decided to fight against the infidel and the impious Christians who trade with them, they were permitted to attack and loot their ships. He also allowed a priest to travel with them for confessing and absolving the evil Christians whom they captured, after such had repented their evil deeds.[57] Alain Demurger suggests that this expedition was connected to the grand master's own crusade plan of 1306, in which he advised the pope to arm ten galleys and send them to defend Cyprus and prevent evil Christians from supplying prohibited goods (such as weapons) to the Muslims.[58] In this case, Himbert Blanc would not have been in France in the winter and spring of 1307, because he was engaged in this expedition in the East.[59] Possibly he came to England later in 1307 to promote another such expedition to the East, only to find himself 'trapped' there when the Templars in France were arrested in October.

Some of the ordinary brothers suffered severely in prison, many dying during the early months of the trial. As persons accused of heresy were regarded as guilty until proven innocent they were treated as excommunicated, cut off from the Church and its spiritual comforts. Particularly vulnerable were the elderly and sick; the majority of those who died had been living at the Templars' houses of Denney (Cambridgeshire) or Eagle (Lincolnshire) before the arrests, where Templars had hospitals for elderly and sick brothers (plate 15).[60] Presumably these houses were regarded as suitable for this purpose because of their locations in the open countryside, away from the smoke and stench of the towns, in exposed areas with cold north-easterly winds.[61] Forcibly detained in the unhealthy town castles and confined indoors, although not chained up like their French counterparts, even the healthiest brothers would have been more vulnerable to sickness, and the infirm quickly succumbed.

Some died within weeks. Adam le Mazun, who had been based at New Temple in London, died on 16 February 1308.[62] Geoffrey Joliffe, from Eagle, died in Lincoln Castle on 25 January 1308.[63] William Scurlagge, knight-brother, who had been based at Balsall (although his white knight's mantle was at New Temple, London), died in January 1308.[64] Roger of Wyke, who had been at Temple Combe in Somerset, died on 15 April 1308.[65]

Others lasted a little longer. John de Vale or du Vaal, who had been based at Eagle, died on 15 July 1308.[66] Patrick of Ripon, formerly *claviger* (key-holder) at Newsam in the West Riding of Yorkshire, died on 29 October 1308.[67] Hugh de Kyrketon or Kirketoft was arrested in Kent in January 1308 and held at Rochester castle. The sheriffs of London recorded that they received custody of Hugh de Kerketoft from the sheriff of Kent on 14 March 1308 and that he died on 1 November 1308.[68] William of Marringe, from Denney, died 6 December 1308.[69] Robert of Halton was another brother who had been based at Eagle and who died in prison, on 29 December 1308.[70] Richard of Hales, formerly commander of Foulbridge in the North Riding of Yorkshire, died on 23 June 1309.[71]

For some who died, no date of death is known. Michael of Karvyle, who is mentioned in the trial proceedings as a brother at Lydley in Shropshire,[72] Adam of Crayk or Creyke,[73] who had been *claviger* at Temple Hirst in Yorkshire, and Henry the Marshal,[74] who had been based at Willoughton, all died before interrogation. William of Herewyk, although not mentioned by the sheriff of Yorkshire as having been arrested in January 1308, was mentioned later in John le Gray's half-yearly accounts of the Templars' Yorkshire houses,[75] but was never interrogated, so presumably died before the interrogations began at York in late April 1310.

More Templars died after the interrogations had begun. Alexander of Althon or Halton, who was based at Bruer, gave evidence at Lincoln but was not interrogated at London and was not absolved in July 1311, so presumably had died.[76] Alexander of Bulbeke, who was based at Denney, was interrogated once and then not mentioned again.[77] John of Cannville or J. of Kanvyle is mentioned in the full record of the English trial proceedings as dead, but his testimony is described in the summary which the papal inquisitors produced for the Council of Vienne.[78] John of Euleye, whose surname is also spelt in the trial records as Heule, Yvleath, Uley or Aley, was based at Combe in Somerset. He died after his first interrogation.[79] Richard of Herdwick, who had been based at the New Temple in London and who had held responsibility in the Order, acting as commander of the New Temple in 1294 and the grand commander's attorney in 1294-5 and 1298-1301, died after the first interrogation.[80] Robert of Cavill or Cammvile, who had been based at Thornton in Northumberland, was not sent to a monastery in August 1311 to do penance, so presumably died before the end of the trial.[81]

Thomas of Toulouse, knight, had been received in around 1266, had been commander of Ireland in 1285 and the early 1290s, a commander in the diocese of York at the beginning of the fourteenth century, and by January 1308 was commander of Upleadon (Bosbury, in Herefordshire). After being interrogated twice, one of his fellow-Templars reported on 3 March 1310 that he was dead, but in fact he was interrogated again on 9 June 1310. However, he died before the end of April 1311.[82] John of Newent lived a little longer: he was imprisoned in Ludgate at the end of April 1311, but was absent from the ceremonies of abjuring heresy and absolution in July 1311.[83]

A few of the Templars from Denney and Eagle lived through the interrogations, but for various reasons were not interrogated. John of Hauwile or Hamil was at Denney. He was not interrogated because, as he was described as *demens* (insane), he was not fit to give evidence.[84] Roger of Lodelawe was also at Denney; in March 1310 he was recorded as having died before being interrogated, at the end of April 1311 he was noted as still alive and imprisoned in Ludgate in London,[85] yet as he did not abjure heresy with the other Templars in July 1311 and was not absolved, presumably he was too ill to be interrogated and died before July 1311. William of Spanneby, royal official in charge of the Templars' properties in Lincolnshire, mentioned that he had arrested Robert of Bernewell, chaplain, at Eagle. Robert was not interrogated, but one Templar mentioned him in March 1310.[86] Robert may have been the same man as William of Barnwell, who was too ill to be brought before the London Council or to be absolved, was assigned to the diocese of Lincoln to do penance but was too ill to be moved to Wardon, the monastery to which he had been assigned, and who died in late August 1311, still unshriven.[87] The bishop of Lincoln's registers record that William of Barnwell was not only very sick and infirm but also deaf.[88] It is odd that Robert of Barnwell disappears from the record after March 1310, while William of Barnwell does not appear until after the trial was over – yet neither were mentioned as fugitives. If Brother Robert Barnwell was known by the English diminutive of his name, 'Bob', and – being sick and deaf – he was not able to speak clearly, Church officials could have misheard his name as 'Bill' – the English diminutive for 'William'.

Another brother arrested at Eagle but never interrogated was John of Saddlecombe. The bishop of Lincoln's register records that he was too ill to appear before the Church Council in London in July 1311, or to be moved to the monastery of Swineshead to which he had been assigned to do his penance. He died early in September 1311, without having abjured heresy, and was not absolved.[89]

Stories were told about the dead brothers that could not be checked. Sir William of Jafford, who was rector of the church of Croft in York diocese and an official of the archbishop of York,[90] said on oath that William of Reynburer, priest of the Order of St Augustine, already deceased, had told him that he had heard the confession of Brother Patrick of Ripon[91] of the Order of the Temple. William of Reynburer had recited what he said Brother Patrick told him about his reception into the Order of the Temple: the ceremony took place in secret; Patrick had to deny God and Christ, spit on the cross, and turn his bare buttocks to it; he was told to worship an image like a calf (not an idol head, as in the official list of charges), and he was then blindfolded and kissed by the other brothers; the brothers also had sexual relations with each other. William of Jafford said that he had heard this account in his own house in the city of York, but as his alleged informant and the Templar in question were both dead, his testimony could not be verified.[92]

Brother Thomas of Redemer of the Dominican friars said that he heard from Brother Reginald of Braybof, also a Dominican, about a certain Templar brother who recently died in Lincoln Castle. According to this tale, the dying Templar had received the consecrated bread from the priest's hand and kept it whole in his mouth until the priest had left, then spat it into his chamber pot and made a woman who was nursing him throw it into the latrine, even though she was unwilling to do so and said that she would rather throw it in the fire. Asked the woman's name, he said that he did not know – so once again this tale could not be checked.[93]

Brother Reginald of Braybof confirmed this story, which he said that he had heard from Brother William of Pilton, subprior of the Dominicans' house at Lincoln. The subprior had heard it from Brother Henry of Celeby, then *lector* (director of the school) of the Dominican Order at St Botolph's church, Lincoln.[94] So this story was already third hand when Brother Reginald told it. William of Pilton did not appear in court, and the offending Templar was never named. As similar stories had been told in the past about groups of heretics and the Jews, this story was no more than the equivalent of the modern urban myth.[95]

Beyond such myths, little evidence survives about the Templars' neighbours' opinions of the Templars during the period of the trial. Eileen Gooder,
in her study of Temple Balsall, noted that a nun of St Mary's, Clerkenwell,
gave an ivory image of the Blessed Virgin Mary to one of the Templars who
was imprisoned in Aldgate.[96] The large crowds who assembled during the
first weeks of July 1311 to hear the Templars of Canterbury Province abjure
heresy and receive absolution suggest that in London there was widespread
popular interest in the case.[97] Yet very few former servants or tenants of the
British and Irish Templars gave evidence during the trial, and those who did
had little to say about the Order.

The neighbours of the New Temple, London, were generally either
favourable or stated that they knew nothing relevant to the case. Three
former servants of the Order gave evidence on disciplinary procedures for
the Order's servants. Other former servants had only rumour to report.[98]
There were distinct advantages in being a tenant of the Templars, as the
brothers and their tenants enjoyed a certain degree of independence from
royal jurisdiction,[99] so it is possible that it was the change in tenants' legal
rights following the dissolution of the Templars which led to a riot at the
Templars' new town of Baldock in Hertfordshire in September 1312. The
riot was set off by the arrival of the king's officer, who came to conduct a
view of frankpledge there and to collect the tolls and other dues from the
annual fair.[100] Perhaps the previous administration at Baldock had been less
strict in enforcing these regulations.

Very few of the witnesses against the Templars were lay people, and hardly
any of them were of noble birth. Miles of Stapleton, an English baron who
had been steward of the king's household and bailiff of Holderness, was
mentioned by Master John of Nassington, official of the archbishop of York,
as having been a guest of the Templars and having heard about their idolatry,
but Miles of Stapleton himself did not appear in court to verify the story.[101]
In Scotland there were a handful of knightly witnesses: Fergus Marshal,
Henry Sinclair and his son William, eight other 'domicelli' or young gentlemen, and three other knights.[102] In Ireland the four lay witnesses were
servants or merchants.

In England the only lay witness of any social standing was John of
Eure, sheriff of York 1310–11, who as lord of Stokesley was overlord of
the Templars' commandery of Westerdale.[103] John of Eure was a northern knight, holding most of his lands in the four most northerly counties
of England: Northumberland, Durham, Cumberland and Westmorland,

which were also the counties which suffered most from Scottish devastation during the Anglo-Scottish war. He was captured by the Scots at the battle of Bannockburn in 1314, and later became a retainer of Earl Thomas of Lancaster, King Edward II's cousin and chief opponent.[104] He was not a major noble, but a man of local importance who went on to play a significant role in the politics of northern England.

Yet although Eure did give evidence against the Templars, he said very little against them. His only accusation was that a book which the commander of Westerdale, William of the Fenne, had lent to his wife to read had contained a document which included heretical doctrines – to judge from his description, this was a Jewish description of Christ, like that in the *Talmud*.[105] When asked about this, Brother William of the Fenne admitted what John of Eure said about the book, but said that he had no idea what was written on the offending document.[106] Perhaps, because John of Eure was a prominent individual who was known to be the Templars' landlord and to have entertained leading Templars to dinner, he was pressurised to bring evidence against them under threat of being charged with their crimes.

The English lay nobility received scarcely any mention in the trial proceedings until Monday 12 July 1311, when four of the Lords Ordainer attended the ceremony of the Templars' abjuration at London: Earl Thomas of Lancaster and Leicester, Humphrey de Bohun, earl of Hereford and Essex, Aymer de Valence, earl of Pembroke and Guy de Beauchamp, earl of Warwick.[107] The Ordainers were a group of twenty-one leading clergy, earls and barons who had come together in March 1310 to control King Edward II's government. The English nobility as a whole were exasperated by the pope's repeated demands for taxes to be levied in England to contribute towards the cost of a crusade. In August 1309 the English nobles in Parliament wrote to Pope Clement V that his demands were infringing the rights of the English king and damaging the religious houses which their ancestors had founded.[108] Because their ancestors had originally given the Templars the lands which the king confiscated at the beginning of 1308, the nobles believed that they should have a voice in what became of the Templars' former property; hence the Ordainers' interest in the outcome of the trial in London. In 1324 they decided in Parliament that because the Templars' lands had originally been given for religious purposes – to defend Christendom and the Holy Land – the lands should be handed over to religious persons, and agreed that the recipient should be the Hospitallers, as instructed by the pope.[109]

The clergy, in contrast could not avoid becoming involved in the trial, because it was an ecclesiastical matter. The bishops were clearly concerned about the Templars' affairs: as a matter of pastoral care, they were responsible for the souls of those within their diocese. Yet, on the whole, the English bishops at this time preferred to remain out of national affairs, and to concentrate on the needs of their diocese. The exception was Robert Winchelsey, archbishop of Canterbury, who was a major figure in the opposition to King Edward II.[110] But even he did not take a leading role in the trial of the Templars, generally delegating his role to the bishops of London and Chichester.

In October 1309 the inquisitors in London, led by Bishop Ralph Baldock of London, declared that 'the case is very dangerous for the whole of the orthodox faith' and that it needed to be settled quickly, but Bishop Ralph himself was present only because the king had ordered him to attend, to ensure that proper procedures were followed. He made formal protests during the course of the Templars' trial, stating that he did not wish to act against the grand commander of the Templars, William de la More.[111] In contrast, John Langton, bishop of Chichester, was anxious to resolve the case, and urged Brother William de la More to confess to the charges so that he could be reconciled to the Church.[112]

The archbishop of York, William Greenfield, was reluctant to go to London or to Lincoln to take part in the trial, because he could not have his archiepiscopal cross carried before him outside his own province. In addition, in autumn 1309 he wrote to London, to the two inquisitors sent by the pope and the clergy whom the pope had appointed judges in the Templars' affair, that he was too busy to come to London, and also unwell. He also complained of delays in the receipt of letters, so that he did not receive a summons to one meeting in London until it was too late for him to set out. On the other hand, he did discuss with his own clergy both the case itself and the problem of runaway Templars; and two of his officials, William of Jafford and John of Nassington, gave evidence against the Templars. He and his clergy were aware of the anxiety of the pope and the inquisitors to obtain confessions from the Templars, but decided not to bring torturers from overseas. Overall, scholars have concluded that Greenfield was unenthusiastic about the Templars' trial.[113]

Although some of the monks who kept a record of current events seem to have believed the charges (such as the authors of the *Flores historiarum* at Westminster and Tintern), some did not (such as Walter of Guisborough's continuator), while others remained neutral (such as the author of the *Vita Edward secundi*, 'Life of Edward the Second').[114] Their views of the trial were not linked to their political views as a whole: the author of the Westminster *Flores*, who apparently approved of the trial, was 'a rabid Lancastrian' – that is, a supporter of King Edward's cousin and rival, Earl Thomas of Lancaster;[115] but Walter of Guisborough's continuator, who also criticised the king, did not support the trial. The friars, however, were another matter, as will be explained in chapter four.

One religious order was notable for its absence from the trial. The Hospital of St John of Jerusalem in the British Isles remained out of the way. No Hospitallers came forward to give evidence either for or against the Templars. The prior of the Hospital in England continued in his normal relationship with the king of England: he was invited to Edward II's coronation in February 1308 with the other ecclesiastical and secular lords of the realm, and he was summoned to attend Parliament with them.[116] On 25 May 1309, Edward II gave the Hospitallers in England the right to export horses, other animals, gold and silver, for the aid of the Holy Land – the Hospitallers were in the process of conquering Rhodes, and needed to be able to export resources from the West. He added that he was making this concession on the pope's request.[117] King Edward and Pope Clement might have given up any hope of saving the Templars, but they were anxious to demonstrate their continued zeal for the Catholic Christian cause in the Holy Land.

Yet although many people in the British Isles were at best unenthusiastic about the trial, there was no rush to defend the Templars. On 2 January 1308, Pope Clement V had written to all Christian clergy stating that no one should show the Templars public or secret help, advice or favour, or give any of them shelter, but should avoid them 'as those suspected of heresy'. Anyone who did help the Templars or give them shelter was pronounced excommunicate, cut off from all Christian society; and the towns, castles, or places where they had been given shelter were placed under interdict, so that all spiritual services by the clergy were suspended.[118] The result was that no one dared to help the Templars openly; no lawyers would plead for them in court, and no one would demonstrate in their support.

Despite the pope's instructions of August 1308 to interrogate the Templars on the charges against them, he did not send his nominees to the British Isles to commence the trial. However, on 4 October 1308 he wrote to King Edward, reminding him that he should hand the Templars' properties over to the Church. Yet the Templar estates were far too valuable for Edward to let them go. He replied that he did not wish to do anything except what he ought and what he knew would be most pleasing to God.[119]

Clarence Perkins suggested that it was this papal pressure which led Edward, at the end of November 1308, to instruct to his sheriffs to arrest any wandering Templars, take William de la More into closer custody and guard the prisoners more carefully.[120] The manors which had been assigned to William de la More were taken back into the king's hands and administered by the king's officials, and the grand commander had to surrender the Order's seal to the king so that the royal officials could administer the Templars' lands.[121] At the beginning of March 1309, Edward ordered a full investigation into the extent and annual value of the Templars' lands, with a view to exploiting this source of income more fully.[122] However, Edward did take steps to ensure that the Templars who had been locked up were properly looked after: in late November and December 1308 he instructed his sheriffs to pay the Templars' pensions of four pence per day from the revenue of their lands.[123]

But the trial itself remained stalled. Pope Clement V seemed to be in no hurry to push matters on, and even the bishops' enquiries in France did not get under way until May or June 1309.[124] It was not until 12 July 1309 that the pope wrote to his appointee judges in England, led by Antony Bek, ordering them to begin enquiries against the Templars there.[125] This letter would have taken several weeks to reach England. Not until the beginning of September 1309 did King Edward send instructions to the constables of York, Lincoln and London to assemble the Templars at their castles for interrogation. At the same time, he ordered the justiciar of Ireland to arrest all Templars still at large and send them and those already in custody to Dublin Castle, to be brought before the investigators of heresy appointed by the pope. In October, John de Segrave, the 'keeper of Scotland', received similar orders.[126] Meanwhile, Antony Bek and his fellow papal judges sent out instructions on the same lines.[127]

Notes

1   *Foedera*, ed. Rymer, vol. 2, pt 1, p. 20.

2   *CPR, 1307–1313*, p. 28; *CCR, 1307–1313*, p. 50; *Itinerary of Edward II*, pp. 27–8.

3   Perkins, 'Trial of the Knights Templars'; *Foedera*, ed. Rymer, vol. 2, pt 1, pp. 18–19, 23–4; *CCR, 1307–1313*, p. 14.

4   On this, see Gooder, p. 88; *Règle*, section 139, trans. Upton-Ward, p. 54.

5   Gooder, pp. 83–4.

6   For example, TNA:PRO E142/11 mem. 1 dorse (Northumberland); TNA:PRO
    E142/13 mem. 2 (Oxford and Berkshire).

7   Gooder, p. 88, citing TNA:PRO E358/20, rot. 6 dorse under 'compotus Henrici de
    Cobham'; MS A, fol. 44v (Wilkins, p. 344). According to MS A, fol. 58r (Wilkins,
    p. 347), Thomas of Loudham was a sergeant-brother at New Temple in London, so
    presumably he had been assigned to that house after his reception.

8   TNA:PRO E142/11 mem. 1 dorse (Northumberland); TNA:PRO E142/13 mem. 2
    (Oxford and Berkshire); TNA:PRO E358/18 rot. 14, front and dorse, rots 15, 16(1)
    (Lincs.); Gooder, p. 89. The six brothers in Hertford Castle in July 1308 (TNA:PRO
    E368/78 rot. 15 dorse; TNA:PRO E358/18 rot. 23(1)) were probably the three at
    Dinsley and three from Essex: from Dinsley Richard Poitevin, Henry of la Paul and
    Robert of the Wolde; from Cressing Roger of Norreis and John Coffyn, with John of
    Sutton from Sutton (MS A fol. 58v, Wilkins, p. 347). The priest Thomas of Burton was
    imprisoned in London (E358/18 rot. 7 (1), under 'expenses').

9   Gooder, p. 89.

10 TNA:PRO E358/20 rot. 40, dorse.

11 MS A, fol. 42v (Wilkins, p. 344).

12 MS A, fol. 129r (Wilkins summarises, p. 372); TNA:PRO E142/18 mem. 1 dorse.

13 Alan J. Forey, 'Desertions and Transfers from Military Orders (Twelfth to Early
    Fourteenth Centuries)', *Traditio*, 60 (2005), pp. 143–200: here p. 183 note 227; Gooder,
    p. 84 and lists on pp. 147–52 (William Scurlage appears twice on p. 147; Henry Paul
    appears twice, pp. 148 and 149; on p. 148, Henry of Sleaford does not appear in TNA:
    PRO E358/18 rot 47 dorse or /19 rot. 47 dorse as stated by Gooder, but in MS A, fol.
    16r (Wilkins, p. 337), is mentioned as commander of Strood in 1294, so was probably
    dead by 1308; on p. 149, John de Hamill and de Hauteville were the same man, but
    John de Kanville has been omitted; on pp. 151–2: Henry de Rochester and Henry
    de Roucliffe were the same man; on p. 152: there was only one Henry de la Ford);
    Clarence Perkins, 'The Knights Templars in the British Isles', *English Historical Review*,
    25 (1910), pp. 209–30: here pp. 222, 224.

14 On the Templars in Wales, see William Rees, *A History of the Order of St John of
    Jerusalem in Wales and on the Welsh Border, including an Account of the Templars* (Cardiff,
    1947), pp. 51–3, 102, note 72.

15 TNA:PRO E142/11 mem. 4. At this time this area was under the lordship of John
    Balliol: *Documents Illustrative of English History in the Thirteenth and Fourteenth Centuries,
    selected from the Records of the Department of the Queen's Remembrancer of the Exchequer*,
    ed. Henry Cole (London, 1844), see notes on index, pp. 129–37.

16 Gooder, p. 84, citing TNA:PRO E358/19 rot. 52 dorse; MS A, fol. 58v (Wilkins,
    p. 347).

17 MS A, fol. 115v (Wilkins, p. 167, misread 'Lodlawe' in place of 'Lydley'). Gooder, p. 149,
    lists only two brothers at Lydley: Henry of Halton, 'deputy preceptor', and Stephen
    of Stapelbrugge, who ran away. MS A, fol. 144v (Wilkins, p. 376) refers to a Brother
    Michael of Karvile at Lydley in around 1304 as well as Stephen of Stapelbrugge.

18 MS A, fol. 96v (Wilkins omits).

19 Gooder, pp. 88–90, 92, 93–4; MS A, fols 39r; 54r–55v, 56r–v (Wilkins, pp. 343, 345–6
    – giving 'William' instead of 'Michael' of Baskerville).

20 These 'late arriving' Templars were not included in the record in MS B, before fol.
    81v; they appear in MS A, fols 54r–57v (Wilkins summarises, pp. 345–6). On Walter of
    Rockley see *CCR, 1307–1313*, p. 177.

21 MS A, fols 32v–33r (Wilkins summarises, p. 342); for his licence to leave see MS A, fol. 88r (Wilkins, p. 357); for the bishop's register see Forey, 'Ex–Templars', p. 19 and note 7.

22 Mentioned by Thomas the Chamberlain, MS A, fol. 13r (Wilkins, p. 335); Thomas of Wonhope, MS A, fol. 84v (Wilkins, p. 356); William of Craucumbe, MS A, fol. 28r (Wilkins, p. 341); Friar Adam de Smeton, MS A, fol. 96v (Wilkins omits); *Register of William Greenfield*, part 4, pp. 286, 337.

23 Stephen of Stapelbrugge: *IEP*, p. 204; was arrested in Wiltshire 10 June 1311 (*CCR, 1307–1313*, pp. 316–17): 'confessed' MS A, fol. 160r–v (Wilkins, pp. 383–4). Brother Thomas of Lindsey: *IEP*, p. 204; MacNiocaill, pp. 198, 222: MS D, fol. 171v (*Annales Londonienses*, ed. Stubbs, p. 176); *Councils and Synods with other documents relating to the English Church*, II: A.D. *1205–1313*, ed. F.M. Powicke and C.R. Cheney, part 2: *1265–1313* (Oxford, 1964), p. 136; Forey, 'Ex–Templars', p. 36. For 'Walter le Rebel' see *Register of William Greenfield*, part 4, pp. 286, 337; for 'Walter le Lung' see *IEP*, p. 204. In default of other evidence, these two could have been the same individual.

24 MS A, fols 84v, 85r (Wilkins, p. 356, omits second). John of Euley, MS A, fol. 45v (Wilkins, p. 344), refers to Thomas Scot, who was probably the same man. For his initial flight, see Brother William Middleton, MS A, fol. 156v (Wilkins, p. 381). Interrogation: MS A, fols 114v–115r, 161r–63v (Wilkins, pp. 367, 384–7); details of second escape: MS A, fol. 162r (Wilkins, p. 385).

25 MS A, fol. 156v (Wilkins, p. 381).

26 *Councils and Synods*, vol. 2, pt 2, ed. Powicke and Cheney, p. 1309, note; *Flores Historiarum*, vol. 3, p. 333.

27 MS A, fol. 156v (Wilkins, p. 381); for the date see *CCR, 1302–1307*, p. 208.

28 MS A, fol. 156v (Wilkins, p. 381, misread as 'Caraton'); interrogation in MS A, fol. 133r (Wilkins, p. 373); *Register of William Greenfield*, part 4, pp. 326–7, no. 2294.

29 MS A, fol. 84v (Wilkins, p. 355); *Register of William Greenfield*, part 4, pp. 286, 337; Forey, 'Ex-Templars', p. 36, n. 101.

30 MS A, fol. 84v (Wilkins, p. 356); *Register of William Greenfield*, part 4, pp. 286, 337, submitted before 1313; Forey, 'Ex-Templars', p. 36, n. 100.

31 Mentioned as a Templar in MS A, fol. 120r (Wilkins omits); Forey, 'Ex-Templars', p. 36 n. 101.

32 MS A, fol. 27r (Wilkins, p. 341).

33 MS A, fols 84v, 85r, 156v (Wilkins, pp. 356, 381); *Register of William Greenfield*, part 4, pp. 286, 337.

34 Henry Pawell, MS A, fol. 85r (Wilkins omits); *Register of William Greenfield*, part 4, pp. 286, 337.

35 John of Poynton: MS A, fol. 85r (Wilkins omits); *Register of William Greenfield*, part 4, pp. 286, 337; Ralph of Bulford: *Register of William Greenfield*, part 4, pp. 286, 337.

36 *Registrum Henrici Woodlock*, p. 403.

37 On this modern myth, see Lord, p. 154; Sharan Newman, *The Real History Behind the Templars* (New York, 2007), p. 394.

38 TNA:PRO E368/78, rot. 72 dorse; TNA:PRO E368/79 rot. 108r; Perkins, 'Trial of the Knights Templars', p. 433 and note 13.

39 J.M.W. Bean, 'Percy, Henry, first Lord Percy (1273–1314)', *ODNB*, vol. 43, pp. 690–1.

40 TNA:PRO SC1/35/74.

41 TNA:PRO E368/79 rot. 107 dorse.

42 MS A, fol. 58r (Wilkins, p. 347).

43 MS A, fol. 125r–v; for date, see fol. 127v (Wilkins, pp. 371–2).

44 TNA:PRO E368/78 rot. 82.

45 TNA:PRO E368/78 rots 41, 82.

46 Perkins, 'Trial of the Knights Templars', pp. 492–3; *Records of Antony Bek*, p. 118, no. 111; pp. 130–1, no. 128; C.M. Fraser, *A History of Antony Bek, Bishop of Durham, 1283–1311* (Oxford, 1957), pp. 165, 172–3, 219; *Foedera*, ed. Rymer, vol. 2, pt 1, pp. 46, 55; *CCR, 1307–1313*, p. 35.

47 TNA:PRO E368/78 rot. 15 dorse.

48 Gooder, p. 89; TNA:PRO E358/18 rot. 7 (1), under 'expenses'.

49 TNA:PRO E358/18 rot. 7 (1), under 'In gardaroba fratris Willelmi de la More'.

50 MS A, fols 134r, 155 (Wilkins, pp. 373, 380). For the English version of his surname, see MS A, fol. 147v (Wilkins omits).

51 *CPR, 1292–1301*, pp. 20, 391 (Brian le Jay died 22 July 1298; William de la More was grand commander by 25 December 1298).

52 MS A, fol. 74r–v (Wilkins, p. 352).

53 See, for example, Edward I's letter of recommendation for William de la More: *CCR, 1302–1307*, p. 208.

54 For William de Warenne as commander of Ireland until early 1308, see Wood, p. 333; *Calendar of the Justiciary Rolls or Proceedings in the Court of the Justiciar of Ireland Preserved in the Public Record Office of Ireland: Edward I, Part 2, XXXIII to XXXV Years*, ed. James Mills, under the direction of the master of the rolls in Ireland (London, 1914), pp. 291, 292, 334, 357; for his pension see *IEP*, p. 217; for his relatives see *Calendar of the Justiciary Rolls or Proceedings in the Court of the Justiciar of Ireland Preserved in the Public Record Office of Ireland: I to VII years of Edward II*, prepared under the direction of the deputy keeper of the public records by Herbert Wood and Albert E. Langman and revised by Margaret C. Griffith of the Public Record Office (Dublin, 1956), p. 36.

55 For a summary of his career, see *Procès des Templiers d'Auvergne*, ed. Sève and Chagny-Sève, pp. 273–4. For his arrest, see Gooder, p. 88, citing TNA:PRO E358/20 rot. 6 dorse under 'compotus Henrici de Cobham'; MS A, fol. 44v (Wilkins, p. 344).

56 Scholars' various theories are summarised by Sève and Chagny-Sève in their *Procès des Templiers d'Auvergne*, p. 246, n. 7: 'Peut-être s'y trouvait-il à cause de ses fonctions…, peut-être s'y était-il rendu par prudence … peut-être comme le laisserait penser une liste de frères en fuit, s'y était-il réfugié'.

57 Demurger, *Jacques de Molay*, p. 210, citing (p. 324 n. 28) *Regestrum Clementis papae V ex Vaticanis archetypis*, edited by monks of the Benedictine Order, 9 vols (Rome, 1885–92), vol. 1, pp. 190–1, nos 1034–36.

58 Demurger, *Jacques de Molay*, p. 210, quoting Jacques de Molay's memorandum in *Vitae Paparum Avenionensium*, ed. Étienne Baluze (Paris, 1630–1718), new edn G. Mollat, 4 vols (Paris, 1916–1927), vol. 3, pp. 145–9, here pp. 148–9; translated by Malcolm Barber and Keith Bate, *The Templars: Selected Sources* (Manchester, 2002), pp. 105–9, here p. 108.

59 Demurger, *Jacques de Molay*, p. 211.

60 Gooder, 'South Witham', p. 90: quoting *VCH: Cambridgeshire*, vol. 2, ed. L.F. Salzman (1948), pp. 259–60; Lord, pp. 63–4, 78.

61 The historian Tanner assumed this for the Hospitallers' house of Chippenham in Cambridgeshire, near Denney, writing that it was: 'used for sick brethren, often removed hither for country air': *The Knights Hospitallers in England: Being the Report*

of Prior Philip de Thame to the Grand Master Elyan de Villanova for A.D. *1338*, ed. Lambert
B. Larking, introduction by John Mitchell Kemble, Camden Society First Series,
65 (1867); henceforth cited as L&K: p. 230, note on p. 78: quoting Tanner, *Notitia
Monastica*, ed. J. Nasmith (Cambridge, 1787), vi.

62 Gooder, pp. 147–52; TNA:PRO E358/18 rot. 7(1), under 'Exp'.

63 Gooder, p. 149; TNA:PRO E358/18 rot. 18 dorse.

64 Mentioned MS A, fol. 119r, 119v (Wilkins, p. 370); Gooder, pp. 89, 147; TNA:PRO
E358/18 rot. 7 (1) on his white mantle.

65 TNA:PRO E142/111 mem. 2 dorse; Gooder, p. 148.

66 Gooder, p. 149, TNA: PRO E358/18 rot. 14. See also ibid., rot. 18 dorse.

67 TNA: PRO E142/18 mem. 1 dorse; Gooder, p. 151.

68 TNA:PRO E358/20 rot. 6 dorse, under 'Compotus Henrici de Cobham: Expensa';
TNA:PRO E358/18 rot. 7(1).

69 Gooder, p. 149; TNA:PRO E358/18 rot. 11; TNA:PRO E358/20, rot. 8(2).

70 TNA:PRO E358/18 rot. 14; Gooder, p. 149.

71 TNA:PRO E142/18 mem. 1 dorse; Gooder, p. 151.

72 MS A, fols 115v, 144v (Wilkins p. 276; omits first reference).

73 TNA:PRO E142/18 mem. 1 dorse.

74 Gooder, p. 148; TNA:PRO E358/18 rot. 15.

75 TNA:PRO E358/18 rot. 31 recto; Gooder, p. 151.

76 MS A, fols 109r, 115v (Wilkins, pp. 366, 367); Gooder, pp. 148–9.

77 MS A, fols 52v, 58r (Wilkins, pp. 345, 347).

78 MS A, fol. 84r (Wilkins, p. 355); MS C, fol. 9v (Schottmüller, p. 95, misread the name
as 'Caunde').

79 MS A, fols 45v, 58v, 84r (Wilkins, pp. 344–5, 347, 355); TNA:PRO E142/111 mem. 2
dorse.

80 MS A, fols 30v, 58r, 84r (Wilkins, pp. 341–2, 346, 355); *CPR, 1292–1301*, pp. 75, 88, 391,
483, 572.

81 MS A, 130r (Wilkins, p. 372: name only); TNA:PRO E142/11, mem. 1, dorse; *Register
of William Greenfield*, part 4, p. 336 n. 2.

82 *Calendar of Documents relating to Ireland, preserved in Her Majesty's Public Record Office*,
ed. H.S. Sweetman *et al.*, 5 vols (London, 1875–86) (henceforth cited as *CDRI*),
vol. 3, p. 30, no. 57; MS A, fols 24r, 29v, 58v, 87v, 90r, 101v–102r, 148v, 149r (Wilkins,
pp. 340, 341, 347, 364–5; other references omitted); although his absence in April 1311
could have been due only to illness, he was not included in the final abjurations and
absolutions of July 1311, as he is not mentioned in MS A, fols 166v–170r (Wilkins,
pp. 390–3) – so was dead by that time.

83 MS A, fol. 102r (Wilkins, p. 365); he is not mentioned in MS A, fols 166v–170r
(Wilkins, pp. 390–3).

84 MS A, fol. 58r (Wilkins, p. 345); and see TNA:PRO E358/18 rot. 11.

85 MS A, fol. 58r, 84r, 102r (Wilkins, pp. 347, 355, 365).

86 TNA:PRO E358/18 rot. 18; MS A, fol. 83r (Wilkins, p. 354); Gooder, p. 149.

87 *CCR, 1307–1313*, p. 365; Forey, 'Ex-Templars', pp. 19, 21, 34–5 (citing the unpublished
registers of the bishop of Lincoln).

88 Personal communication from Alan Forey, 13 December 2007. I am very grateful to
Dr Forey for this information.

89 TNA:PRO E358/18 rot. 18; Forey, 'Ex-Templars', pp. 19, 21, 34–5.

90 For William of Jafford's offices, see: *Register of William Greenfield*, part 1, p. xxvii, p. 6, no. 22, p. 237, no. 563, etc.; ibid., part 4, p. 319, no. 2285, etc., and *passim*.

91 Patricius de Ripen, *claviger*, was arrested at Temple Newsam in January 1308: TNA: PRO E142/18 mem. 1 dorse. He died 29 October 1308: Gooder, p. 151.

92 MS A, fol. 91v–92r (Wilkins, p. 359); cited in MS C, fols 1v, 2r, 5r, 6r (Schottmüller, pp. 79, 81, 87, 89).

93 MS C, fol. 4r (Schottmüller, pp. 84–5).

94 MS C, fols 2v, 4r (Schottmüller, pp. 81, 85).

95 Told against heretics: Malcolm Barber, 'Propaganda in the Middle Ages: the Charges against the Templars', *Nottingham Medieval Studies*, 17 (1973), pp. 42–57, here p. 46; Norman Cohn, *Europe's Inner Demons: the Demonization of Christians in Medieval Christendom* (London, 1975), pp. 48–9. Told against Jews: Robert I. Moore, *The Formation of a Persecuting Society: Power and Deviance in Western Europe, 950–1250* (Oxford, 1987), pp. 38–9; Matthew Paris, *Chronica majora*, ed. Henry Richards Luard, Rolls Series 57 (London, 1872–83), vol. 3, p. 115.

96 Gooder, p. 113, quoting *Documents illustrative of English History*, ed. Cole, 'Corrodia', pp. 215–16.

97 MS A, fols 165r–v, 168r, 168v (Wilkins, pp. 389, 391).

98 Neighbours: MS A, fols 60r–62v (abridged in Wilkins, pp. 348–9). Servants: MS A, fols 97v, 99r (Wilkins, pp. 362, 363, gives names only). Other servants: MS A, fols 153v (Wilkins, p. 379); MS A, fols 158v–159r (Wilkins, p. 382).

99 Perkins, 'Knights Templars in the British Isles', pp. 213–18.

100 *CPR, 1307–1313*, pp. 535–7, 539–40. Frankpledge was a system for keeping law and order. When boys reached adulthood they were placed in a group of ten, a 'tithing', in which every member was answerable for the good conduct of, or the damage done by, any one of the other members (see *Oxford English Dictionary Online* (http:// dictionary.oed.com/); henceforth cited as *OED Online*). The local lord was responsible for checking annually that every adult male was in a tithing – this was called 'view of frankpledge'.

101 MS A, fol. 91v (Wilkins, p. 358); A.J. Musson, 'Stapleton, Miles, first Lord Stapleton (*d.* 1314)', *ODNB*, vol. 52, pp. 259–80.

102 MS A, fol. 158r (Wilkins, p. 382).

103 MS A, fol. 91v (Wilkins, p. 358); *Calendar of Inquisitions post Mortem preserved in the Public Record Office, prepared under the superintendence of the Deputy Keeper of the Rolls*, vol. 5, *Edward II* (London, 1908), pp. 406, 411, 412; J.R. Maddicott, *Thomas of Lancaster 1307–1322: A Study in the Reign of Edward II* (Oxford, 1970), p. 63.

104 Maddicott, *Thomas of Lancaster*, pp. 41–3, 45, 54–5, 204–6, 274; J.R.S. Phillips, *Aymer de Valence, Earl of Pembroke 1307–1324: Baronial Politics in the Reign of Edward II* (Oxford, 1972), pp. 106, 125–7, 207, 255.

105 *The Babylonian Talmud, Seder Nezikin: Sanhedrin*, vol. 1, 43a, pp. 281–2.

106 MS A, fol. 91v (Wilkins, p. 358).

107 MS A, fol. 168r (Wilkins, p. 391).

108 *Councils and Synods*, ed. Powicke and Cheney, vol. 2, pt. 2, pp. 1236–1240, esp. 1239.

109 James Davies, *The Baronial Opposition to Edward II: its Character and Policy. A Study in Administrative History* (London, 1918, repr. 1967), p. 290.

110 On this, see Kathleen Edwards, 'The Political Importance of the English Bishops during the Reign of Edward II', *English Historical Review*, 59 (1944), pp. 311–347, here pp. 313–15.

111 MS A, fols 9r, 74v, 81v, 87v, 167r, 169v (Wilkins omits first reference, pp. 352, 356, 390, 392); *Foedera*, ed. Rymer, vol. 2, pt 1, p. 88; *CCR, 1307–1313*, p. 230. I am grateful to Jeffrey Hamilton for drawing this final reference to my attention.

112 MS A, fol. 166r (Wilkins, p. 390). On Bishop John, see M.C. Buck, 'Langton, John (*d.* 1337)', *ODNB*, vol. 32, pp. 512–13.

113 Roy Martin Haines, 'Greenfield, William (*c.*1255–1315)', *ODNB*, vol. 23, pp. 590–2; *Register of William Greenfield*, part 4, pp. 97–8, 99–100, 281–2, 283–4, 292–5, 306–7, 349, nos 1886, 1890, 2260, 2268, 2273, 2274, 2279 (end), 2324; ibid., part 5, pp. xxxiii–xl; *Chronicle of Walter of Guisborough*, pp. 392, 395; *Councils and Synods*, ed. Powicke and Cheney, vol. 2, pt. 2, p. 1338. For William of Jafford and John of Nassington see pp. 57–8 above.

114 *Chronicle of Walter of Guisborough*, pp. 386–95; *Flores Historiarum*, vol. 3, pp. 143, 144–148 (Westminster manuscript); pp. 331–4 (Tintern manuscript); *Vita Edwardi Secundi*, pp. 80–1.

115 Edwards, 'Political Importance of the English Bishops', p. 330; Antonia Gransden, 'The Continuations of the Westminster *Flores* from 1265 to 1327', *Mediaeval Studies*, 26 (1974), pp. 472–80, here pp. 483–4.

116 *Foedera*, ed. Rymer, vol. 2, pt 1, p. 27.

117 Ibid., p. 75. Edward II took the cross in 1313 with King Philip IV of France, his children and nobles, but none of them ever went on crusade: Christopher Tyerman, *England and the Crusades, 1095–1588* (Chicago and London, 1988), pp. 241–4.

118 *Register of William Greenfield*, part 4, pp. 307–10, no. 2280.

119 *Foedera*, ed. Rymer, vol. 2, pt 1, pp. 59, 65.

120 Perkins, 'Trial of the Knights Templars', p. 433.

121 TNA:PRO E368/79 rot. 115 dorse.

122 *Foedera*, ed. Rymer, vol. 2, pt 1, p. 70; *CCR, 1307–1313*, p. 94; Clarence Perkins, 'The Wealth of the Knights Templars in England and the Disposition of it after their Dissolution', *American Historical Review*, 5 (1910), pp. 252–63: here pp. 258–9. See also Agnes M. Leys, 'The Forfeiture of the Lands of the Templars in England', *Oxford Essays in Medieval History presented to Herbert Edward Salter* (Oxford, 1934), pp. 155–63; Hamilton, 'Apocalypse Not', pp. 91–2.

123 *CCR, 1307–1313*, p. 90; TNA:PRO E368/79 rots 107 dorse, 108 dorse.

124 Barber, *Trial of the Templars*, 2nd edn, pp. 130–4.

125 *Register of William Greenfield*, part 4, p. 292, no. 2272 (July 12, 1309).

126 *CCR, 1307–1313*, pp. 175–7, 179, 181, 187, 189; *Foedera*, ed. Rymer, vol. 2, pt 1, pp. 88, 90, 91, 92–4, 99, 100.

127 Fraser, *History of Antony Bek*, p. 173; *Records of Antony Bek*, pp. 155–6, 157, nos. 144, 145, 147.

3

The Templars' Lands
in Royal Hands

When the king's sheriffs arrested the Templars in the second week of January 1308 and took the Templars' possessions into the king's hands, King Edward II of England acquired control of a considerable acreage of land. The Templars had administered their land in western Europe through a system of administrative centres, called (in Latin) *preceptoriae* or (in French) *commanderies*, each of which represented a manor, effectively a large farm house with its estates. The official (*preceptor* or *commandeur*) in charge of this administrative centre was responsible not only for that manor but also for a number of other subordinate manors or smaller farms, churches and small areas of land. He employed managers and workers, authorised expenditure and collected the revenue from these estates. The surplus of income over expenditure would be submitted to the grand commander of England once a year at the provincial chapter meeting – which by the late thirteenth century was usually held at Dinsley in Hertfordshire – and a proportion of the total income (the *responsion*) from the grand commandery of England would be sent to the Order's headquarters in the East. However, after the Templars' arrests, the sheriff of each county in England took over these responsibilities, and the surplus of income over expenditure was paid into the royal exchequer.

Historians of the Templars have tended to talk rather glibly of 'preceptories' of the Templars, as if this were an official term.[1] This is misleading. First, they are using the Latin term from the legal documents, rather than the 'commanderies' which the Templars themselves would have used in everyday speech. Second, there was no official usage of the term. The word was used to designate a house which was a centre of administration, which would also be where brothers were received into the Order of the Temple. However, with economic and social change, shifting patterns of population and the climate change of the late thirteenth and early fourteenth centuries, those houses which were centres of administration in the early thirteenth century might no longer be so in the early fourteenth. Some houses where brothers had been received into the Order in the late thirteenth century – suggesting that they were commanderies then – no longer had any Templars in residence by the start of 1308, and some had even been leased out and were no longer controlled by the Templars.

For example, a brother had been received in the chapel at the Templar's house at Addington in Surrey in 1291, but subsequently the Templars had leased Addington to one John Blebury or Bloebury for life. The account of the sheriff of Sussex and Surrey covering the period from the arrests to Michaelmas 1308, ends with the note that he was not submitting an account for the *maner' de Adyngton* because when the Templars were arrested, the manor with its stock had been handed over to John of Blebury, chaplain, 'who was enfeoffed a long time before the aforesaid arrest by the aforesaid master and brothers, for John to hold for his lifetime'. In 1324, Parliament assigned Addington with the Templars' other properties to the Hospital of St John, but the Hospitallers had difficulty in recovering the manor from John of Blebury. They persisted and eventually he admitted that the land was theirs and that his claim on it would end on his death. Having recovered the land, the Hospitallers held it until the dissolution of their Order in England in 1540.[2] This case is an illustration of the Hospitallers' determination to track down and obtain all the lands which had belonged to the Templars, no matter how obstinate the current holder or obscure the records.

Again, South Witham, a sizeable house of the Templars in south-west Lincolnshire, had been abandoned by the Templars before 1308 and was not specifically mentioned during the trial proceedings.[3] Wetherby, in the West Riding of Yorkshire, had been a significant Templar house and, during the trial, one of the non-Templar witnesses mentioned the chapel and sleeping accommodation and indicated that in the late 1280s there were many brothers resident; but in 1308 there were no brothers living there, and by 1338 the house was combined with nearby Ribston.[4] In 1292 Copmanthorpe near York had a commander, who was also custodian of the Templars' mills at York – in 1297 the commander of Copmanthorpe was one Robert of

Rygate – but by 1308 there were no Templars at Copmanthorpe.[5] Keele in Staffordshire had a single brother in 1308, who was called 'commander', but the income of this house was apparently very small; the king's officials accounted for it with the income from Lydley and the other Templar properties in Shropshire.[6]

A Templar house might have only one brother in residence, yet in fact be a wealthy and important commandery. Whitley, a Templar house near Hirst, south of the River Aire, is overlooked by modern studies of the Templars in the British Isles, but had a commander and accommodated William of Grafton, commander of Yorkshire, for the early months of 1308. In January 1308 its total value was assessed at £130 15s. 10d.[7] This was an impressive sum compared with, for example, the commandery of Penhill in the North Riding of Yorkshire (plate 22), which was assessed at £67 19s. 5d., or even nearby Temple Hirst at £124 8s. 7d. The wealthiest house in Yorkshire was Faxfleet in the East Riding (plate 16), assessed at £290 4s. 10½d., followed by Ribston in the West Riding at £267 13s. 2d. (plate 23) and Newsam in the West Riding, which was assessed at £174 3s. 3d.[8]

The fact that there were no brothers permanently resident at a Templar house did not mean that it was in decline. Evelyn Lord has noted that, to judge from the royal keepers' accounts, in 1308 the estate at Rothley in Leicestershire was the Templars' most valuable estate in England – yet no Templars were arrested there. The commander, Thomas of Walkington, was arrested at Temple Balsall in Warwickshire, where apparently he was also commander. Evidently the Templars were running their estates at Balsall and Rothley under a single management – not because the estates were poor or run down, but because they presented few management problems and did not require more.[9] It seems that at last the Templars had accepted the advice of successive Church Councils and were using their estates in the West to finance fighting men in the East, rather than supporting large numbers of non-fighters in the West.[10]

The point at issue, then, for historians studying the Templars' properties in the British Isles in 1308, is not which houses were called commanderies or had been called commanderies in the past, but what was actually happening at those houses. Were there any Templars in residence? Were the houses leased out to tenants? What problems were associated with these houses (for example, did they suffer from flooding)? How did the king's officials administer them?

The following Templar properties in England had at least one Templar in residence, permanently or on a part-time basis, at the beginning of January 1308:[11]

1. Aslackby, Lincolnshire (2 Templars)
2. Balsall, Warwickshire (4)
3. Bisham, Berkshire (1)
4. Bruer, Lincolnshire (4)
5. Combe, Somerset (3)
6. Cowton, North Riding of Yorkshire (3)
7. Cressing, Essex (2)
8. Denney, Cambridgeshire (13)
9. Dinsley, Hertfordshire (3)
10. Duxford, Cambridgeshire (3)
11. Eagle, Lincolnshire (8)
12. Ewell, Kent (2 + 2 visitors)
13. Faxfleet, East Riding of Yorkshire (4)
14. Foulbridge, North Riding of Yorkshire (2)
15. Garway, Herefordshire (2)
16. Guiting, Gloucestershire (2)
17. Hirst, West Riding of Yorkshire (2)
18. Keele, Staffordshire (1)
19. Lydley, Shropshire (3)
20. Newsam, West Riding of Yorkshire (3)
21. New Temple, Middlesex (8)
22. Penhill, North Riding of Yorkshire (1)
23. Ribston, West Riding of Yorkshire (3)
24. Rockley, Wiltshire (1)
25. Rothley, Leicestershire (1)
26. Sandford, Oxfordshire (4)
27. Shipley, Sussex (2)
28. Strood, Kent (1)
29. Sutton, Essex (1)
30. Thornton, Northumberland (4)
31. Upleadon, Herefordshire (2)
32. Westerdale, North Riding of Yorkshire (1)
33. Whitley, West Riding of Yorkshire (1)
34. Wilbraham, Cambridgeshire (2)
35. Willoughton, Lincolnshire (3)

The sheriffs' inventories give a vivid picture of everyday life at a Templar commandery on a single morning in January 1308. Consider, for example, Foulbridge commandery in North Yorkshire (plate 17). It is still a working farm; the farmhouse includes the Templars' thirteenth-century hall. It is situated in the valley of the River Derwent to the south of the North Yorkshire Moors, and the modern visitor can walk along public rights of way across the flat, marshy land, to the modern 'foul bridge' across the River Derwent. The pattern of lanes and bridle paths converging on Foulbridge suggest that it held more importance in the past as a crossing point over the river than it has today.

In the fourteenth century, Foulbridge was far from being isolated from Christian life. The next community, two miles to the west, was a house of Benedictine nuns at Yedingham; five miles to the north-east was a house of Cistercian nuns of Wykeham; both of these were also next to the River Derwent. Two Templars were arrested at Foulbridge in 1308: Richard of Hales, the commander, and Richard of Ripon, *claviger* or keyholder.[12] One of the Franciscan friars who gave evidence against the Templars in England recounted a third-hand derogatory story about Brother Robert of Raygat (or Basset, or Rygate) which he said originated with a former servant at Foulbridge. He also told a derogatory story about Richard of Hales, whose confession he said he used to hear. Richard of Hales died before giving a formal testimony, on 23 June 1309.[13]

All this information – the modern site, the references to the house in the trial proceedings – helps us to create an image of the Templars' house, but the sheriff's inventory of Foulbridge adds a new and vivid dimension to the picture. The inventory was taken on the Wednesday after Epiphany (6 January) 1308, by Geoffrey of St Quintano and John of Hotham on behalf of the sheriff, and Brother Richard of Hales, the commander.[14]

There was a chapel, a chamber, a larder, a cellar, a hall, 'le malthous', a grange or barn, a forge, a kitchen, a granary and 'le Tendlathe' – the final two buildings stored grain. The chapel had the most valuable contents: there was a silver chalice gilded with gold, a missal, four vestments for the chaplain, a service book containing the daytime 'hours' or prayers for each hour – but one service book was at the subordinate house at Allerston, five miles distant to the north-west – two covers for the altar, two towels for the priest, two phials, one silver pyx for the eucharistic host, four crosses – two with images of Christ and two without – a censer, two iron candelabras, two tunics for the deacons, two surplices, a cope for the choir (*j capa pro coro*), a lenten veil for the altar, an antiphoner, five prayer books of various types – graduals, psalters and an ordinal – two little bells, two great bells and two basins with iron chains. In the chamber there was a great chest, which was empty. In the larder there were twenty-nine bacons and two beef carcasses. In the cellar there were three tuns, two barrels and two old casks. In the hall there were five tables, each worth five shillings, and a wash-basin. In the malthouse was a bake-oven, a basin and pipe-work, a quantity of oats, five vats, three barrels and sacks, a press and other equipment for brewing. One of the earthenware pots which should have been in the kitchen was currently at Allerston. In the forge there were a smithy and a bellows, a hammer, three pairs of tongs and a wrench. In the barn there were estimated to be eighty quarters[15] of oats in sheaves, eight quarters of wheat in sheaves and ten quarters of maslin (mixed rye and wheat). In the chaff-house there were twenty quarters of maslin in sheaves. In the granary there were eight quarters of malted oats.

The officials then went on to see what was growing in the fields and what animal stock the commandery owned. Growing in the field at Foulbridge and Wydale (2¾ miles to the north-east in Snainton Dale on the south flank of the moors) there were 120 acres of wheat and maslin. There were eleven cows, one bull, two bullocks, one steer, two three-year-old bullocks, five steers and eight two-year-old bullocks, two heifers two years old and nine calves of one year. There were four old sows, one old boar, thirty-six old hogs and ten piglets; and there were 759 wethers (neutered male sheep), 659 ewes and 300 young rams.

Finally, the officials moved on to the haulage power of the commandery: thirty-two oxen, six mules and two asses. To be pulled there were six ploughs with fittings and six without, two carts with iron tyres and fittings, and two old carts with fittings. Spades, forks, and other farm implements were recorded last.

The officials then went to the smaller farms dependent on Foulbridge. They recorded the acreages sown with wheat and maslin at Allerston, as well as the wheat, maslin and oats in sheaves and the beans and peas stored in the barn. There were also oxen for the plough and four carthorses. At Wydale was a grange or barn containing wheat and barley in sheaves. The total value was £54 3s. 2d.[16]

A further report on the value of the manor of Foulbridge was produced in 1309: the manor was worth 40s. a year, and there was also a windmill, but it was empty and rendered nothing. The brothers had a chaplain who celebrated mass each year at the manor, and alms were given to all comers.[17]

Every single item within a house was assigned a value, but at this distance in time it is impossible to know how accurate the valuations were. Some items were probably overvalued. On 1 December 1311, Adam of Hoperton, former custodian of the manors of the Templars in the county of York, handed over to the sheriffs, Alexander of Cave and Robert of Amecotes, the Templars' mills by the castle of York, complete with the inventory taken at the time of the Templars' arrests. He noted that the gilt chalice in the chapel had been valued at the time of the arrests at 100s. (£5), 'but it is not worth so much'.[18] It is difficult to know now why the chalice at York Castle mills was initially valued at 100s., while that at Cowton was worth only one mark[19] (two-thirds of a pound) – as Cowton was a more important house, we might expect it to have had more valuable equipment. Again, it is not clear what the *Liber infirmorum* (book of the sick) at Combe in Somerset could have been – a herbal, or perhaps a list of sick people in the parish who were to be prayed for – but a value of 12d. seems rather low for any book in this period.[20]

Nothing was found in the Templars' houses in the British Isles to support the allegations against them. For example, despite the claims by some non-Templars during the trial that there were idol-heads in England, no such heads were found.[21] It is possible that the gilt heads mentioned by these witnesses were actually reliquaries, each containing the skull of a saint; but the inventories do not specifically mention such reliquaries. Relics were recorded at New Temple in London and a *phylatorium* (reliquary) in the chapel at Sandford in Oxfordshire (plate 24).[22] A second-hand story related by the Austin friar Adam of Smeton suggests that there was a portable altar at Sandford commandery which contained relics, and which the Templars used to venerate before setting out on a journey.[23]

Given that the leading Templars were knights, it might seem surprising that hardly any weapons were found in the Templars' houses. At New Temple in London there were a few crossbows and swords, one sword listed as being among the possessions of Brother William de Hertford (elsewhere surnamed 'Hereford'), another among the possessions of Brother Thomas of Standon, and a third in Brother Richard of Herdwick's room. There was also in the dormitory an Irish axe belonging to Brother William (possibly a souvenir of his travels), which the sheriffs of London handed over to him with his sword and other possessions from the dormitory. But apparently Brothers Thomas and Richard did not get their swords back – their possessions were handed over to James le Boteler and William of Basyng, then sheriffs of London.[24] At Combe in Somerset there was a crossbow worth 7d. and at Shipley in Sussex there was a haketon or padded tunic, two sets of plates, two gorgets, a bascinet, a pair of mailed gauntlets, a pair of greaves, a pair of cuisses – value of all 20s. 6d. Also, there were two helmets, two bows with arrows, and a battle axe, value of these 4s. 9d.[25] This lack of weapons and armour indicates that the Templars in Britain were not normally armed. Clarence Perkins and Evelyn Lord suggested that they had been allowed to take their weapons with them when they were arrested,[26] but the inventory of the New Temple reveals that although some property was handed over to its former owners, much was not. If the Templars had taken their weapons with them, these would have been confiscated when the Templars were formally locked up, late in 1308. In fact, the royal records do not record large numbers of swords or quantities of armour coming into the king's hands at that time.

As men who had taken religious vows, the Templars in western Europe were not permitted to bear weapons; they could carry weapons only to defend Christians and Christendom against the enemies of Christ. Contemporary pictures of the Templars in western Europe show them dressed like monks, with long robes and wearing the cap of a religious man, rather than dressed as warriors.[27] In this case, it is reasonable to question why there were *any* weapons in Templar houses in 1308. It is possible that the swords in New Temple were ceremonial swords, not intended for fighting. The armour at Shipley could have been a gift to the Templars by one of their supporters, intended to be sent out to the East to help the crusading cause. Overall, it is clear that the Templars in Britain were not heavily armed.

The problem of corruption among sheriffs had long been a problem for the English government.[28] At Garway in Herefordshire (plate 18) there were two Templars in residence at the time of the arrests: the commander, Philip de Meux, and William of Pokelington. The sheriff, Walter Haklut or of Hakluy, recorded that he had been given the gift of a horse, a palfrey which had belonged to Brother Philip, but sadly it had broken its leg in the stable and died within a month.[29]

It soon became clear that the king could not simply hold on to the Templars' estates and do nothing with them; management decisions had to be made. As a religious Order, the Templars had been given churches from which they could take both the property revenues and the 'spiritualities' – the dues owed to the Church. They also had the right to appoint or 'present' the priest. On 24 March 1308 the king, acting on behalf of the Templars, presented to the church of Cardington in Shropshire one John Mahen of Norton; in May he presented a priest to the Templars' church of Ewell in Kent; in June, a priest was presented to the Templars' church of Baldock in Hertfordshire.[30] The right to appoint parish priests to the Templars' churches gave the king a means of rewarding clergy who had served him well.

Another obligation was the payment of corrodies. These were usually regular payments made to persons who had made a substantial donation to the Order in return for their board and lodging, or other day-to-day support, for the rest of their lives. Alternatively, a corrody could be a gift by the Templars of board and lodging for life to a former employee of the Templars – the equivalent of a regular pension.[31] The Templars had had a great many corrodians living in their houses, or associated with them, and the king's officials found themselves besieged with demands for payments. For example, in May 1310, Michael of the Grene complained to the king that he had granted Brother William de la More (representing the Order of the Temple) sixty acres of arable land and eight acres of meadow at Wycombe, in return for which the Templars had to maintain him with board and lodging, and if they failed to do so he was entitled to have his land back. As they had not fulfilled their side of the agreement they had returned his land to him. However, when the Order was arrested, the sheriff of Buckinghamshire – who assumed that he was simply renting his land from the Templars – confiscated his property with the Templars' possessions. The king ordered that Michael's land should be returned to him.[32]

There were some expenses connected with maintenance of the Templars' properties. In December 1308 the king ordered the sheriffs of London to repair the roof of the New Temple, London; if there was not enough money available from the Templars' own land, they must pay for the repairs out of other income. After floods on the River Thames had damaged the Templars' mills at Withyfleet, on the south bank of the Thames just upriver from Southwark, King Edward instructed the sheriff in June 1309 to send twenty oaks from Lilleston, a Templar manor in Middlesex, to repair the mills. In 1312 the mills again required repair; the king authorised expenditure up to £10.[33]

Despite such problems, the king also saw the Templars' property as a useful source of money to meet pressing needs. As Edward II was still paying off his father's debts, he was in constant need of additional funds. The lands of Walter Langton, bishop of Coventry and Lichfield, were also currently in the king's hands while the bishop was tried for extortion, corruption and trespass.[34] On 28 February 1308, Thomas of Bernham, sheriff of Lincolnshire, came before the treasurer and barons of the exchequer with a letter, which stated that Francesco Cose and Francesco Grandon, *socii* and *mercatores* (fellows and merchants) of the Society of the Bardi of Florence, and Ponche Portenare and Giacomo Enrici of the Society of the

Portenare of Florence, owed on their own behalf and on behalf of their societies to William de la More, master of the knighthood of the Temple in England, and his brothers, the sum of £476 6s. 8d., as payment for wool from the Templar houses of Bruer, Willoughton and Eagle. The wool had been sold by the Templars and received by these Italian wool merchants on 15 August 1307.[35]

At this time the Italian wool merchants still dominated the English wool trade, although the Flemish trade was rising in importance. 'Forward-selling' of wool to merchants had been a common practice among both monastic and secular wool-producers in England since at least the early thirteenth century, but compared to the Cistercians and Augustinian canons, the Templars had entered into very few such contracts.[36] Now this contract became a means for Edward II to reduce his own debts. Since the arrest of the Templars and confiscation of their assets, money due to the Templars was due to the king. So, for example, the king owed money to the Society of the Bellardi of Lucca. On 1 July 1308 the Italian wool merchants' debt to the Templars was made over to Giovanni Vanne, merchant of the Bellardi, and the Bardi and Portenare merchants were directed to pay their debts to Giovanni Vanne.[37]

As for future years' wool, the king sent instructions that it should also be used to pay his debts. On 8 May 1308 he told the sheriff of Leicester to have the Templars' sheep shorn and send the wool to Bruer in Lincolnshire (plate 14), to be handed over to 'our clerk' William of Spanneby, custodian of Bruer, in return for a receipt stating how much wool he had delivered. The same instructions were sent to the sheriffs of Nottingham and Huntingdon. On 26 May William of Spanneby was instructed to give the wool to Giovanni Vanne and his *socii*, merchants of the Bellardi society of Lucca, in payment of the debts of Edward I and Edward II. The same instructions were sent to the king's bailiff in Bustlewick in Holderness and to the sheriff of Surrey and Sussex, regarding the wool from the Templars' and Walter Langton's lands. On 2 May 1309, William of Spanneby was instructed that all the wool from Temple Bruer was to be given to Henry Nasard, Frenchman and merchant of London, in part payment of the king's debts. The same instructions were sent to the sheriff of York, custodian of the Templars' lands in Yorkshire.[38]

Those owing the Templars money for wool could be slow to pay it. On 15 November 1309, two merchants of Beverley in Yorkshire who still owed £312 to the grand commander of the Temple in England for wool which they had bought from him, were instructed to pay it to Lord Henry Percy, because the king owed Lord Henry money. But on 23 February 1310 this instruction was revoked; the money was now to be paid directly to the king, which was done.[39]

In order to administer the Templars' lands to the best effect, the king appointed keepers (such as William of Spanneby) for many of the houses. In June 1308, Edward sent instructions to his justiciar in Ireland to draw supplies of food from the Templars' former properties in Ireland for his forthcoming campaign in Scotland. The same instructions went to the sheriffs of Cambridgeshire and Huntingdonshire: the latter were instructed to send 500 quarters of wheat, 1,000 quarters of oats and 500 quarters of malt; this was to be ready and delivered by 15 August. In the event, the expedition did not take place, allowing King Robert Bruce of Scotland to keep the lands which he had recently conquered in the south of Scotland.[40]

As well as using former Templar income to pay his debts, Edward II gave some of the Templars' property to his friends and allies, with gifts to the elder and younger Hugh Despensers. He also gave Guy of Beauchamp, earl of Warwick, the lease of four Templar manors in Warwickshire.[41]

The Templars' houses could also provide accommodation for the king's use. On 6 November 1308, King Edward II wrote to the royal custodian of Bisham, Robert of Halstede, to inform him that *dilecta nobis* ('the lady dear to us') Elizabeth Bruce – wife of Robert Bruce (now Robert I of Scotland) – who had been captured by King Edward I's supporters in Scotland in September 1306, was coming to stay at Bisham (plate 13) and should be allowed to make use of the woods and water for hunting and hawking, and everything on the estate while she was there. Although Elizabeth was a prisoner, the king took pains to ensure that her stay would be a pleasant one. She was still at Bisham on 15 October 1310, but by 6 February 1312 Edward was giving instructions for her to be received at Windsor Castle, and later in that year she moved to Shafton. Elizabeth was not released until after the English defeat at Bannockburn, when she was freed in exchange for the earl of Hereford, captured after the battle.[42]

All in all, the king found many uses for the Templars' properties: to ease his problems of money supply, to supply his army, to reward his friends and allies, and to accommodate noble prisoners. While Clarence Perkins calculated that revenue from the Templars' lands only provided four per cent of royal earnings in these years, it was nevertheless an additional, uncommitted income at a time when most of the king's money was already committed.[43]

So useful was this windfall that Edward went to every length to exploit it to the full. On 1 March 1309 the king instructed the sheriffs to make enquiries about any other money, precious objects and other goods which had belonged to the Templars in his counties and to take them into royal hands. Three days later he told the treasurer and barons of the exchequer to make a complete investigation of the Templars' lands, their extent and what they were worth each year, and for this to be sent to the exchequer.[44] On 27 April he appointed the abbot-elect of St Albans abbey to survey the king's manors and the Templars' former manors to the south of the River Trent, to establish what they were worth. On 6 May the king instructed his officials Ralph of Monte Caniso and John of Kirketon to find out how his official William Inge, who was acting as keeper for the Templars' lands in Hertfordshire, was getting on with his duties. What state were the Templars' lands in? What were they worth? When they had made a full report, they should submit it to the treasurer and barons of the exchequer.[45]

Yet Edward could not use the Templars' lands unchallenged. Back in August 1308, when Pope Clement V had composed the bull *Faciens misericordiam* which ordered that the Templars be formally interrogated, he had also issued a bull stating that he wanted to protect the Templars' properties because they had been given to protect the Holy Land and defend Christendom against its enemies (*Deus, ulcionum dominus*). The pope had entrusted these properties to the care of the patriarch of Jerusalem (Antony Bek, bishop of Durham), the archbishops of Canterbury and York and the bishop of Lincoln. They had full papal authority over these properties and should prevent anyone taking anything from them. If anything was taken and not returned on demand, they should inform him at once. It is not clear when this letter reached England, although a copy dated 26 November 1309 is in the register of the archbishop of York.[46]

If the letter arrived in England with the two papal inquisitors in late summer 1309, this would explain why Edward suddenly became anxious about the damage to Templar property – most of which he had caused himself. On 27 September 1309 he wrote to his officials Alan of Goldingham and John of Meldfield, stating that since the Templars' arrests, some of the goods and chattels belonging to the Templars of Essex and Hertfordshire had been taken and removed. They were to find out who had done this and the value of the goods and chattels so taken, find out where they went and where they were now. The accounts that the sheriff of Essex and

Hertfordshire had submitted to the exchequer had recorded extensive sales – even the palfrey belonging to the commander of Dinsley in Hertfordshire, which had been found safely stabled at Ware, had been sold and the sale recorded in the accounts for Cressing in Essex. Now that the papal inquisitors had arrived in England and were enquiring into the Templars' affairs, perhaps Edward was merely 'covering his back' to forestall the inevitable enquiries into what had become of the Templars' properties while they were in the king's hands. He ordered similar investigations in Norfolk, Suffolk and Yorkshire, and these continued into March 1310.[47]

The inventories of the Templars' lands, the 'extents' drawn up by the sheriffs in 1309–10, the testimonies of outsiders and various pieces of royal correspondence offer an insight into the network of contacts between a Templar house and its local community.[48] Such contacts could take many forms, but could simply involve outsiders travelling regularly through the Templars' property. The trial testimonies indicate that the Templars allowed others to enter their houses on a regular basis and gave lodging to outsiders.

It is difficult to identify guest houses or lodgings for visitors in the surviving sites of Templar and Hospitaller houses in the British Isles. The Hospitallers' English priory sent a report to Rhodes in 1338 which indicated that every Hospitaller commandery in England and Wales incurred heavy expenses lodging travellers, but there is no mention of guest-houses.[49] The report included eight former Templar commanderies that had passed into Hospitaller possession and incurred annual expenses in lodging travellers: Wetherby in Yorkshire, Eagle, Bruer and Willoughton in Lincolnshire, Garway in Herefordshire, Wilbraham in Cambridgeshire, Templecombe in Somerset and Sandford in Oxfordshire.[50] As these houses were lodging travellers in 1338, they had probably done so three decades earlier, at the time of the Templars.

The trial proceedings offer some information about hospitality given by individual houses. Brother Richard of Bokingham, a friar, gave testimony that he and his comrade on the road had stayed at the Templar house of Faxfleet (plate 16), along with many other people. They were lodged in a room next to the Templars' dormitory. In the middle of the night the Templar key-holder got them out of bed and sent them to stand in the hall with many others while the master and brothers held chapter in the chapel, where the grand commander of England and commander of London were receiving a new brother.[51] Perhaps the crowd in the hall was made up of the new Templar's friends and relations, who had come to witness his admission into the Order, although Brother Richard did not say as much.

It is striking that Brother Richard and his comrade were lodged within the house adjoining the Templars' own rooms – not in a separate guesthouse, as was normal in monasteries. If his account is true, far from being more secretive than other religious Orders, the Templars were more open in allowing non-members access to their houses. Similar arrangements were in use at the Templars' house at Arles in the lower Rhône valley, where the guest room was in the Templars' own residential wing of the house, between the commander's chamber and the room for sick knights.[52]

Faxfleet is situated on the north bank of the River Humber in southern Yorkshire, at the confluence of the Rivers Ouse and Trent, directly opposite the town of Alkborough on the south bank of the Humber. This would have been an obvious place for a ferry service across the Humber, carrying passengers who were travelling north or south. An inquest of 1323 into the rights of the Templars' manor here identified a right to a 'water passage of the Humber' worth 18*d*. a year, which could have been a toll on those who crossed the river here, or the right to run boats across the Humber or up and down the river.[53]

Another outsider, one Nicholas of Hynton, notary of London, described how he was invited into the New Temple (plate 19) for a drink by Brother Peter of Ottringham.[54] His story assumed that there was nothing unusual about an outsider being invited into the New Temple, an assumption supported by the testimony of Brother Michael of Baskerville, commander of the New Temple in London. When asked about the time of day that the Order held chapter meetings, Brother Michael replied that it was about the first hour (around 6.00 a.m., after dawn), after mass had been said, and that any of the people could come to mass.[55]

'People' could refer to servants of the brothers, or outsiders from the local community. Brother Michael did not specify which he meant, but his testimony indicates that access to the New Temple was not tightly restricted. As merchants, nobles and kings kept their property in the treasury of the house,[56] they would need to be able to obtain access to it at reasonable hours. After 1330, a succession of legal cases came before the king regarding a public right of way through the middle of the court of the New Temple, from the main road to the bank of the Thames, from where any person could take a boat up the Thames to Westminster. It had been the Templars' responsibility to maintain the jetty, known as 'Temple Bridge', so that outsiders could use this route to Westminster. The king commanded the mayor of London to ensure that the gates of the New Temple were kept open from sunrise to sunset to allow the public to pass through to the jetty, implying that this had been the Templars' custom.[57] The customary thoroughfare, which had existed since 'time out of mind', was not only for persons on foot but for carrying goods 'by wains (carts), horses and otherwise', and any free man of London could request passage through the New Temple at night for the carriage of goods, although not by cart.[58] As the River Thames is tidal, it would sometimes be necessary for merchants to carry their goods down to the wharf in the middle of the night in order to catch the tide.

Brother Michael of Baskerville's evidence that 'people' attended mass in the chapel of New Temple indicates that the Order's chapels were used by the Order's servants and/or by outsiders from the locality. When Pope Innocent II had in 1139 granted the Order the privilege of having its own chapels, he specifically stated that this was to enable the brothers to worship separately from non-members of the Order,[59] yet other evidence from the British trial proceedings suggests that outsiders did enter Templar chapels on a regular basis.

Brother Adam of Smeton, an Austin friar, reported a conversation that he had had with an old man who had worked twenty years for the Templars at their commandery at Sandford in Oxfordshire. The old man had said that when the Templars had to go on journeys, they used to get up early in the morning and go into their chapel. Going up to the altar, they took a great stone tablet out of it, like a small portable altar. They placed this on the altar and all knelt before it and adored it and lay on the ground before it groaning. The old man had often seen this. At such times, no secular person (presumably he meant no non-member of the Order) was permitted to enter the chapel except on important business.[60]

This testimony may well have been true; the obvious explanation for the old man's story was that the stone that lay within the altar stone contained holy relics, which the Templars venerated before setting out on an important journey, a normal action for devout Catholic Christians.[61] If the story were true, presumably it was also true that outsiders were excluded from the Templars' chapel only during the brothers' private services.

One Nicholas of Redemer, Dominican friar, said that he had heard from the Lady of Stiteton near Keele, wife of Lord William of Bereford, knight and justiciar of the lord king, that one of her servants had told her that he had been bearer of a letter addressed to a Templar at Balsall (Warwickshire). When he entered the chapel (plate 12) he saw a Templar baring his buttocks to the cross on the altar.[62] Neither the lady nor her servant came forward to confirm this story, which was probably invented. On the other hand, the fact that the messenger in the story could simply walk into the chapel without having to get permission suggests that outsiders were normally able to enter the Templars' commandery chapels.

Outsiders also came to Templar houses to receive charity. The Order's regulations stated that the Templars should give their unused food and clothing to the poor.[63] Individual houses of the Temple in Britain also gave regular alms to the local poor and needy over and above this requirement. The local men on oath ('jurors'), who in 1309 reported on the value of the Templars' former manor of Foulbridge in north Yorkshire, stated that alms were given on three days each week to all comers;[64] similar alms were given at Cressing in Essex.[65] Such almsgiving must have been very valuable to the local poor, especially in the deteriorating climatic conditions of the early fourteenth century, when harvests failed and food became short. Another means by which Templar houses contributed towards the local communities was through paying corrodies to former donors and employees.[66]

A Templar commandery would employ a large number of outsiders both inside and outside the house. Eileen Gooder has assessed the royal keepers' accounts for Balsall (Warwickshire) and South Witham (Lincolnshire).[67] Taking into account only the full-time labourers, she established that at Balsall there were nineteen full-time labourers, with two more men taken on at harvest time. The labourers were paid partly in cash and partly in food.[68] In addition, there were part-time seasonal workers such as the 'fifteen women collecting straw for four days' mentioned in passing in the first year of the keeper's accounts.[69] After the Templars' arrests, these jobs disappeared. At Balsall the keepers gradually reduced the workforce and the stock, and in 1313–14 – before the land was handed over to the Hospitallers – everything moveable and all the stock was sold, so that Balsall was probably left 'near-derelict'.[70] At South Witham, Gooder noted that there were eight labourers, plus twelve ploughmen and a bailiff, and three shepherds who were paid from the neighbouring Templar commandery of Bruer. The king appointed a keeper who sold off the stock and in 1309 on royal orders handed the commandery over to a new owner.[71]

At Faxfleet, John of Crepping, who was keeper of the Templars' lands in Yorkshire, reported in 1308 that he had paid wages in grain to one reeve, one granger, one carpenter, one smith, one miller, fourteen ploughmen, two carters, one oxherd, one custodian of the horses, one swineherd, eight shepherds, one cook and dairyman and one harvest overseer. They were paid from 14 January to 24 June (twenty-three weeks), a total of sixty-five quarters seven bushels[72] at a rate of one quarter per twelve weeks. There was also a woman who collected milk for the lambs from 3 March to 5 May (nine weeks), who was paid one quarter – which would be one quarter, five-and-a-half bushels per sixteen weeks. Another woman who collected milk for the lambs from 3 March to 14 April received three bushels for the six weeks. Then there were ten women who worked milking the ewes from 5 May to 24 June (seven weeks), who were paid four quarters and three bushels. There was one shepherd from Etton, who looked after the sheep from the Templars' commandery of Etton grazing on the pastures of Faxfleet, from 24 March to the 15 June (twelve weeks), and was paid one quarter.[73]

John of Gray was keeper of the Templar lands in Yorkshire after John of Crepping. His reports for the following year include four lists of wages paid, covering a full year. Those employed at Faxfleet included a reeve, a granger, a stockman, a carpenter, a smith, a miller, a cook and dairyman, an overseer of the ploughmen, fourteen ploughmen, two carters, one oxherd, one horsekeeper, seven shepherds and a swineherd. There were also ten women who milked the ewes, and two peasants who looked after the flocks.[74]

Alexander of Cave and Robert of Amecotes, who followed John of Gray as keepers in Yorkshire, reported sales of stock but not the payment of wages, and finally reported that on the king's instructions they had delivered all the moveables at Faxfleet to Johanna, widow of Alexander Comyn.[75]

Faxfleet was the major Templar house in Yorkshire at the time of the arrests,[76] so it is not surprising that it employed a significant number of people. It is not clear what became of the estates when the king passed the property of the house to others, but the loss of the regular and seasonal employment offered by the Templars would have been a blow to the labourers of the area and their families.

Individual Templar houses could be responsible for local environmental matters. On 18 November 1308, King Edward II wrote to John of Shadworth, custodian of the former Templar lands in Essex, stating he understood that the dykes and ditches on the sea coast that belonged to the Templars' tenements in Sutton, which the brothers used to maintain against flooding by the sea, had deteriorated so far that unless steps were taken urgently the coastal land would be flooded by the sea. John of Shadworth was to have the dykes and ditches repaired without delay from the incomes from Sutton. This was despite the fact that during the period 12 February – 29 September that year John had already spent 103s. and a halfpenny on repairing the ditches and dykes.[77] At a time of deteriorating climatic conditions, the need for effective flood defences on the east coast of England and on the Somerset coast became urgent, yet it is clear from the government records of 1313 to 1327 that in many areas there was no one responsible for ensuring continued maintenance of these defences. Where there was a locally responsible body such as the Templars, it could take precautionary measures before a serious problem of flooding arose – but the dissolution of the Templars meant that there was no longer anyone on the spot at Sutton with the authority to take quick action. In a similar vein, on 23 May 1311 the king commanded the keeper of the Templars' lands in Southwark to repair the river bank there.[78]

Clearly Templar houses could play an important role in their locality, although some houses did more than others to benefit the local area. Overall, the loss of the employment, social care and travel accommodation which resulted from the dissolution of the Templars must have been a sad blow to many of their neighbours.

Notes

1 For example, Gooder, p. 84. Eileen Gooder was a brilliant local historian. Her legalistic insistence on the 'preceptory' is, however, misleading.

2 MS A, fol. 51r and MS B, fol. 81r (Wilkins, p. 345); TNA:PRO E358/18 rot. 13 dorse; BL Cotton MS Nero E vi, fol. 100r–v; L&K 1338, p. 95.

3 Gooder, 'South Witham', pp. 80–95.

4 MS A, fol. 92r (Wilkins, p. 359); L&K 1388, p. 137. For the inventory of this house, see TNA:PRO E142/18 mem. 11. For the sheriff's list of arrests (no Templars were arrested at Wetherby), see TNA:PRO E142/18 mem. 1 dorse.

5 For Robert of Rygate, see MS A, fol. 92r (Wilkins, p. 359); 'Houses of Knights Templar', *VCH, York*, vol. 3, ed. William Page (1974), pp. 256–60, section 68. For the inventory of the house, see TNA:PRO E142/18 mem. 12. For the sheriff's list of arrests (no Templars were arrested at Copmanthorpe), see TNA:PRO E142/18 mem. 1 dorse.

6 Lord points out that Keele was on a major road (now the A525) and adds that the Templars charged toll on packhorses passing through (Lord, pp. 99–100, quoting C. Harrison, *Essays on the History of Keele* (Keele, 1986), pp. 6–14, and TNA:PRO E358/19 – no roll number given, but must be rot. 36). One Templar was arrested at Keele in 1308, the commander Ralph Tanet (Gooder, p. 149; TNA:PRO E358/20 rot. 6).

7 For the commander of Whitley, see TNA:PRO E142/18 mem. 1 dorse; for William of Grafton's stay there, see TNA:PRO E358/20 rot. 40 dorse; for the inventory, see TNA: PRO E142/18 mem. 8. Whitley is not mentioned by Gooder, nor by Lord. For the currency: until 1971 a pound sterling (£) was worth 20 shillings (s.), and each shilling contained 12 pence (d.).

8 TNA:PRO E142/18 mm 4, 17, 18, 15, 7.

9 Lord, p. 133; inventory at TNA:PRO E142/105; ed. T.H. Forbrooke as 'Rothley: I. The Preceptory', in *Transactions of the Leicestershire Archaeological Society*, 12, pp. 32–34; for the commander, see Gooder, pp. 26, 92, 102.

10 For such urgings from the English clergy, see Matthew Paris, *Chronica majora*, vol. 4, p. 291; Richard Mepham, dean of Lincoln, at the Second Council of Lyon, 1274, in *Councils and Synods*, ed. Powicke and Cheney, vol. 2, pt 2, p. 815; Provincial Council of Canterbury, 1292, in ibid., p. 1106.

11 The list which follows and the numbers of brothers are based on MS A, fols. 58r–v; TNA:PRO E142/11 mem. 1 dorse; TNA:PRO E142/18 mem. 1 dorse; *CCR, 1307–1313*, p. 177; Gooder, pp. 147–50, and her references; and see Appendices 1 and 2.

12 TNA:PRO E142/18 mem. 1 dorse; the latter is Richard de Ripton at MS A, fol. 132r. On Foulbridge commandery, see David Knowles and R. Neville Hadcock, *Medieval Religious Houses: England and Wales*, 2nd edn (Harlow, 1971; henceforth cited as K&H), p. 292; see also Janet Burton, 'The Knights Templar in Yorkshire in the Twelfth Century: A Reassessment', *Northern History*, 27 (1991), pp. 26–40: here p. 38. There is a very brief notice on the house in *VCH, York*, vol. 3, ed. William Page (London, 1913), p. 258; see also *Survey of the County of York taken by John de Kirkby, commonly called Kirkby's Inquest. Also Inquisitions of Knights' Fees, the nomina villarum for Yorkshire, and an Appendix of Illustrative Documents*, Surtees Society 49 (1866), here p. 141; E.J. Martin, 'The Templars in Yorkshire', *Yorkshire Archaeological Journal*, 29 (1927–9), pp. 366–385, here pp. 370, 372, 383; Lord, pp. 87–8.

13 MS A, fols 92r, 97r–v (Wilkins, p. 359; omits second reference); Gooder, p. 151.

14 TNA:PRO E142/18 mem. 14.

15 According to the *OED Online*, a quarter in this context is eight bushels, and represented one-fifth of a wey or load (perhaps originally a fourth of a wey). The *OED Online* defines a wey as: 'A standard of dry-goods weight, varying greatly with different commodities'.

16 TNA:PRO E142/18 mem. 14.

17 TNA:PRO E142/16 mem. 15.

18 Adam of Hoperton's report is printed as 'Original documents relating to the Knights Templars no. II', in *The Gentleman's Magazine and Historical Review*, ed. Silvanus Urban, new series 3 (old series 203) July–December 1857, p. 520. For the original inventory of January 1308, see TNA:PRO E142/18, mem. 6.

19 For the chalice at Cowton see TNA:PRO E142/18 mem. 16.

20 TNA:PRO E142/111 mem. 7.

21 MS A, fol. 98v, 99v (Wilkins, pp. 362–3); MS C, fol. 7v (Schottmüller, p. 92); MS D, fol. 188v (*Annales Londonienses*, ed. Stubbs, p. 194).

22 T.H. Baylis, *The Temple Church and Chapel of St Ann*, p. 145; Lord, p. 33; for the reliquary at Sandford, see: TNA:PRO E142/13 mem. 3.

23 MS A, fol. 96v (Wilkins omits).

24 The inventory at New Temple is summarised by Lord, pp. 26–30; for the detail, see TNA:PRO E358/18 rot. 7(1).

25 For Combe, see: TNA:PRO E142/111 mem. 7; for Shipley, see TNA:PRO E142/15 mem. 5 (H 1); printed in translation by W.H. Blaauw, 'Sadelescombe and Shipley, the Preceptories of the Knights Templars in Sussex', *Sussex Archaeological Collections relating to the History and Antiquities of the County*, 9 (1857), pp. 227–74, here p. 254. The translation here is my own.

26 Perkins, 'Wealth of the Knights Templars', p. 255; Lord, p. 30.

27 For example, the image of two Templars playing chess from King Alfonso X of Castile's book *Libro de Ajedrez, dados y tables*, in Biblioteca del Monasterio ed El Escorial, ms T.I 6, fol. 25; the image of Templars on the tomb of Don Felipe in the church of Villasirpa, Palencia; the image of a Templar with Renart the Fox in Paris, Bibliothèque National de France, MS Fr. 25566 fol. 173 and MS Fr. 372 fol. 59 (all reproduced in Nicholson, *Knights Templar: A New History*, pp. 48, 125–7); the image of a Templar reproduced in Alain Demurger, *Les Templiers. Une chevalerie chrétienne au moyen âge* (Paris, 2005), plate 3; the funerary slabs reproduced in plates 2 and 3, on which see: Francesco Tommasi, 'Fonti epigrafiche dalla *domus Templi* di Barletta per la cronotassi degli ultimi maestri provinciali dell'ordine nel regno di Sicilia', in *Militia Sacra: Gli ordini militari tra Europa e Terrasanta*, ed. Enzo Coli, Maria de Marco and Francesco Tommasi (Perugia, 1994), pp. 167–202.

28 William Alfred Morris, *The Medieval English Sheriff to 1300* (Manchester, 1927), pp. 275–85; Richard Gorski, *The Fourteenth-century Sheriff: English Local Administration in the Late Middle Ages* (Woodbridge, 2003), pp. 107–119.

29 MS A, fol. 58v (Wilkins, p. 347); TNA:PRO E358/18 rot. 2; TNA:PRO E358/19 rot. 25.

30 *CPR, 1307–1313*, pp. 57, 67, 79, 93, 100, 113, 134, 135, 139, 142, 202, 206, 286, 335, 141, 391, etc.; *CCR, 1307–1313*, p. 94.

31 Alan Forey, 'Provision for the Aged in Templar Commanderies' in *La Commanderie: Institution des ordres militaires dans l'Occident médiéval*, ed. Anthony Luttrell and Léon Pressouyre (Paris, 2002), pp. 178–83; on corrodies, see also Gooder, 'South Witham', p. 85.

32 *CCR, 1307–1313*, pp. 214–15.

33 *CCR, 1307–1313*, pp. 90, 467; TNA:PRO E368/79 rot. 111.

34 Roy Martin Haines, 'Langton, Walter (*d.* 1321)', *ODNB*, vol. 32, pp. 523–5.

35 TNA:PRO E368/78 rot. 41 dorse; *Advance Contracts for the Sale of Wool, c. 1200–c. 1327*, ed. Adrian Bell, Chris Brooks and Paul Dryburgh, List and Indexes Society 315 (Kew, 2006), pp. 148–9, no. 179.

36 T.H. Lloyd, *The English Wool Trade in the Middle Ages* (Cambridge, 1977), pp. 60–102; *Advance Contracts*, pp. i–vii, esp. p. vi.

37 TNA:PRO E368/78 rot. 41 dorse; *Advance Contracts*, pp. 148–9, no. 179.

38 TNA:PRO E368/78 rot. 84; E368/79 rot. 121 dorse; see also Perkins, 'Wealth of the Knights Templars', pp. 255–6 and notes. On Henry Nasard, see Natalie Fryde, *The Tyranny and Fall of Edward II, 1321–1326* (Cambridge, 1979), p. 166; Eilbert Ekwall, 'Introduction chapter V: the subsidies and the London population: 1: immigration into London', *Two Early London Subsidy Rolls* (Lund, 1951), pp. 43–71 (http://www.british-history.ac.uk/report.aspx?compid=31907).

39 *CCR, 1307–1313*, pp. 184, 195; *CPR, 1307–1313*, p. 210.

40 *CCR, 1307–1313*, p. 81; Hamilton, *Piers Gaveston*, p. 71; G.W.S. Barrow, *Robert Bruce and the Community of the Realm of Scotland* (London, 1965), pp. 262, 258–61.

41 James Davies, *The Baronial Opposition to Edward II: Its Character and Policy; a study in administrative history* (London, 1918, repr. 1967), p. 88 and n. 15, pp. 143–4; Fryde, *The Tyranny and Fall of Edward II*, p. 31; *CPR, 1307–1313*, p. 331; see also p. 337; Maddicott, *Thomas of Lancaster*, p. 91.

42 TNA:PRO E368/79 rot. 107; *CCR, 1307–1313*, pp. 284, 394, 493, 511; *Foedera*, ed. Rymer, vol. 2, pt 1, pp. 155, 182. On Elizabeth's custody, see also Barrow, *Robert Bruce*, pp. 227–30, 330; *CPR, 1307–1313*, p. 500; *CCR, 1307–1313*, pp. 39, 281, 394, 493, 511, 535.

43 Perkins, 'Wealth of the Knights Templars', pp. 258–9. See also Leys, 'Forfeiture of the Lands of the Templars', pp. 155–63; Hamilton, 'Apocalypse Not', pp. 91–2.

44 TNA:PRO E368/79 rot. 120 recto; *Foedera*, ed. Rymer, vol. 2, pt 1, p. 70; *CCR, 1307–1313*, p. 94.

45 *CPR, 1307–1313*, pp. 112, 131; *Foedera*, ed. Rymer, vol. 2, pt 1, p. 21.

46 *Register of William Greenfield*, part 4, pp. 302–6, no. 2279.

47 *Foedera*, ed. Rymer, vol. 2, pt 1, p. 92; TNA:PRO E358/18 rot. 22 dorse; *CPR, 1307–1313*, pp. 203, 213, 242, 246.

48 What follows is discussed in more detail in my article 'Relations between Houses of the Order of the Temple in Britain and their Local Communities, as Indicated during the Trial of the Templars, 1307–12', in *Knighthoods of Christ: Essays on the History of the Crusades and the Knights Templar, Presented to Malcolm Barber*, ed. Norman Housley (Aldershot, UK and Burlington, VT, 2007), pp. 195–207.

49 L&K 1338, pp. 5–101, *passim*; Roberta Gilchrist, *Contemplation and Action: the Other Monasticism* (London and New York, 1995), p. 92, is confident of two identifications, but cf. *VCH Hertford*, vol. 3, ed. William Page (London, 1912), p. 349; *VCH, Wiltshire*, ed. D.A. Crowley, vol. 13: *South-West Wiltshire: Chalke and Dunworth Hundreds* (London, 1987), p. 95 and plate facing p. 97. For the problem as it relates to the Templars, see Alan J. Forey, 'The Charitable Activities of the Templars', *Viator*, 34 (2003), pp. 109–41, here pp. 127–8.

50 L&K 1338, pp. 137, 149, 155, 158, 164, 186, 192, 198.

51 MS A, fol. 97r (Wilkins omits).

52 Damien Carraz, *L'Ordre du Temple dans la basse vallée du Rhône (1124–1312): Ordres militaires, croisades et sociétés méridionales* (Lyon, 2005), p. 267.

53 TNA:PRO E142/30 mem. 1.

54 MS A, fol. 94r (Wilkins omits).

55 MS A, fol. 56r (Wilkins, p. 346).

56 See, for example, *Close Rolls of the Reign of Henry III preserved in the Public Record Office, 1247–1251* (London, 1922), p. 283; Annals of Dunstable, in *Annales Monastici*, ed. Henry Richards Luard, Rolls Series 36, vol. 3 (London, 1866), pp. 222–3; Agnes Sandys, 'The Financial and Administrative Importance of the London Temple in the Thirteenth Century', in *Essays in Medieval History presented to Thomas Frederick Tout*, ed. A.G. Little and F.M. Powicke (Manchester, 1925), pp. 147–62.

57 *CCR, 1327–1330*, p. 580; *CCR, 1330–1333*, p. 102; *Foedera*, ed. Rymer, vol. 2, pt.2, A.D. 1327–1344, pp. 774, 805.

58 *CCR, 1374–1377*, pp. 26–7.

59 *Papsturkunden für Templer und Johanniter*, ed. Rudolf Heistand (Göttingen, 1972), no. 3.

60 MS A, fol. 96v (Wilkins, p. 362, gives only this witness's name).

61 For the reliquary at Sandford, see TNA:PRO E142/13, mem. 3. For the Catholic Church's ambiguous attitude towards the veneration of relics, see Kathleen Kamerick, *Popular Piety and Art in the Later Middle Ages* (New York and Basingstoke, 2002).

62 MS C, fol. 3r (Schottmüller, p. 82); for the chapel, see Gooder, pp. 67–8.

63 *Règle*, sections 19, 29, 62, 65, 94, 97, 129, 153, 188, 189, 199, 370, 371; trans. Upton-Ward, pp. 24, 27, 34, 35, 43, 51, 57, 65, 67, 102.

64 TNA:PRO E142/16 mem. 15.

65 *Cartulary of the Knights of St John of Jerusalem in England, Secunda Camera: Essex*, p. 56, doc. 85, from British Library Cotton MS Nero E vi, fol. 304r; see also Forey, 'Charitable Activities of the Templars', p. 118.

66 See above, p. 77.

67 Gooder, pp. 31–63; Gooder, 'South Witham', pp. 80–95. See also P. M. Ryan, 'Cressing Temple: its history from Documentary Sources', in *Cressing Temple: A Templar and Hospitaller Manor in Essex*, ed. D.D. Andrews (Chelmsford, 1993), pp. 11–24.

68 Gooder, pp. 31–3.

69 TNA:PRO E358/19 rot. 40(1) recto.

70 Gooder, pp. 43, 61.

71 Gooder, 'South Witham', pp. 85–6.

72 According to the *OED Online*, a bushel is a measure of capacity used to measure dry goods such as grain or fruit. It contains four pecks or eight gallons. The modern imperial bushel, laid down in Great Britain in 1826, contains 80 pounds of distilled water; the earlier Winchester bushel, in common use in Britain from the sixteenth century and still used in North America, contains 77.627413 pounds of distilled water. Eight bushels equal one quarter.

73 TNA:PRO E358/20 rot. 40 recto.

74 TNA:PRO E358/18 rots 31, 33 recto; TNA:PRO E358/20 rot. 34 recto.

75 TNA:PRO E358/18 rot. 45 recto; TNA:PRO E358/19 rot. 29 recto; see also *CPR, 1307–1313*, p. 569.

76 Listed first by the sheriff in his account of the arrests, Faxfleet housed four brothers including a priest, more than any other Yorkshire house; and the Templars' Yorkshire records were kept there: TNA:PRO E142/18 mm 1, 13.

77 2 Edward II, Lord Treasurer's remembrancer, memoranda rolls: TNA:PRO E368/79 rot. 107 recto; TNA:PRO E358/18 rot. 22 (2), under Sutton: Exp'n'.

78 *CCR, 1307–1313*, p. 312.

4

The Interrogations in England

The beginning of the interrogations of the Templars in October 1309 coincided with the start of an unusually cold winter. The Thames froze so hard that people could cross on foot or walk upriver to Westminster, hunt hares with dogs and play sports on the ice.[1] The bitter cold was a memorable backdrop for the trial in London.

The pope had specified in August 1308 that the judges of the Templars in the British Isles were to be the patriarch of Jerusalem (Antony Bek, bishop of Durham), and the archbishop of York (William of Greenfield); the bishops of Lincoln (John Dalderby), Chichester (John Langton) and Orléans (Raoul); the abbots of the monasteries of Lagny (Dieudonné), Paris diocese, and St Germain des Prés (Pierre), near Paris; Master Sicard de Vaur, canon of Narbonne, papal chaplain and auditor of causes in the papal curia, and Guy of Wych or de Vichio, rector of the church of Hayes, diocese of London. Antony Bek, bishop of Durham 1283–1311, had been created patriarch of Jerusalem by Pope Clement V in February 1306. He had taken the cross with the intention of embarking on the crusade that was being planned in 1306, and had clearly impressed Pope Clement with his enthusiasm. Although his title was largely honorary because Latin Christendom had lost Jerusalem in 1244, as patriarch of Jerusalem Bek had spiritual authority over the Order of the Temple and so was the most suitable person to take charge of the trial in England. Bek himself seems to have had some sympathy for the Order, as he intervened on behalf of William de la More and got him out of prison. He took no active part in the interrogation of the Templars, and died on

3 March 1311, before the final dissolution of the Order in England – but he did correspond with the king over the issues which arose between the inquisitors and the king during the course of the trial.[2]

The three other English clergy appointed as judges in the case played a larger role in the trial. The archbishop of York has already been considered in chapter two. John Dalderby of Lincoln was a university-educated, conscientious diocesan bishop; John Langton of Chichester was chancellor of England. Both were later Ordainers, and helped to draw up a scheme of reform for King Edward II's government.[3]

The two inquisitors sent by the pope to conduct the case in England were Abbot Dieudonné of Lagny and Sicard de Vaur. Dieudonné had become abbot of the sixth-century abbey of Lagny-sur-Marne, east of Paris, in 1306. In 1318 Pope John XXII (1316–34) would promote him to bishop of Castres (a town in the Languedoc, to the south of Albi, east of Toulouse and north-west of Narbonne), where the same year he issued a condemnation of some beliefs ascribed to the radical Spiritual Franciscan movement, declaring them to be heretical. He died in 1327; by his will, he set up an institution for the care of twelve paupers.[4] His career suggests that he was a conscientious administrator and a pious man, determined to stamp out heresy.

Sicard de Vaur was probably from Lavaur, a town between Toulouse and Albi in the Languedoc, whose rulers in the early thirteenth century had been Cathar heretics. He would, then, have been very familiar with the Church's war against heresy. Sicard was a canon lawyer, who had previously acted as lieutenant for the French king's sénéchal of Carcassonne in the Languedoc. In 1303 he was described as 'clerk of the king of France'.[5] He remained an 'auditor of causes' in the papal palace throughout the pontificate of Clement V's successor, John XXII. His task as auditor was to hear and examine legal cases submitted to the pope, but not to make a decision unless the pope specifically delegated jurisdiction to him.[6] Again, his administrative and legal experience would have stood him in good stead for his task in the British Isles. But neither of the pope's appointees had previous experience of working in the British Isles.

The others named by the pope played no role at all in the trial. Guy of Wych or Vichio had been rector of Hayes since at least 6 October 1296, but he had died by September 1309.[7] Two others were excused from taking part. Raoul, bishop of Orléans, who was a former clerk of the king of France, had been made bishop in 1308 and died in 1311;[8] Pierre of Courpalay had become abbot of the sixth-century abbey of St Germain des Prés in the Parisian suburbs in 1303 and would continue in his post until 1334.[9]

On 13 September 1309 King Edward II issued a document instructing all his officials and faithful people to ensure safe conduct for the abbot of Lagny and Sicard de Vaur, who had been sent by the pope to conduct the investigations into the Templars. The king also issued instructions to the bishops, stating that the trial would take place at London, Lincoln and York. The Templars were each to be taken to one of these three places, and the bishops of Lincoln, London and York must be present in person at the trial proceedings in their respective cities. On the following day, the king wrote to his sheriffs, informing them of the arrival of the pope's investigators, and ordering them to have the Templars escorted to the appropriate venue: those in the south and west of England to London, those from the Midlands to Lincoln, and those from Yorkshire and the north to York. He then wrote to the constables (officials in charge) of York Castle, Lincoln Castle and the Tower of London, telling them to receive the Templars when they arrived and to put them into safe and secure custody.[10]

Money was a pressing problem. The expenses of the trial must be paid – yet the king of England still held the Templars' lands and would not release their revenues to pay for the trial. On 3 September, Abbot Dieudonné and Sicard de Vaur had written to their colleagues in the trial – the bishops of Durham, Lincoln and Chichester, and the archbishop of York – explaining that they had been sent by the pope to conduct the investigation into the Templars, that they were incurring vast expenses, and that they needed ten gold florins a day. To meet this expense, a tax must be imposed on the clergy, both the secular clergy – bishops and parish priests – and all the monks and other religious Orders. The tax should be one penny on each mark sterling of revenue and profits – that is, one penny on each 160 pence. 'Revenue and profits' would be assessed as for the calculation of the tithe, the tax of one tenth on incomes which the Church levied on everyone. Half of this new tax was to be paid within two months.[11] The clergy were not anxious to pay, and the bishops would still be chasing up the overdue payments after the inquisitors had left England in May 1311.[12]

On 26 September 1309 Antony Bek and his colleagues, Archbishop William Greenfield of York, Bishops John Dalderby of Lincoln and John Langton of Chichester, along with Abbot Dieudonné of Lagny and Sicard de Vaur, sent instructions summoning the Templars of England and Wales for interrogation.[13] A week later Bishop John of Chichester, Abbot Dieudonné

of Lagny and Sicard de Vaur sent a letter to their associates in the trial setting a date of 16 February 1310 for a Church Council to be held in London
to decide the Templars' fate.[14] Their planning was premature – the Council
would not make that decision until July 1311.

The Interrogations Begin

On Friday 17 October 1309 the inquisitors were waiting in the chapter hall
of the priory of Holy Trinity, London.[15] This was a house of Augustinian
canons, priests who followed a religious lifestyle similar to monks. The
two papally-appointed inquisitors, Abbot Dieudonné and Sicard de Vaur,
were present, and with them Ralph, bishop of London, whom the king
had ordered to attend the proceedings. With these three were three notaries
public: two were from France and had probably accompanied the pope's
inquisitors to England – Pons de Curte, rector of the church of Saint-
Pierre-du-Monastère, Albi diocese and Berengar Brossini, rector of the
church of Vimenando, Rodez diocese – the third was English, Adam, called
'of Lindsey', who came from a family of notaries public.[16]

Notaries public appeared in English records from the thirteenth century
onwards. They drew up legal documents for public record and held 'authority as a writer of public instruments from either the pope or the emperor'.[17]
The notaries at the trial of the Templars drew up two formal copies of each
interrogation in the province of Canterbury; these were copied into two
bound volumes, one of which survives complete in the Bodleian Library,
Oxford (here called MS A), while the other is a fragment in the British
Library, London (MS B).

The two versions of the testimonies were not identical. Some information is in one manuscript but not the other, for example, the fact that there
was a chapel at the Templars' house in Addington (MS B, folio 81r) or the
number of years that John of Euleye had been a Templar (MS B, folio 78r).
Some information is phrased differently: for example, where MS A uses the
word *cingula* for the woollen belt worn by the Templars over their shirts,
MS B uses *cordula*.[18] There were also some important differences. When
Brother William of Chalesey or Chelesey was asked about the statement in
the papal letter that said the brothers in France had confessed to the charges,
he replied, according to MS A, that he did not know what they confessed,

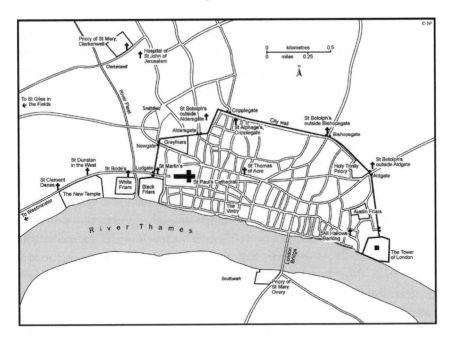

Map of locations in London mentioned in the trial proceedings.

and if they confessed such things he said that he did not reckon them to be Christians.[19] However, the corresponding passage in MS B records that he replied that he did not know what they confessed, but if they confessed, they were not Christians: a much more definite statement.[20]

As the testimonies were given in French or English,[21] but were recorded in Latin, the notaries would have translated individual words differently (such as *cingula* or *cordula*), but could also change subtle nuances of meaning. In addition, notaries recorded only information that they believed to be relevant, and discarded the rest.[22] The differences between these two manuscripts indicate that the records of the brothers' testimonies are only a general guide to what they actually said.

On Friday 17 October the inquisitors and notaries were waiting for the reeves of the Tower of London to bring the Templars who were imprisoned in the Tower (plate 31). When the Templars arrived, the inquisitors told them that their trial would begin on Monday 20th. The Templars asked for a postponement to Wednesday 22nd. Having eventually agreed on Tuesday 21st, the Templars came on that day to the chapter house of Holy Trinity, London.[23] The interrogations formally began two days later.

For the first three days, 23–25 October, three of the Templars were interrogated without being put on oath, as if on a 'test run'. The record of these initial interrogations does not mention the three inquisitors, but gives a list of churchmen who were present during the proceedings. In July 1308 the pope had specified that two canons, two Dominicans and two Franciscans should join each bishop in his inquiries against the Templars; for these hearings there was one canon and four friars: Ralph of Canterbury, Augustinian canon and prior of the house of Holy Trinity where the trial was taking place; John of Wrotham, prior of the Dominican friars of London; Peter of Kenington, *lector* and Master of Holy Theology, of the same Order; Robert of Basingstoke, guardian (official in charge of a sub-division of a province) of the Franciscan friars of London, and Thomas Rundel, master of the Franciscan friars.[24] As the friars had played a leading role in the war against heresy since their foundation in the early thirteenth century, their involvement in the trial was to be expected. What was surprising was that friars would also be the leading witnesses against the Templars.

The first interrogation under oath began on Saturday 25 October with Ralph Barton, chaplain and custodian of the chapel in the New Temple, London; his interrogation continued until 28 October. Ralph, and each of his fellow-Templars when their turn came to be interrogated, had to swear on the gospels to tell the truth, not only about himself but also about individual Templars and the Order as a whole. Ralph had nothing to say which would incriminate his Order, but finally he was asked about the death in 1301 of Walter the Bachelor, former grand commander of Ireland, at the New Temple in London (plates 20–21). The inquisitors wanted to know whether Walter had been killed for refusing to agree to the Templars' heresies, as suggested in charges 70–74. Ralph said that he knew nothing except 'that he was placed in prison and in fetters and he died there; and he has certainly heard that some duress was done to him, but since he is chaplain he did not involve himself in those matters on account of the danger of breaching canon law' – as a priest, Ralph could not be involved in the shedding of blood. He said that Walter was not buried in the cemetery 'because he was regarded as excommunicate on account of the disobedience that he had committed against the Order', which could have meant that he had refused to conform to the alleged heretical practices in the Templars.[25]

Forty-three Templars were questioned in the first series of interrogations, which lasted until 17 November. Proceedings took place at the priory of Holy Trinity until the final day, when the last four witnesses were interrogated in the chapel of St Mary Barking, near the Tower of London.[26] From this time, the trial in London became peripatetic, moving from one location to the next on an almost daily basis (plates 33, 34, 36, 37). The records of the trial proceedings do not explain why this was; perhaps, as the interrogations continued for far longer than the inquisitors initially planned, they had difficulty in finding suitable locations that were available for their use.

This first series of interrogations did not produce much information to support the charges against the Templars. The brothers denied all wrong-doing, and several asserted that the confessions obtained from Templars in France, on which the current interrogations were based, were untrue. They also denied that there had been widespread suspicion about the Order before the trial began. The grand commander of the Auvergne, Himbert Blanc, stated that if the grand master had confessed to absolving Templars of their sins, even though he was not a priest, then he had lied; and all the French Templars who had confessed before the cardinal and pope to the charges had lied. William of the Forde and Richard of Herdwick agreed that the Templars who had confessed had lied, while John Coffin agreed that the grand master had lied about absolving sins; Peter of Ottringham agreed with them. Henry Paul, when asked why the brothers had not tried to correct the errors in the Order, said (according to one record of the proceedings) that he had never known such errors; the other record has him stating that there never were such errors. Robert of Sautre stated, when questioned on the 38th and 39th charges, that he did not know about any suspicion against the Templars, and that if he had known, he would never have entered the Order. He also said that if the French Templars had con-fessed to the charges, then they had lied, with which Thomas of Staundon, William of Warwick and William of Welles agreed.[27]

The inquisitors tried to persuade the Templars to abandon their vows to the Order, concentrating their efforts on some of those who had not been in the Order more than two years at the time of the initial arrests. After all, if the Order was guilty as charged, these brothers who claimed to be innocent should leave it. Brother Philip de Meux, Thomas of Burton and Thomas of Staundon (who had respectively joined the Order five, three and four years ago), replied individually that they would prefer to die rather than leave. John of Euleye, William of Warwick and William of Pokelington, who had all joined three years previously, firmly refused to leave. Thomas of Loudham, who had joined the Order only eleven days before the arrests, refused to leave even though he had enough money to support himself.[28]

But the inquisitors did not ask Brother Roger of Dalton to leave, even though he had joined less than four years ago and later turned out to have a grudge against those who had admitted him. On 6 February 1310, in the course of the second round of interrogations, Roger of Dalton complained that his reception had cost him sixty marks, and he had never received anything from the Order in return. This reference to payment on entry to the Order suggests simony (a payment for spiritual things, which the Church forbade), but it is more likely that Brother Roger had paid a 'passagium', a sum towards the costs of his voyage to the East, just as the Hospitallers paid – and yet had never been sent abroad.[29]

Rather than confessing to heresy, some brothers made statements which showed their piety. When they were asked about the cord that they wore around their waists, three Templars stated that St Bernard, abbot of Clairvaux abbey in France, had laid down the regulation about cords.[30] St Bernard (plate 5) had been one of the composers of the Order's rule in 1129;[31] section 21 of the 'primitive rule' of 1129 instructs Templars to wear their underwear and belts even when they are sleeping. Although Bernard was not in fact the founder of the Order, the Templars' connection to this renowned saint showed that their Order was based on excellent spiritual authority. Later, one of the Templars who had been imprisoned at Lincoln stated that Bernard had written the Order's Rule.[32]

The inquisitors' failure in London may have had a knock-on effect across the Channel. On 12 November the papal commissioners in France began their inquiry into the Templars' affair; it is possible that it was the English Templars' denials of the charges which eventually encouraged the French Templars to defend their Order.[33] The French Templars' defence collapsed after many were burned at the stake in May 1310 for going back on the confessions which they had made under torture – because they had recanted their confessions, they were lapsed heretics.[34] The English Templars fared better.

The papal inquisitors, Abbot Dieudonné and Sicard de Vaur, had initially hoped to get the investigation cleared up quickly. On 9 November they had written to Archbishop William Greenfield of York informing him that they were going on to Lincoln on 24 November and would then proceed to York, unless the archbishop had already completed the interrogations by then.[35]

But when the interrogations finished on 17 November it was clear that they would have to spend much more time on the trial in London before they could go anywhere else. In fact, they did not get to Lincoln until the following March, and did not reach York until April. The trial in Scotland – which the papal inquisitors had delegated to other judges – opened on 17 November 1309.[36]

On 24 November 1309 a Provincial Church Council of the clergy of the province of Canterbury met at St Paul's cathedral in London. The Council was supposed to discuss the Templars' affair, but there were no confessions to discuss. The Council decided to send three bishops with the two papal inquisitors to the king to ask him to allow the bishops to proceed against the Templars 'in a better way'. On 17 December, the Provincial Council was prorogued until 23 September 1310, to give the inquisitors time to gather more evidence.[37]

'A better way' meant torture, for clearly the English Templars were not going to confess to anything voluntarily. But the inquisitors were up against the law of the land. English law was common law, based on custom and precedent, rather than Roman law, as used in France and in canon (Church) law. The author of the thirteenth-century English legal treatise *The Mirror of Justices* had contended that heresy was *lèse majesty*, damage to the king's majesty, and so a matter for the king's courts, not the Church courts.[38] As English common law and the king's courts did not use torture as a method of gathering evidence, the inquisitors could not find anyone willing to act as torturers in the Templars' case.

So the king had to act. On 15 December 1309, Edward issued instructions that the interrogators should be allowed to torture the Templars if necessary and, on 8 February 1310, he wrote that the knight William de Dien had been appointed to oversee the proceedings against the Templars and help the inquisitors – that is, to oversee torture. William de Dien or Dene was probably the same as the former royal seneschal in Agen whom Edward had summoned in November 1307 to brief him about the Templars' case.[39] Presumably the inquisitors expected William de Dien to give them all assistance. Yet by 16 June 1310 the inquisitors were complaining that neither William nor the prison guards were helping them as they should, implying that no one was prepared to torture the Templars.[40]

At the same time, Edward had other problems which were nothing to do with the Templars. On 13 December 1309 he had sent instructions to all the sheriffs to arrest people who spread false rumours to cause discord or stir up the nobles of the kingdom. This was partly because Edward was taxing his subjects to pay for the Scottish war – even though there was currently a truce – and partly because of his friend Piers Gaveston. Edward's nobles considered that they were his traditional advisors and should act as the king's counsellors and receive gifts in return for their service. But Edward preferred to give his gifts to Gaveston, and to take Gaveston's advice. In effect, this was a dispute over who would control the country: the king or his leading subjects. Under severe pressure from the English nobles and clergy, Edward had agreed in May 1308 that Gaveston would be exiled to Ireland; Archbishop Winchelsey of Canterbury had enforced this by pronouncing a sentence of excommunication on Gaveston if he should return from Ireland.

Gaveston had acted in Ireland as the king's lieutenant. In June 1309 Edward won his friend a pardon, and Pope Clement absolved him. Although Archbishop Winchelsey was still opposed to the favourite's return, and many of the leading nobles loathed him, Gaveston returned to England. But the earls of Arundel, Lancaster, Lincoln, Oxford and Warwick refused to attend a Parliament to discuss the next Scottish campaign if Gaveston was present, and Edward found that he was losing control of the situation.[41]

The Second Stage of the Trial

With no confessions and no torturers to force confessions, the inquisitors had to look elsewhere for evidence. In the course of the thirteenth century, investigators of heresy had reinterpreted the old rules of evidence required by Roman law and hence by canon (Church) law. Roman law required 'undoubted indications' of guilt, but as heresy is essentially a hidden crime – being concealed within the soul – there was often no visible evidence of it. So the inquisitors of heresy reinterpreted the old rules about using public reputation or *fama* ('fame' or 'infamy') to meet the need. If 'public reputation' could be an 'undoubted indication', the inquisitors need only find solid evidence of the Templars' public reputation in the British Isles. But they had to be careful, because Roman law did forbid the use of hearsay, and 'public reputation' could all too easily be simply hearsay evidence.[42] In the case of the trial in the British Isles, most of the evidence gathered by the inquisitors from non-Templars turned out to be rumour, slander and unsupported juicy anecdotes.

The bishop of each diocese took testimonies from witnesses who came forward, and sent these to the inquisitors to be included in their final report. The inquisitors who conducted the investigations in Ireland and Scotland also questioned non-Templars and produced a report of their evidence.[43] Procedures for these enquiries were laid out in a document of 25 May 1310 in which Archbishop William Greenfield of York instructed his official to question the parish priests, monks and friars who used to hear the Templars' confessions, clergy and laity who were in the Templars' service, and their household servants and friends.[44] On the following 20 June he commissioned two rectors to go to the area around the Templars' manors of Ribston, Wetherby and Newsam in the West Riding of York-shire and summon the people named on a list which was included with their instructions, but which is now lost. These were people who were said to have been in the Templars' service in the past. The rectors should ask them if they ever served the Templars, and if so where and when, and when they had left their service. The rectors should ask whether any Templars were received into the Order while they were in the Templars' service, and if so whether they were received at night and whether the witness was present. They should also be asked whether they knew anything about the reception ceremonies, and generally whether they knew, or had heard or seen anything about the Templars which made them suspect that they were guilty of the alleged abuses. The replies were to be recorded in writing under the two rectors' seals and sent to the archbishop by 29 September 1310. Those questioned were to be warned that they should not talk about their testimony, on pain of excommunication; this was to prevent 'copycat' testimonies.[45] But of course witnesses could agree beforehand on a single story.

To judge from the archbishop's instructions, potential witnesses were found by the officials asking around the area of a commandery. People who had had any sort of dealing with the Templars would find themselves under pressure to give evidence against them, even if they knew virtually noth-ing about the Order. The witnesses could also include people who had put themselves forward because of a grudge against the Templars, or those who wanted to gain attention for themselves, gossips and seekers of reward. It is not surprising, then, that the evidence of the non-Templar witnesses was largely rumour, second or third-hand stories or wildly horrific fantasies. Eventually, these testimonies formed the bulk of the summaries of the trial produced for the Church Councils at Vienne and London.

The examination of the non-Templar witnesses from London began immediately after the interrogations of the Templars, on 19 November 1309 in the chapel and later in the chapter house of the priory of Holy Trinity. In all seventeen witnesses, lay and religious men, gave evidence: the first ten in November, followed by another seven on 9 January in the parish church of St Dunstan West. A few of the witnesses had damning evidence, but most were favourable towards the Templars.[46]

The first witness was Master William the Dorturer, notary public of London,[47] who had attended some of the Templars' chapter meetings at Dinsley, presumably to produce legal documents for the Templars in his professional capacity. He observed that receptions and chapter meetings did start before dawn. The following witness, Master Gilbert of Bruer,[48] clerk, said that he had never regarded any of the Templars' dealings as suspicious, except that they could be unduly strict with punishment of their brothers. Later interrogation suggested that he was referring to the Templars' practice of flogging their servants for minor faults.[49]

Robert the Dorturer, notary public of London, then gave evidence against the Templars.[50] Most of his evidence was vague or related to deceased persons. For example, when asked whether he knew anything about the accusations of sodomy in the Order, he stated that Brother Guy of Forest, former grand commander of England,[51] and a man called Robert, whose surname he did not know, used to shut themselves up in a chamber after lunch in the New Temple at London, with one Brother Hugh (possibly Hugh Peraud, the visitor of the Order). He implied that they were indulging in homosexual acts. He went on to say that Guy of Forest had wanted to sodomise him in his chamber, but he fled. He knew the name of one Templar who had been received at night, Roger of Reile, 'who is dead and who was received at night at London', but he himself had never been to a Templar reception ceremony. When he was asked how the inquisitors could best find out the Templars' secrets, he replied that they should ask William Borne 'who sometimes lodges at London in the house of Adam the Dorturer, and sometimes stays at Isleworth'. Yet William Borne never appeared to give evidence.

Robert the Dorturer's allegations can be checked on one point: he was asked whether the Templars believed it was not a sin to acquire property for the Order unjustly. He replied that he did not know, except in relation to certain pastures at Isleworth 'which they acquired unjustly from certain men of this country and beyond what they were accustomed to have there'.[52]

Isleworth is a parish in Middlesex on the River Thames. In 1300–1 Earl Edmund of Cornwall had given rents in Isleworth to the master and brothers of the Temple in England, with common rights of pasture and heath in the hundred of Isleworth.[53] If Robert's complaints were connected to this gift, the Templars did have a valid right to hold them; but perhaps he was referring to additional pastures that they had acquired since. It is interesting that in January 1304 Robert the Dorturer gave the Templars the site of a dwelling-house in Charing (*La Cherryng*) in the parish of St Martin-in-the-Fields. During the legal investigation that had to precede a donation to a religious Order, the jurors explained that the land actually belonged to the Templars, and Robert the Dorturer was only returning to them what was already theirs.[54] They did not say why he was doing this. Possibly the two parties had disagreed over Robert's tenancy, and this was why he later came forward to give evidence against the Templars.

Adam the Dorturer, layman, knew nothing against the Templars; apparently his lodger William Borne had told him nothing. Ralph of Rayndon, an old layman, knew nothing against the Order. William Lamberd, former envoy of the Templars, believed that they were innocent of the charges against them.[55]

On the following day, Nicholas the Crier, layman of London, explained that he knew nothing against the Templars and said that they never held chapters before daylight. Lord Ralph of London knew nothing about the Templars but remarked on their secrecy. Lord Richard of Barton, priest, stated that: 'he knows nothing about these things which are contained in the said charge, except what is good and honourable'.[56] On the day after that, Master Philip Walrand, advocate of the Templars and priest, stated that he knew nothing against the Templars, 'nor has he observed anything about them that smacks of unbelief'.

The gathering of evidence continued after Christmas, with seven witnesses agreeing that they knew nothing about the Templars which was relevant to the case. John of Hoddington, rector of the church of St Mary le Strand, said that it was well known that the Templars held chapter meetings at night, and Vicar Thomas of St Martin-in-the-Fields believed that the secret reception ceremonies were suspicious, but none of the others had anything to say against the Templars.[57]

Meanwhile, following the king's instructions to the sheriffs to search out missing Templars, the first series of interrogations of the Templars recommenced. On 27 January 1310 at the chapel of St Mary Barking, John of Stoke, William of Hereford and Michael of Baskerville came forward to be questioned.[58] John of Stoke had been treasurer of the New Temple, and as such would have been responsible for the care of much of the wealth of London's merchants, as well as of the king and nobility. Nothing was said about his actions in this role, but as he had probably made enemies as well as friends in the course of his work it is not surprising that he received a thorough cross-examination.[59] In particular, the interrogators were interested in the death of Walter the Bachelor. Ralph of Barton's testimony could have implied that Walter was killed for refusing to submit to the alleged abuses. So Brother John of Stoke was asked about his involvement in Walter the Bachelor's death.

> He replied that he was buried just like any other Christian, except that he was not buried in the cemetery but in an open space in the house at London, and that he was confessed by Brother Richard of Grafton, Priest, who is in Cyprus,[60] and he believes that he will have received Christ's Body, although he does not know, and he says that he and Brother Ralph of Barton, who is [imprisoned] in the Tower of London, carried him to be buried at dawn, and he was in prison, as he believes, for 8 weeks. Interrogated as to whether he was buried in the Order's habit, he replied that he was not. Interrogated as to why he was buried outside the cemetery, he replied, because he was regarded as excommunicate. Interrogated as to why he was excommunicate, he replied that he believes that, according to their statute or general opinion, whoever furtively pilfers the goods of the house and does not acknowledge their crime is regarded as excommunicate.[61]

John of Stoke, then, made it clear that Walter the Bachelor was not punished for refusing to commit the alleged abuses but for theft. Yet it is possible that it was John's involvement in this affair that gave the inquisitors a 'hold' over John and finally forced him, on Thursday 1 July 1311, into making a confession.[62] John was also asked whether he thought the Templars required any reforms. He answered that new members should have a year's probation, and that their receptions should be public.

The mention of English brothers being overseas seems to have aroused the inquisitors' interest, because they later asked Brother William of Hereford if he knew of any English brothers overseas. William replied that there were English brothers in Cyprus: Roger de la More, knight, Richard of Grafton, chaplain, and Brother John, knight. Sadly for the inquisitors, none of these Templars had confessed to any of the abuses.[63]

Walter of Rockley was the last Templar interrogated on the original list of eighty-eight charges, at Holy Trinity, London on 18 March 1310, and like his colleagues he maintained that the Order had done nothing wrong.[64] By this time the other Templars in London had been interrogated three times.

Re-questioning the Templars

Having failed to get any substantial evidence of guilt from the Templars, on 29 January 1310 the inquisitors in London had produced a second set of questions, twenty-five in all. These were based on the premise that the Order of the Temple was a tightly organised institution, with a top-down command structure. All the Templars followed the same rule and statutes, which were established by the grand master (argued the inquisitors). Indeed, the grand master and the visitor had recently visited England, and held a chapter and laid down new statutes. All the Templars had the same reception ceremony. The grand master in France and the leading officials of the Temple in France had confessed – admittedly under torture or the threat of torture – to the charges against the Order. Therefore all the Templars must be guilty of the abuses of which they were charged.[65]

The English Templars disagreed. Their statutes, they said, were not drawn up by the grand master but by the general chapter of the Order on Cyprus.[66] Some Templars indicated that their rules came from the papal court in Rome.[67] As for the grand master and visitor, the English Templars had seen them or heard of their visit, but they knew nothing about the alleged abuses. Hugh of Tadcaster added that he saw Hugh Peraud at Temple Bruer, but could not understand what he said because he did not understand French.[68]

This second set of questions also asked about the procedures for absolution and penance, both for brothers and for servants (*servientes laici*) of the Order, and here the Templars did show uncertainty. It was clear that many of them did not understand the difference between a sin against God and an infringement of the Order's own regulations – only a priest could absolve a Templar of a sin, but the grand master, or visitor, or a commander could let them off for infringing the regulations. The question asked whether 'any Brother of theirs might absolve from the sin of perjury any lay servant when he came to discipline in the hall and a Serving Brother flogged him while saying "in the name of the Father and of the Son and of the Holy Spirit"'.

The point had been raised by some of the outside witnesses, notably Gilbert of Bruer, who stated that the Templars had once flogged his father because he had committed a crime against the Order.

[Gilbert of Bruer] says that while the brothers from the whole household of that house in which he had served were seated at table, or otherwise, a man who fell short by stealing half a loaf, perhaps, or badly guarding or managing the things which were in his keeping, came into the middle of the hall in the presence of all after taking off his hood and belt, and the keyholder of the house said in the common tongue: 'Friends, this servant of the house acknowledges that he has transgressed against the establishments of the house & against his oath. Therefore he has come with humility to the justice of the house, begging that you pray for him', and afterwards the brother gave him three blows with a leather scourge, saying, 'in the name of the Father & of the Son & of the Holy Spirit'. Questioned whether this flogging was done in the name of absolution or from what cause, he says that they called it 'the justice of the house' and thought that such a person was then corrected from the transgression of breaking the oath that he had made to them, and the witness believes that it seems to the servants that then they are absolved, because, even though they are laymen, the brothers say that they have the power of doing these things and other things by the authority of letters conceded to them by the apostolic see.[69]

Gilbert of Bruer's story was corroborated by the testimonies of Robert the Dorturer, Osbert Carter and William Boggis – William speaking from personal experience of being flogged – William the Dorturer, Gilbert of Chapemoa, who had been a servant of the Templars for many years, and William Provost, an Englishman working in Scotland.[70] It appeared from these accounts that lay members of the Order had been claiming the right to absolve sins, as if they were priests.

Some Templars, such as Peter of Ottringham, knew that laymen could give absolution only from crimes against the Order, not from broken oaths or other sins; others knew that only a priest could absolve sins.[71] Brother William of Egeldon explained that a servant who broke the Order's regulations would be scourged, and the scourger said, 'In the name of the Father & the Son', etc. 'But he is not absolved through this scourging, although the scourger enjoins him to say the "Our Father"'. William of Warwick, Ralph of Malton and John of Sutton agreed.[72]

But William of the Ford declared that when a servant broke the Order's regulations, 'the brother keyholder absolved him, and this was always the custom', and Richard Poitevin agreed.[73] Both of these were senior brothers within the Order of the Temple in England, who had attended many reception ceremonies and had held senior office in England. William of the Ford had joined the Order forty years before the interrogations, had acted as the grand commander's attorney, and was commander at Denney at the time of the arrests; Richard Poitevin was received forty-two years previously. He had been commander of the Temple in England in May 1282, acting as lieutenant for grand commander Robert of Turville. In January 1308 he was based at Dinsley. By July 1311 he was so old and decrepit that he was physically unable to appear in court.[74] The fact that two such senior brothers took this view indicates that the Templars in England had become confused over what constituted a sin and what was a crime.

As the Templars were told when they were received into the Order that they would be serving God in the Order, it would not be surprising if some came to believe that any misdemeanour against the Order was a sin against God. As their servants were effectively members of the household, they were also serving God through the Order of the Temple. Late medieval employers had a deep concern for the personal lives of their employees, treating them as the equals of their own children, and punishing them as if they were their own children.[75] But the Templars' failure to distinguish between service for their institution and service for God would be fatal for the Order of the Temple in Britain.

It was in the middle of this second set of interrogations, on 4 February 1310 in the church of St Alphage at Cripplegate (plate 34), that Bishop Ralph of London first made a formal statement of his protest 'that he did not intend to be present at the aforesaid examinations insofar as they were done against the Master or against the Order in the role of examiner, but solely as a witness'.[76] While one of their number declared that he was washing his hands of responsibility for proceedings – he was present only because the king had commanded it – the other inquisitors decided that one reason they could not get confessions was that the Templars were imprisoned together and could confer and agree on what to say. At the beginning of March 1310 Edward II sent out orders to the officials responsible for guarding the Templars, telling them to follow the inquisitors' instructions as regards to keeping the Templars locked up separately and anything else (which would include allowing the Templars to be tortured, although the king did not say as much). In addition, he sent instructions to the constable of the Tower of London that the inquisitors wanted the Templars to be imprisoned separately, and that he had ordered William de Dien to make sure that this was done. William de Dien was to survey the premises to ensure that they were suitable as a secure prison.[77]

The third round of interrogations of the Templars in London, 3–4 March 1310, was based on a set of four questions which sought to establish that all the Templars in the British Isles knew each other and all had been received in the same way. Thus, if one or two brothers confessed that they had denied Christ when they entered the Order, all the Templars in the British Isles must have been received like that. A fifth question was added: 'why are deceased brothers buried secretly?'[78] The question was prompted by allegations from outside witnesses regarding the Templars' burial customs. A rector in the diocese of Lincoln had alleged that Templars were not buried like Christians, suggesting that their graves could be difficult to identify.[79] Another priest, this time in Scotland, one Robert, chaplain of Kirkliston, had alleged that no one ever knew where a Templar was buried or whether he had died a good (that is, Christian) death.[80] A later French writer, perhaps echoing opinion during the time of the trial, wrote that dead Templars were burned and new Templars ate the ashes.[81]

The Templars responded that they were not buried secretly (plates 2–4) and, after the first four had hotly denied it, the question was dropped.[82] Brother John of Coningston said he had never seen any brother buried except those who had died in the Tower of London, and he saw the bones of Brother Brian le Jay buried; but so far as he had heard, anyone could watch Templars being buried. William of the Ford stated that he had been custodian of the infirmary at Eagle near Lincoln, and during his period in office sixteen brothers had died and were buried in the presence of the vicar of Eagle, Robert of Keal, Vicar John of Swinderby, Robert of Gonerby and many others, sometimes as many as a hundred. Roger of Noreys said that he saw two brothers – Robert Carpenter and W. the Marshal[83] – buried at Cressing, and listed those present, including members of these brothers' family. There were, he said, as many as sixty people there. But the point remained that Templar tombs – like those of the Hospitallers and Teutonic Order[84] – were not marked by impressive funerary slabs, and it is likely that most outsiders did not know which Templars were buried where.

On 8 and 9 June 1310 the London trial returned to Holy Trinity, London, for the fourth and final interrogation of Templars from the southern part of Canterbury province.[85] The Templars were asked about how the grand commander gave absolution in chapter meetings and which words he used. It was clear from their answers that this was the main point of weakness among the English brothers; they were confused about the theological details of absolution and penance and the role of a priest.

While the interrogations of Templars continued in London, King Edward II's authority was still under attack from his magnates. In February 1310 he issued orders that no one was to come armed to Parliament – particularly not his cousin, Earl Thomas of Lancaster. Thomas was already a leading figure in the opposition to Edward, and his opposition would eventually lead to open rebellion, battle and his death at Boroughbridge in 1322.[86] The magnates demanded reform, and in March 1310 Edward II had to agree to the appointment of twenty-one Ordainers who had full power to reform the kingdom and his household, and to control his finances.[87]

In April, Antony Bek and his colleagues met Edward and asked him to hand over the Templars' properties to them, so that they could administer them and the revenues would go to the Church. This was, after all, what Pope Clement V had commanded back in August 1308. Edward replied that he could not do so unless he had the consent of his magnates – for this was now a matter for the Ordainers. The pope's appointees continued to badger him, but early in April Edward left Westminster for Windsor, not returning to Westminster until June. Meanwhile, the king's councillors insisted that they could not make a decision during the king's absence.[88] So the situation remained unresolved, for neither king nor magnates wished to enforce the pope's mandate. Those Templar lands which Edward did not hold himself, or which he had not given to his friends, were in the hands of the noble families who had originally granted them to the Order, and they were not willing to return them to the Church. If the Church no longer wanted the Templars, the Templars' patrons wanted their land back.

The Trial in Lincoln

Meanwhile, the inquisitors had gone to Lincoln to interrogate the Templars there. As long ago as 27 October 1309, Bishop John Dalderby of Lincoln had written to King Edward to make arrangements for bringing the Templars into court when the papal inquisitors arrived in Lincoln.[89] On 9 November 1309, the inquisitors had written to Archbishop William

Greenfield of York informing him that they were going on to Lincoln on 24 November.[90] The interrogations at last began on 31 March 1310, and lasted until 1 June 1310.[91]

Proceedings took place in the lovely thirteenth-century chapter house of Lincoln cathedral. Constructed during the second quarter of the thirteenth century, this is a ten-sided hall with a fine vaulted ceiling. It is sited on the north side of the cathedral; the entrance opens off the cloister (plate 35). Apart from the bishop and the two papal inquisitors, there were some notaries present to take two copies of the testimonies, as at London, and Master Walter of Wermington, who was a canon of Lincoln cathedral and would later be one of three representatives the bishop of Lincoln appointed to represent him at the Council of Vienne.[92]

The Templars who were interrogated at Lincoln came from the commanderies of Lydley (Shropshire), Keele (Staffordshire), Balsall (Warwickshire), Rothley (Leicestershire) and Aslackby, Bruer, Eagle and Willoughton (Lincolnshire). They all insisted that the Order of the Temple was an orthodox Catholic Christian religious Order, and that the charges against them were false. There was no suspicion against them (they said), they could reveal the details of their reception ceremony to anyone, and they could confess their sins to any priest. There was some disagreement over whether or not they swore not to leave the Order, but the general consensus was that they did not swear; they only promised not to leave without permission from a superior. As for the belts that they wore over their shirts, they generally agreed that they were worn for decency's sake (to keep their clothes tidy), but one brother, Robert of Amoldon, explained that the belt he wore had touched a column in the church at Nazareth. He did not specify which column this was, but in Ireland the Templar Richard of Burthesham, who had been received into the Order at Tripoli in Syria, described it as being in the chapel of the Blessed Mary (Jesus' mother). Other Templar witnesses said that this was the column against which she lent when she received the annunciation. Presumably the 'chapel' was the cave-shrine beneath the Church of the Annunciation. Robert of Amoldon had been received into the Order at Dinsley in Hertfordshire, but as he later remarked that he had seen Grand Master Jacques de Molay and visitor Hugh Peraud overseas, perhaps he himself had touched his belt to the holy column while he was overseas.[93]

The last brother cross-examined at Lincoln on the eighty-eight charges, on 10 April 1310, was Brother Thomas Totty, one of the most notorious of the runaways. He appeared wearing his mantle – the sign that he was a member of the Order – although one of the notaries recorded that he had been carrying it secretly while he was on the run.[94] Like his colleagues, he insisted that the Order was innocent as charged, but there were some oddities in his testimony. He said that he was received by Brother William Forest – no such brother had ever been grand commander of England; presumably he meant Guy Forest. One notary recorded that he was received twenty-eight years ago, the other twenty-seven years ago.[95] Thomas Totty's testimonies would continue to be dogged by such errors.

Thomas Totty was clearly more aware of the intricacies of canon law than some of his colleagues. On charges 24–8, regarding absolution of sins by lay members of the Order, he stated that the grand master could absolve brothers from failure to obey the Rule and observances of the Order, but not from sins. He agreed that he had sworn not to leave the Order without permission from a superior, he wore the cord over his shirt for decency's sake, there were no regulations against revealing the details of the reception ceremony or confessing to non-Templars, and until recently there was no rumour against the Templars.

The trial at Lincoln continued on 1 June with a second set of questions about the Templars' absolution procedures, but Thomas Totty was not there to answer.[96] He later explained that he had been so terrified by Abbot Dieudonné of Lagny that he had run away,

> because the abbot of Lagny at Lincoln where he examined him asked him if he wished to confess other things, and when he replied that he did not know what else to say without lying, the abbot, putting his hand on his breast, swore by God's Word that he would make him confess before he escaped from his hands, as he said.

Desperate to escape, the witness met the sheriff of Lincoln and the custodian of Lincoln Castle, handed over forty florins and was then allowed to leave in broad daylight.[97]

The enquiries into the detail of the Templars' absolution ceremonies produced widely varying answers. John of Whaddon and Henry de la Vole said they had never heard that the grand master could absolve anyone. Some other brothers simply quoted the relevant passage from the Order's regulations for the holding of ordinary chapter meetings. Several brothers said that they had never been in a chapter meeting – they had all been in houses with fewer than four brothers, where weekly chapter meetings were not held.[98] Only Thomas of Walkington, commander at Rothley and Balsall, said anything which would have interested the inquisitors. He had seen the grand commander of England at Balsall having a Templar flogged three times for a misdemeanour, with the words: 'In the Name of the Father & the Son & the Holy Spirit' – 'may God remit [the punishment due] to you, and we remit it; and go to the brother priest who will absolve you'.[99] This agreed with some accounts given at London, but although it was clear that a priest actually gave the absolution, the inquisitors were uneasy about the use of the words 'in the name of the Father and the Son and the Holy Spirit', which seemed to imply that this was a religious ceremony and so outside the authority of a layman. Thomas of Walkington also said that he saw Brother 'Dalfin de Viana' at a general chapter in England collecting money to support the Holy Land.[100] This was presumably Brother Guy Delphin of Auvergne province, who would have come to England to collect the province's annual monetary contribution to the Order's work in the East. But it is not clear which year this occurred. The priest William of Winchester had also seen Brother 'Delphin' and also Brother Aimo d'Oiselay, who was marshal of the Temple by 1307, but this was when he was in France, so before 1302–3.[101] The inquisitors noted these points as evidence of contact between the English brothers and the French province.

After two interrogations, the Templars at Lincoln had not confessed anything significant. They were not formally interrogated again until the end of March 1311, after they had been moved to London. Interrogations took place at St Martin's church, Ludgate and St Botolph Bishopgate (plate 36) and were based on twenty-eight questions similar to those which the Templars in London had been asked in spring 1310, although the questions were in a different order and slightly rephrased for greater clarity.

Many of these Templars thought that the Order's rule was laid down at the papal court.[102] Henry de la Vole and the chaplain William of Winchester said that the Templars had had their regulations since the Order was first founded.[103] Ralph of Tanet said that the Order's procedures were laid down by statute, confirmed by the Roman (i.e. papal) Court and approved by the Order and brothers.[104] Several Templars stated that they knew nothing about the book which contained the Order's customs about absolution and confession, some adding that this was because they were laymen – although by the early fourteenth century it was not unusual for knights to be able to read.[105] Brother John of Whaddon, chaplain, stated that the only book the Templars had was their rule, 'which was made and given to them by the blessed Bernard [of Clairvaux]'.[106]

On the subject of punishments, John of Balsall stated that the grand commander could absolve from the sin of perjury, and he did not know what the keyholder said when he flogged a servant for his misdemeanours, but he could confirm the punishment, as he saw a certain Nicholas flogged, horsekeeper of Balsall.[107] Other brothers confirmed the punishment without giving specific examples; Richard of Newent stated that he had been keyholder for almost thirty years, and had spoken the words 'in the name of the Father, etc.' when he flogged a servant, as stated in the charge.[108]

The Trial in York

While proceedings continued in Lincoln, Abbot Dieudonné of Lagny and Sicard de Vaur had travelled on to York, where interrogations of the Templars began on 24 April 1310 and continued until 4 May. A year previously Archbishop Greenfield had summoned his clergy to a Council to be held in May 1310 to discuss the Templars' case. But as the interrogations were not completed until 4 May, the Council decided to postpone business until May 1311.[109] Around the same time, a papal bull arrived in England, dated 4 April 1310, announcing that Pope Clement V had postponed the opening of the Church Council at Vienne until October 1311.[110]

Interrogations began in the archbishop's hall, then moved into the chapter house of York Minster. Constructed in the second half of the thirteenth century, the chapter house is an octagonal hall with a magnificent vaulted ceiling. It is entered through a vestibule leading off the north transept of the cathedral.[111]

The Yorkshire Templars each insisted that their Order was innocent of all heresy, but the inquisitors found some of their statements very interesting. For example, thirteen of the twenty-three Templars interrogated at York agreed that they were not permitted to reveal the details of their reception into the Order to anyone, because this was one of the secrets of chapter.[112] However, Templars who did reveal these details were not killed; the worst that happened to them was to lose their habit and be put in prison.[113] Four Templars stated that they should not reveal the details of their reception because it was part of the chapter meeting, but there was no actual restriction.[114] But three brothers – Thomas of Staunford, Roger of Sheffield and John of Ebreston – believed that they could reveal the details of their reception to anyone.[115] All the brothers agreed that there was no restriction on their confessing to outsiders, except for Thomas of Staunford, who was able to quote from the Rule: 'where they could have a brother chaplain they should not confess to inferior priests without the licence of him [the priest] or the master, because the aforesaid brother chaplain has power over the brothers like that of a bishop or archbishop; and it is not otherwise forbidden to them.'[116]

Thomas of Staunford, who had joined the Order thirty years before in Cyprus, held views on the charge of lay absolution which were different from those held by the Templars interrogated at London and Lincoln.[117] He said that a grand commander who was a knight, or the visitor, could absolve brothers from the seven deadly sins if they asked for mercy in a chapter meeting, and the commander and convent then gave them penance. A Templar who had been absolved in a chapter meeting did not need to confess further to a priest, unless the commander sent him. When asked for what things the commander would send them to priests, he said 'secret carnal lapses'. He added that the priest would also absolve the Templars for other things, except for simony and violence against priests. According to canon 15 of the second Lateran Council (1139), anyone who used violence against a priest or member of a religious Order would be excommunicated, a sentence which only the pope could remove.[118]

Brother Thomas of Staunford was wrong: a layman could not absolve anyone from sin. As the Templars' chapter was composed of laymen, it could not absolve Templars; only a priest could do so. If these were the Yorkshire Templars' actual practices, then the Order in Yorkshire was in need of reform. But the brothers held different interpretations of the regulations. Brother Henry of Kerby, who followed Thomas of Staunford, understood the difference between 'faults relating to God and the soul', which had to be absolved by a priest, and other faults, which the master could absolve in a chapter meeting.[119] After Brother Henry came Brother Ralph of Ruston, priest, who had joined the Order twenty-three years earlier in Sicily and had another original interpretation of the master's right to absolve faults.

The grand commander and visitor, said Brother Ralph, who were knights, absolved brothers from any grave sins admitted in a chapter meeting, while for other sins the master sent them to the brother priest. Brother Ralph was unable to explain the difference between the sins absolved by the master and those absolved by a priest. When asked whether Templars absolved by the master later confessed the sin to the priest, he replied that some did but others did not. Then he said that 'just as an abbot can absolve persons of his convent, so the master can absolve persons of his convent'. Brother Ralph was showing his ignorance: abbots were priests, but the master of the Order of the Temple was a layman, and so had no right to absolve sins. To damn the Templars further, Ralph stated that he believed the other brothers agreed with him on this.[120] In fact, the three brothers who followed Brother Ralph differed in their opinions.[121] The inquisitors would go on to note this heretical view of absolution in their summary of the Templars' testimonies, and it was part of the evidence against the Templars included in the summary of the case which they sent to the papal commissioners for consideration at the Council of Vienne.[122]

Apart from this confusion over proper procedures for absolution, and their insistence that the reception ceremony was part of the secret aspect of chapter meetings, the Yorkshire brothers' testimonies were unspectacular. On 1 June 1310, the archbishop authorised two of his clergy, Henry of Botelesford (his penitencier), and John of Hemingburgh (dean of the cathedral), to hear the Templars' confessions and to give them penances, although he himself would absolve them of their sins. However, as the archbishop wrote in spring 1311 to the clergy of the province of York, the Templars had not confessed to any heresy.[123]

Outside Witnesses

As the inquisitors had found little substantial evidence against the Templars, they would have to rely on the Templars' public reputation to convict them. The evidence of around 170 non-Templar witnesses was collected by the archbishop of York's officials and similar officers in each diocese. Yet hardly any of the evidence brought against the Order was firsthand. Some had originally been recounted by persons unknown to the witness, and because many of those involved – both the witnesses' informants and the Templars mentioned – were dead, their stories could not be checked. Many accounts seem to be myth, testimonies constructed by the witness to meet the expectations of the inquisitors.[124] A few contain some accurate information.

Two friars told stories of pious Templars who were deliberately sent overseas to be killed.[125] The tale echoed the complaint of Ponzard de Gizy, commander of Payns, in France:

> Again, if a minor brother says anything to a commander of *bailies* [a commandery or other area of responsibility] that annoys him, the commander bribes the provincial commander to send the poor brother overseas to die, or to some foreign land where he does not know what to do and he is forced to die out of grief and poverty; and if he leaves the Order and is caught, he is put in prison.[126]

The friars' accusations suggested that the Templars 'punished' devout brothers by sending them overseas to die. Yet the Order had lost so many warriors in the last twenty years, suffering severe losses at the fall of Acre in 1291 and again at the fall of Arwad Island in 1302, that it would not have been surprising if some people in the West believed that any good knight who joined the Templars would be killed.

Richard of Bokingham's story of his involvement in a reception ceremony at Faxfleet has been discussed in chapter three; the core of this story could be true, although it is 'dressed up' to appear suspicious. Another partially true account was told by Brother Adam of Smeton, an Austin friar, about the Templars at Sandford in Oxfordshire. As described in chapter three, Brother Adam stated that he had met an elderly man who had served at the commandery of Sandford and who described the Templars' veneration of a stone slab which – from his description – was a portable altar containing relics. While they were doing this, no one was allowed into the chapel.[127] Although this was all reasonable behaviour for Catholic Christians, Adam presented it as heretical.

Three friars told a story about a Templars' sister who came to prepare her dead brother's body for burial. Although she had been strictly instructed not to undress the body, she did so in order to wash it, and discovered a cross embroidered on the Templar's underpants, demonstrating that the Templars dishonoured the cross. One of these friars said that he had heard the story from a certain woman, whose name he did not know, in his church in Lincoln.[128] Two friars told a second- or third-hand story about a dying Templar in Lincoln Castle who was being cared for by a woman, which they had heard from a friar in Lincoln.[129] Another friar told a story of Templars staying with a married woman in York; when she took their clothes for washing she found a cross on the underpants of one of them.[130] These stories were inherently unlikely, as the Templars' own Rule and customs would not allow them to lodge with or be cared for by a woman, the Templars had their own house at York where they would have lodged, the Order had its own hospitals for sick brothers at Denney and Eagle where brothers could be cared for; and, according to the Order's Rule, a dead brother would be prepared for burial by his Order.[131] However, the stories reflect women's stereotypical gendered roles within society (as carers, suppliers of hospitality and laundry services, and responsible for laying out the dead),[132] and allowed a means for the secret events to become known, for the woman could have repeated the story.

A Dominican and an Augustinian friar stated that they had heard, first or second hand, that an unnamed Templar commander had denied the resurrection of the dead, but although both indicated others who could corroborate their claims, no one appeared to support them. A similar accusation was brought in 1327 against an Irish rebel leader, as if this was a standard charge against those in political or religious disfavour.[133]

Several testimonies from Yorkshire were incorporated into the full record of the trial proceedings, testimony to the efficiency of the archbishop of York's officials.[134] Apart from John of Eure, sheriff of York, and William Jafford, who have already been noted in chapter two, these included two Franciscan friars: Robert of Ottringham, and Geoffrey of Nafferton, priest, who had both served the Templars at Ribston. Geoffrey explained that while he was at Ribston, the Templar William of Pokelington had been received into the Order there. Geoffrey had had to get out of bed to celebrate mass for the Templars in chapel at the beginning of the reception ceremony, but was then sent out. He went on to describe an exchange between himself and the keyholder who was guarding the door, over whether he should be allowed to watch the ceremony. In fact, Ribston chapel (which still stands: plate 23) is a small building, and by the time that William of Pokelington and the other five brothers mentioned by Geoffrey and himself were in the chapel, it could have been crowded.[135] At the time, the priest probably saw nothing unreasonable in being asked to leave the crowded room for the part of the ceremony which did not concern him. Only under questioning from the inquisitors did he realise that he had to produce a reason for having left the ceremony, or be accused of abetting heretics.

The vast majority of the non-Templar witnesses were unimportant people. One such was Agnes Cocacota or Louekata,[136] who lived with her husband Robert 'in the suburb of London, near some elm trees which are on the right-hand side of the street which goes towards St Giles (-in-the-Fields, now in London's West End). An otherwise unknown Franciscan friar of London, one John of Bercia, told the interrogators a long and involved story, which he said Agnes had told him, about idol worship and obscene activity at a Templar chapter meeting at Dinsley. The tale included the murder of a Templar who refused to spit on the cross – he was dropped down a well. Unusually, the interrogators had Agnes brought into court to confirm her tale, which she did with gusto. She added various colourful details such as the well being sixty fathoms (360 feet, nearly 110 metres) deep. Probably the wells at Dinsley were extremely deep – the modern well in the nearby village of Preston is 226 feet deep[137] – but even Agnes's vivid account was second hand. She said that her husband had heard the tale from Walter, a former servant of a former commander of the New Temple in London, but as the servant was never brought into court to repeat his story, it remains just that – a story.

Agnes's story combined a number of familiar elements from accusations against heretics, such as the black idol, kissing the backside of said idol, and repeated spitting on the cross as a routine part of life in the group. With these she included actual elements from the real history of the Templars: the brother who had entered to save his soul, the brothers' secret judgements, and the imprisonment and death of Templars who had committed crimes. All of this made her testimony more satisfactory to her interrogators, but less convincing to modern historians.[138]

Agnes Cocacota and her friend John of Bercia were not the most obscure witnesses against the Templars. Even the majority of the friars are otherwise unknown. Of seventy-seven witnesses against the Templars in England, only twenty-two of them made their mark elsewhere;[139] of forty-four witnesses against the Templars in Ireland, additional information is available about only twelve;[140] of fifty-two witnesses in Scotland, only nine appear in other sources.[141] Given that none of this evidence was substantial, it is difficult to deduce why witnesses came forward. As discussed already, some could have been under pressure to show that they had not abetted heretics. Some could have hoped for financial reward. Clergy could have hoped for promotion. The friars may also have hoped to distract attention from problems within their own Orders.

The trial testimonies show that the mendicant friars – Franciscans, Dominicans, Carmelites and Austin friars – acted as priests for the Templars in Britain and Ireland.[142] This was essential for the spiritual wellbeing of the Templars, because before the arrests the Order had only eleven priests of its own in the British Isles.[143] As priests who heard the Templars' confessions and conducted chapel services for them, the friars should have known about the Templars' alleged heretical practices and either taken action themselves to correct the Templars or reported them to the local bishop. Yet they had done nothing until King Philip IV of France acted against the Order in autumn 1307. As a result, the mendicants themselves would have been under suspicion for not reporting heresy. In addition, the Franciscan friars were already under suspicion of heresy because of the debates over the importance of absolute poverty;[144] perhaps they accused the Templars of heresy so as to clear themselves of suspicion.

Like the Franciscans, the Dominican friars had problems with heretical ideas, discipline and misbehaviour within their Order during the early fourteenth century. From time to time the writings of Dominicans at the University of Paris were investigated and condemned for heresy: this happened to John Quidort in 1305/6 and Durand of St Pourçain in 1314.[145] In 1314 a group of English Dominicans complained to Brother Berengarius, then Master of the Order, at the Council at London about 'certain most insane abuses contrary to divine and human law, which are practised in the said Order, and other enormities, which cannot be tolerated without heretical depravity' – these included concealing suicides by making effigies of brothers who had killed themselves and pretending that the brothers were still alive but sick; then claiming that the sick brother had died a natural death and giving the effigy Christian burial. They also complained about inhumane imprisonment of brothers.[146] Bringing accusations against the Templars would have distracted attention from the friars' own failings.

Overall, both the Franciscans and Dominicans had aroused the anger of the secular clergy. Sometime during the years 1305–10, the rectors of the London churches wrote to the archbishop of Canterbury to complain that the friars were overstepping their rights and taking over the work and income of the secular clergy.[147] All the more reason, then, for the friars to speak up against the Templars, so proving themselves enemies of heresy and good Christians, and deflecting other criticism. In contrast, at the University of Paris the Franciscan and Dominican friars supported the Templars as an exempt Order of the Church, against King Philip IV of France.[148]

In the case of the Carmelite friars, their testimonies against the Templars may reflect their Order's weak position. The Second Church Council of

Lyons (1274) had declared that no religious Order founded after 1215 should be allowed to continue – this included the Carmelites. The friars had to reform their Order and work hard to prove their loyalty to the papacy, for only the papacy could decide whether their Order would continue. They also wanted to demonstrate their concern about recovering the Holy Land, although they were not actually involved with crusading. Even though Pope Boniface VIII had assured the Carmelites that they would not be abolished, not until 1326 did Pope John XXII confirm their status as mendicant friars.[149] The Carmelites in the British Isles in 1308–11 could have damaged their Order if they had defied papal commands, so some demonstrated their loyalty and closeness to the papacy by speaking against the Templars. Some did believe in the Templars' guilt: one of the English Carmelites, William of Radinges, wrote a book claiming that the Templars were guilty of the charges against them, but his work has not survived.[150]

The Austin friars in the British Isles, in contrast, were very dependent on the monarch. Like the Dominicans, this Order valued study and learning very highly, and perhaps the friars' criticism of the Templars stemmed partly from horror of the Templars' ignorance of theology.[151] But overall the friars would certainly have been anxious to distance themselves from the Templars, whose heresies they should have known about and reported to the ecclesiastical authorities.

The Inquisitors' Continued Efforts

Having failed to get any substantial confessions out of the Templars in London, and disappointingly vague evidence from the non-Templar witnesses, the inquisitors resorted to their French colleagues. At some point copies of the confessions of two Templars who had been received in England but arrested in France – where they were interrogated under torture and confessed to the charges – arrived in England. The inquisitors included them with the evidence against the English Templars, and presented these confessions in the final summaries of the trial proceedings as if they were the confessions of Templars in England.[152]

The inquisitors hoped that such confessions would swing the trial in their favour. In a letter to the archbishop of Canterbury written before 16 June 1310, they stated that the Templars' confessions from France and other countries should be publicised in England to win popular opinion in support of the trial of the Templars, and read to the Templars to encourage them to confess. In addition, as the grand commander of the Auvergne, Himbert Blanc, refused to confess to having received any brothers into the Order by making them deny Christ or spit on the cross, the inquisitors in the Auvergne sent to England the confessions of those Templars whom Himbert Blanc had received into the Order. Brother Himbert was interrogated on the contents of these confessions in an attempt to make him confess – but he refused to co-operate.[153] However, as the three English brothers who made confessions in June 1311 did produce some material reminiscent of the French confessions, they may have been influenced by them.[154]

The inquisitors' letter to the archbishop of Canterbury had much more to say about the progress of the trial. Suspecting that the English Templars had discussed and agreed their defence in advance, they wanted to bring them into Church custody and prevent their having contact with each other.[155] They also claimed that they were being thwarted at every turn because the king's ministers were bribing the king to give the proceedings no assistance.[156] Although the knight William de Dien had been appointed at their request to oversee the Templars and to assist the inquisitors, neither he nor anyone else was prepared to carry out the investigation effectively. The archbishop replied that Sir William de Dien was their own choice, and if they were not happy with him they should nominate someone else.[157]

Finally, the inquisitors explained that they were about to leave England, their task completed.[158] Whether or not Abbot Dieudonné and Sicard de Vaur did leave at that time (King Edward did not issue any safe conduct documents for them), they were back in England by 13 October.[159]

Some of the inquisitors' suggestions on how to make the trial proceedings more effective were put into action. The bishop of Winchester instructed his clergy to read out the papal letters against the Templars from their pulpits each week, and the king – who was on his way to Scotland for a campaign against Robert Bruce – gave way on the question of custody. An anonymous note of 10 August 1310 recorded that the king had approved the inquisitors' petition regarding the Templars' imprisonment; the Templars would be handed over into Church custody and all the Templars in Lincoln Castle would be brought down to London for interrogation.[160] On 26 August 1310, Edward II wrote from north-east England to John of Crumbewell, constable of the Tower of London, instructing him to hand the Templars over to the sheriffs of London to be guarded and to be brought for interrogation when requested by the inquisitors. He also wrote to the sheriffs of London, telling them to have the Templars guarded by men appointed by the bishops and inquisitors, in prisons approved by the bishops or inquisitors, and to allow the inquisitors to do what seemed suitable 'following ecclesiastical law' – in short, they were to allow the Templars to be tortured. The Templars' pension of four pence a day would be paid to their guards, who should pass it to the Templars.[161]

The Council of the Providence Canterbury, which had been postponed from 17 December 1309, met again on 23 September 1310 at St Paul's cathedral, London, to discuss the Templar affair. The Templars' testimonies to date were read out to the delegates, with the statements of the outside witnesses. After lengthy debate, it was agreed that the Templars should be imprisoned separately in various places in London and cross-examined again over the charges and with new questions. The same should be done with the Templars at Lincoln. If the Templars refused to confess to anything, then they should be tortured, but without mutilation or permanent damage, or severe loss of blood. On 14 November the Council was dissolved until 23 April 1311.[162]

Meanwhile, on 6 October 1310 Edward, now in the lowlands of Scotland, had repeated his instructions of 26 August to the constable of the Tower, but with more detail as to where the Templars were to be imprisoned. The Templars, he wrote, were to be kept in the gates of London and the houses which had formerly belonged to John of Bakewell and to the Friars of the Sack (whose London house had been abandoned by 1305) or other suitable places in the city of London. He also instructed the sheriffs of London to take the Templars into their custody and guard them, to produce them when required by the inquisitors and then return them to prison. The king repeated his instructions on 23 October, and wrote the same to the mayor and bailiffs of the city of Lincoln and the constable of Lincoln Castle.[163]

However, these instructions were not followed. The sheriffs of London informed the king that he could not use the gates of London as prisons because they were not royal property; they belonged to the city of London. So on 22 November 1310 Edward wrote from Berwick-upon-Tweed to the mayor and aldermen of the city, ordering them to hand the gates over to the sheriffs so that they could be used as prisons for the Templars, including those who were soon to arrive from Lincoln. He wrote to the sheriffs telling them that if the gates were unsuitable, they must find other accommodation for the Templars; he would pay the necessary costs. He also instructed the mayor and aldermen to keep the Templars apart; they must be properly guarded and produced when required, and the guards must allow the investigators 'to do whatever is required by ecclesiastical law' and then take the Templars back to custody. The king would pay all expenses.[164] But apparently the Templars at Lincoln were still in Lincoln Castle on 12 December 1310.[165]

Eventually the Templars at Lincoln did travel to London, where their final interrogation took place between 30 March and 2 April 1311.[166] As discussed already, they confessed nothing significant, except that some thought that lay members of the Order could absolve brothers from sins. The inquisitors had not yet found any substantial evidence against the Order in the British Isles, and the Church Council to decide the Templars' final fate was due to open at Vienne in October that year.

Notes

1 *Annales Londonienses*, ed. Stubbs, p. 158.
2 Perkins, 'Trial of the Knights Templars', pp. 492–3; *Records of Antony Bek*, p. 118, no. 111; pp. 130–1, no. 128; C.M. Fraser, *A History of Antony Bek, Bishop of Durham, 1283–1311* (Oxford, 1957), pp. 164–5, 172–3, 219, 223, 225; *Foedera*, ed. Rymer, vol. 2, pt 1, pp. 46, 55; *CCR, 1307–1313*, p. 35; for his career, see also C.M. Fraser, 'Bek, Antony (I) (*c.*1245–1311)', in *ODNB*, vol. 4, pp. 862–4.
3 For the career of William Greenfield, archbishop of York 1306–1315, see Roy Martin Haines, 'Greenfield, William (*c.*1255–1315)', in *ODNB*, vol. 23, pp. 590–2; for the career of John Dalderby, bishop of Lincoln, 1300–20, see Nicholas Bennandt, 'Dalderby, John (*d.* 1320)', in *ODNB*, vol. 14, p. 925; for the career of John Langton, bishop of Chichester, 1305–37, see M.C. Buck, 'Langton, John (*d.* 1337)', in *ODNB*, vol. 32, pp. 512–13.
4 *Gallia Christiana in provincias ecclesiasticas distributa: qua series et historia archiepiscoporum, episcoporum, et abbatum franciae vicinarumque ditionum*, ed. Gaucher and Scévole de Sainte-Marthe, Denis de Sainte-Marthe, *et al.*, 16 vols (Paris, 1715–1865), vol. 1, col. 67; vol. 7, cols 502–3.
5 Barber, *Trial of the Templars*, 2nd edn, p. 344 n. 16.
6 Bernard Guillemain, *La Cour Pontificale d'Avignon (1309–1376): Étude d'une Société*, Bibliothèque des Écoles Françaises d'Athènes et de Rome, 201 (Paris, 1962), p. 348. The definition of 'auditor' is given by William H.W. Fanning in *The Catholic Encyclopedia*, vol. 2 (New York, 1907); see also Guillemain, *La Cour Pontificale d'Avignon*, pp. 346–9.
7 *Registrum Roberti Winchelsey*, vol. 1, pp. 141–2. On the village of Hayes, see *VCH, Middlesex*, vol. 1, ed. J.S. Cockburn, H.P.F. King and K.G.T. McDonnell (London, 1969), p. 139. For Guy's death, see: *Records of Antony Bek*, p. 155, no. 145.
8 *Gallia Christiana*, vol. 8, cols 1471–2.
9 Ibid., vol. 1, col. 457.

10 *Foedera*, ed. Rymer, vol. 2, pt 1, pp. 88, 90, 91; *CPR, 1307–1313*, p. 190; *CCR, 1307–1313*, pp. 175–7, 230.

11 *Register of William Greenfield*, part 4, pp. 295–7.

12 *Registrum Henrici Woodlock*, pp. xxxv, 406, 415–16, 565, 567, 568; *Registrum Simonis de Gandavo*, p. 408.

13 Fraser, *History of Antony Bek*, p. 173; *Records of Antony Bek*, pp. 155–6, 157, nos. 144, 145, 147.

14 *Register of William Greenfield*, part 4, pp. 299–301, no. 2277.

15 MS A, fol. 10v (Wilkins, p. 333).

16 Probably Adam son of Adam of Sweyny de Boterwik, called 'de Lindeseia', whom C.R. Cheney noted as a notary public between 1289 and 1305: C.R. Cheney, *Notaries Public in England in the Thirteenth and Fourteenth Centuries* (Oxford, 1972), pp. 29, 46, 88, 103, 118, 121, 128–9. Cheney, p. 88, suggests that he was married and that Henry Adams, called 'de Lindeseia', who appears as a notary public in 1320 and 1325, was his son.

17 Cheney, *Notaries Public*, pp. 3, 37–8.

18 For example, MS A, fols 31r, 37v, 38r, 39r; MS B, fols 72r, 74r–v.

19 MS A, fol. 29v.

20 MS B, fol. 71v.

21 MS A, fols 88v, 168r.

22 See MS A, fol. 18v; MS B, fol. 68r (Wilkins, p. 339).

23 MS A, fol. 11v (Wilkins, p. 334).

24 Barber, *Trial of the Templars*, 2nd edn, p. 124; MS A, fols 11v–13r (Wilkins, pp. 334–5, abridged). For further information about all these clergy see the detailed footnotes to my edition of MS A, fol. 12r, in *The Trial of the Templars in the British Isles*, ed. Helen Nicholson, vol. 2.

25 MS A, fols 13r–16v, fol. 16v on Walter the Bachelor (Wilkins, pp. 335–7); Wood, p. 333.

26 MS A, fol. 54r (Wilkins, p. 345).

27 MS A, fol. 17r–v; fol. 48r–v; fol. 21v; fol. 31v; fol. 38r; MS B, fol. 74r; MS A, fol. 40v; MS B, fol. 75r; MS A, fols 41r, 42r–v; MS A, fols 41v, 50v, 54r (Wilkins omits all).

28 MS A, fol. 42r (Wilkins, p. 344); MS A, fol. 46v; MS B, 78r; MS A, fol. 50v; MS B, fol. 79v; MS A, fol. 44v (Wilkins omits all these); MS A, fol. 44v; MS B, fol. 78r (Wilkins, p. 344); MS A, fol. 47r (Wilkins omits).

29 MS A, fol. 77v (Wilkins omits). For the *passagium* ('payment of passage') see MS A, fol. 93v, a testimony taken from the French trial proceedings (Michelet, *Procès*, vol. 2, p. 400; Wilkins, p. 361, mistranscribes); and for analysis, see Helen J. Nicholson, 'International Mobility versus the Needs of the Realm: The Templars and Hospitallers in the British Isles in the Thirteenth and Fourteenth Centuries', in *International Mobility in the Military Orders, Twelfth to Fifteenth Centuries: Travelling on Christ's Business*, ed. Jochen Burgtorf and Helen J. Nicholson (Cardiff, 2006), pp. 87–101, here pp. 99–100, n. 53.

30 MS A, fols 24v, 25v, 34r (Wilkins, p. 340, omits rest).

31 *Règle*, sections 5 and 6; trans. Upton-Ward, pp. 20–21.

32 Brother John of Whaddon: MS A, fol. 120r (Wilkins omits).

33 Barber, *Trial of the Templars*, 2nd edn, pp. 139–40. My thanks to Khudeza Siddika for this suggestion.

34 Barber, *Trial of the Templars*, 2nd edn, pp. 141–83.

35 *Register of William Greenfield*, part 4, pp. 301–2, no. 2278.

36 MS A, fol. 155 (Wilkins, p. 380).

37 *Councils and Synods*, ed. Powicke and Cheney, vol. 2, pt 2, pp. 1241–3, 1264–1274.

38 *The Mirror of Justices*, ed. William Joseph Whittaker, Selden Society, 7 (1895), pp. 59–60. In the second decade of the fourteenth century this work was included in a compilation of English legal treatises by Andrew Horn: see Jeremy Catto, 'Andrew Horn: Law and History in Fourteenth-century England', in *The Writing of History in the Middle Ages: Essays presented to Richard William Southern*, ed. R.H.C. Davis and J.M. Wallace-Hadrill (Oxford, 1981), pp. 373–4. The *Mirror's* opinion may have been drawn from Roman law; in the fifth-century Theodosian Code, heretics received the same punishment as high treason: *The Theodosian Code and Novels and Sirmondian Constitutions*, trans. Clyde Pharr (Princeton, 1952), Bk 16.1.4 (p. 440); 16.4.1 (p. 449); 16.5.40 (p. 457).

39 *CPR, 1307–1313*, pp. 208–9; *CCR, 1307–1313*, p. 196; *Foedera*, ed. Rymer, vol. 2, pt 1, p. 104. See also Barber, *Trial of the Templars*, 2nd edn, p. 217.

40 *Foedera*, ed. Rymer, vol. 2, pt 1, p. 100; *CPR, 1307–1313*, pp. 208–9; MS B, fol. 80r; summarised by Perkins, 'Trial of the Knights Templars', p. 487. The inquisitors' problems in finding torturers in England are discussed by Barber, *Trial of the Templars*, 2nd edn, pp. 221–28; Perkins, 'Trial of the Knights Templars in England', pp. 435–6, 438–43, 445, 447.

41 Hamilton, *Piers Gaveston*, pp. 43–77.

42 Paul Hyams, 'Due Process versus the Maintenance of Order in European Law: the Contribution of the *ius commune*', in *The Moral World of the Law*, ed. Peter Coss (Cambridge, 2000), here p. 82.

43 These were assembled together in MS A, fols. 91r–100r (Wilkins, pp. 358–64, much abridged), a section which comprises some testimonies summarised from elsewhere in MS A, presented before the inquisitors in Ireland (MS A, fol. 91r–v) or Scotland (fol. 93r); some testimonies sent by the inquisitors in France (fols 93r–94r), some given to a third party such as the bishop of Hereford (fol. 96v) or of Lincoln (fol. 97r); groups of testimonies came from specific dioceses such as Canterbury (fols 95v–96r), York (fols 91v–92r), or Lincoln (fol. 94r–v); others came from a specific religious order, such as the Franciscan friars (fol. 92v) or the Carmelites (fols 95r–v, 96r); and one group of testimonies was submitted in writing (fol. 92r–v). Some testimonies were repeated.

44 *Register of William Greenfield*, part 4, p. 286, end of no. 2271.

45 Ibid., pp. 334–5, no. 2301.

46 MS A, fols 60r–62v (Wilkins, p. 348–9).

47 MS A, fol. 60r (Wilkins, p. 348). For more information on this individual, see the footnote on my edition of MS A, fol. 60r, in *The Trial of the Templars in the British Isles*, vol. 2.

48 MS A, fols. 60r–v (Wilkins, p. 348); gave evidence again later, MS A, fols 96v–97r (Wilkins omits), when he stated that his father, Lord Ranulph of Ryrol, had been in the Templars' employment. For further information see the footnote to my edition of MS A, fol. 60r, in *The Trial of the Templars in the British Isles*, vol. 2.

49 MS A, fols 96v–97r (Wilkins omits).

50 MS A, fols 60v–61r (Wilkins, p. 348). Cheney, *Notaries Public*, p. 46, suggests that he was related to William the Dorturer.

51 Grand commander by 10 March 1272: *CPR, 1266–1272*, p. 635.

52 MS A, fol. 60r–61v (Wilkins, p. 348).

53 TNA:PRO C143/31/4 and C143/34/4.

54 TNA:PRO, C143/44/5 mem. 2.

55 MS A, fol. 61r–v (Wilkins, p. 348).

56 MS A, fols 61v– 62r (Wilkins, pp. 348–9).

57 MS A, fol. 62v (Wilkins, p. 349).

58 MS A, fols 54r–56v (Wilkins, pp. 545–6, abridged).

59 Sandys, 'Financial and Administrative Importance of the London Temple', pp. 147–62. The New Temple also housed legal records: *Select Cases: the Court of King's Bench under Edward I*, ed. G.O. Sayles, Selden Society 55 (1936), p. cxxiii.

60 For Brother Richard, priest and Englishman on Cyprus, see Gilmour-Bryson, *Trial of the Templars in Cyprus*, pp. 81–3 and note 34, p. 99 and note 140, pp. 175–8 and listed on p. 448, and the note on my edition of MS A, fol. 55r, in *The Trial of the Templars in the British Isles*, vol. 2.

61 MS A, fol 55r–v (Wilkins, pp. 345–6).

62 MS A, fol. 164r–v (Wilkins, pp. 387–8).

63 MS A, fol. 56r (Wilkins omits); Gilmour-Bryson, *Trial of the Templars in Cyprus*, pp. 99, 107–8, 235–8, 258–61.

64 MS A, fols 56v–57r (Wilkins, p. 346, abridged).

65 MS A, fols 63v–64v (Wilkins, pp. 349–50). For the answers to these questions, see MS A, fols 64v–81v (Wilkins summarises, pp. 350–2).

66 MS A, fols 64v–65r, 65v, 66r, 66v, 68v (Wilkins, pp. 350–1; he omits most of this).

67 MS A, fols 66r, 67r, 68v (Wilkins omits).

68 MS A, fol. 68v (Wilkins omits).

69 MS A, fols 96v–97r (Wilkins omits).

70 MS A, fols 97r, 97v, 98r, 99r–v, 158v (Wilkins omits).

71 MS A, fol. 64v–65r, 68r, 72r, 72v, 73v, 75v, 76r–v (Wilkins, pp. 350–1).

72 MS A, fols 69r, 77r–v, 79r (Wilkins omits).

73 MS A, fol. 71r, 71v, 74v (Wilkins omits).

74 William of the Forde: MS A, fols 21r, 58r, 168r (Wilkins, pp. 340, 347, 391); *CPR, 1292–1301*, pp. 75, 313; Richard Poitevin: *CPR, 1281–1292*, pp. 20, 24; MS A, fols 19v, 58v, 168v (Wilkins, pp. 339–40, 347, 391).

75 For a discussion of what it meant to be a servant in England in the late Middle Ages, and employer-servant relations, see P.J.P. Goldberg, 'What was a servant?' in *Concepts and Patterns of Service in the Later Middle Ages*, ed. Anne Curry and Elizabeth Matthew (Woodbridge, 2000), pp. 1–20; on punishments, see p. 18; P.J.P. Goldberg, 'Masters and Men in Late Medieval England', in *Masculinity in Medieval Europe*, ed. D.M. Hadley (London, 1999), pp. 56–70, here p. 61; and for an example of punishments at Kilkenny in the fourteenth century, see *Borough Customs, I*, ed. Mary Bateson, Seldon Society 18 (London, 1904), p. 62.

76 MS A, fol. 87v (Wilkins, p. 352); *CCR, 1307–1313*, p. 230.

77 *CCR, 1307–1313*, pp. 196, 200, 206; *Foedera*, ed. Rymer, vol. 2, pt 1, pp. 104–5.

78 MS A, fols 81v–86r (Wilkins, pp. 352–6). For the burial customs of religious orders in Britain at this time see *Requiem: The Medieval Monastic Cemetery in Britain*, ed. Roberta Gilchrist and Barney Sloane (London, 2005).

79 Richard Berards, MS A, fol. 94v (Wilkins omits).

80 MS A, fol. 158r (Wilkins, p. 382).

81 Barber, *Trial of the Templars*, 2nd edn, p. 206.

82 MS A, fol. 82r–v (Wilkins, p. 353).

83 The identify of this W. Marshal is unclear; see my note on MS A, fol. 82v, in *The Trial of the Templars in the British Isles*, vol. 2.

84 For Hospitaller tombs, see Anthony Luttrell in *Sacra Militia*, 3 (2002), pp. 25, 40. The Teutonic Order's tombs at their headquarters at Marienburg (now Malbork, Poland) are plain stone slabs marked with a simple cross.

85 MS A, fols 87v, 89v, 90v (Wilkins, pp. 356–8).

86 J.R. Maddicott, 'Thomas of Lancaster, second earl of Lancaster, second earl of Leicester, and earl of Lincoln (*c.*1278–1322)', *ODNB*, vol. 54, pp. 288–95.

87 *Foedera*, ed. Rymer, vol. 2, pt 1, pp. 102–3; Hamilton, *Piers Gaveston*, pp. 77–80; Michael Prestwich, 'The Ordinances of 1311 and the Politics of the Early Fourteenth Century', *Politics and Crisis in Fourteenth-Century England*, ed. John Taylor and Wendy Childs (Gloucester, 1990), pp. 1–18.

88 *Itinerary of Edward II*, pp. 58–60; *Records of Antony Bek*, pp. 158–9, no. 150; Fraser, *History of Antony Bek*, pp. 223–4.

89 TNA:PRO SC1/33/118.

90 *Register of William Greenfield*, part 4, pp. 301–2, no. 2278.

91 MS A, fols 103r–116r (Wilkins, pp. 365–8).

92 MS B, fol. 76r; *Councils and Synods*, ed. Powicke and Cheney, vol. 2, pt 2, pp. 1289, 1351 n. 7.

93 MS A, fols 105v, 121r (Wilkins, pp. 366, 370); MS A, fol. 135r (Wilkins, p. 135); *Procès*, ed. Michelet, vol. 1, p. 419; Schottmüller, p. 65; Denys Pringle, *The Churches of the Crusader Kingdom of Jerusalem: a Corpus*, vol. 2, L–Z (Cambridge, 1998), pp. 116–140, here p. 121.

94 MS B, fol. 76v.

95 MS A, fols 114v–115r (Wilkins summarises, p. 367); MS B, fol. 76v.

96 MS A, fols 115r–16r (Wilkins, pp. 367–8).

97 MS A, fol. 162r (Wilkins, pp. 385–6).

98 MS A, fols 115r–16r (Wilkins, pp. 367–8); *Règle*, section 385; trans. Upton-Ward, p. 105. For the regulations on absolutions in chapter meetings, see *Règle*, sections 538–40; trans. Upton-Ward, pp. 140–1.

99 MS A, fol. 115v (Wilkins, pp. 367–8).

100 Michelet, *Procès*, vol. 1, pp. 415–20, vol. 2, pp. 219, 237, 254, 280; *Le procès des Templiers d'Auvergne*, ed. Sève and Chagny-Sève, pp. 235, 242. Sève and Chagny-Sève list his offices: he had been commander of Jussy-le-Chaudrier (Cher, 1298), Lespinaz (Indre-et-Loire, 1304), and Celles (1304–7): ibid., p. 282.

101 MS A, fol. 116r (Wilkins, p. 368). For information on the career of Aimo d'Oiselay I am indebted to Jochen Burgtorf.

102 MS A, fols 118r, 123r, 124r, 124v (Wilkins, p. 369 for the first only).

103 MS A, fols 119r, 122v (Wilkins omits).

104 MS A, fol. 122r (Wilkins omits).

105 John of Wakeleye, MS A, fol. 118r; Henry of la Volee, fol. 119r; Brother Thomas of Walkington, fol. 119v; Robert of Hameledon, fol. 120v; Brother John of Balsall, fol. 121v; Henry of Halton, fol. 121v; Ralph Tanet, fol. 122r; Brother Richard of Bistelesham, fol. 123r; John of Eagle, fol. 124r (Wilkins omits all); Elspeth Kennedy, 'The Knight as Reader of Arthurian Romance', in *Culture and the King: the Social Implications of the Arthurian Legend: Essays in Honor of Valerie M. Lagorio*, ed. Martin B. Shichtman and James P. Carley (New York, 1994), pp. 70–90; Michael Clanchy, *From Memory to Written Record: England, 1066–1307* (London, 1979), pp. 182–201.

106 MS A, fol. 120r (Wilkins omits).

107 MS A, fol. 121v (Wilkins omits).

108 MS A, fols 122r, 123v (Wilkins omits).

109 *Register of William Greenfield*, part 4, pp. 328–30, no. 2297; part 5, p. xxxvi.

110 *Register of William Greenfield*, part 4, pp. 327–8; *Councils and Synods*, ed. Powicke and Cheney, vol. 2, pt 2, p. 1284 and n. 4.

111 MS A, fols 125r–133r (Wilkins summarises, pp. 371–3).

112 MS A, fols 125r, 125v, 126v, 127r, 127v, 128v, 129r, 131r, 131v, 132r (Wilkins, p. 371 for first; omits the rest); for the regulation on not revealing the proceedings of chapter meetings, see *Règle*, sections 223, 225, 391, 418, 550–1; trans. Upton-Ward, pp. 72, 73, 107, 112, 143.

113 MS A, fol. 127v: the opinion of Stephen of Radenhall, commander (*preceptor*) of Westerdale. Wilkins omits, and (p. 272) misreads the office as *presbiter*.

114 MS A, fols 128r, 129v, 132r (Wilkins omits).

115 MS A, fols 126r, 133r (Wilkins omits).

116 MS A, fol. 126r (Wilkins omits); *Règle*, section 269; trans. Upton-Ward, p. 70. See also Henry Kerby, MS A, fol. 126v, and John of Walpole, fol. 129r, who denied the charge but said that the Templar chaplains had received from the pope greater power of absolving than other priests. Stephen of Radenhall, fol. 127v, said that they were allowed to have their own priests but they could confess to others.

117 MS A, fol. 126r (Wilkins, p. 372).

118 For a case of simony in the Order of the Temple, see *Règle*, sections 544–9; trans. Upton-Ward, pp. 142–3. On the sins which could be absolved only by the pope, see: Johannes Baptist Sägmüller, 'Ecclesiastical Privilege', *The Catholic Encyclopedia*, vol. 12 (New York, 1911); *Decrees of the Ecumenical Councils*, ed. Norman P. Tanner (London, 1990) (http://www.piar.hu/councils/ecum10.htm#canons).

119 MS A, fol. 126v (Wilkins omits).

120 MS A, fol. 127r (Wilkins omits).

121 MS A, fols 127r, 131v (Wilkins omits).

122 MS A, fol. 91r (Wilkins, p. 358); MS C fol. 4v (Schottmüller, p. 86).

123 *Register of William Greenfield*, part 4, p. 327, no. 2296; *Chronicle of Walter of Guisborough*, pp. 391–2.

124 Gilmour-Bryson, 'The London Templar Trial Testimony', pp. 44–61; Arnold, *Inquisition and Power*, pp. 11–12.

125 Robert of Maidenesford, MS A, fol. 95v; Roger of Ware, fol. 96r; for a variation on the story, see Robert of Dofeld, fol. 97v (Wilkins omits all).

126 *Procès*, ed. Michelet, vol. 1, pp. 37–8.

127 MS A, fols 96r–v, 97r; see above, chapter three, p. 83.

128 MS C, fols 2v, 3r (Schottmüller, pp. 81–3).

129 MS C, fols 2v, 4r (Schottmüller, pp. 81–2, 84–5).

130 MS C, fol. 2v (Schottmüller, p. 82).

131 *Règle*, sections 61, 62, 70, 71, 563, 578–82, 625; trans. Upton-Ward, pp. 34, 36, 146, 149–51, 160–1; on these houses, see appendix 2.

132 See, for example, Carole Rawcliffe, *Medicine and Society in Later Medieval England* (Stroud, 1995), pp. 205–13; Helen Nicholson, 'Women in Templar and Hospitaller Commanderies', in *La Commanderie*, ed. Luttrell and Pressouyre, pp. 131–2 and notes 22–3, citing especially: P.J. Goldberg, *Women, Work and Lifecycle in a Medieval Economy: Women in York and Yorkshire c. 1300–1520* (Oxford, 1992), p. 135;

1. The tomb of King Edward II of England at Gloucester cathedral; the effigy dates from around 1330. Copyright: Nigel Nicholson.

2. Templar tombstones showing Templars are very rare. The tombs shown in plates 2 and 3 come from the kingdom of Sicily, and are now in the museum of Barletta. Plate 2 is the tomb of the Templar Gioberto, master of the Temple in Sicily, who died 13 March 1287. Reproduced by permission of the *Comune di Barletta*.

3. The tomb of the Templar Simone di Quincy, master of the Temple in Sicily, who died 7 June 1307. For further information on these tombs, see Francesco Tommasi, 'Fonti epigrafiche dalla *domus Templi* di Barletta per la cronotassi degli ultimi maestri provinciali dell'ordine nel regno di Sicilia', in *Militia Sacra: Gli ordini militari tra Europa e Terrasanta*, ed. Enzo Coli, Maria de Marco and Francesco Tommasi (Perugia, 1994), pp. 167-202. Reproduced by permission of the *Comune di Barletta*.

4. The tomb of the Templar Gerard de Villers (d. 1273), at Villers-le-Temple, in Flanders. Copyright: Denys Pringle.

5. Templar images of St Bernard, abbot of Clairvaux. Many Templars regarded him as founder of their Order. From a Templar altarpiece, now in the Museum of La Palma, Mallorca. Reproduced by permission of the museum.

6. Athlit or Castle Pilgrim, from inland. Henry Danet, grand commander of Ireland, informed his interrogators that an (unnamed) commander of this castle had received Templars into the Order here in a blasphemous ceremony like those of which the Templars were accused. Copyright: Denys Pringle.

7. Arwad island, otherwise known as Ruad, looking across the sea the short distance to Tortosa. The Templars set up a base here early in the fourteenth century, but in October 1302 the naval forces of the Mamluk sultan of Egypt sacked the island and took the Templars prisoner or killed them. Copyright: Paul Crawford.

8. The site of the fortress of Maraclea, viewed from the shore. Templar brother Thomas Totty of Thoroldby described an attack on the fortress by crusaders, the king of Cyprus and the Templars, during which the Christians were taken by surprise by the Muslim army. Copyright: Jochen Burgtorf.

9. The Templars' tower at Paris. In June 1306 King Philip IV of France took refuge here from the Parisians who were rioting against his monetary policies. Pen and ink drawing of 1785, from the collection of Hippolyte Destailleur (1822-1893). BnF Est. Rés. Ve-53h-Fol. Shelfmark: IFN-7744847. Copyright: Bibliothèque Nationale de France.

10. The memorial to Jacques de Molay on the Pont Neuf, Paris. Copyright: Nigel Nicholson.

11. The Templars' ruined chapel at Balantrodoch (now Temple) at Midlothian, Scotland. Copyright: SUAT Ltd.

12. The chapel at Temple Balsall, constructed in the thirteenth century. A second-hand story told by one of the witnesses against the Templars suggested that any visitor to Balsall could enter the chapel to pray. Copyright: Nigel Nicholson.

13. Bisham today, by the River Thames opposite Marlow. The Templars' hall, dating from around 1260, survives as part of the modern house. King Edward II used Bisham to house a royal prisoner, Queen Elizabeth of Scotland. Copyright: Nigel Nicholson.

14. The chapel at Temple Bruer. A centre of arable farming today, in the early fourteenth century Bruer was noted for its wool production. Copyright: Nigel Nicholson.

15. Eagle, Lincolnshire. In the Templars' time, this was a house for old and sick brothers; it later became one of the Hospitallers' most important English houses. Copyright: Nigel Nicholson.

16. Faxfleet farm today; view from the sea wall. Note the expanse of wheat fields. Copyright: Nigel Nicholson.

17. The exterior of the modern farm at Foulbridge. The modern farmhouse incorporates the Templars' thirteenth-century hall. Copyright: Nigel Nicholson.

18. Garway church: the sheriff of Herefordshire reported that he had received the gift of a horse from the commander here, but the horse died shortly after. The commandery now appears to be 'off the beaten track', but in 1338 the Hospitallers reported that many travellers came through Garway seeking lodging. Copyright: Nigel Nicholson.

19. The exterior of New Temple Church, London, showing the twelfth-century circular nave and the thirteenth-century chancel. The pillar in the centre of the courtyard is a modern memorial to the Templars, surmounted with their symbol of two knights on one horse. Since the early seventeenth century the church has belonged to the Inner and Middle Temple Inns of Court, London. Copyright: Nigel Nicholson.

20. The interior of the small room halfway up the stairs in Temple Church, London, where 'tradition states' that Walter the Bachelor, disgraced grand commander of Ireland, was imprisoned and died. Copyright: Nigel Nicholson, by permission of the Hon. Societies of the Inner and Middle Temple.

21. Looking up from the chancel of Temple Church, London, towards the window of the small room where Walter the Bachelor is supposed to have been imprisoned. Copyright: Nigel Nicholson, by permission of the Hon. Societies of the Inner and Middle Temple.

22. The excavated ruins of the Templars' chapel at their commandery of Penhill, North Riding of Yorkshire, contains tombs – presumably of the Templars who once lived there – before the altar (front right), but there is now nothing to show that there were ever images or writing on the tombs. Copyright: Nigel Nicholson.

23. Dawn over Ribston Hall at Little Ribston, West Riding of Yorkshire. The chapel of St Andrew (centre) still has its thirteenth-century doorways, but the rest has been rebuilt since the Templars' time. Copyright: Nigel Nicholson.

24. Sandford today: Oxford Thames Four Pillars Hotel, Sandford-on-Thames, Oxfordshire; incorporating the barns and chapel of the Templars' former commandery of Sandford. Reproduced by permission of Oxford Thames Four Pillars Hotel. Copyright: Nigel Nicholson.

25. Acorn Bank, on the site of Temple Sowerby in Cumbria, on the main road south from Scotland. There were no Templars here in early 1308; probably it was in the front line of the Anglo-Scottish war. Like the other Templar houses in the British Isles, the house is set in gently rolling agricultural land. Copyright: Nigel Nicholson.

26. Temple house, Co. Sligo, Ireland. No Templars were in residence here at the time of the arrests in February 1308. Copyright: Denys Pringle.

27. The medieval keep of Oxford Castle, the prison to which the sheriff of Oxfordshire and Berkshire took the Templars of Sandford and Bisham after their arrests early in January 1308. Copyright: Nigel Nicholson.

28. The Norman keep of Canterbury Castle, where William de la More and his companions, arrested at Ewell in Kent, were imprisoned in January 1308. Copyright: Nigel Nicholson.

29. The ruins of Hertford Castle, where the Templars of Hertfordshire and Essex were imprisoned in the summer of 1308. Copyright: Nigel Nicholson.

30. The west gate of Lincoln Castle. Eventually all the Templars from the northern counties of the province of Canterbury were imprisoned in this castle. In April 1310 Thomas Totty walked free with his gaoler's permission. Copyright: Nigel Nicholson.

31. The Tower of London: by the end of 1308, all the Templars from the south of England were to have been imprisoned here; in fact some did not arrive until spring 1310. Copyright: Nigel Nicholson.

Oriens

Occides

Letha

Brachiũ maris

Sepretrio

32. Edinburgh in 1550, from Sebastian Munster, *Cosmographei* (Basel: H. Petri, 1550), lxiiii. The trial of the Templars in Scotland took place at Holyrood Abbey (on hill, left) in November 1309. Edinburgh Castle is on the hill to the right. Reproduced by courtesy of Historic Cities Project (http://historic-cities.huji.ac.il), The Hebrew University of Jerusalem, The Jewish National and University Library; and by permission of the Shapell Family Digitization Project and the Eran Laor Cartographic Collection.

33. St Botolph Aldgate, London. Trial proceedings took place at this church on 3 and 6 February 1310. Originally constructed in the thirteenth century, the church was rebuilt in 1741–4. Behind the church stands the early twenty-first-century office block 30 St Mary Axe, popularly known as 'The Gherkin'. Copyright: Nigel Nicholson.

34. The remains of the fourteenth-century tower of the church of St Alphage outside Cripplegate: trial proceedings took place at this church on 4 February and 4 March 1310. Copyright: Nigel Nicholson.

35. The exterior of the thirteenth-century chapter house of Lincoln cathedral. The Templars from the northern counties of the province of Canterbury were interrogated here, 31 March–1 June 1310. Copyright: Nigel Nicholson.

36. St Botolph Bishopgate, London. In early February 1310 the Templars who had been imprisoned in London were interrogated here. At the end of March and beginning of April 1311, the Templars who had been held at Lincoln were interrogated for a third time; proceedings generally took place at St Martin's church, Ludgate, but on 1 April the trial was relocated to this church. Originally constructed in the twelfth or early thirteenth century, the church was rebuilt in 1727-9. Copyright: Nigel Nicholson.

37. The church of All Hallows Barking today; trial proceedings took place here on 29 April and 5 July 1311. The church was originally founded from Barking Abbey in Essex in the late seventh century and has been considerably rebuilt since the middle ages, but some of the medieval fabric survives. Copyright: Nigel Nicholson.

38-9. Southwark Cathedral, exterior and interior; formerly the priory of St Mary Overie, Southwark. Trial proceedings took place here on 29 June and 6 July 1311. Built in the thirteenth century, the cathedral is still very much as it was during the Templars' trial. Copyright: Nigel Nicholson.

P.J. Goldberg, 'Women's Work, Women's Role in the Late Medieval North,' in *Profit, Piety and the Professions*, ed. M.A. Hicks (Gloucester, 1980), pp. 34–50; Henrietta Leyser, *Medieval Women: A Social History of Women in England, 450–1500* (London, 1995), p. 151.

133 MS A, fol. 94v (Wilkins omits): 'nos moriemur sicut alie bestie'; ibid., fol. 95r (Wilkins, p. 361): 'nullus homo post mortem habet animam plus quam canis'; Anne R. Neary, 'Ó Tuathail, Adam Dubh (*d.* 1328)', in *ODNB*, vol. 42, pp. 114–15; Jacobi Grace Kilkenniensis, *Annales Hiberniae*, ed. and trans. Richard Butler (Dublin, 1842), pp. 106–7: 'negavit mortuorum resurrectionem'; *Il Registro di Andrea Sapiti, procuratore alla curia avignonese*, ed. Barbara Bombi (Rome, 2007): 'dicunt hominem simul mori in corpore et anima'. Adam and his followers also denied the king of England's right to rule Ireland and criticised papal policy. See also Callan, '"No such art"', pp. 266–89.

134 The majority appear in MS A, fols 91v–92r (Wilkins, pp. 358–9).

135 MS A, fols 43v, 99r (Wilkins, pp. 344, 362–3).

136 MS A, fol. 98r–v (Wilkins, p. 362); MS C, fols 3r and 7v (Schottmüller, pp. 83, 92).

137 Details of the well from English Heritage Images of England, IoE number 162885 (http://www.imagesofengland.org.uk/); well, wellhead gear and wellhouse, the Green (west side), Preston, North Hertfordshire, Hertfordshire.

138 The black idol: *Heresies of the High Middle Ages*, ed. Wakefield and Evans, no. 3A, p. 75; no. 3B, p. 79; Norman Cohn, *Europe's Inner Demons: The Demonisation of Christians in Medieval Christendom*, rev'd edn (London, 1993), pp. 48–9. Kissing idol's backside: *Heresies of the High Middle Ages*, ed. Wakefield and Evans, no. 42B, p. 254; Cohn, *Europe's Inner Demons*, pp. 40–1, 49. The pious Templar: Matthew Paris, *Chronica Majora*, vol. 5, pp. 149–50; the secret judgements and punishments: *Règle*, sections 553–4, 573; trans. Upton-Ward, pp. 144, 148; Roger of Howden, *Gesta Regis Henrici Secundi*, ed. William Stubbs, 2 vols, Rolls Series 49 (London, 1867), vol. 2, pp. 47–8; *idem*, *Chronica*, ed. William Stubbs, 4 vols, Rolls Series 51 (London, 1868–71), vol. 2, p. 354 (translated by Henry T. Riley as *The Annals of Roger de Hoveden, comprising the History of England and of other Countries of Europe from A.D. 732 to A.D. 1201*, vol. 2: *A.D. 1181 to A.D. 1201* (London, 1853), p. 98); death in prison of Walter the Bachelor, former commander of Ireland (above, chapter 4). For modern assessment, see for example Gilmour-Bryson, 'The London Templar Trial Testimony'; on the unoriginality of the typical witness in a heresy trial, see Arnold, *Inquisition and Power*, pp. 74–6.

139 William the Dorturer, Gilbert of Bruer, Robert the Dorturer, Philip Walrand, John of Nassington, John of Eure, William Jafford, John of Dunstable, Adam of Overton, Hugh of Ayesbury, John of Lacock, John of Prestbury, John of Blaxan, Robert of Maidenesford, Thomas of Mepham, Thomas, rector of Staplehurst church, Roger, rector of Godmersham parish church, William, vicar of St Clement's church at Sandwich, Richard of the Hewse, W. of Radinges, Roger of Ware, Laurence of Sandwich.

140 Richard Balybyn, Philip de Slane, Master Philip of Herdele, Roger of Eton, William de Hothim, John the Marshal, Hugo the Luminour, Nicholas of Kilmainham, Thomas of Ratho, Roger Kymayman, Ralph Kilmaman, John Le Palmere.

141 Adam of Wedale, Fergus Marshal, Lord Henry of Sinclair, William of Ramsey, Hugh of Rydale, William Bisset, William of Preston, John of Wigmore senior, William of Sinclair.

142 See MS A, fols 91v, 92r–v, 94v, 96r, 97r–v, 151r, 153r–v (Wilkins, pp. 359, 378, 379; omits the rest).

143 William of Kilros was the only Templar priest in Ireland in 1308. In England, Ralph of Barton, Thomas of Burton, William of Warwick, John of Stoke, John of Whaddon, William of Winchester, Ralph of Evesham and Ralph of Ruston were priests (MS A, fols 13r–v, 36r, 49v, 54r, 106v, 110v, 111r, 126v; Wilkins, pp. 335, 342, 345, 366, 372) while the priest Roger of Stowe (MS A, fol. 32r; Wilkins, p. 342) was a former Templar. The Templar priest Robert of Bernewelle (Gooder, p. 149; TNA:PRO E358/18 rot. 18) was too ill to be interrogated.

144 David Burr, *The Spiritual Franciscans: From Protest to Persecution in the century after Saint Francis* (Philadelphia, 2001); Michael Robson, *The Franciscans in the Middle Ages* (Woodbridge, 2006), pp. 101–7, 119–219.

145 William J. Courtenay, 'Inquiry and Inquisition: Academic Freedom in Medieval Universities', *Church History*, 58 (1989), pp. 168–81, here pp. 175, 177.

146 A.G. Little, 'A Record of the English Dominicans, 1314', *English Historical Review*, 5 (1890), pp. 107–12, and 6 (1891), pp. 752–3.

147 *Councils and Synods*, ed. Powicke and Cheney, vol. 2, pt 2, pp. 1255–63.

148 Paul Crawford, 'The University of Paris and the Trial of the Templars', in *The Military Orders*, vol. 3: *History and Heritage*, ed. Victor Mallia-Milanes (Aldershot, 2008), pp. 115–122.

149 Frances Andrews, *The Other Friars: The Carmelites, Augustinian, Sack and Pied Friars in the Middle Ages* (Woodbridge, 2006), pp. 13–21, 49, 50; Andrew Jotischky, *The Carmelites and Antiquity: Mendicants and their Pasts in the Middle Ages* (Oxford, 2002), pp. 15–17, 36–7, 40 and n. 141, 45–78.

150 MS A, fol. 96r (Wilkins omits): William of Radinges, doctor of theology. John Bale recorded that William of Radinges wrote two books, one entitled: 'Against the Templars in England', but this does not survive: Richard Copsey, 'An Anonymous Chronicle from the Carmelite House, Calais', in *idem*, *Carmel in Britain: Studies on the Early History of the Carmelite Order*, vol. 2: *The Hermits from Mount Carmel* (Faversham and Rome, 2004), pp. 51–73, at p. 55.

151 Andrews, *Other Friars*, pp. 102–4, 148–51.

152 MS A, fols 92v, 93r–94r (Wilkins, pp. 359, 360–1); MS C, fols 1r, 2v, 11v (Schottmüller, pp. 79, 81, 100); MS D, fols 178v, 179r (*Annales Londonienses*, ed. Stubbs, pp. 184–5).

153 MS B, fol. 80v; MS A, fols 100v–101r, 170r (Wilkins, pp. 364–5, 393).

154 MS A, fols 160r–164v (Wilkins, pp. 383–8).

155 See comment at the bottom of MS A, fol. 92v (Wilkins, p. 359); MS B, fol. 80v; summarised by Perkins, 'Trial of the Knights Templars', p. 488.

156 MS B, fol. 80r; summarised by Perkins, 'Trial of the Knights Templars', p. 487.

157 On William de Dien see *CPR, 1307–1313*, pp. 208–9; *CCR, 1307–1313*, p. 196; *Foedera*, ed, Rymer, vol. 2, pt 1, p. 104.

158 MS B, fol. 80v; summarised by Perkins, 'Trial of the Knights Templars', p. 488.

159 *CPR, 1307–1313*, p. 289; see also their letter of 20 November 1310 at TNA:PRO SC1/35/113; and their letter to the archbishop of York, enclosing a letter from King Philip IV of France dated 1 November 1310: *Register of William Greenfield*, part 4, pp. 318–19, no. 2284; *Register of Walter Greenfield*, part 5, p. xxxvi.

160 *Registrum Henrici Woodlock*, pp. 468–9; TNA:PRO SC1/32/35; published in *Select Cases in the Court of King's Bench under Edward I*, vol. 2, ed. G.O. Sayles, Selden Society 57 (1938), p. cxlii (k). For this Scottish campaign, which most of the English nobles refused to join, see Hamilton, *Piers Gaveston*, pp. 81–6.

161 *Foedera*, ed. Rymer, vol. 2, pt 1, p. 115; *CCR, 1307–1313*, p. 279.

162 *Councils and Synods*, ed. Powicke and Cheney, vol. 2, pt 2, pp. 1285–6, 1290.

163 *Foedera*, ed. Rymer, vol. 2, pt 1, pp. 117–19; *CCR, 1307–1313*, pp. 285, 290; 'Friaries: The friars of the Sack', *VCH, London*, vol. 1: *London within the Bars, Westminster and Southwark*, ed. William Page (London, 1909), pp. 513–14.

164 *Foedera*, ed. Rymer, vol. 2, pt 1, p. 119; *CCR, 1307–1313*, pp. 291, 308.

165 *Foedera*, ed. Rymer, vol. 2, pt 1, p. 120.

166 MS A, fols 117r–124v (Wilkins, pp. 368–71).

5

The Trial in Scotland: Mixed Reactions

The trial of the Templars in Scotland opened on 17 November 1309.[1] At this time the Anglo-Scottish war was in full spate. King Robert Bruce had held his first Parliament at St Andrews in March 1309, and King Philip IV of France had made diplomatic overtures to the Scottish king. But King Robert did not control the whole of Scotland, and some of the nobles wanted to return to the situation as it had been in 1304, before Robert Bruce's assassination of John Comyn. Lothian, the area where the trial in Scotland took place, was still under King Edward's control, but it had come under heavy attack in December 1308, and continued under severe pressure in the months that followed.[2]

Edward II's father, Edward I, had conquered the independent kingdom of Scotland, but various contenders to the Scottish throne wished to re-establish the kingdom. Robert Bruce was one of those claimants; early in 1306 he had murdered John Comyn, whose claim was arguably better than his own. Bruce had been crowned king of Scotland at Easter 1306, and in the winter of 1307/8 defeated the Comyns and established control over a large part of the kingdom of Scotland. Edward II should have led his army north to deal with Bruce, but in 1308 he had cancelled his projected campaign (French diplomats negotiated a truce) and, although there had been some Scottish raids against the north of England, in 1309 he made another truce rather than go to war. In 1310 Edward II led a campaign north but few of his nobles accompanied him and he achieved little. Bruce then went on the offensive. In 1311 he advanced south into Tynedale, burnt Corbridge, and only withdrew when the men of the county offered him two thousand pounds. He also ravaged Cumbria and captured English-held fortresses in Scotland. The Scots would finally capture Edinburgh in March 1314.[3] The situation in Scotland was so unsettled in November 1309 that the questioning of non-Templar witnesses in Scotland over the Templars could not be properly completed.[4]

The military threat from the Scots certainly encouraged Edward to retain the Templars' properties as a source of useful income and supplies for his military campaigns in the north. Yet Edward II's problems in Scotland were not simply military. He also had to counter Robert Bruce's 'propaganda', and prevent the pope from acknowledging Bruce as king. In 1306 Pope Clement V had excommunicated Bruce for his murder of John Comyn. So far as the pope was concerned Bruce's coronation was invalid; Edward II was still rightful king of Scotland. But as the Scottish clergy began to lobby the pope in support of Bruce, Edward's position became less secure. In 1310 a group of Scottish clergy issued a statement that Bruce had the right to be king because he had saved and restored the kingdom by his sword.[5] If Edward wished to retain papal acknowledgement of his authority in Scotland, he must show the pope that he was worthy to be king, by protecting the Church and repressing heresy; which would include obeying papal commands to prosecute the Templars.

Presumably the Templars in Scotland had been arrested early in 1308 and their lands taken into the king's hands, although no inventory survives. They had apparently been held in custody in Scotland.[6] It is difficult to know what property the Templars held in Scotland beyond their two commanderies, Balantrodoch (now Temple) in Midlothian (plate 11) and Maryculter near Aberdeen. As noted in the introduction, the best guide to the Templars' properties in 1308 is the Hospitallers' rental of 1539–40, which includes many properties called 'Temple lands'; but at some locations this simply indicates that they had 'Temple rights' of tenure and privileges of not paying certain dues.[7] Other Templar properties in Scotland included a parish church at Inchinnan in Renfrewshire, some three miles north of Paisley in the western lowlands of Scotland; property at East Fenton and Peffer in East Lothian, that is, east central Scotland in the region of Dunbar and Haddington; property at Gullane and Sandenisdene, also in East Lothian (Gullane is on the coast five miles west-south-west of North Berwick, while Sandenisdene is two miles south of Haddington); property at Falkirk in Stirling in central Scotland, some twenty-five miles east-north-east from Edinburgh, at Swanston in

Midlothian, a few miles due south of Edinburgh, and at Glasgow in western central Scotland; property at Liston (now Kirkliston) in West Lothian, around ten miles west of Edinburgh; and a saltworks in the carse of Callander (Callander is in Perthshire, on the edge of the Scottish Highlands, around fifteen miles north-east of Stirling).[8] So while the Templars had many small properties in Scotland, their holdings were scattered and insubstantial. Before the Edwardian conquest, the Templars in Scotland had had their own commander: Brian le Jay, who had done homage to King Edward I on 29 July 1291. The Templars in England agreed that the commander of the Templars in Scotland was subject to the grand commander of England, and should attend the English provincial chapter meetings. But by November 1299, when Brother Walter Clifton joined the Templars, there was no separate commander for Scotland, an indication of the decline of the Order in Scotland since 1291.[9]

On 23 September 1309 at London, the patriarch of Jerusalem, Antony Bek, the archbishop of York, the bishops of Lincoln and Chichester, Abbot Dieudonné of Lagny and Sicard de Vaur, had written to Lord William de Yetham, dean of Dunblane, Hugh of Selkirk, archdeacon of Brechin, and John de Solerio, canon of the church of St Radegund in Poitiers, a papal clerk. They cited Pope Clement V's letters of 12 August 1309, which authorised them to join the bishop of St Andrews in an investigation into the affairs of the Templars in Scotland. But, they said, they were prevented from going personally to Scotland, so they were delegating their powers throughout the Scottish cities and dioceses to the addressees, or to two or one of them.[10]

Possibly they chose the dean of Dunblane in preference to his bishop, Nicholas Balmyle, because the latter was a supporter of Robert Bruce and had attended his Parliament in March 1309; John Kinninmonth, bishop of Brechin, was also in favour of Scottish independence and a supporter of Bruce, so his archdeacon was selected instead.[11] But in the event neither of these dioceses were represented in the trial, which was conducted by the bishop of St Andrews and John de Solerio or Solercio, with William of Spottiswode, 'notary by imperial authority', making the official record.[12]

William Lamberton, bishop of St Andrews 1297–1328, had taken a leading part in the coronation of King Robert I. He had been imprisoned by King Edward I of England and was released only in August 1308. By the terms of his release he had to remain within the diocese of Durham, but Lamberton based himself on the River Tweed and managed to maintain good relations with both the king of Scots and the king of England. In 1308 he was involved in the Anglo-Franco-Scottish truce negotiations, and in the winter of 1309/10 he again negotiated on the English side with the Scots. In February 1310 he was at King Robert's court at Fife, and later in the year he was able to hold a synod at St Andrews. When Edward II was told that Lamberton was in Scotland, he gave him permission to remain there.[13] So at the time of the trial of the Templars, Bishop William Lamberton of St Andrews was trusted by both Scots and English, and hence was an ideal person to head the investigation.

On 3 October 1309, King Edward II of England wrote to his bailiffs and remaining faithful subjects in Scotland, informing them that the pope had appointed John de Solercio to investigate the Templars. On 6 October he instructed John of Segrave, custodian of his lands in Scotland, to arrest any Templars who had not yet been detained and to have them taken to some place 'wherever seems best', and guarded, so that they could be brought before the papal investigators.[14]

The trial in Scotland took place in Holyrood Abbey in Edinburgh (plate 32). King David I of Scotland had founded the abbey in 1128 for Augustinian canons; it was so named because it owned a relic of the True Cross.[15] There were only two men wearing the Templars' habit in Scotland, both English by origin,[16] and they gave their evidence on 17 November.[17]

Walter of Clifton and William Middleton had both been received into the Order in England, and neither gave any indication that they had been out of the British Isles during their careers in the Templars. They were not questioned on each point individually, as in England and Ireland, but their testimonies were taken as a whole. The interrogators were particularly interested in what contacts the Templars had with Templars overseas, and in the details of their receptions. Walter of Clifton, who was commander of Balantrodoch, gave a blow-by-blow account of the reception ceremony. He also explained that the grand commander of England received his instructions from the grand master on Cyprus, and from the statutes and observances laid down by the Order's general chapter. He agreed that the grand master and the visitor did visit England (but not, apparently, Scotland). He believed that the grand master, visitor and commanders, could absolve sins 'and he said that the said grand master had this power from the grace of the lord pope'. He agreed that there was great suspicion against the Order because of the secrecy of reception ceremonies, and he confirmed that there was no period of probation and that he had sworn never to leave the

Order. But his testimony indicated that there was no heresy in the Order, simply poor practice.[18]

William Middleton explained that he was from Newcastle in England, and that he was received into the Order of the Temple on St Euphemia's day (16 September), seven years previously. However, as he also stated that he was received into the Order by Brian le Jay, then commander of England – who was killed at the battle of Falkirk in July 1298 – he must have been in the Order for at least twelve years. During that time, he had been stationed in England and at Maryculter and Balantrodoch in Scotland. He did not explain why he had left Maryculter and come south to Balantrodoch, but perhaps it was a result of the war after the murder of John Comyn in 1306.

William Middleton agreed that the grand commander of England received his instructions from overseas; he received them from the grand commander of France, who received them from the grand master on Cyprus. The grand commander of England went to the chapter meeting of the province of France once each five years. The grand master would send the visitor to England, although he did not go to Scotland; he had also come to England himself, and William had seen him absolving sins – but the grand master then sent the Templars he had absolved to a priest. William explained how on his last visit, the visitor, Hugh Peraud, had removed some commanders from their positions and replaced them. His account of the reception ceremony was the same as his colleague's.[19]

Some non-Templars also gave their evidence. The leading non-Templar witnesses in Scotland were drawn from a small circle: there were Franciscan and Dominican friars, and the abbots and some monks of Dunfermline, Newbattle and Holyrood – all monasteries founded by the kings of Scotland. Given the political situation in Scotland, it is not surprising that men from religious houses that supported the Scottish monarchy would give testimony against a religious Order which had traditionally supported the English monarchy. Then there were several secular clergy, some nobles (a few of whom were favourable towards the Order), and some ex-servants of the Order. Almost all the witnesses were from the area around Edinburgh and the Templars' house at Balantrodoch. There were no witnesses from the area of the Templars' northern Scottish commandery at Maryculter, near Aberdeen. As King Robert Bruce had captured Aberdeen Castle from the English in June or July 1308, and Forfar Castle at the end of 1308,[20] presumably that area was still in too much turmoil in November 1309 for the papally-authorised investigators to make their enquiries there. It is interesting that the official record notes which witnesses were of English origin – as if this might have prejudiced their testimony.

The non-Templar witnesses generally agreed that they knew little or nothing about the Templars, but they thought that the accusations against them were true, 'due to the clandestine reception of their brothers and their profession, and the nocturnal celebration of their Chapters'.[21] This information must have been based on hearsay rather than personal experience, because there had been no Templar receptions in Scotland for many years: Brother William Middleton, who had been in the Order for at least seven years, had never seen a reception.[22] As there were only two Templars in Scotland, there would have been no chapter meetings. In fact, there were never many Templars in Scotland, although a number of Scottish brothers were in English houses or abroad.[23]

The first witness was Abbot Hugh of Dunfermline. Dunfermline abbey, about fifteen miles north-west of Edinburgh, had been founded in around 1070 by King Malcolm Canmore and Queen Margaret of Scotland and refounded by King David I. Many of the monarchs of Scotland were buried there; Robert Bruce would eventually lie among them.[24] Abbot Hugh admitted that he knew nothing certain about the Templars, but he had heard that the charges against them were true. He believed this because of their centralised administration, with visitors overseeing the whole Order and the commanders being called to chapter meetings overseas. As he had never heard of any receptions in Scotland, he could not comment.[25] The following witnesses all agreed with him, adding a few points of their own.

Robert of Kidlaw,[26] doctor of canon law, added that he was suspicious of Brother Walter of Clifton's testimony, because his description of the reception ceremony was so different from that in the papal bull. According to this line of thought, the Templars could not clear themselves of the allegations against them no matter what they said in answer to the charges; if their testimony differed from the pope's account, it must be the Templars who were lying, for the pope (Robert Kidlaw believed) would not lie. Robert Kidlaw also added that the Templars were publicly accused of acquiring others' property unjustly. He had personal experience of this, because the Templars had failed to pay tithe (the tenth of income due to the Church) on a mill in a parish of his.[27] As the Templars were exempted by papal privilege from paying tithes, this hardly counted as acquiring other persons' property. So far as they and the pope were concerned, no tithe was owed from this mill.

Brother Patrick, prior of the Dominican friars of Edinburgh, added that he had seen the Templar brothers William and Walter come to confess their sins to Dominican friars after they had been accused of the alleged crimes and arrested. But, he said, he had not seen the Templars confess to friars elsewhere, nor had he heard that Templars confessed to them. Andrew of Douracd, guardian of the Franciscan friars of Haddington, agreed.[28] In fact, his colleagues in England and Ireland could have informed them that they had received Templars' confessions.

Brother Adam Hercton or Henton of the Franciscan friars had a story from his childhood about how all the boys in school used to shout 'Beware the Templars' kiss'. Adam said he now realised that the cry referred to the alleged illicit kisses of the Templars' reception ceremony. The inquisitors considered that this was a useful piece of evidence, and it was later copied into their summaries of the outside witnesses' evidence, and sent to the papal commissioners who were preparing the case for the Church Council at Vienne.[29]

Adam of Wedale, monk of the abbey of Newbattle, complained that the Templars wanted to take over their neighbours' land and goods legally or illegally, and that they never gave hospitality to the poor, only to the rich because they were afraid of the rich, and that they did not give alms.[30] Wedale is the old name for the valley of the Gala Water; the church of St Mary of Wedale is in the village of Stow, approximately thirteen miles south-east of Balantrodoch/Temple and sixteen miles south-east of Newbattle. In 1354 an Adam of Wedale, perhaps a relative of this one, was a witness to a charter which set out how the Templars of Balantrodoch had, at the end of the previous century, forcibly evicted the landowner Christina of Espertoun from her property. The historian John Edwards, writing in 1908, suggested that Adam of Wedale's evidence in 1309 was alluding to this recent case.[31]

Robert, chaplain of Kirkliston – a village around eight miles west of Edinburgh where the Templars had held property – said that he had heard Templars who had been a long time in the Order say that no one ever knew where a Templar was buried or whether they died a good death – that is, their graves were unmarked (but see plates 2–4) and he did not know whether they had given their last confession and been absolved before their death. He also said that the Templars were always against the Church as much as they could be, presumably referring to legal disputes over tithe payments and land rights.[32]

Master John of Lindsey, rector of the church of Ratho (eight miles from Edinburgh, south of Kirkliston), as well as agreeing with the abbot of Dunfermline, said that he knew from experience that the brothers of the Order of the Temple were usurers, because he sold them a chalder (ninety-six bushels) of oats for five shillings and, because he did not have the grain, they forced him to repay the price twice over.[33] If the rector sold the Templars grain that he did not have, it is not surprising that the Templars demanded compensation – but they had demanded punitive compensation, rather than being satisfied by a simple repayment.

A priest, John of Liberton (a village some three miles south of Holyrood Abbey) said that he had stayed with the brothers of the said Order for two years, celebrating mass for them. Several times he saw them confess and hear mass with Christian devotion – at least, it seemed that they were pious. However, he believed the Templars of the kingdoms of England and Scotland were accused of the same crimes as the brothers of their Order overseas because their reception ceremonies, religious habit, statutes and observances were all the same, and the same official, the visitor, watched over all of them. He had never been able to find out anything about the Templars' method of reception and profession, because the ceremony was secret, and so – he said – he had always been suspicious of them.[34]

Nine servants of the Templars agreed that Templar laymen absolved people who had been excommunicated, on the excuse that this was a privilege which they held from the pope; and that the Templars held chapter meetings at night. An Englishman, William Provost, agreed that the Templars absolved excommunicates.[35] Nicholas, vicar of Lasswade (a village around four-and-a-half miles north of the Templars' commandery at Balantrodoch), said that he had heard the brothers of the Order of the Templars saying, when the bishop had excommunicated their people, that they would absolve them because, they said, they had full power over these things.[36]

One of the lay nobles, Fergus Marshal – who may have held land in Dumfriesshire – told a story about his grandfather, who had joined the Templars in his old age, hale and hearty with his dogs and hawks, and three days later was dead. Fergus claimed that the Templars had killed him because he had refused to submit to their foul practices. The papal inquisitors thought his allegation so valuable that they included it in their later summaries of the case.[37] Yet Fergus's grandfather was probably elderly when he entered the Order of the Temple. It was common for noblemen to enter the Order when they were very near death, for they could then be certain of the best spiritual care as they set off on their last journey to meet their Maker. However, as they would will the bulk of their property to the Order in return for the care they received, their family might well resent their entering the Order, and might dispute the gift in an attempt to recover it. So Fergus's claim that the Templars murdered his grandfather could have been an attempt to recover his grandfather's lands from the Templars. An earlier occasion, when a nobleman's family disapproved of his entering the Order of the Temple, and the nobleman died shortly after entering, was described in the knight Philip of Novara's account of John the Old Lord of Ibelin entering the Order of the Temple in the Holy Land in 1236.[38] As the senior member of the powerful Ibelin family, John had been one of the most powerful nobles in the Catholic Christian kingdoms of Jerusalem and Cyprus. In that instance the Templars were not accused of killing the Old Lord after he entered their Order, but the family's disapproval of his decision to join the Templars was very clear.

In contrast to Fergus, a few of the Scottish nobles were favourable towards the Templars. Lord Henry de St Clair or Sinclair, and Lord Hugh of Rydale, two neighbours of the Templars of Balantrodoch, expressed their good opinion of the late local commander:

> Lord Henry Sinclair said that he had seen the commander of Temple on his deathbed, receiving the eucharist very devoutly, so far as onlookers could judge. Then Lord Hugh of Ryedale said that the same commander used to give gifts because he did not go to the General Chapters, and he believed that he did this so that he would not have to assent to the crimes that had now been confessed by the superiors of his Order.[39]

Henry Sinclair of Roslin had sworn homage to King Edward I of England in 1291 and he is listed in the so-called Ragman Rolls as one of those who did homage to Edward I in 1296. By 1316 he was a supporter of Robert Bruce, and in 1320 he was one of the signatories of the Declaration of Arbroath.[40] Hugh of Rydale also appears in the Ragman Rolls, although he was not on the list of those who swore homage to King Edward I in 1291.[41] These Scottish nobles' testimonies show that some of the Templars' closest neighbours in Scotland had a good opinion of them.

However, Henry Sinclair's son William, who also gave evidence during the trial with other young lords, did not have such a good opinion of the Templars. The young nobles agreed that it was suspicious that the Templars held reception ceremonies in secret when other religious Orders had public reception ceremonies to which family and friends were invited, with a feast afterwards. Echoing Adam of Wedale, they added that the Templars did not willingly give hospitality to poor people, but gave it only to the wealthy and powerful because they were afraid of them. The Templars were also very eager to acquire other people's goods for their Order by legal or illegal means. Lastly, they stated that their ancestors claimed that if the Templars had been faithful Christians, they would not have lost the Holy Land – which was not what Henry Sinclair had said. William Sinclair clearly had a personal interest in the Holy land. He died in 1330 on crusade in Spain with James Douglas, while taking the heart of the late King Robert I to Jerusalem.[42] But his testimony in 1310 was apparently based on hearsay rather than personal knowledge.

Three other 'young gentlemen', Alan of Wallingford, Roger of Sutton and William of Dishforth, said that they had no personal knowledge of the Templars except that they had seen them living a devout way of life and devotedly hearing masses. They had heard that one brother disappeared in each chapter meeting, and no one knew what happened to him; and Alan of Wallingford told a story of a friend, a scholar at Oxford, whose uncle was a Templar and refused to tell him about the Order's reception ceremony.[43]

The story that a Templar was murdered in each chapter meeting as a sacrifice to the devil was mentioned by the Templar commander in Ireland, Brother Henry Danet, as something he had heard from outsiders. Certainly three of the outside witnesses did tell stories of this sort. William, vicar of the church of St Clement of Sandwich, had heard a story from a former servant about a Templar having disappeared during a chapter meeting at Dinsley. Two friars had also heard it: Nicholas of Irton heard that a Templar was given to the devil in each general chapter, while Alexander of Barllo said at Carlisle that he had heard that one Templar always died in each chapter.[44] Two of the Templars who 'confessed' at the end of the trial in the British Isles told similar stories: Brother Thomas Totty said he had been told by some of his friends that the devil took a brother each year; Brother Stephen of Stapelbrugge had also heard tell that the Templars lost one brother in each general chapter meeting. But a former servant of the Order in Ireland, who had formerly been in Cyprus, stated that this was untrue: the Templars were counted in and out of chapter and the numbers always tallied.[45] This accusation that a person was always missing from the general chapter could suggest that the Order kept one place in chapter free for the 'invisible guest' – their heavenly king, Christ.

All in all, the Scottish testimonies were mixed. Some outside witnesses showed friendship towards the Templars; some showed resentment born of old disputes. Other witnesses simply wanted to distance themselves from the accused Order as quickly and thoroughly as possible. The record of the investigation concluded with the words: 'This inquisition could not be carried out with more formality because of enemies' attacks and the continuous tempest of war.'[46] The investigation was hastily wound up and the written records sent back to London to be combined with the full record of the proceedings from the British Isles.

No records survive of any final decision by the bishops of Scotland on the Templar affair. Apparently some sort of decision was reached, as a report from the Council of Vienne stated that early in December 1311 'prelates of Scotland' at the Council had voted with those who wished to hear the Templars' defence. Professor Donald Watt, in his study of Scottish Church Councils in the Middle Ages, concluded that two Scottish bishops were present at the Council of Vienne. But the Scottish bishops alone did not decide the fate of the two Scottish Templars; they were taken to the Provincial Church Council at York, 24 May–30 July 1311. On 29 July twenty-four Templars appeared before the Council and abjured all heresy, were absolved of all their sins and reconciled with the Church. On the following day the Council decided that they should be assigned to monasteries to perform penance. The names of the twenty-four are set out in a royal letter of 1 September 1311: the final two names are William of Middleton and Walter of Clifton.[47]

Notes

1   MS A, fol. 155 (Wilkins, p. 380).
2   G.W.S. Barrow, *Robert Bruce and the Community of the Realm of Scotland* (London, 1965), pp. 261-2, 266, 268, 274, 278; Michael Brown, *The Wars of Scotland, 1214–1371* (Edinburgh, 2004), pp. 203-7.
3   Barrow, *Robert Bruce*, pp. 234-79; Hamilton, *Piers Gaveston*, p. 71; M. McKisack, *The Fourteenth Century, 1307–1399* (Oxford, 1959), pp. 32-3; B. Webster, *Medieval Scotland: The Making of an Identity* (Basingstoke, 1997), pp. 81-2.
4   MS A, fol. 159r (Wilkins, p. 383).

5 *Anglo-Scottish Relations, 1174–1328: Some Selected Documents*, ed. E.L.G. Stones (Edinburgh, 1965), pp. 140-3, no. 36; Menache, *Clement V*, pp. 269-75.

6 To judge from Brother Walter of Clifton's comments, MS A, fols 155, 156r-v (Wilkins, pp. 380-1): he had been in the Order for ten years, the last three years (i.e. since November 1306) at Balantrodoch.

7 *The Knights of St John of Jerusalem in Scotland*, ed. Ian B. Cowan, P.H.R. Mackay and Alan Macquarrie, Scottish History Society 4th ser. 19 (Edinburgh, 1983), pp. 11, 12, 14, 17-20, 25-6, 28-31, 35.

8 D.E. Easson, with David Knowles and R. Neville Hadcock, *Medieval Religious Houses: Scotland, with an Appendix on the Houses in the Isle of Man* (London, 1957; henceforth cited as Easson), p. 132; *Knights of St John in Scotland*, ed. Cowan, Mackay and Macquarrie, pp. xviii, xix, lvii, 69-70, 224.

9 E.L.G. Stones and Grant G. Simpson, *Edward I and the Throne of Scotland, 1290–1296: An edition of the record sources for the Great Cause*, 2 vols (Oxford, 1978), vol. 2, p. 126; charge 25 in MS A, fols 66r-81v and charge 6 in MS A, fols 117r-124v (Wilkins, p. 369 only; omits rest); MS A, fol. 159 (Wilkins, p. 380).

10 *Records of Antony Bek*, p. 155, no. 144.

11 Barrow, *Robert Bruce*, pp. 264, 371-2, 375.

12 MS A, fol. 155, 159r (Wilkins, pp. 380, 383).

13 D.E.R. Watt, *Medieval Church Councils in Scotland* (Edinburgh, 2000), p. 107; Barrow, *Robert Bruce*, pp. 212-13, 215-16, 217, 264, 373-4.

14 *Foedera*, ed. Rymer, vol. 2, pt 1, p. 94; *CCR, 1307–1313*, p. 181.

15 Easson, p. 75. The remains of the abbey are today in the care of Historic Scotland.

16 MS A, fol. 155 (Wilkins, p. 380).

17 MS A, 155-156v (Wilkins, pp. 380-1).

18 MS A, fols 155-156v (Wilkins, pp. 380-1).

19 MS A, fols 156v-157r (Wilkins, p. 381).

20 Barrow, *Robert Bruce*, pp. 259-60.

21 MS A, fol. 157v (Wilkins, p. 381).

22 MS A, fol. 157r (Wilkins, p. 381).

23 *Knights of St John in Scotland*, ed. Cowan, Mackay and Macquarrie, pp. xix-xx.

24 Easson, p. 51.

25 MS A, fol. 157v (Wilkins, pp. 381-2).

26 Mr Richard Armitage has identified this (personal communication, 3 November 2004) as Kidlaw, East Lothian, about twelve miles north-east of Balantrodoch (Temple). I am very grateful to Mr Armitage for allowing me to refer to his research on the persons and places mentioned in the Templar trial proceedings for Scotland.

27 MS A, fol. 157v (Wilkins omits).

28 MS A, fol. 157v (Wilkins, p. 382).

29 MS A, fol. 157v (Wilkins, p. 382); MS A, fol. 93r (Wilkins, p. 360); MS C, fol. 5r (Schottmüller, p. 87); MS D, fol. 184v (*Annales Londonienses*, ed. Stubbs, p. 190).

30 MS A, fol. 157v (Wilkins, p. 382).

31 J. Edwards, 'The Templars in Scotland in the Thirteenth Century', *Scottish Historical Review*, 5 (1908), pp. 20, 21; I am very grateful to Richard Armitage for pointing this out. For Wedale, see *The Buildings of Scotland*, ed. Nikolaus Pevsner; *Lothian except Edinburgh*, ed. Colin McWilliam (London, 1978), p. 442.

32 MS A, fol. 158r (Wilkins, p. 382).

33 MS A, fol. 158r (Wilkins omits).

34 MS A, fol. 158r (Wilkins omits).

35 MS A, fol. 158v-159r (Wilkins, pp. 382-3).

36 MS A, fol. 158r (Wilkins omits).

37 MS A, fol. 158r-v (Wilkins omits); see also MS A, fol. 93r (Wilkins, p. 360); MS C, fol. 8v (Schottmüller, pp. 93-4; MS D, fol. 189v (*Annales Londonienses*, ed. Stubbs, p. 195). Two individuals named 'Fergus Marshal' appear in the Ragman Rolls in 1296: *Calendar of Documents Relating to Scotland*, ed. Joseph Bain, vol. 2 (London, 1884), pp. 181, 185, nos 771, 810. A 'Fergus Marshal' appears as a juror at an investigation at Dumfries: ibid., pp. 411-12, no. 1588; and a 'Fergus Marshal' held the barony of Dalmellington in East Ayrshire in 1302-4: ibid., p. 425, no. 1608. A 'Fergus Marshal', knight, appeared as a witness of royal charters for King Robert I in 1316 and 1318: *Acts of Robert I, King of Scots, 1306-1329*, ed. Archibald A.M. Duncan (Edinburgh, 1988), pp. 377, 421, nos 99, 143. I am very grateful to Richard Armitage for these references.

38 Filippo da Novara, *Guerra di Federico II in Oriente (1223-1242)*, ed. Silvio Melani (Naples, 1994), p. 210, section 116 (212).

39 MS A, fol. 158v (Wilkins omits).

40 Stones and Simpson, *Edward I and the Throne of Scotland*, p. 367. These references in the Ragman Rolls and the Declaration of Arbroath were traced by Richard Armitage. See also A.A.M. Duncan, *The Nation of Scots and the Declaration of Arbroath (1320)* (London, 1970), p. 34; Barrow, *Robert Bruce*, pp. 340, 427; Fiona Watson, 'Sinclair, Sir William (*d.* 1299-1303)', *ODNB*, vol. 50, pp. 768-9.

41 Stones and Simpson, *Edward I and the Throne of Scotland*, p. 368.

42 MS A, fol. 158v (Wilkins, p. 382); Barbara E. Crawford, 'Sinclair family (*per.* 1280-*c.* 1500)', *ODNB*, vol. 50, p. 735.

43 MS A, fol. 158v (Wilkins omits).

44 MS A, fol. 141r (Wilkins omits); MS A, fols 92v twice, 95v-96r (Wilkins omits first two stories, final story p. 361).

45 MS A, fol. 161r-v (Wilkins, pp. 384-5); MS A, fol. 153v (Wilkins, p. 379).

46 MS A, fol. 159r (Wilkins, p. 383).

47 Watt, *Medieval Church Councils in Scotland*, pp. 108, 110; *CCR, 1307-1313*, p. 373.

6

The Trial in Ireland:
'All the Templars are Guilty'

In the modern age, the Irish Sea appears to be a barrier between Britain and Ireland. Yet the Irish Sea can be travelled relatively easily in good weather, and during the Middle Ages it acted as a highway for travellers. It was common for a prominent figure in English politics to go to Ireland or to be sent to Ireland to get out of trouble. To escape the anger of King John, William de Braose fled to Ireland in 1208-10;[1] Richard Marshal went to Ireland during his quarrel with King Henry III in 1234;[2] Piers Gaveston was sent to govern Ireland in 1308 because King Edward II's nobles wanted him out of England;[3] while a few fourteenth-century writers suggested that when King Edward II took to the sea on 20 October 1326, in order to flee the army of his estranged wife Isabelle and her partner Roger Mortimer, the king intended to flee to Ireland.[4] With such a tradition, it is not surprising that some Templars had also fled to Ireland early in 1308.

Although the kings of England since John had claimed the title of 'Lord of Ireland', the English government in Ireland was not in fact under close royal control. Kings of England tended to leave their representatives in Ireland to get on with the job of administration as best as they could, without royal interference. The native Irish continued their traditional conflicts, and engaged in war against the Cymro-Norman and Anglo-Norman incomers. By the early fourteenth century, those same incomers regarded themselves as different from their ancestors on the other side of the Irish Sea, and as belonging to Ireland, not to Britain.

So the trial of the Templars in Ireland was rather different from that in Britain. To begin with, although the trial was based on a short list of around eighty-eight charges as in England, the list of charges used in Ireland was the same as that used elsewhere in Europe, while that used in England had errors and omissions. The English Templars were not asked whether they held chapter meetings at night, but the Templars in Ireland were (and replied that they did not). The Irish Templars were asked why they had not informed holy Mother Church of the heresies in the Order, whereas the English Templars were not asked this.[5] Unlike their colleagues in England, rather than grouping the charges under subheadings, the inquisitors initially asked the brothers to answer each charge individually, so the records of the proceedings are lengthy and longwinded. Unlike England, any Templar who was 'just visiting' and was not a regular member of a commandery in Ireland, was not cross-examined; whereas in England, all Templars present in the country on the day of the arrests, and still alive by the time the inquisitions began almost two years later, were included in the investigation. Finally, unlike England, there is no evidence that the Templars were required to abjure or 'swear off' all heresies. Herbert Wood wrote in 1906 – almost two decades before the destruction of the Irish medieval records – that there was no record of the Irish Templars being sent to monasteries to do penance, as was done in England. They remained in prison until Michaelmas term 1312, when Henry Danet was released on bail.[6] Wood surmised that the other Templars in Ireland were released shortly afterwards. He did not discover where they went after this, although a regular pension was paid to them.[7]

The Arrests

King Edward II of England sent instructions on 20 December 1307 to John Wogan, his justiciar or chief minister in Ireland, to arrest the Templars, make an inventory of their possessions, and keep the Templars in custody but not in harsh conditions until such time as he should order otherwise. The writ reached the justiciar on 25 January 1308; the Templars were arrested on 3 February 1308.[8] As in England, the sheriffs took inventories of the Templars' possessions at each of their houses. Unlike in England, no record has survived of where the Templars were arrested, but the inventories mention a few brothers.

The beds of Peter of Malvern the commander, Walter of Jonely or Chonesby, Adam of Langeport and William the chaplain were at Kilcloggan in Co. Wexford. Hugh of Broghem or Broughton was custodian of Kilsaran in Co. Louth. Thomas le Palmer helped to take the inventory at Kilbarry in Co. Waterford, while Ralph of Bradley, commander of Crooke in the same county, was present while an inventory was taken there. Brother Richard (who could have been Richard of Burthesham or of Upleadon) was custodian of Cooley (Templetown) in Louth; the inventory at Clonaulty in Co. Tipperary was taken in the presence of William de Warenne, custodian of that house; Robert of Pourbrigge was custodian of Rathronan in Co. Tipperary and Athkiltan in Co. Carlow.[9] However, no Templars were mentioned in the inventories for other houses, such as Baligaueran (Gowran) in Co. Kilkenny, Templehouse in Co. Sligo, Clontarf near Dublin, Rathbride and Kilcork in Co. Kildare.[10]

There were probably no Templars living at Templehouse in Co. Sligo in 1307 (plate 26) because of the constant warfare in the area, but they did own the church there, which was worth 40s. a year to them. The inventory of the animals – six draught animals and one horse – and two ricks of oats, sixteen acres of sown wheat and an iron plough-share – was taken by Ewan ap Madoc and William Bynor of Wales, who reckoned this to be worth 73s. 8d.[11] At the other end of the scale was Clontarf near Dublin, with goods worth £125 17s. 7d., including a book of the gospels in French and a copy of the 'Brut' in English (presumably Layamon's *Brut* – the English translation and adaptation of Geoffrey of Monmouth's *Historia Regum Britannie*), three shillings in cash, three swords worth three shillings, three chests worth six shillings, and precious plate in the chapel (two chalices, one gilded with gold, two cups and a partly-made cup), robes for the priest and service books.[12]

As in England, King Edward II exploited the Templars' property to meet his immediate financial needs. On 19 June 1308 the king sent instructions to John Wogan and the treasurer of the exchequer in Dublin to provide supplies for his forthcoming expedition to Scotland. Among other sources of supply, the justiciar was to supply from the Templars' property in Ireland 1,000 quarters of wheat, 1,000 quarters of oats, 200 quarters of beans and peas, 300 tuns of wine, three tuns of honey, 200 quarters of salt and 1,000 stockfish. At the same time the king ordered the English sheriffs to supply materials from the Templars' lands in England.[13] In 1309 the sheriff of Co. Louth was instructed to let Reginald Irpe, the king's *provisor* (collector) of food in the Drogheda area, have £26 from the grain of the manor of Kilsaran and the other Templar lands in his county, for purchasing food for the king's forthcoming expedition to Scotland.[14] In February 1310 the sheriffs of Louth, Meath, Dublin and Kildare received instructions to take all the grain from the former Templar manors in their territory (except for Kilsaran in Co. Louth) and send it to Drogheda or Dublin to the king's collectors of food for his forthcoming campaign in Scotland.[15]

As in England, in autumn 1309 the sheriffs and the keepers of the Order's lands in Ireland were instructed to draw up a record of the extent of the Templars' lands, so that the king would know exactly what the Templars had owned and what it was worth. The investigations continued until the following spring.[16] As in England, there was also maintenance to be done on the Templars' former properties. John of Kent, who had been entrusted with the care of the Templars' manor of Cooley in Co. Louth, complained that two millstones were missing from the manor's mill. As a result, the manor's tenants had to grind their grain elsewhere, and the manor lost revenue. However, there were two suitable millstones at Clontarf, near Dublin, so instructions were dispatched to Walter of Thornbury, chancellor of Ireland and current holder of that manor, to send the two millstones to Cooley, and he would be recompensed for this expense.[17]

Like in England, not all the Templars who were arrested lived long enough to be interrogated. Two apparently died before Michaelmas (29 September) 1308, for they were recorded as present when the inventories were taken, but were not recorded at Michaelmas 1308 as receiving a pension: Peter of Malvern, commander of Kilcloggan in Co. Wexford, and Thomas le Palmer at Kilbarry in Co. Waterford. On the other hand, Thomas of Rathenny and Michael of Sutton were not mentioned in the inventories but were recorded as receiving a pension; they probably died before February 1310, as they were not interrogated.[18]

Yet there were other Templars who were definitely alive throughout the period 1307-11, but were not interrogated. Brother Thomas of Lyndeseye or Lindsey, aide (*socius*) to Brother Henry Danet, grand commander of Ireland, fled to Ireland before the Templars were arrested, and was in Ireland in 1308–9. He was involved in taking the inventory at Kilsaran in February 1308, and in collecting debts due to the Templars at Kilsaran, Tipperary, Waterford and Kildare, and he received a pension as a Templar. He was not interrogated in Ireland. He returned to England in April 1312, where the

Church Council allowed him to abjure all heresy, absolved him and sent him to a monastery to do his penance as a Templar.[19]

The royal justiciar and his administration in Ireland knew Thomas of Lindsey was in Ireland because the exchequer was paying him a pension. As aide to the Templar grand commander in Ireland, he must have been prominent in Templar affairs. So why was he not interrogated? Possibly he was exempted because he was an outsider, and the Anglo-Irish clergy in Dublin considered that it was the responsibility of the inquisitors in England to interrogate him, not those in Ireland.

Brother Stephen of Stapelbrugge, listed in the record of pension payments from the Irish exchequer as aide to William de Warenne, former Templar grand commander of Ireland, was almost certainly the same man as the commander of Lydley in Shropshire who had fled before the arrests.[20] There is no indication in the surviving records as to how Stephen of Stapelbrugge had escaped from England. Friar Adam of Smeton's story of his leaving Hopesay at Shropshire at the crack of dawn might conjure up images of a breakneck flight across Wales to the western coast, then bribing a ship's captain to take him to Ireland – but the Irish record indicates that his arrival in Ireland was above board and legal, that he held an official position in the Order as the aide to the former grand commander of Ireland, and he was entitled to a pension. Of course there is a remote possibility that there were two Templars in the British Isles in 1308 named Stephen of Stapelbrugge – but this is not very likely. The surname is rare, and the Stephen of Stapelbrugge in Ireland held a prominent post yet was not interrogated, indicating that (like Thomas of Lindsey) he was an outsider. However, for whatever reason, Brother Stephen chose to return to England before the trial in England had ended. He was arrested in Wiltshire, England, on 10 June 1311, and taken to London, where he was interrogated and confessed to some of the charges against the Templars.[21]

A Templar named Walter le Long, or le Lung ('the tall') was mentioned in the Irish exchequer records as receiving his pension in Ireland in 1308–9, but was not interrogated. This man was not mentioned elsewhere, but Archbishop William Greenfield of York mentioned a 'Walter le Rebel' as one of the English Templar fugitives. Walter was not an uncommon name, but it is possible that Walter called 'the rebel' was also known as 'the tall', and that this was another English Templar who sought refuge in Ireland.[22]

William de Warenne was grand commander of the Temple in Ireland from 1302 to early 1308, and as such was mentioned by three of the outside witnesses during the trial.[23] At the time of the Templars' arrest in Ireland, he was commander of Clonoulty.[24] Even though Warenne was still alive in 1312,[25] he was not interrogated with the other Irish Templars in spring 1310. He was related to Edmund le Botiller, who was lieutenant justiciar of Ireland in 1304–5, 1312–14 and 1315–18, but details of the relationship are not known.[26] He may have been an illegitimate descendent of William de Warenne IV (d. 1240), earl of Surrey, and Matilda, daughter of Isabel de Clare, countess of Pembroke and William Marshal I. Matilda had married first Hugh Bigod, earl of Norfolk, and second William de Warenne IV; her daughter Isabel by the first marriage married John fitz Geoffrey and was maternal grandmother of Edmund le Botiller or Butler.[27] Warenne's relationship to Edmund le Botiller could explain why he was exempted from the humiliation of being interrogated as an alleged heretic. The friars who gave evidence against the Templars in Ireland were particularly hostile towards Warenne; this antagonism may have been prompted by his escape from interrogation.

Adam of Langport was a different case. He was mentioned in the inventories of February 1308 at Kilcloggan in Co. Wexford, and he was interrogated, but he was not listed in the exchequer payments as receiving a pension,[28] although why he was not entitled to a pension is not clear.

It is interesting that the English king's government in Ireland was prepared to pay the Templar fugitives from England a pension, even though the inquisitors in Ireland did not interrogate them. If they reported these fugitives' location to the inquisitors in England, the inquisitors in England did not record the fact.

After 14 April 1309 the pensions ceased. Instead, King Edward II's justiciar and council in Ireland handed over the manors of Kilcloggan, Crooke and Kilbarry to Brother Henry Danet, grand commander of Ireland, and his brother Templars; the Templars were to support themselves on the revenues of these manors, rather than relying on a government pension. On 16 February 1310 – ten days after the trial in Ireland had begun – the seneschal of Wexford received instructions to hand over custody of the manor of Kilcloggan to two worthy men nominated by Brother Henry Danet of the Order of the knighthood of the Temple, as Henry was coming to Dublin 'for certain reasons' (that is, to be interrogated). The custodians were to manage the manor and keep account of its revenues, which were intended to support Brother Henry and his brethren. Similar instructions were issued to the sheriff of Waterford in relation to the Templars' manors of Crooke and Kilbarry.

The Interrogations

On 29 September 1309, King Edward II wrote to his bailiffs and faithful subjects in Ireland to inform them that the patriarch of Jerusalem, the archbishop of York, the bishops of Chichester and London, the abbot of Lagny and Sicard de Vaur were coming to Ireland to conduct the trial of the Templars. In the event, these officials appointed judges-delegate to come to Ireland in their place: Thomas of Chaddesworth or Chedworth, dean of Dublin, and two canons: Bindus de Bandinell, of St Paul's church, Florence diocese, and John Balla, of Clonfert church. These three received a royal safe conduct on 29 September 1309.[29]

The archbishop of Dublin was not involved in the Templars' trial in Ireland, as there was no archbishop of Dublin at this time. Richard of Haverings, who had been appointed by the pope in 1307, was never consecrated and resigned in 1311; instead, Walter Calf, bishop of Kildare, appointed commissioners as required.[30] At this time, Thomas of Chaddesworth was acting as deputy of the absentee archbishop-elect of Dublin. He was also the collector of the papal tax of one-tenth of ecclesiastical incomes, and lieutenant of the royal treasurer of Ireland. In addition, he was involved in another heresy trial: that of Philip of Braybrooke, canon of Holy Trinity, who on 4 September 1310 was found guilty by the archbishop-elect of Dublin of being a relapsed heretic, and sentenced to do penance.[31] Maeve Callan, the scholar who has most recently studied this case, describes Philip of Braybrooke's sentence as 'quite lenient': he was sentenced to a year under custody in All Hallows Priory, Dublin (in effect, a year's 'exile' in a rival religious house), with fasting on Wednesdays and Fridays.[32] Of the other two inquisitors, one had presumably accompanied the two papal inquisitors to England, while the other was a local man.

King Edward II also instructed John Wogan on 29 September 1309 to detain all the Templars in Ireland who had not yet been locked up, and to have them taken to Dublin and put under guard in the king's castle there until they were required for the trial. The king sent a letter to the archbishop-elect of Dublin, instructing him or his representative to be present in person during the proceedings against the Templars – Thomas of Chaddesworth took on this responsibility.[33]

The trial proceedings took place in St Patrick's cathedral in Dublin, beginning on 6 February 1310 and ending on 6 June.[34] As directed by the pope, other clergy were present during the proceedings in addition to the three inquisitors. Some of these also had a personal interest in the trial, either because they had received former Templar property or because they gave evidence against the Templars.

One of those listed as present during the Templars' trial was Master Philip of Herdele, officer of the court of Archdeacon Matthew of Bela.[35] On 17 November 1309, Master Philip of Erdelee (the same man) had been given custody of the Templars' former house at Kilsaran, Co. Louth. However – according to Master Philip – the previous custodian, Stephen Gernoun, was unwilling to surrender it, and defended his position with armed force. Stephen denied the accusation, stating that he had surrendered the houses as soon as he received instructions to do so, and demanded a formal inquiry.[36] With such an interest in the Templars' property, Master Philip could hardly have been an impartial observer at their trial.

Three leading friars were present during the interrogations of the Templars and also gave evidence against them. These were Brother Richard Balybyn, former minister of the Dominican friars in Ireland;[37] Brother Roger of Eton or Heton, guardian of the Franciscan friars of Dublin;[38] and Brother Walter Prendergast, lector of the Franciscan friars of Dublin.[39] Again, they could hardly be impartial witnesses when they themselves were giving evidence against the Templars.

Master William of Hothum, also present during interrogations,[40] did not give evidence against the Templars, but was involved with them outside the courtroom. In Michaelmas term 1312, William of Hothum was one of the guarantors for Henry Danet when the latter was released on bail. As chancellor of the Irish exchequer in 1312–17, and keeper of the office of treasurer of Ireland from 1313–14,[41] William of Hothum was a man of influence and authority in Ireland, and would have been a valuable friend for the Order; but, again, he was not a wholly impartial witness of the proceedings.

But not all those present during the interrogations were involved elsewhere in the Templars' affair. Master John the Marshal, canon of Kildare,

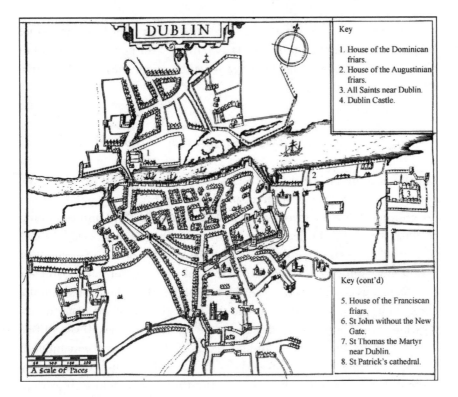

Key

1. House of the Dominican friars.
2. House of the Augustinian friars.
3. All Saints near Dublin.
4. Dublin Castle.

Key (cont'd)

5. House of the Franciscan friars.
6. St John without the New Gate.
7. St Thomas the Martyr near Dublin.
8. St Patrick's cathedral.

Map of locations in Dublin mentioned in the trial proceedings, based on John Speed's Map of the Countie of Leinster with the Citie Dublin described, 1610.

was a witness of the interrogations of the Irish Templars and present at the final summing-up of their testimonies on 23 May 1310, but did not give evidence against them.[42] He may or may not have been related to the great Marshal family, whose direct male line had died out in 1245. A Master John le Marshal, canon of Kildare, was a donor and patron of the Hospital of St John the Baptist outside Newgate, Dublin; if this was the same man, he appears to have been a charitable individual, supportive of religious Orders.[43]

Brother Philip of Slane, lector of the Dominican friars in Dublin, acted as a witness of the Templars' trial, but did not give evidence against them.[44] He later had a prominent career in government service, acting as a messenger and diplomat, and by Easter 1318 he was a member of the king's council in Ireland. In 1321 Pope John XXII made him bishop of Cork, on the king's request.[45] Trusted by both king and pope, Philip of Slane could have acted as an impartial witness to the Templars' trial.

The others present during the proceedings, Hugh of St Leger and Peter Wylyby, rector of the church of Balygriffyn,[46] do not appear in other records, so it is not possible to judge whether or not they were impartial observers of events.

The Testimonies

Fourteen Templars in Ireland were interrogated three times. In the course of the first set of interrogations several brothers amended their testimonies, but except for the priest, William of Kilros, and the grand commander, Henry Danet (whose surname was also written as 'Tanet' and 'Hanet')[47] none said anything to indicate that the brothers were heretics. The Templars in England had agreed that the commander of the Templars in Ireland was subject to the grand commander of England, and that the commander in Ireland should attend the English provincial chapter meetings, but several pointed out that in fact he did not come every year.[48] The Templars in Ireland, however, did not admit that the grand commander in England had any authority over them. But like the Templars in England, some did seem to be confused about the Order's procedures regarding confession and penance.[49]

Brother William of Kilros, the only chaplain of the Order in Ireland, said that the grand master absolved Templars of their penance, and that Templars went to the chaplain to confess only minor sins, confessing major sins in chapter meetings – in this he was agreeing with Brother Ralph of Ruston, chaplain in Yorkshire.[50] When the grand master heard the confession of a Templar brother (said William), he ordered the brother chaplain to absolve him from his sins, although the chaplain would not hear the confession. If this were true, it would indicate sloppy procedures within the Order, but was an error of ignorance rather than heresy. William referred to the death of Walter the Bachelor, and said that there had long been general suspicion against the Templars because they came to power so quickly and were so friendly with the Muslims. As he did not state that he had been in the East, this comment must have been based on hearsay rather than personal experience.[51]

Brother William related that a Templar brother who was staying at 'Killofan' (possibly Kilsaran in Co. Louth), whose name he did not know, was a sodomite and was placed in the infirmary of the commandery and died there. As the Templar remained nameless, this story could not be checked. Brother William also complained that priests in the Order of the Temple could not be promoted above the level they held when they entered the Order.[52] If this were true, it would help to explain why one of the priests in England (William Beche) had left the Order some time shortly before the arrests;[53] but a few Templars did become bishops elsewhere, suggesting that Brother William's complaint was not wholly justified.[54]

Brother Henry Danet informed the inquisitors that he had joined the Templars at Bruer in Lincolnshire, seven years ago at the next Eve of the Purification of the Blessed Virgin Mary.[55] The Purification is on 2 February, and Brother Henry gave his testimony on 18–25 February 1310,[56] so the next Eve of the Purification would be 1 February 1311. If Brother Henry had been in the Order for seven years on 1 February 1311, he joined on 1 February 1304. He said that he had spent a year-and-a-half in England (until the start of August 1305), then went overseas, where he spent two-and-a-half years, and finally came to Ireland where, he said, he would have been for three years at the next Eve of the Purification (1 February 1311).[57] In this case, he had arrived in Ireland 1 February 1308, only two days before the arrest of the Templars in Ireland. As he came from 'overseas', he could have come from France or the East; as he had avoided arrest, presumably he had come directly from Cyprus, where the pope's instructions to arrest the Templars did not arrive until May 1308.[58]

Brother Henry did not confess to any of the heresies described in the charges, but he stated that some brothers of the Order overseas were guilty as charged. He had heard that a Brother Hugh of Empures, who was lieutenant-marshal at Tortosa in Syria, had left that castle three days before it fell to the Mamluks of Egypt, abandoned Christianity and joined the sultan of Egypt. He had also heard that a certain commander of Castle Pilgrim (plate 6), one of the Templars' major castles in the kingdom of Jerusalem, had received many brothers into the Order of the Temple in a ceremony which included denying Christ, but he could not name any of them.

At a chapter meeting in Cyprus, Henry Danet had seen (he said) a Brother Hugh de la Roche, who did not believe in the sacraments of the Church and who was imprisoned as punishment. He had also seen many brothers from Catalonia and the kingdom of Portugal who did not believe in the sacraments. He had never heard of any Templar adoring a head as alleged, but he had heard that a Templar from Catalonia owned a bronze head with two faces that would answer questions put to it. Although he did not make use of it, Brother Henry knew that many lay people in that region possessed similar heads for answering questions and did make use of them.[59]

Henry also believed that the Burgundian commanders were particularly guilty of usurping the power of priests to absolve sins. Both the grand master Jacques de Molay and the Order's marshal, Aimo d'Oiselay, were from Burgundy.[60] Was Brother Henry saying that this was a fault in the grand master's own area of origin (after all, the grand master had confessed to it), but nowhere else? Brother Henry added that he had often heard from lay people that when there was a shortage of food the Templars used to eat one of their brothers in chapter, but that this was untrue.

Yet when he was asked why the Templars had failed to correct the errors within their Order, Brother Henry replied that he did not believe such errors existed; he had never heard of them. Brother Henry's testimony was so inconsistent that some of his evidence must have been untrue. His confusion led Clarence Perkins to conclude that he had been tortured, but there is no definite evidence that torture was used against the Templars in Ireland.[61]

Some of Brother Henry's testimony had some basis in fact. Brother Hugh of Empures or Ampurias, in Catalonia, was a real Templar commander. The so-called 'Templar of Tyre' (who was really the former secretary of Grand Master William de Beaujeu) recorded that in 1302 the Templars surrendered Arwad island, just off Tortosa (plate 7), to the Mamluks on the advice of Brother Hugh of Ampurias; the Mamluk commander, who had promised the Templars safe conduct to wherever they wanted to go, broke his word and had them all taken as prisoners to Cairo.[62] As Arwad was known as 'the isle of Tortosa', presumably Brother Henry had confused the town with the island and was referring to Brother Hugh of Ampurias's fatal advice to surrender the island. Henry could have heard this story after he arrived in the East, which would have been in the winter of 1305/6. Perhaps it was this incident that led him to depict the Catalans as bad Christians.

Although Brother Henry said that the Templars did not adore idol heads, he alleged that many Catalans owned a bronze head that answered questions. Here he again appears to have muddled his information. It was not the Catalans who had a reputation for skill at divination or magical practices, but the people of the city of Toledo in the neighbouring kingdom of Castile.[63] Toledo possessed a library containing Greek and Arabic scientific texts, including material on astrology, medicine and magic, where scholars from western Europe went to study. King Alfonso X of Castile (1252–84), 'the wise', had produced many books of science and magic drawing on classical texts such as those in the library.[64] Brother Henry Danet could have confused the Castilian capital's reputation as a centre for the study of magic with his own dislike of the neighbouring Catalans, and hence accused the Catalans of practising magic.

None of Henry Danet's colleagues supported his claims. Brother Richard de Burchesham or Burthesham, who had been received in Tripoli in Syria,[65] said nothing about Templar heresies in the East. The trial in Cyprus produced no confessions from the Templars, nor did outsiders produce any evidence that the Order was heretical.[66] None of the Templars interrogated in the kingdom of Aragon (of which Catalonia formed a part) confessed to the charges, even under torture. Overall, the trial on the Iberian Peninsula produced no evidence that the Templars were guilty.[67]

If Brother Henry's accusations were baseless, why did he blacken his Order's reputation? He may not have been physically tortured, but his position was vulnerable. The grand commander he had replaced in Ireland – William de Warenne – had been excused interrogation for reasons not recorded. Brother Henry was an outsider, originally from England, with no knowledge of Ireland, the Irish or the Anglo-Irish – neither of those two groups had much love for the English. According to two of the friars who gave evidence against him, he had been a close associate of the grand master of the Order, who had confessed to heretical practices, and he had been given the command of Ireland for life as a reward for his services.[68] If that were the case, then Henry Danet must have been in France with the grand master prior to 13 October 1307, yet had somehow evaded arrest. His own evidence indicated that he had come to Ireland directly from Cyprus. By giving the court scandalous stories about the Templars in the East, he distracted his judges from looking more closely into his own recent history.

The other Templars in Ireland had less to say, but did produce some information which interested the inquisitors. In general, they denied all the charges against them, but all fourteen brothers interrogated in Ireland (seven or eight of whom had been received in England) confirmed that they were not allowed to talk about their receptions.[69] All of them agreed that they should not reveal their receptions to outsiders, but had never heard of anyone being punished for doing so. Richard of Burtlesham, Henry of Aslackby, Robert of Pourbrigge and Henry of the Ford agreed that they were forbidden to confess their sins to anyone except to their own priests.[70]

Eight others said if a Templar priest was available, they were not allowed to confess to another priest; but usually no Templar priest would have been available.[71]

The Irish Templars were also asked about the death of the former grand commander of Ireland, Walter the Bachelor, at the New Temple in London, which had already been investigated during the trial in London. Robert of Pourbrigge, John of Faversham and Henry of the Ford had heard that Walter the Bachelor had been punished with death at the New Temple in London because of his disobedience; Henry Danet had heard that he had suffered a death sentence because he had taken the Order's property; Adam of Langport and Walter of Choneby (or Joneby) agreed.[72] If the inquisitors had been hoping for evidence that Brother Walter was murdered for refusing to deny Christ (for example), they were disappointed.

On 2 May 1310, the fourteen Templars who had been interrogated assembled in St Patrick's cathedral in Dublin before the inquisitors and Master John of Kildare to hear their evidence read back to them. The Templars were then asked whether they were prepared to stand by what they had said; they replied that they were. Then outside witnesses stepped forward, swore an oath on the gospels to tell the whole truth, and gave their evidence against the Order.

Non-Templar Witnesses

The majority of the non-Templar witnesses in Ireland were friars, led by the current guardian or chief official of the Franciscan friars in Ireland (Roger of Heton or Eton), and the former guardian of the Dominicans (Richard of Balybyn). Each of these was followed by a number of his friars: twelve Franciscans and seven Dominicans.[73] They had little specific evidence against the Templars, but all agreed that because of the Templars' crimes, 'scandal has arisen among the people and peril threatens souls'.

Roger of Heton declared that the Templars in Ireland must be guilty as charged, because the grand master and some of the commanders of the Temple in France had confessed to the charges, and all the Templars agreed that they all followed the same statutes and the same reception ceremony, which was secret – and therefore the Templars in Ireland must be using the same blasphemous reception ceremony as the brothers in France had confessed to. The Franciscan friar Walter Waspayl claimed to have spoken to a fellow-Franciscan, one William of Denedale, who had been in Paris when a knight of the Temple had confessed to the 'evil method of profession' in the reception ceremony.[74] The Franciscan friar William the Butler related how, when he was at Clontarf assisting his fellow-friar (possibly Hugh the Luminour, on whom see below) celebrate mass, none of the Templars had looked up at the Elevation of the Host, but all looked at the floor; they did not listen to the reading of the gospel (of course, it being in Latin, they could not understand it) and they did not wish the priest to speak the words of the mass giving them God's peace.[75]

Richard Balybyn noted that Henry Danet had been overseas with the grand master, had acted as the grand master's aide, and the grand master had been so impressed by his service that he had given him 'great honour, mounts, clothing and also other equipment and the command of the whole of the Order in Ireland for his lifetime if he wished'. Therefore, he said, Brother Henry must have shared in the grand master's crimes.[76] His fellow-Dominicans all agreed with him.

Some of these friars were men of some influence inside or outside their Order. Hugh the Luminour, Franciscan friar of Dublin, would in 1323–4 accompany his fellow Franciscan Symon Simeonis on a journey to the Holy Land, and die on the journey. His willingness to undertake that journey suggests that his evidence against the Templars was at least partly prompted by a genuine concern over the loss of the holy places to the Mamluks. His evidence was that he had often been at the Templars' commandery of Clontarf, near Dublin, and there had seen Brother William de Warenne (who would then have been grand commander of Ireland) refuse to look at the consecrated bread when it was raised up by the priest during the service of the mass.[77] Perhaps Brother William looked away because he felt unworthy to look on Christ's Body, but the friar considered that a pious Christian should have looked straight at his God.

A few other friars who spoke against the Templars were also responsible officials of their Orders. Nicholas of Kilmainham had been superior of the Franciscans' house in Dublin in 1306. Thomas of Ratho, Dominican friar, appeared in the government records for October 1307 acting for his Order, as did Ralph Kilmainham, guardian of the Franciscan house in Dublin in 1303. Ralph believed that Brother Henry Danet must be guilty as charged because he had lived overseas with the Templars who had confessed to these crimes. Friar Roger of Kilmainham, who would be guardian of the

Franciscan house at Dublin by 1325–6, gave evidence about Walter the Bachelor, late grand commander in Ireland.[78]

After the two great Orders of friars came lesser, but locally influential, Orders. There was Brother Thomas, abbot of the house of St Thomas the Martyr near Dublin, with Simon, prior of that house, and four canons (priest-brothers).[79] Following the same logic as that used by Roger of Heton, these canons all insisted that the Templars must be guilty, but without any specific evidence.

Then there was Gilbert the Reeve, prior of the religious house of All Saints near Dublin, with his colleagues Brothers John Gay and Philip of Kenefeke.[80] Prior Gilbert and Brother John followed the same logic as Roger of Heton, but Brother Philip had also heard that Brother William de Warenne had called Jesus the son of a whore – which would have indicated Jewish beliefs, if it were true.[81]

Roger, prior of the friars of the Order of St Augustine, appeared with his brother-friars Henry Walsh, David Long and John of Waterford.[82] Prior Roger followed the same logic as Roger of Heton, but added that Brother Henry Danet had lived with the grand master for a year and more, very intimately and familiarly. As the grand master had acknowledged – according to the papal bull – that he had committed the horrible crimes contained in the bull, and he had made Brother Henry grand commander of Ireland, then Brother Henry was probably guilty as charged.[83] Henry Walsh gave evidence that:

> Lord Thomas the Chaplain who had served the Templars at Waterford says that a certain man whom he saw in that house did not confess during two years, to his knowledge, and that on Good Friday he did not venerate the Cross, nor did the other seculars confess at the proper time in the Good Friday service. And if he had cooked food, he would rather let it rot than have it given to the poor.[84]

Regretfully, Friar Henry Walsh could not give the name of this evil Templar, nor did Thomas the Chaplain appear to present his evidence himself.

Finally, John the Palmer, prior of the house of St John the Baptist without the New Gate, Dublin, appeared with his fellow-canons.[85] This priory and hospital of St John the Baptist was a house of *fratres cruciferi* (cross-bearing brothers), canons of the Order of St Augustine.[86] The prior and canons all followed the same logic as Roger of Heton and repeated that the Templars were guilty as charged and that this had led to great scandal in the Church and peril of souls.

These witnesses' hostility is puzzling, because they had virtually no solid evidence against the Templars. At first glance, the opposition to the Templars in Ireland could seem to arise from racial tensions. The Irish-born friars had a past record of opposition to the English king, and in fact many Irish Franciscans would support the Scottish Edward Bruce's invasion of Ireland in 1315, while within the mendicant Orders in Ireland there were severe tensions between Irish and Anglo-Irish brothers, sometimes result-ing in open violence.[87] In contrast to the friars, the Templars in Ireland were either drawn from the Anglo-Irish and Cymro-Irish populations or had come directly from England[88] – none bore Irish names. In addition, the Templars served the English government in Ireland and the grand com-mander before Henry Danet, William de Warenne, was related to the great Anglo-Norman Botiller/Butler family – another possible reason for Irish racial dislike of the Templars.

However, none of the names of the friars who gave evidence against the Templars in Ireland were clearly Irish. Instead, they either had surnames which implied English or Welsh origin, or they originated from the area around Dublin. Although the Irish-born Anglo-Irish did not love incom-ers from England (such as Henry Danet), the main factor which the friars could have held against the Templars was that their former commander had been spared interrogation, so the charges of heresy were not being properly investigated. They also shared a motivation with their English brethren: they had acted as priests for the Templars in Ireland and should have known about the alleged heresies and reported them, so now they were trying to distance themselves from the Templars by giving evidence against them. Perhaps the less important friars were pressurised by their superiors into making some sort of statement, or possibly they hoped to win favour or advancement by testifying against the Order. Only Brother Hugh the Luminour later showed a personal interest in the state of the Holy Land.

As well as these religious men, four laymen gave evidence. Two men who had travelled in Cyprus and were possibly merchants (Robert of Hereford and Michelm of Bras) spoke against the Templars, based (they claimed) on what they had seen of the Order there.[89] Robert of Hereford said that nine years before in Cyprus he had heard about the secret reception ceremonies, while Michelm of Bras had heard that Templars who wished to leave the Order had a large stone hung around their neck and were drowned. This punishment does not appear in the surviving copies of the Templars' Rule. The claim may refer to the gospels, Matthew 18 v. 6, Mark 9 v. 42 and Luke 17 v. 2, where Jesus stated that if anyone caused the downfall of a child (a human child or a child in faith) it would be better for that person to have a millstone tied about their neck and to be drowned in the sea. Were the Templars told that those who abandoned the Order were causing the downfall of their brothers? But the punishment would be a metaphorical or spiritual one, not involving an actual millstone.

Michelm of Bras also described how the Templars made loans and accepted property such as villages, land or tenements, as collateral for the loan. They would receive rent or other revenue from the village, land or tenement, but would not put that towards paying off the debt. He then described a loan made to one Raymond Viscount on Cyprus, which was guaranteed on a village three leagues from the town of Nicosia. The Templars held this village for seven years. Michelm indicated that it was a terrible thing to deprive a lord of his village for so long, but in fact the Templars were providing a valuable service in supplying cash when it was most needed.

Raymond Viscount may have been related to the former viscounts of Tripoli; the 'Viscount' family on Cyprus were well-established, but not among the top nobility.[90] The chronicle of the 'Templar of Tyre' mentions him as commander of a Cypriot naval raid on Egypt; on 26 April 1306 he was one of the Cypriot lords involved in the formal suspension of King Henry II of Cyprus and, on 3 June 1306, he witnessed a grant of privileges to the Venetians by Lord Amaury, who had taken over the government of Cyprus. He is mentioned under May 1308 by the later chronicler Amadi, in the latter's account of the arrest of the Templars: the discussion between Amaury and the Templars at the village of Nissou, on the road between Limassol and Nicosia, was followed by Raymond Viscount going with the Templar leaders to Nicosia.[91] Possibly Nissou, which is a few miles to the south of Nicosia, is the village Michelm of Bras mentioned as having been mortgaged by Raymond to the Templars. Perhaps Raymond's command of the raid of 1303 left him short of money and forced him to resort to the Templars for a loan. Michelm, however, saw the Templars as an enemy of Christendom, and claimed that people on Cyprus said Acre and many other cities and castles were lost because of the Templars. The hostile testimonies of Robert of Hereford and Michelm of Bras were not supported by the evidence from Cyprus, where all the lay witnesses were very favourable towards the Templars.[92]

A former servant of the Templars who had been on Cyprus, Thomas of Broghton, had some favourable and some unfavourable things to say about the Order. He had heard about the sinister kisses and the secret reception ceremonies and that many had been placed in sacks and drowned in the sea, but it was not true that a Templar died in each chapter meeting – the brothers were counted in and out of the chapter, and the numbers always matched. He had heard a story about a Templar who was imprisoned for some reason in the Templars' house at Limassol on Cyprus and who had escaped to the Order of the Hospitallers by being rolled up in a linen cloth.[93] Adam Latimer, a layman, repeated two stories about William de Warenne trying to prevent the men under his authority from going on pilgrimage because he regarded this as an excuse to avoid work, and threatening to burn the crosses of the churches of Holy Trinity, St Patrick, and the images of the Blessed Virgin Mary.[94]

The evidence gathered from the trial in Ireland was a little more useful to the papal inquisitors than that from England and Scotland, as two Templars apparently had serious grudges against certain aspects of the Order – Henry Danet against the Burgundians and Catalans; William of Kilros against lack of opportunities for promotion. But the outside witnesses' complaints against the Order were largely rumour, with little factual content.

The End of the Trial in Ireland

On 14 July 1310 King Edward II granted safe conduct through Ireland to the three judges-delegate there, who were then on their way back to England.[95] As in England and Scotland, the Irish testimonies were recorded by notaries as they were given, and later copied into the full record of the trial proceedings. The inquisitors in London made extensive use of the Irish testimonies. Henry Danet's evidence was incorporated into the summary of outsiders' evidence which was sent to the papal commissioners preparing for the Church Council of Vienne, while the confused comments of some of his brethren were used to prove that the brothers were not permitted to discuss their reception ceremonies or to confess to any priest outside the Order.[96]

No record survives of any Church Council in Ireland which decided the Templars' case, nor is there any record of the Templars in Ireland abjuring all heresies as they did in England. The manors of Kilcloggan, Crooke and Kilbarry remained under the control of the Templars until Michaelmas 1311, when the Templars handed the manors back to the justiciar and Council. From Michaelmas 1311 to 7 April 1314, King Edward II's exchequer in Ireland continued to pay pensions to the Templars. Then the responsibility was handed over to the Hospitallers, who had been given the Templars' properties in Ireland.[97]

Henry Danet had been released on bail in Michaelmas term 1312.[98] No records survive of the fate of his fellow-Templars in Ireland, but presumably all of them received similar treatment. As for any Templars who had fled to Ireland from England, and who had not (like Stephen of Stapelbrugge and Thomas of Lindsey) gone back to England, presumably they ended their lives in peaceful obscurity in Ireland.

Notes

1   Sidney Painter, *The Reign of King John* (Baltimore, 1949), pp. 238–50; W.L. Warren, *King John* (London, 1961), pp. 186–7; Seán Duffy, 'John and Ireland: The Origin of England's Irish Problem', in *King John: New Interpretations*, ed. S.D. Church (Woodbridge, 1999), pp. 221–45.

2   Maurice Powicke, *The Thirteenth Century, 1216–1307*, 2nd edn (Oxford, 1962), pp. 53–5, 57–8; D.J. Power, 'Marshal, Richard, sixth earl of Pembroke (*d.* 1234)', *ODNB*, vol. 36, pp. 813–15.

3   Hamilton, *Piers Gaveston*, pp. 50–66.

4   Sources in Paul Dryburgh, 'The Last Refuge of a Scoundrel? Edward II and Ireland, 1321–7', in *The Reign of Edward II: New Perspectives*, ed. Gwilym Dodd and Anthony Musson (Woodbridge, 2006), pp. 119–39, here p. 119. Dryburgh refers to 'a historical tradition in which Ireland acts as a refuge for those fleeing persecution in England'.

5   For this charge used elsewhere, see Schottmüller, p. 122, charge 75.

6   Callan, '"No such art"', p. 55, n. 133, citing Philomena Connolly's forthcoming edition of the justiciary roll for 6–7 Edward II. William of Hothum, chancellor of the Irish Exchequer, was one of Danet's guarantors.

7   Wood, pp. 357–9. The pension was still being paid, at a quarter of the original rate, when the responsibility for paying it passed to the Hospitallers, 7 April 1314: Callan, '"No such art"', p. 55.

8   Wood, pp 346–48; Martin Messinger, 'The Trial of the Knights Templar in Ireland', unpublished M.Phil. thesis, University College Dublin, 1988, pp. 16–17; *Foedera*, ed. Rymer, vol. 2, pt 1, p. 23; *Calendar of the Justiciary Rolls, I to VII years of Edward II*, pp. 23–4.

9   MacNiocaill, pp. 191, 192, 196, 199, 200, 205, 207, 209, 212, 214.

10 Ibid. pp. 210, 211, 216–17, 216, 217,

11 Ibid. p. 211; Aubrey Gwynn and R. Neville Hadcock, *Medieval Religious Houses in Ireland* (London, 1970; henceforth cited as G&H) pp. 330–1.

12 MacNiocaill, pp. 214–15.

13 *CPR, 1307-1313*, p. 81.

14 'The Memoranda Roll of the Irish Exchequer for 3 Edward II', ed. David Victor Craig, unpublished Ph.D. thesis, University of Dublin, 1984, vol. 2, pp. 57–8, A 99. This covers the period 7 July 1309–6 July 1310.

15 'Memoranda Roll of the Irish Exchequer, 3 Ed II', ed. Craig, vol. 2, p. 256, nos A729–732; p. 264, no. A768.

16 Ibid. pp. 77, 85, 132–3, 222, nos A159, A178, A318, A645.

17 'Memoranda Roll of the Irish Exchequer, 3 Ed II', ed. Craig, vol. 2, pp. 446–7, no. A1367.

18 MacNiocaill, pp. 199, 207; *IEP*, p. 204.

19 *IEP*, p. 204; TNA:PRO E101/235/13; MacNiocaill, pp. 198, 222; MS D, fol. 171v (*Annales Londonienses*, ed. Stubbs, p. 176); *Councils and Synods*, ed. Powicke and Cheney, vol. 2, pt 2, p. 136; Forey, 'Ex-Templars in England', p . 36.

20 *IEP*, p. 204; TNA:PRO E101/235/13; mentioned as a fugitive MS A, fols 13r, 28r, 84v, 96v (Wilkins, pp. 335, 356, 341, omits last); *Register of William Greenfield*, part 4, pp. 286, 337.

21 *CCR, 1307-1313*, pp. 316–17; Alan Forey, 'Desertions and Transfers from Military Orders (Twelfth to Early-Fourteenth Centuries)', *Traditio*, 60 (2005), pp. 189 and n. 261; 'confessed' MS A, fol. 160r–v (Wilkins, pp. 383–4).

22 *IEP*, p. 204; *Register of William Greenfield*, part 4, p. 337.

23 See Wood, p. 333; *Calendar of the Justiciary Rolls, Edward I, XXXIII to XXXV Years*, ed. Mills, pp. 291, 292, 334, 357; MS A, fols 151r, 153r, 153v (Wilkins, p. 378 only).

24 MacNiocaill, p. 205.

25 *IEP*, p. 217.

26 Wood, p. 333; *Calendar of the Justiciary Rolls, I to VII years of Edward II*, p. 36.

27 Robin Frame, *English Lordship in Ireland, 1318–1361* (Oxford, 1982), p. 344; George Edward Cokayne, *The Complete Peerage of England, Scotland, Ireland, Great Britain and the United Kingdom, Extant, Extinct or Dormant*, new edn, ed. Vicary Gibbs, 13 vols (London, 1910–59), vol. 5, pp. 433–4, vol. 9, p. 590, vol. 12.1, p. 502.

28 MacNiocaill, p. 200; MS A, fols 145r–146r, 149v, 150r (Wilkins, p. 376 only); *IEP*, p. 204.

29 Quoted by M.H. MacInerny, 'The Templars in Ireland', *The Irish Ecclesiastical Review*, 5th series 11 (1913), pp. 225–245, here p. 245; Wood, p. 351; Messinger, 'The Trial of the Knights Templar in Ireland', p.17; *Foedera*, ed. Rymer, vol. 2, pt 1, p. 93; *CPR, 13071313*, p. 192.

30 MS A, fol. 150r; *A New History of Ireland*, vol. 9: *Maps, Genealogies, Lists: A Companion to Irish History, II*, ed. T.W. Moody, F.X. Martin and F.J. Byrne (Oxford, 1984), p. 314.

31 'Memoranda Roll of the Irish Exchequer for 3 Edward II', ed. Craig, vol. 2, pp. 9, 337, 385, 414, nos 34, 1021, 1214, 1268; Callan, '"No such art"', pp. 56, 100–36, 427–8.

32 Callan, '"No such art"', p. 100.

33 *Foedera*, ed. Rymer, vol. 2, pt 1, p. 93; *CCR, 1307-1313*, p. 179.

34 MS A, fols 143r, 155; for year see Wood, p. 354. For the location, see MS A, fol. 135r (Wilkins, p. 374).

35 MS A, fol. 155; Wilkins, p. 380.

36 'Memoranda Roll of the Irish Exchequer, 3 Edward II', ed. Craig, vol. 2, pp. 92, 352, nos A193, A1064.

37 MS A, fols 135r, 151v (Wilkins, pp. 374, 378–9). He also appears in *IEP*, pp. 171, 189, and *CDRI*, vol. 5, p. 166, no. 577, and p. 52.

38 MS A, fols 137v, 141r, 151r (Wilkins gives only the last, p. 378). According to the
Kilkenny Chronicle, *frater Rogerus de Heytoune* (probably the same) died in 1315: BL
Cotton MS Vespasian B. xi, fol. 131, printed in Robin Flower, ed., 'Manuscripts of Irish
Interest in the British Museum', *Analecta Hibernica*, 2 (1931), p. 335; Callan, '"No such
art"', p. 25, n. 5.

39 MS A, fols 137v, 141r, 146r, 151r (Wilkins gives only the last, p. 378). On the
Prendergasts see, for example, *The Oxford Companion to Irish History*, ed. S.J. Connelly,
2nd edn (Oxford, 2002), p. 483.

40 MS A, fol. 141r (Wilkins omits).

41 James F. Lydon, 'The Enrolled Account of Alexander Bicknor, Treasurer of Ireland,
1308–14', *Analecta Hibernica*, 30 (1982), pp. 7–46, here p. 19 and n. 8, and p. 20); *IEP*,
pp. 222, 225, 228, 231–2, 235, 241, 245, 249; Callan, '"No such art"', p. 55, n. 133, citing
Philomena Connolly's forthcoming edition of the justiciary roll for 6–7 Edward II.

42 MS A, fol. 150r (Wilkins, p. 378).

43 *Registrum Chartarum Hospitalis Sancti Johannis Baptistae extra Novam Portam Civitatis
Dublin; Register of the Hospital of St. John the Baptist without the New Gate, Dublin*, ed.
Eric St. John Brooks (Dublin, 1936) pp. 146–9, nos 210–14.

44 MS A, fols 135r, 137r, 137v, 141r (Wilkins, pp. 374, 375, 376; omits last).

45 *IEP*, pp. 242, 245, 257, 267, 253, 295, 307; Urban Flanagan, 'Papal Provisions in Ireland,
1305–78', *Historical Studies*, 3, ed. James Hogan (London and Cork, 1961), pp. 92–103, at
p. 100. For further information see Margaret Murphy, 'Slane, Philip (*d.* 1327)', *ODNB*,
vol. 50, p. 904.

46 Hugh of St Leger: MS A, fols 135r, 137r, 137v, 141r (Wilkins, pp. 374, 375, 376, omits
last); Peter Wylyby: MS A, fols 141r, 155 (Wilkins, p. 380 only).

47 Hanet: MS A, fols 148r, 149v; Tanet: MS A, fol. 151v. Wilkins read 'Tanet' throughout:
pp. 358, 376. The surname 'Danet' probably does not relate to a place of origin, but
means 'son of Daniel': Charles Wareing Bardsley, *A Dictionary of English and Welsh
Surnames* (New York, 1901), p. 230; 'Tanet' is an emphatic form of the same name:
ibid., p. 736.

48 MS A, charge 25 on fols 66r–81v; variant opinions on fols 66v, 67r, 67v, 68r; charge 6
on MS A, fols 117r–124v (Wilkins, p. 369 only; omits rest).

49 The testimonies have been analysed by Messinger, 'Trial of the Knights Templar in
Ireland', pp. 25–43, and by Callan, '"No such art"', pp. 57–84.

50 MS A, fols 148v, 150r (Wilkins p. 377, with omissions and some differences). See also
MS A, fol. 127r (Wilkins omits).

51 MS A, fol. 149v, 150r; Wilkins, p. 377.

52 Ibid.

53 MS A, fol. 13r (Wilkins, p. 335: misread 'exivit' as 'extitit').

54 For Richard, Templar bishop of Lavello in southern Italy, see *Regesta Honorii papae
III*, ed. Petrus Pressutti, 2 vols (Rome, 1888, repr. Hildesheim, 1978), vol. 2, p. 429, no.
5969; for Umbert, Templar bishop of Paneas (Banias or Banyas in northern Galilee,
called Caesarea Philippi in classical times), see Marie-Luise Bulst-Thiele, *Sacrae Domus
militiae templi Hierosolymitani magistri: Untersuchungen zur Geschichte des Templerordens
1118/9–1314* (Göttingen, 1974), p. 254.

55 MS A, fol. 139v (Wilkins, p. 376). Much of the material which follows on Henry Danet
is discussed in Helen J. Nicholson, 'The Testimony of Brother Henry Danet and the
Trial of the Templars in Ireland', *In Laudem Hierosolymitani: Studies in Crusades and*

Medieval Culture in Honour of Benjamin Z. Kedar, ed. Iris Shagrir, Ronnie Ellenblum and Jonathan Riley-Smith (Aldershot, 2008), pp. 411–23.

56 MS A, fols 141r, 148r (Wilkins, pp. 376–7); Messinger, 'Trial of the Knights Templar in Ireland', p. 24.

57 MS A, fol. 139v (Wilkins, p. 376).

58 Barber, *Trial of the Templars*, 2nd edn, p. 253; citing Étienne Baluze, *Vitae Paparum Avenionensium*, ed. G. Mollat, vol. 3 (Paris, 1921), pp. 84–6.

59 MS A, fol. 141r (Wilkins omits); see also MS A, fol. 91r (Wilkins, p. 358).

60 Alain Demurger, *Jacques de Molay: Le crépuscule des templiers* (Paris, 2002); for information on Aimo d'Oiselay I am indebted to Jochen Burgtorf.

61 Perkins, 'Trial of the Knights Templars', pp. 444–5; Callan, '"No such art"', pp. 68, 69, 81–4, argues that torture was not used.

62 *Cronaca del Templare di Tiro (1243–1314): La caduta degli Stati Crociati nel racconto di un testimone oculare*, ed. Laura Minervini (Naples, 2000), 241 (477), 401–2 (637–8), pp. 198, 310; *The 'Templar of Tyre', Part III of 'Deeds of the Cypriots'*, trans. Paul Crawford (Aldershot, 2003), pp. 101, 161, and notes. On Hugh, see also Alan Forey, 'The Military Orders and the Ransoming of Captives from Islam (Twelfth to Early Fourteenth Centuries)', *Studia Monastica*, 33 (1991), pp. 259–79: here pp. 262–3; reprinted in his *Military Orders and Crusades* (Aldershot, 1994), article 6.

63 For the speaking brazen head as a stock image, see Lynn Thorndike, *A History of Magic and Experimental Science during the first Thirteen Centuries of our Era*, vol. 2 (New York, 1923), p. 825, and Nicholson, 'Testimony of Henry Danet', pp. 419–20.

64 Jean Jolivet, 'The Arabic Inheritance', in *A History of Twelfth-Century Philosophy*, ed. Peter Dronke (Cambridge, 1988), pp. 113–148; and 'Bio-biographies', in ibid., pp. 443–44, 447–54; Alejandro García Avilés, 'Two Astromagical Manuscripts of Alfonso X', *Journal of the Warburg and Courtauld Institutes*, 59 (1996), pp. 14–23; *Picatrix: the Latin Version of the Ghâyat Al-Hakîm*, ed. David Pingree (London, 1986), III XI 54, 56, pp. 160–1, IV IX 33, p. 229.

65 MS A, fol. 134r; Messinger, 'Trial of the Knights Templar in Ireland', p. 26; Wilkins, p. 373.

66 Schottmüller, pp. 147–400; Gilmour-Bryson, *Trial of the Templars in Cyprus*, esp. pp. 30–1 on the 'vague though unsubstantiated remarks' by the prior of the Order of the Hospital of St John of Jerusalem.

67 Forey, *Fall of the Templars in the Crown of Aragon*, pp. 86–7. For the interrogations of the Templars in the Iberian Peninsula, see (for example) Josep Maria Sans i Travé, *La Defensa dels Templers Catalans: Cartes de fra Ramon de Saguàrdia durant el setge de Miravet* (Lleida, 2002); Josep Maria Sans i Travé, 'L'inedito processo dei Templari in Castiglia (Medina del Campo, 27 aprile 1310)', in *Acri 1291: La fine della presenza degli ordini militari in Terra Santa e i nuovi orientamenti nel XIV secolo*, ed. Francesco Tommasi (Perugia, 1996), pp. 227–64; Josep M. Sans i Travé, *El Procés dels Templers catalans: Entre el turment i la glòria* (Lleida, 1991); Gonzalo Martínez Diez, *Los templarios en la Corona de Castilla* (Burgos, 1993), pp. 192–252; Aurea Javierre Mur, 'Aportación al estudio del proceso contra el Temple en Castilla', *Revista de Archivos, Bibliotecas y Museos*, 69 (1961), pp. 47–100. I am indebted to José María Pérez de las Heras for his generosity in supplying me with information about the trial in Spain.

68 MS A, fols 151v, 153r–v (Wilkins, pp. 378–9, omits rest).

69 MS A, fols 136r, Richard of Burtesham (received in Tripoli); 137v, Henry of Haslakeby (received at Aslackby); 139r–v, Robert of Pourbrigge (received in Ireland); 141v, Henry Danet (received at Bruer); 142r, Henry Mautravers (received at Guiting); 143v,

John Romayn (received in Ireland); 144r, Hugh Brogham (received at Bruer); 145r, Ralph Bradley (received at Lydley); 145v, Adam of Langeport (received in Ireland); 146v, Richard of Upleadon (probably received at Upleadon); 148r, Walter of Chuesby (received at Ribston); 148v, John of Faversham (received at London); 149r, William of Kilros (received in Ireland); 149r Henry de la Ford (received in Ireland) (Wilkins, p. 375, omits the rest).

70 MS A, fols 136r, 137v, 139v, 149r–v (Wilkins, p. 375 only); and see MS A, fol. 91r (Wilkins, p. 358).

71 Henry Danet, John Romayn, Hugh of Brogham, Ralph of Bradley, Adam of Langeport, Richard of Upleadon, Walter of Chuesby, and John of Faversham: MS A, fols 141v, 143v, 144r–v, 145r, 145v, 146v, 148r, 148v (Wilkins omits all).

72 MS A, fols 139r, 141v, 145v, 148r, 148v, 149r (Wilkins omits all).

73 MS A, fols 151r–v, 152v–153r (Wilkins, pp. 378–9); MS A, fols 151v–152r (Wilkins, p. 379).

74 MS A, fol. 151r (Wilkins, p. 378).

75 MS A, fol. 153r (Wilkins, p. 379).

76 MS A, fol. 151v (Wilkins, p. 378 – mistranscribed).

77 MS A, fol. 151r (Wilkins, p. 378). On this witness, see Marios Costambeys, 'Symon Simeonis (*fl.* 1322–1324)', *ODNB*, vol. 52, p. 589.

78 Nicholas of Kilmainham: *Materials for the History of the Franciscans in Ireland, A.D. 1230–1350*, ed. E.B. Fitzmaurice and A.G. Little, British Society of Franciscan Studies 9 (Manchester, 1920), pp. 72–3: citing *CDRI*, vol. 4, p. 317, no. 660; vol. 5, p. 166, no. 578; see also for 1299, 1305–6, 1306, 1307, *IEP*, pp. 155, 182, 189, 197. Thomas of Ratho: *CDRI*, vol. 5, p. 200, no. 682; given as Thomas de Rathtouthe in *IEP*, p. 197. Ralph of Kilmainham: *IEP*, p. 171; MS A, fol. 153r (Wilkins omits). Roger of Kilmainham: *IEP*, pp. 310, 315; MS A, fol. 152v (Wilkins omits).

79 MS A, fol. 152r (Wilkins, p. 379). On this house, see A.L. Elliot, 'The abbey of St. Thomas the Martyr, near Dublin', reprinted in *Medieval Dublin: the Living City*, ed. Howard Clarke (Dublin, 1990), pp. 62–76, esp. p. 64; G&H, pp. 5, 172–3; J.T. Gilbert, *Register of the abbey of St. Thomas, Dublin*, Rolls Series 94 (London, 1889).

80 MS A, fol. 153r (Wilkins omits). On this house, see G&H, pp. 154, 171–2. See also my note on Brother Gilbert the Reeve: MS A, fol. 153r, in *The Trial of the Templars in the British Isles*, vol. 2.

81 *The Babylonian Talmud: Yebamoth*, translated into English by Israel W. Slotki (London, 1936), vol. 1, p. 322. In 1328 the Irish military leader Adam Dubh Ó Tuathail was burned at the stake outside Dublin for heretical beliefs, including the accusation that Mary the Lord's Mother was a whore ('asseruit Mariam matrem domini esse meritricem'), suggesting that such accusations were not unusual in Ireland against political opponents: Neary, 'Ó Tuathail, Adam Dubh', pp. 114–15; Jacobi Grace, *Annales Hiberniae*, pp. 106–7; *Il Registro di Andrea Sapiti*, pp. 104–5; Callan, '"No such art"', pp. 266–89.

82 MS A, fol. 153r–v (Wilkins omits).

83 MS A, fol. 153v (Wilkins omits).

84 Ibid.

85 Ibid.

86 See Charles McNeill, 'Hospital of St. John without the Newgate, Dublin', reprinted in *Medieval Dublin: The Living City*, pp. 77–82; R. Neville Hadcock, 'The Order of the Holy Cross in Ireland', in *Medieval Studies presented to Aubrey Gwynn, S.J.*, ed. J.A. Watt, J.B. Morrall and F.X. Martin (Dublin, 1961), pp. 44–53; G&H, pp. 210, 212;

Mark Hennessey, 'The priory and hospital of New Gate: the evolution and decline of a medieval monastic estate', in *Common Ground. Essays on the Historical Geography of Ireland Presented to T. Jones Hughes, M.A., M.R.I.M.*, ed. William J. Smyth and Kevin Whelan (Cork, 1988), pp. 41–54. On Prior John the Palmer, see *Calendar of Entries in the Papal Registers Relating to Great Britain and Ireland: Papal Letters*, ed. W.H. Bliss and J.A. Twemlow, 9 vols (London, 1893–1915), vol. 2, p. 343.

87 Niav Gallagher, 'Two Nations, one Order: the Franciscans in Medieval Ireland', *History Ireland*, 12.2 (2004), pp. 16–20; John Watt, *The Church in Medieval Ireland* (Dublin, 1972), pp. 64, 78–80.

88 Nicholson, 'International Mobility versus the Needs of the Realm', pp. 87–101.

89 MS A, fol. 153v–154r; Wilkins, pp. 379–80.

90 For what follows, I am indebted to Professor Peter W. Edbury of Cardiff University for his help in identifying this individual, and for the possible context of the loan.

91 *Cronaca del templare di Tiro*, ed. Minervini, p. 300; *Recueil de l'Orient latin*, 11 (1905–8), p. 442; L. de Mas Latrie, *Histoire de l'île de Chypre sous le règne des princes de la maison de Lusignan*, 3 vols (Paris, 1852–61), vol. 2, p. 103; 'Chronique d'Amadi', in *Chroniques d'Amadi et de Strambaldi*, ed. R. de Mas Latrie, 2 vols (Paris, 1891–3), vol. 1, pp. 285–6; cf. Florio Bustron, 'Chronique de l'île de Chypre', ed. R. de la Mas Latrie in *Collection des documents inédits sur l'histoire de France: Mélanges historiques*, 5 (1998), p. 167.

92 See Gilmour-Bryson, *Trial of the Templars on Cyprus*.

93 MS A, fol. 153v (Wilkins, p. 379).

94 MS A, fol. 153v (Wilkins omits).

95 *CPR, 1307-1313*, p. 267.

96 MS A, fol. 91r (Wilkins, p. 358); MS C, fols 1v, 3v, 9r–v (Schottmüller, pp. 79, 84, 95); MS D, fols 175r, 181r, 187r, 190v–191r (*Annales Londonienses*, ed. Stubbs, pp. 181, 187, 193, 196–7).

97 *IEP*, pp. 209, 217, 220, 223; 'Memoranda Roll of the Irish Exchequer, 3 Ed. II', ed. Craig, vol. 2, p. 246, nos A678, A679; Wood, p. 359.

98 Callan, '"No such art"', p. 55, n. 133, citing Philomena Connolly's forthcoming edition of the justiciary roll for 6–7 Edward II.

7

The End of the Trial
in the British Isles

By the beginning of April 1311, the inquisitors had amassed a large pile of evidence, although most of it was either denials (from the Templars) or unsubstantiated hearsay (from outsiders). This evidence had to be arranged to make a case against the Order.

In all, 108 Templars were interrogated in the British Isles. Until the end of June 1311, none confessed to any of the charges regarding denial of Christ, idolatry, disbelief in the sacraments, and sodomy. Two brothers in Yorkshire and six in Ireland did confess to charges 24–9, which stated that the grand master and other lay commanders of the Order could absolve them of their sins; but the great majority denied these charges. A few Templars had agreed that they absolved servants, who were not members of the Order, of crimes against the Order as if they were absolving sins 'in the name of the Father, and of the Son, and of the Holy Spirit'. All the Templars in the British Isles confirmed charges 34–7, that those received into the Order were forced to swear not to leave the Order (although some said that they did not swear, but only promised); that newly-received brothers were regarded at once as full members of the Order, without having a year of probation, and that receptions took place in secret with no one present except brothers of the Order of the Temple. Some Templars also confirmed charge 72, that they should not reveal the method of their reception to anyone, and charge 75, that they were not to confess their sins to anyone outside the Order. But they all insisted that these things were done for honourable reasons and there was nothing untoward or heretical in the Order.

The issues of promising not to leave the Order and confessing only to Templar priests were both in the Order's Rule. The Hospitallers, Teutonic Order and Order of Santiago also had regulations forbidding members from leaving their orders. Although religious Orders generally had a period of probation, the military religious Orders did not, because of the need to recruit brothers quickly after losses on the battlefield. The lack of a probationary year could have damaged the brothers' education, but it was not necessarily heretical.[1]

Whether or not they could reveal the method of their reception depended on whether the reception had formed part of a chapter meeting. The Templars' rule forbad discussion of chapter proceedings with anyone who had not been present – again, this was a regulation also enforced by other military religious Orders.[2] The Templars interrogated in London and Lincoln did not know of any regulation against discussion of receptions, but those at York and in Ireland thought that this fell under the regulation covering chapter proceedings, although they did not know of anyone who had been disciplined for breaking it.

All agreed that receptions were held without any outsiders being present, with certain qualifications. In his initial interrogation, without being put on oath, Brother William Raven stated that when he was received at dawn in the chapel of Temple Combe around five years previously, about 100 secular persons had been present;[3] however, when he was interrogated on oath he agreed that receptions took place without outsiders being present.[4] Brother Hugh of Tadcaster explained that brothers were received into the Order with only other Templars present, with doors open but guarded by a Templar so that secular persons could not enter; yet outsiders would have been able to watch proceedings from outside the open doors.[5] William of Chalesey confirmed that the doors were kept open.[6] Brother Thomas the Chamberlain stated that the door was closed behind him when he entered the chapel to be received into the Order, but the other door of the chapel – which opened into the commandery cemetery – was left open, as no one would come in that way.[7] The testimony of Friar Richard of Bokingham about a reception ceremony at the Templars' commandery of Faxfleet in Yorkshire offers additional information: Richard described a crowd of non-Templars, including himself, waiting outside the chapel while the grand commander and brothers held a chapter meeting inside; at the end of the meeting the grand commander and brothers came out, leaving the newly-admitted brother behind in the chapel; then Brother Richard entered and celebrated mass.[8] Geoffrey of Nafferton, a parish priest, also reported that he had celebrated mass for the Templars in the chapel at Ribston in connection with a reception ceremony, but in his case he had had to get out of bed to celebrate mass at the beginning of proceedings, then had had to leave the chapel and wait in the hall outside while the applicant for reception entered, and the doors were shut behind him.[9]

Possibly Templar reception ceremonies took place in two stages, the first in a public space, such as the commandery hall, in the presence of family and friends of the applicant; then the Templars and the applicant proceeded into the chapel, leaving all the others outside, for the second part of the ceremony – and the door could be left open or closed. This might explain how William Raven could have 100 guests at his reception to the Order (in his first interrogation), yet have none but Templars present (in his second interrogation).

During the proceedings in Scotland a group of young gentlemen expressed their amazement that Templars' reception ceremonies were secret, as they had seen men join other religious Orders where the ceremony was public, with friends, relations and neighbours present and a great feast afterwards.[10] There is some evidence that, outside the British Isles, outsiders could attend Templar reception ceremonies. One German Templar who was arrested and interrogated within France stated that in Germany honest, respectable outsiders could attend.[11]

As the Templars were clearly not following normal religious practice if they excluded outsiders from any part of the reception ceremony, the inquisitors asked the brothers in the British Isles to explain their practice. Ralph Barton, prior of the New Temple in London, thought that receptions were secret because the first founders of the Order had wished it; Thomas the Chamberlain believed that it was written in their regulations.[12] Yet nothing in the Templars' Rule specifically supports this belief. Perhaps these brothers meant that as receptions took place as part of a chapter meeting, and non-Templars were excluded from chapter meetings, receptions also had to be private affairs. That was the opinion of Himbert Blanc, grand commander of the Auvergne, although he considered that the secrecy had been a mistake.[13]

Perhaps outsiders were kept out of receptions in order to maintain an atmosphere of solemnity. As discussed in chapter three, some comments in the English proceedings by both Templars and non-Templars indicate that Templar chapels were normally open to outsiders[14] – so the door could be kept shut or guarded during reception ceremonies to prevent outsiders from wandering in and disrupting proceedings. This would have fitted with the contemporary concept of chivalry as a spiritual vocation, where the ceremony of knighting included an all-night vigil in church beforehand.[15] Yet, if this were the case, at least one of the senior brothers should have said as much; but they did not. In any case, excluding outsiders from the admission ceremony was not in itself a heretical practice, and all the Templars in the British Isles insisted that nothing dishonourable happened during the reception of brothers to the Order.

The Templars in England and Scotland either knew nothing about or dismissed charges 82–5 (on the truth of French Templars' confessions). Some declared that those confessions had been extracted by torture.[16] In Ireland, in contrast, the Templars agreed that the French Templars had confessed to the charges – but that did not mean that they themselves would confess to them.

Overall, the only point on which the Templars of the British Isles were out of line with then-current Catholic canonical practice was the question of whether laymen could absolve sins. This was a theological point that the Templars could hardly be expected to understand, because they were uneducated laymen. Presumably their error was a genuine misunderstanding over what constituted a sin and what a failure to keep the Order's Rule of life. After all, the Templars might have argued, as the whole Order was established to serve Christ, a crime against the Order must also be a sin against Christ.

Summing-Up

On 22 April 1311 the Templars who had been interrogated in London and Lincoln, and were now all imprisoned in the city of London, appeared before the inquisitors to hear the evidence against them.[17] Although the documents from the trial do not specifically identify this list of evidence, it may have been the summary which appears on folio 91r of MS A.[18] This refers to charges having been proven, but it is remarkably difficult to tie up the evidence listed here with actual testimonies.

For example, the summary states: 'They swore not to reveal how they were received: proved by seven witnesses.'[19] Which seven witnesses? The Templars interrogated in London and Lincoln all denied this charge; two stated that they swore not to reveal the secrets of chapter, but believed that the reception ceremony was not part of the secrets of chapter.[20] Nineteen Templars interrogated at York took the line that the reception ceremony was part of the secrets of chapter which must not be revealed to outsiders.[21] Four Templars at York denied the charge completely.[22] All fourteen Templars interrogated in Ireland, seven or eight of whom were received into the Order in England, stated that they were not allowed to talk about their receptions, but had never heard that anyone was punished for doing so.[23] Overall, it is clear that a certain number of Templars did make this statement, but the details in the summary do not tie up to actual testimonies.

The summary also claimed: 'That they are forbidden to confess except to their own priests, proven by four witnesses.'[24] Four Templars in Ireland agreed that this was true,[25] but eight said that it was true only if a Templar priest were available.[26] In Yorkshire, four Templars stated that they should not confess to an outsider if a Templar priest was available, because a Templar priest was the equivalent of a bishop or archbishop for them, but they were not forbidden to confess to outsiders.[27] The other English Templars all denied it, but the summary ignored their denials.

If this summary of the evidence was the one read out to the Templars on 22 April, it is not surprising that when the Templars heard it they were extremely angry. On 29 April 1311 a group of the Templars who were imprisoned in the Tower of London went to the church of All Hallows Barking (plate 37), to submit their defence to the inquisitors. They made a statement of faith like that in the Apostles' Creed (which is still used in daily services by the Catholic and Protestant Churches) and insisted: 'that we believe as the Holy Church believes and teaches us, and that our religious Order is founded on obedience, chastity, living without personal property, aiding to conquer the holy land of Jerusalem with the force and power that God has given us.' They denied all heresy and asked for justice.

> And if we have done anything wrong in any word in our cross-examinations through ignorance of the meaning, as we are lay people, we are ready to submit to Holy Church. And we wish to live and die like good Christians in the faith of Holy Church, like Him who died for us on the Blessed Cross. And we firmly believe all the sacraments of Holy Church. And we pray you, for the sake of God and the salvation of your souls, that you judge us just as you wish to answer before God for yourselves and for us.

They ended by asking for their full testimonies to be read out to them and to the people, presumably because the summary misrepresented what they had said.[28]

The inquisitors went round the gates of London, where the rest of the Templars were imprisoned, and asked them whether they endorsed the statement of defence; they all agreed that they did. Clearly the brothers were not prepared to give up their Order without a struggle.

Perhaps partly in response to this defence, and because Abbot Dieudonné and Sicard de Vaur had to start preparations for their final return to the papal court, the inquisitors now began to produce a report on the trial proceedings in the British Isles, which they would submit to the papal commissioners who were preparing for the Church Council of Vienne. The basis of this report, which is now in the Vatican Archives, was the summary of the Templars' testimonies on folio 91r of MS A.[29] Yet the inquisitors had to admit that they had obtained virtually no useful information from the British and Irish Templars. They were forced to resort to a rather contrived piece of logic, as follows: (a) the Templar brothers Robert de Saint-Just and Geoffrey of Goneville, interrogated in France, had confessed that they had been received in England, and that they had been received with the alleged abuses;[30] (b) all the English brothers insisted that the same method of reception was in use everywhere; (c) therefore, the inquisitors argued, all the brothers in England must also have been received with the abuses.[31] This ignored the fact that torture, or the threat of torture, had been used on Robert de Saint-Just and Geoffrey of Goneville when they were cross-examined in France, so that their testimonies were unreliable; while it had not been used on the English brothers, who insisted that there were no abuses in the Order.

Unlike the full versions of the trial proceedings, where the testimony of each witness is set out in turn, the inquisitors' report presents a summary of the evidence grouped together under subheadings. Charges 1–77 against the Order were divided into eighteen groups, and the evidence collected for each group was listed, with the names of witnesses.

The interrogations in Britain and Ireland against the Templars had been based on a short list of around eighty-eight charges. But in France, Cyprus and Brundisi, for example, a longer list of charges was used.[32] The inquisitors in the British Isles referred to this longer list of charges for their report. For charges 14 and 15, regarding the adoration of a cat, they found that they had collected no evidence,[33] and they had also failed to ask whether or not the Templars gave alms to the poor, for this charge had not been included in the short list of charges.[34] On the other hand, the longer list gave a correct version of charge 63, regarding chapter meetings being held at night.[35]

The bulk of the evidence in the inquisitors' report came from non-Templar witnesses. Those compiling the report did not completely ignore the Templars' denials, but they played the denials down, so that readers are given the impression that the evidence against the Templars was at least as strong as that in their favour – whereas the full versions of the Templars' testimonies show that the Templars' denials far outweighed the evidence against them. The compilers of the report did not question how probable an anecdote was; if they found a story told against the Order which supported one of the charges, they included it in their collection of evidence. Yet they omitted all outside evidence that was in the Templars' favour.[36] The material in the report was probably taken directly from the original bishops' reports rather than from the full records of the trial proceedings, as the report includes information which is not in the full official records.[37] Even the numbering of the witnesses is different. For example, William of Jafford, rector of Croft, is witness 4 in the full record, but 64 in the inquisitors' report.[38]

Sometimes the report gives additional information which reveals a seemingly plausible story in the full record to be less reliable than it first appeared. For instance: in the full record, Nicholas of Chinon, Franciscan friar, heard the story that he related from Brother Robert of Tregumham of the same Order; in the inquisitors' report we discover that Brother Robert had heard it from 'a certain lady whose name the witness does not know', and as the Templar commander and his son who are the centre of the story also remain unnamed, as does the commandery, and Nicholas tells us that everything occurred in the greatest secrecy, the whole tale appears very unlikely.[39] The compilers of the report also found some additional witnesses: four Dominican friars, Brothers Thomas of Redemer, Reginald of Braybof or Bray, John Taltet and Nicholas of Redemer.[40] Yet as all their evidence was based on hearsay, being stories which they had heard from someone who had heard it from someone else, this evidence did not strengthen the case against the Templars.

Given the care with which it was compiled, it is a pity that we do not know what contribution, if any, the contents of this report eventually made to the proceedings at the Council of Vienne.[41]

Having completed their report for the Council of Vienne, the two papal inquisitors made ready to depart. The last appearance of Abbot Dieudonné and Sicard de Vaur in the trial was on 5 May 1311 at the hearing of some late non-Templar testimonies at St Paul's cathedral (plate 40).[42]

On 10 May 1311 King Edward II sent Robert of Kendale, constable of Dover Castle and warden of the Cinque Ports, instructions to allow the abbot of Lagny and Sicard de Vaur to leave from the port of Dover with their households, horses, equipment, gold and silver vessels and other things, without being searched.[43] On 24 May 1311 Abbot Dieudonné and Sicard gave a receipt for £1,156 4s. 10d. from the province of Canterbury, £315 14s. 9d. from the province of York and 50 marks from Ireland, which they had received for the expenses they would have incurred from 1 June 1309 when they set out from the papal court to England, until 1 August 1311 when they were to arrive back. They said that they were content with this payment and would ask for no more, but they allowed the archbishop and bishops to punish the clergy who had failed to pay the tax towards their expenses.[44]

Templar Confessions

The last stage of the interrogations was about to begin. The final paragraph of the trial proceedings describes the inquisitors' efforts to discover the truth, including: 'ways found and contrived for provoking the said brothers to reveal the truth … and also severe and cruel lay persons sometimes exercising the death sentence, sent to bring terror to them'.[45] Did this mean that the brothers were tortured? One of the three Templars who produced a 'confession' indicated that they were. On 23 June 1311 Stephen of Stapelbrugge stated that he had not made his confession from fear of death, nor from any fear of torture, but only from concern about the salvation of his soul – but the fact he mentioned that torture had not affected his confession shows he had in fact been tortured.[46]

Yet only three Templars in the British Isles did 'confess', and they were in a particularly weak position. The first two, Stephen of Stapelbrugge and Thomas 'Totty' of Thoraldby, had evaded capture and/or escaped after being arrested. Their failure to come forward when summoned indicated guilt, and neither could give a satisfactory explanation as to why they had previously failed to give themselves up. The third, John of Stoke, priest, had been present at the burial of Walter the Bachelor, former grand commander of Ireland.[47] John, who was also treasurer at the New Temple in London, had initially been slow to come forward to give testimony, and possibly there were unanswered questions about his financial management at the New

Temple, which the merchants of London and many English nobles used as a safe-deposit.[48] Despite these confessions and any pressure or threats of torture brought to bear, the other Templars in the British Isles maintained their innocence of the charges and the grand commander of England, William de la More, refused to admit to any errors.

Stephen of Stapelbrugge was interrogated on 23 June 1311.[49] Having taken the oath to tell the whole truth, he explained that there were two receptions into the Order of the Temple, the first good and the second bad. If true, this would account for the discrepancy between the Templar testimonies in the British Isles and those in France, described in the papal bull *Faciens misericordiam* – the French Templars would have been talking about the second reception, in which the Templars denied Christ, His Mother and all the saints and spat on the cross, while the Templars in the British Isles were referring to the first one. However, only Stephen and, a few days later, John of Stoke referred to these two receptions. Thomas Totty, who followed Stephen, said that he had been received in one ceremony which had two stages.

Stephen gave the names of those present at his second reception – grand commander Brian le Jay and Brothers Thomas of Toulouse, Richard of Herdwick and Roger of Ryeley – all dead – and Ralph of Malton, called 'the Carpenter', and Thomas Totty, whose confession would follow his own. Stephen also depicted Thomas Totty as one of the two brothers who forced him to deny Christ, by threatening him with a sword. Uniquely for the brothers in Britain, Stephen was asked about the Templars' alleged worship of a cat, to which he replied: 'that in England they do not adore a cat or an idol so far as he knows, but he has certainly heard tell that they adore a cat and idol in overseas parts'. On the charge that they had to swear not to leave the Order, he agreed that this was true, but added that the superior of the Order gave permission for any Templar to leave the Order who could not keep the vow of chastity or other regulations; effectively denying the accusation. Brother Jean de Villiars, examined at Poitiers at the end of June 1308, had said something similar: he had left the Order because he was young and could not bear to abstain from women.[50]

Stephen said he had heard that overseas, when Templars refused to deny Christ and spit on the cross, they would be killed, but he had never known this to happen in England. Asked about Walter the Bachelor's death, he said that the former commander had died in prison from torture but not because he refused to deny or spit. On the charge of sodomy, he had heard that Brother Robert of Hameldon used to abuse a young Englishman. Robert of Hameldon or Amoldon had been at the Templars' commandery of Balsall, and was interrogated initially at Lincoln,[51] but despite Stephen's allegation, there is no record that he was questioned about this alleged affair, and on 12 July 1311 he was allowed to abjure all heresy with his fellow Templars, although he was given a harsh penance to perform.[52] Brother Stephen had also heard that the Templars lost a brother in each general chapter, an accusation we have met before in Scotland and Ireland.[53] After concluding his confession, he knelt before his interrogators and begged for the mercy of Holy Church, 'saying that he did not care about the death of the body or other torture but only about the salvation of his soul'.

On Friday 24 June, Brother Thomas Totty – who had been on the run since giving his testimony in Lincoln in April 1310 – presented himself before Archbishop Winchelsey and asked for mercy. His confession was heard on the following day at the church of St Martin's in the Vintry.[54] His first testimony had denied that there was any heresy in the Order. He now continued to maintain that the Order was innocent, but changed his statement in a few respects. In April 1310 he had denied the charge that the Templars were forbidden to confess to anyone but Templar priests; he now said that they were forbidden to confess to the friars. He said that before his reception certain of his friends scoffed at him because he wanted to join an Order in which the devil each year snatched away one brother – a story already heard elsewhere.[55] Another story which Brother Thomas may have picked up from the non-Templar witnesses was that the grand master had three idol-heads stored in various places in England.[56] He also mentioned that once, when he was in battle against the Saracens, he had lost the cord which he wore over his shirt because it broke; he was later punished for losing the Order's property. Although Stephen of Stapelbrugge had said that Brother Thomas was present at his second (heretical) reception, Thomas denied this; he had been present at Stephen's one and only reception, he said.

Thomas claimed to have been present at the papal court when the leading French Templars confessed, in July–August 1308. He had been able to travel through France without being arrested because (he said) he had written permission from the grand commander of England to travel around in plain clothes, with his Templar habit hidden under secular clothing, to find out information which would be useful to the Order.

No other Templar, however, endorsed Thomas Totty's story that he was an undercover spy for his Order.

After Thomas Totty's testimony on Saturday, he did not appear for a few days. On the following Monday, at the bishop of London's palace near St Paul's cathedral, Brother Stephen abjured all heresy.[57] On the Tuesday, Thomas Totty continued his confession at the church of St Mary of Southwark (plates 38, 39).[58] The fact that he now changed his story considerably suggests that he had been tortured in the meantime.

He still agreed that he had been received at Keele, but now gave a different date for his admission into the Order. At his first interrogation he had said that he joined the Templars twenty-eight years earlier; now he said it was sixteen years before – so he could have joined in 1282, before the Templars' loss of their possessions in the Holy Land, or in 1295, after the Holy Land was lost. He also gave a different list of witnesses at his admission, and explained that his reception ceremony had been in two parts. The first part followed the Rule, but the second involved the receptor (Guy of Forest) and two of the witnesses – whose names he changed during the course of his testimony – threatening him with swords and forcing him to deny Christ and spit by the cross, and to deny the Blessed Virgin Mary and spit on her image – but, said Thomas, instead he had kissed her feet. He claimed that 'Grand Master Guy of Forest' had taught him the Order's regulations – but Guy of Forest was never grand master of the Order; he was grand commander of England. He told stories against Guy of Forest's successor, Brian le Jay, who had died in battle against the Scots in 1298: Brian le Jay had reportedly said that Jesus Christ was not true God and true Man, and that the smallest hair of the beard of one Saracen was of greater value than the whole body of Thomas Totty, and he had refused to give alms to the poor in the name of the Blessed Virgin Mary. As both Guy of Forest and Brian le Jay were long dead, Thomas could slander them without implicating himself.

The master, said Thomas, absolved brothers from major sins; the priest absolved only minor sins, and penance in the Order was slight. Brother John of Hauville had had two receptions (one good, the second heretical) – but as John of Hauvile was insane and did not give evidence during the trial, this allegation could not be checked.[59] Thomas claimed that fifty or sixty years ago a French grand commander of England – either Brother Amblard of St Romain or Humbert Peraud, but he did not know which – had introduced the heretical errors to the English Templars – but there is no other evidence for this accusation.[60]

Thomas Totty went on to give evidence about the Templars' actions in the Holy Land. He claimed to have seen three instances of the Templars in the East agreeing to the Christians' defeat when they fought alongside the king of Cyprus's army against the Muslims. The first time was during a naval battle, in which Brother Thomas claimed he was acting as standard bearer (*gonfanier* in Old French) for the Templars. According to Thomas, he saw that the Templar ships held back from the fray, while the crusaders and King Henry II of Cyprus fought desperately. He asked 'the master of the Temple's army' (an odd expression, suggesting either that Brother Thomas did not know the title of the officer who commanded the Templars in naval operation, or that he was deliberately vague) why the Templars did not attack, and was told to shut up, so he 'leapt out of the galley in which he was with the men assigned to him to help the oppressed Christians'.[61] Possibly the galleys could have been lashed together in a row to form a barrier to the enemy or a fighting platform, and Thomas leapt off his own galley and ran down the row of galleys towards the fighting line; possibly he meant his audience to understand that he and his men got into a smaller boat and rowed across the water to join in the battle; but his account is not clear.

Thomas's second story concerned a raid on the coastal fortress of Maraclea (plate 8), involving the crusaders, the king of Cyprus and the Templars. In the summer of 1300, a fleet of sixteen vessels and some smaller vessels equipped by King Henry of Cyprus, the Temple and the Hospitallers did indeed raid the coasts of Egypt, Palestine and Syria, attacking Alexandria, Acre, Tortosa and Maraclea.[62] Thomas complained that the Templars did not go on shore with the other forces but remained on their ships. This would have been a reasonable military tactic, to protect the force against sudden attack from the sea. In fact, in Thomas's account, the Mamluks attacked by land, taking everyone by surprise. Thomas complained that the Templars were slow to help their compatriots, but it would of course take some time for the Templars to disembark and join the battle.[63]

Thomas's third point was regarding a clause in the Order's Rule that if any brother attacked the Saracens without leave he should lose his habit. This was true. The prohibition on charging without permission was part of the Order's famous military discipline that won it great admiration during the crusaders' march through Asia Minor during the second crusade. The Order's Rule was emphatic on the point.[64] The Hospitallers had an identical regulation – but Thomas never mentioned the Hospitallers, although at this time they were at least as involved in naval warfare as the Templars. It was essential for the Order's strength and effectiveness as a military force to charge together with a single object, rather than acting like secular knights and charging as it pleased them, in confusion and for their own glory. Yet, although he claimed to have fought the Muslims, Brother Thomas did not understand this.

Brother Thomas's lack of comprehension of basic military discipline and his failure to mention the Hospitallers indicate that in fact he had never been in the East and had never experienced military action with his Order. Overall, his evidence was inconsistent and unverifiable, but it was what the interrogators wanted. A few days later, at St Paul's cathedral, Thomas Totty formally abjured all heresy.[65]

On Thursday 1 July 1311, at St Martin's church in the Vintry, John of Stoke made his confession. He stated that his reception into the Order was honourable and correct, but a year and fifteen days after his admission, at the Templars' commandery at Garway in the Welsh March, he had been summoned into the presence of Grand Master Jacques de Molay, who was then in England. The grand master commanded that he prove his obedience by denying Christ, and two French Templars with him threatened John with swords to force him to obey. One of the two was John of St George, who was a sergeant-brother on Cyprus at the time of the arrests and who did not confess to any heresies,[66] so John of Stoke's testimony lacked corroborative evidence. But the confession was remarkably similar to those given by the French Templars who confessed – under the influence of torture – to irregularities at their reception into the Order. As such, it fulfilled the inquisitors' requirements.[67] On the following Saturday, 5 July, in the same church, John of Stoke made a formal statement abjuring all heresy.[68]

With this success behind them, the English inquisitors could hope that all the Templars would now break their silence and confess. On the same day as John of Stoke abjured all heresy, the bishop of Chichester and the officers of London, two legal experts, a theologian and two notaries, went to the church of All Hallows Barking to speak to Brother William de la More. They hoped that the grand commander would confess and be reconciled to the Church, but the latter insisted that he was innocent.[69]

Concluding the Trial: Church Councils

Even though the grand commander refused to give in, the three confessions were enough to allow the Church authorities to reach a conclusion to the Templars' affair. The notaries in London produced another summary of the testimonies from the trial, even shorter than the report they had sent to the papal commissioners for the Council of Vienne – on which it was based. It alluded to the three Templar confessions without giving details, left out personal names, and abbreviated witness statements so carelessly that hearsay was presented as firsthand testimony. The notaries also included an outline of *Faciens misericordiam*, as if readers needed to be reminded that the trial of the Templars in Britain had been undertaken on papal command. This new short summary could have formed the justification for the dissolution of the Templars in England.

The effect of abridging material from the earlier report was to make the evidence against the Templars appear much stronger. For example: in the earlier report, Brother Adam of Smeton's story about the Templars of Sandford clearly stated that an old servant of the Templars told him the tale;[70] in this short summary the account was amended so that it appeared that the old servant himself had spoken in court. Again, the third-hand evidence given by William of Jafford, about a dying Templar who had confessed his idolatry and sodomy to a now-deceased Austin friar, appeared in this short summary as a firsthand Templar confession – to the confusion of at least one modern historian.[71] A reference to 'witness no. 24' now became '24 witnesses', so that what had been one man's story now appeared to be widespread rumour; later, 'witness no. 23' became '23 witnesses'.[72] The compilers made good use of the friars' stories about the sick Templar who had spat the communion host into a urinal, the dead Templar whose sister found a cross on his underpants, and Agnes Cocacota's tale of dark deeds at Dinsley. They also introduced a new accusation: 'four witnesses confirm that the Templars gave the ecclesiastical sacraments to excommunicated men' – evidence which had never been mentioned in the earlier records of the trial.[73]

Nothing in this short summary states why it was produced, but it was most likely intended for the Provincial Church Council which met in London to decide the fate of the Templars in England. The council began on 27 June 1311 and continued until 13 July. The fact that the summary would have had to have been produced very quickly, to be ready before the end of the Council, could explain the lack of detail and over-simplification of evidence. Ostensibly, the summary provided the Council with an abridgement of the evidence from the trial, to enable the Council to debate the proceedings and come to an informed decision on what to do about the Templars. Because it distorted, exaggerated and omitted evidence it did not do this, but by reinforcing the presumption of the Templars' guilt it allowed the Council to reach a decision. The Templars were allowed to abjure heresy, were absolved of all sin and reconciled to the Church, and were given penance to perform as if they had been guilty of all the heresies they denied.

Only one copy of this short summary survives, in a history of London which was written in the early fourteenth century by a citizen of the city. The famous nineteenth-century constitutional historian William Stubbs named this history the *Annales Londonienses* ('London Annals'), because so much of the content relates to London.[74] Although the author/compiler did not put his name on his work, modern historians agree he was Andrew Horn, a wealthy fishmonger, warden of the fishmonger's guild, lawyer and finally chamberlain of the city of London from 1320 to his death in 1328.[75] As London was a location for the trial of the Templars in the British Isles, and given the importance of the New Temple as a financial centre and the interest of the people of London in the final phases of the trial,[76] it would be reasonable for a well-informed commentator on current events in London to include an official summary of the evidence against the Templars, pro-duced for the Provincial Council.

Although the Templar trial proceedings do not record the Council's deliberations, its decisions were evident from what followed. On Tuesday 6 July 1311 the Church Council met at Southwark. Brothers Philip of Meux, knight, Thomas of Staundon, Henry Paul, Roger of Dalton and Thomas of Loudham – all brothers who had been in the Order for only a short time – asked for mercy and stated that they wanted to be allowed to abjure all heresy.[77] On Friday 9 July 1311 at the lodging of the dean of St Paul's, another thirteen Templars – who had joined the Order between ten and three years before their interrogations and had 'confessed nothing except that there was vehement rumour against them and the impossibility of purging themselves of the accusations' – asked for mercy and, like their brother-Templars, asked to be allowed to abjure all heresy.[78]

Their requests were granted: on the same day at the bishop of London's palace next to St Paul's cathedral, in the presence of the archbishop of

Canterbury, the other bishops of the province of Canterbury and the clergy and people of the city of London, both groups of Templars who had asked for permission to abjure heresy did so. The wording of their abjuration in the official record was a little different from that used by the three brothers who had confessed. Each of the five Templars who had been in the Order for only a short time acknowledged: 'it is a great error regarding the sacrament of penance to believe that a brother who is a layman can absolve brothers from sins or remit sins by the power of God and the authority of the pope, as it is said was done before this time in chapter among the brothers of the Order', and stated that he had been so defamed by the charges of heresy that he could not clear his name, and so submitted himself to the justice and mercy of Holy Church. Each promised to swear off all heresy and to perform whatever penance he was given; to keep the Christian faith in future and persecute heresy; and that if he ever broke his word, he should be treated as a heretic.[79]

These five, and the thirteen who had followed, were then absolved from their sins and formally reconciled to the Church.[80] The absolution, however, was only conditional: they still had penance to perform.

On the following day, eight elderly Templars – although one had been in the Order for only four years – recited a formal abjuration before the Council in which they too admitted they had been so defamed by the allegations against them that they could not clear themselves, and submitted to the mercy and justice of the Church.[81]

On Monday 12 July the archbishop and bishops and the whole Council assembled again. There was also a great crowd of people from the city of London, as well as Earl Thomas of Lancaster, the king's cousin, Humphrey de Bohun, earl of Hereford, Aymer de Valence, earl of Pembroke and Guy de Beauchamp, earl of Warwick. Along with several of the bishops at the Council, these earls represented the Lords Ordainer, who were currently working on the list of ordinances, the government reforms which they wished to introduce; they produced a draft list a month later, on 3 August 1311.[82] The official record does not explain why they were present. As they themselves had a claim on much of the Templars' land, which their ancestors had originally given to the Order, perhaps they came to ensure that their interests were represented at the Council. Nineteen Templars appeared before the Church Council that day and abjured all heresy.[83] On the following day, at the chapel of St Mary Barking next to the Tower of London, five old and decrepit Templars who were too infirm to travel across London to

St Paul's cathedral abjured heresy, gave their confessions privately, and were absolved and reconciled to the Church.[84] Later that day, back in the bishop of London's palace, seven more Templars abjured heresy.

There was some discussion in the Council over the phrasing of the absolution, as the bishops could hardly absolve men who had not yet been found guilty. Eventually it was decided that absolution must be provisional: 'if you have been excommunicated, we absolve you'. This settled, fifty of the Templars who had abjured heresy stood on the steps at the west door of St Paul's cathedral, and the bishops absolved them and reconciled them to the Church.[85]

The Church Council decided to assign each Templar to a monastery to carry out his penance.[86] No decision was made on the grand commander, William de la More, because the pope had reserved the right to pass judgement on him.[87] Himbert Blanc, grand commander of the Auvergne, also remained in prison. Although he had denied all heresy, because his brothers in the Auvergne had brought incriminating evidence against him, the inquisitors in England regarded him as guilty but unrepentant. The punishment for obdurate heresy was burning at the stake, but for the time being the Council decided to take no further action against Brother Himbert.[88]

On 29 July 1311 at the Provincial Council of the province of York, the Templars of Yorkshire and Scotland abjured all heresy and were reconciled to the Church. The council had opened on 24 May 1311 at York to discuss the Templars' affair, with the bishops of northern England and Scotland, and doctors of theology and canon law to advise on the theological aspects of the case. After two adjournments, the Council finally got down to business on 28 July, with Master Robert Pickering, canon of York, in the chair; Archbishop William Greenfield had already left for the Council of Vienne.[89]

On 29 July twenty-four Templars came before the Council in the chapter house of York Minster. They admitted that they had been defamed by the charges in the papal bull and that they could not clear themselves of the accusations. On bended knee they begged to be readmitted to the Church and said that they would do whatever was required. So they were given a form of words to say, while touching a copy of the gospels. They each said in their mother tongue:

On these four holy gospels, I detest and abjure all heresies, and especially those contained in the papal bull, by which I have been defamed; and

I promise from henceforth to observe the catholic and orthodox faith, which the holy Roman Church holds, teaches and preaches. Thus God me help and these holy gospels of God.

When they had sworn this, they went to the west door of the cathedral and knelt. Bishop Thomas of Whithorn, with four other clergymen in attendance, absolved them from the heresies in the papal bull and all others, and readmitted them to the Church and the sacraments. The Templars then came back into the chapter house and were formally freed from royal custody and taken into the custody of the Church.[90]

On the following day, the Provincial Council at York decided to send the Templars to individual monasteries in York Province to do their penance.[91] Robert of Pickering delegated the task of sending the Templars to monasteries to John of Nassington, who had earlier given evidence against the Templars.[92] The final proceedings at York were recorded in Archbishop Greenfield's register, and a copy was made by Henry William of Edeslawe, notary public, which was despatched to the pope for his records.[93]

This was effectively the end of the trial of the Templars in England. Although the Order had not been formally dissolved, all the Templars were dispersed to perform their penance. Their property remained in the king's hands. The records of the Church Council that decided the Templars' case in Ireland have not survived, but in autumn 1312 the grand commander of Ireland was released from prison on bail.[94] There is no record of the Irish Templars being sent to monasteries to do penance, but they received a regular pension.[95]

The Fate of the Templars' Property

From 15 July 1311 onward, King Edward II issued instructions to his sheriffs and bailiffs to co-operate with the bishops in delivering the Templars to their assigned monasteries and ensuring that those monasteries received the money due for the Templars' support. Such instructions continued over the next two years, while the king retained the Templars' lands.[96]

In October and November 1311 the king sent out information to all his faithful subjects explaining to whom he had entrusted the Templars' lands. In some cases these were royal officials responsible for collecting and accounting for the revenues; in others, the king had given the Templars' estates to an individual who could keep the revenues for himself.[97] The king also granted Templar estates to his friends and allies.[98] Edward was not the only landlord in England to act as if the Templars' lands now belonged to him; his cousin, Earl Thomas of Lancaster, confiscated all the lands which the Templars had been leasing from him.[99]

In fact, Edward and his nobles needed the Templars' properties to assist them with more pressing matters. On 11 October 1311 – faced with the alternative of civil war – Edward II gave his royal assent to the reforms required by the Lords Ordainer. They demanded that Gaveston be exiled from all the English king's territories, that policy and official appointments should be decided by the barons in Parliament, and restricted Edward's ability to raise money without going through Parliament. The limitations on the king's right to take goods and money when he needed them would have made the Templars' properties even more valuable to Edward. Gaveston went into exile again on 4 November, but was back in England by early 1312. Over the next few months, as the king and Lords Ordainer realised that war was unavoidable, Edward used the Templars' properties to aid his preparations: on 21 January 1312 he instructed the keeper of the Templars' manor of Ribston, Yorkshire, to send from the produce of the manor 100 quarters of wheat, ten-and-a-half quarters of barley, twenty oxen, eighty sheep and two carts with iron-hooped tyres to Gaveston's castle at Knaresborough, to reinforce that castle.[100] In March, Archbishop Winchelsey excommunicated Gaveston for returning to England, and the opposition clergy and earls laid out their campaign against the king and his favourite.[101]

Meanwhile, on 22 March 1312, Pope Clement V dissolved the Order of the Temple 'not by way of condemnation but by papal provision'; the Order had not been found guilty, but its reputation had been so blackened that it could not continue. This dissolution was published on 3 April. On 2 May, in the bull *Ad Providam*, Pope Clement V recapped on his earlier bull and announced that all the Order's possessions were to be kept for their original purpose: to help the Catholic Christians in the Holy Land and defend them against the enemies of the Christian faith. With the exception of the properties in the Iberian Peninsula, he was giving the former assets of the Templars to the Hospitallers, who would continue the war in the East. On 15 May Clement wrote to King Edward and the archbishops and bishops and nobles of England with this mandate.[102]

The pope's command probably did not reach Edward until after Gaveston's death on 19 June 1312, which was followed by further military manoeuvrings on the part of both the king and his opponents.[103] The king authorised the sale of timber from the Templars' estates and ordered payments to be made from the Templars' revenues directly into the Wardrobe or the Chamber, his private accounts. Stock from the Templars' lands in Warwickshire and Leicestershire was taken for the royal household; hay and oats were to be sent for the king's horses at the next Parliament. Templar lands were given to the king's allies.[104] At the start of August, Edward wrote to the prior of the Hospital of St John of Jerusalem, forbidding him to make any attempt to obtain the Templars' lands, 'because the execution of the papal mandate, if it happens, will be manifestly prejudicial to us and the royal dignity of our crown'. [105]

Civil war was finally averted by the mediation of two of the earls, the pope's representatives who had brought the instructions regarding the Templars' lands to Edward, and Count Louis of Évreux, brother of King Philip IV of France. Formal peace was made on 20 December 1312.[106] On 17 October 1312 Fulk de Villaret, grand master of the Hospital of St John of Jerusalem, had announced that he was sending his representatives to the West to take over custody of the former Templar properties.[107] Edward furiously resisted the papal command to hand the properties over to the Hospitallers, until the arrival in England in November 1313 of the Hospitallers' representatives. One was Albert von Schwarzburg, former marshal (military commander) of the Hospital, then commander of the Hospital on Cyprus and now grand commander of the Hospital and lieutenant of the grand master in Europe, while the other was Leonard of Tibertis, prior of Venice and general procurator of the Hospital. Albert was from a noble family, descended from the counts of Schwarzburg of Thüringia and Saxony; perhaps his noble pedigree and the influence which he could wield as a result impressed the king. In addition, Pope Clement agreed to make Edward a private loan of 160,000 florins, an agreement which was confirmed on 20 January 1314. Although Edward continued to protest that he feared the danger to his kingdom and his subjects if he handed over these properties to the Hospital, he finally agreed to do so.[108]

On 5 December 1313 Albert of Schwarzburg and Leonard of Tibertis issued a statement that the king of England had handed over to them all the former property of the Knights Templar insofar as he was able, and he had ordered his subjects to restore to them the former Templars' properties that they held. They stated that they were satisfied, and that they relinquished all claims on himself and his heirs and would not seek anything more over these properties. Yet many properties, such as Bisham in Oxfordshire, Bruer in Lincolnshire, Combe in Somerset, Faxfleet, Hirst and Newsam in Yorkshire and even New Temple itself were in fact still in the hands of the king or of the local landowner (see Appendix 2). It would be many years before the Hospitallers obtained many of these properties, and some never came back to them.

Notes

1 Promising not to leave the Order: *Règle*, section 676; trans. Upton-Ward, p. 17; confessing only to the Order's priests: *Règle*, section 354; trans. Upton-Ward, p. 98. Forey, 'Desertions and Transfers', pp. 143–5; Forey, 'Novitiate and Instruction', pp. 1–17.

2 *Règle*, sections 225, 418, 550; trans. Upton-Ward, pp. 73, 112, 143; *Cartulaire général de l'Ordre des Hospitaliers de Saint-Jean de Jérusalem, 1100–1310*, ed. Joseph Delaville le Roulx, 4 vols (Paris, 1894–1906), nos 2213.82, 3396.24; *Die Statuten des Deutschen Ordens nach den Ältesten Handschriften*, ed. Max Perlbach (Halle, 1890), p. 83, no. 3.

3 MS A, fol. 11v (Wilkins, p. 334).

4 MS A, fol. 22r–v (Wilkins, p. 340).

5 MS A, fol. 25v (Wilkins, p. 341).

6 MS A, fol. 29r (Wilkins omits).

7 MS A, fol. 13r (Wilkins, p. 335).

8 MS A, fol. 97r (Wilkins omits).

9 MS A, fol. 99r (Wilkins, pp. 362–3).

10 MS A, fol. 158v (Wilkins, p. 382).

11 Barber, *Trial of the Templars*, 2nd edn, p. 70, citing H. Prutz, *Entwicklung und Untergang des Tempelherrenordens* (Berlin, 1888), p. 327; also mentioned by Riley-Smith, 'Were the Templars Guilty?', p. 115.

12 MS A, fols 13r, 14v–15r (Wilkins, pp. 335. 336).

13 MS A, fol. 17r (Wilkins, p. 338).

14 See chapter three.

15 Maurice Keen, *Chivalry* (New Haven and London, 1984), pp. 65, 79.

16 Confessions in France were seen as unreliable: MS A, fols 73r, 75v; some specified that this was because torture had been used on them to force them to confess: MS A, fols 73v, 126v, 129r (twice), 131r, 133r.

17 MS A, fol. 101v.

18 MS A, fol. 91r (Wilkins, p. 358). Alternatively, the historian Maeve B. Callan suggested that this summary was drawn up for the reconvened Provincial Council of Canterbury, which resumed on 23 April 1311 at St Paul's cathedral in London: Callan, '"No such art"', p. 75; for this council, see *Councils and Synods*, ed. Powicke and Cheney, vol. 2, pt 2, p. 1298.

19 MS A, fol. 91r (Wilkins, p. 358).

20 MS A, fols 43v, 55r (Wilkins omits).

21 MS A, fols 125r, 125v, 126v, 127r, 127v, 128r, 128v, 129r, 129v, 130r, 131r, 131v, 132r, 132v, 133r.

22 MS A, fols 126r, 130r, 130v, 133r.

23 MS A, fols 136r, 137v, 139r–v, 141v, 142r, 143v, 144r, 145r, 145v, 146v, 148r, 148v, 149r.

24 MS A, fol. 91r (Wilkins, p 358).

25 MS A, fols 136r, 137v, 139v, 149r–v.

26 MS A, fols 141v, 143v, 144r–v, 145r, 145v, 146v, 148r, 148v.

27 MS A, fols 126v, 126v, 127v, 129r.

28 MS A, fols 101v–102r (Wilkins, pp. 364–5).

29 As Malcolm Barber has noted, 'the material upon which the summaries for the Council of Vienne were based would almost certainly have had to be sent to the commission sitting at Malaucèn' (near Orange in southern France) 'before late June 1311' – so the report now in the Vatican archives must have left England before John of Stoke and his colleagues made their confessions at the end of June and early July: Barber, *Trial of the Templars*, 2nd edn, pp. 352–3, n. 11. For the commission preparing for the Council, see ibid., p. 260. The report is now at the Vatican, Archivio Segreto Vaticano, MS Armarium XXXV 147 (MS C).

30 MS A, fols 93r–94r (Wilkins, pp. 359–61); MS C, fol. 1r–v, 2v (Schottmüller, pp. 79, 81); see also the final summary: MS D, fol. 179r (*Annales Londonienses*, ed. Stubbs, p. 185).

31 MS C, fol. 11v (Schottmüller, pp. 99–100).

32 For the long list of charges, see Schottmüller, pp. 119–124.

33 MS C, fol. 3v (Schottmüller, p. 83). In fact, William of Thorp (MS A, fol. 29v) stated that he had never known anyone to adore a cat.

34 MS C, fol. 11v (Schottmüller, p. 101).

35 MS C, fol. 8v (Schottmüller, p. 93).

36 For example, MS A, fols 61r–62v, witnesses 4–17 (Wilkins, pp. 348–9).

37 MS A, fols 91v–99v (Wilkins, pp. 358–64, abridged); the testimony of Thomas of Witringham or Wintersham in MS C, fol. 3v (Schottmüller, p. 84), has more information than his testimony in MS A, 92r, including giving the name of his informant.

38 MS A, fol. 91v (Wilkins, p. 359); MS C, fol. 5r (Schottmüller, p. 79).

39 MS A, fol. 92r (Wilkins, p. 359); MS C, fol. 8v (Schottmüller, p. 94).

40 MS C, fol. 2r–v (Schottmüller, pp. 80–2).

41 On this, see Barber, *Trial of the Templars*, 2nd edn, p. 261.

42 MS A, fol. 99v and 100r (Wilkins, p. 363).

43 *CCR, 1307-1313*, p. 351.

44 *Registrum Simonis de Gandavo*, vol. 1, p. 408.

45 MS A, fol. 170r (Wilkins, p. 393).

46 MS A, fol. 161r (Wilkins, p. 384).

47 See MS A, fol. 55r–v (Wilkins, p. 346).

48 MS A, fols 35r, 58r (Wilkins, pp. 342, 347); Sandys, 'Financial and Administrative Importance of the London Temple', pp. 147–62.

49 MS A fol. 160r–v (Wilkins, pp. 383–4).

50 Finke, *Papsttum und Untergang*, vol. 2, p. 330.

51 MS A, fols 105v, 120v (Wilkins, pp. 365, 370).

52 MS A, fol. 168v (Wilkins, p. 392); *Registrum Simonis de Gandavo*, vol. 1, p. 404.

53 See above, chapter five.

54 MS A, fols 161r–162v (Wilkins, pp. 384–6).

55 See above, chapter five.

56 MS A, fol. 98v, 99v (Wilkins, pp. 362–3); MS C, fol. 7v (Schottmüller, p. 92); MS D, fol. 188v (*Annales Londonienses,* ed. Stubbs, p. 194).

57 MS A, fols 164v–165r (Wilkins, p. 388).

58 MS A, fol. 162v (Wilkins, pp. 386–7).

59 MS A, fol. 58r (Wilkins, p. 347).

60 MS A, fol. 163v (Wilkins, p. 387). Amblard of St Romain was master in England from 1262–66: Bulst-Thiele, *Sacrae domus,* p. 235, note 11. Imbert de Perowe or Peraud first appears as 'master of the knighthood of the Temple in England' in the English government records early in 1268 (*Close Rolls of the Reign of Henry III, AD 1264–1268,* p. 514) but on 16 June 1271 he was leaving England for the Holy Land, presumably to give up his office (*CPR, 1266-1272,* p. 542), as by 10 March 1272 Guy of the Forest was master or grand commander in England (ibid., p. 635). He had previously been grand commander of the Templars' province of France, and also held the grand commandership of Aquitaine simultaneously with England: Bulst-Thiele, *Sacrae domus,* p. 300, note 29. He went on to become visitor of the Order. Hugh de Peraud was his nephew. I am indebted to Jochen Burgtorf for his help with establishing Imbert de Peraud's career.

61 MS A, fol. 163v (Wilkins, p. 387).

62 Silvia Schein, 'The Templars: the Regular Army of the Holy Land and the Spearhead of the Army of its Reconquest', in *I Templari: Mito e Storia,* ed. Giovanni Minnuci and Franca Sardi (Siena, 1989), pp. 15–25, here p. 23.

63 MS A, fol. 163v (Wilkins, p. 387).

64 MS A, fol. 163v (Wilkins, p. 387); *Règle,* sections 163, 613–15, trans. Upton-Ward, pp. 99, 157–8; Odo of Deuil, *De profectione Ludovici VII in orientem,* ed. Virginia G. Berry (New York, 1948), pp. 124–8, 134.

65 MS A, fol. 165v (Wilkins, p. 389).

66 MS A, fol. 164r–v (Wilkins, pp. 387–8); Schottmüller, pp. 153, 205, 346; Gilmour-Bryson, *Trial of the Templars in Cyprus,* pp. 53, 134–5, 349–52.

67 On this repetition of familiar material by witnesses in heresy trials, see Arnold, *Inquisition and Power,* pp. 74–6.

68 MS A, fol. 166r (Wilkins, pp. 389–90).

69 MS A, fol. 166r (Wilkins, p. 390).

70 MS C, fol. 7r–v (Schottmüller, pp. 91–2).

71 MS D, fols 178v, 184r–v, 186r, 187r (*Annales Londonienses,* ed. Stubbs, pp. 184, 190, 192, 193). This story is cited as a firsthand Templar confession by Michael C. Prestwich, 'The court of Edward II', in *The Reign of Edward II: New Perspectives,* ed. Gwilym Dodd and Anthony Musson (Woodbridge, 2006), p. 71.

72 MS D, fols 184v, 189v (*Annales Londonienses,* ed. Stubbs, pp. 190, 195).

73 MS D, fol. 184r (*Annales Londonienses,* ed. Stubbs, p. 190).

74 *Annales Londonienses,* ed. Stubbs, p. xxviii.

75 Ibid., pp. xxii–xxvii, xli; Catto, 'Andrew Horn: Law and History in fourteenth-century England', in *The Writing of History in the Middle Ages,* ed. Davis and Wallace-Hadrill, pp. 367–91; Jeremy Catto, 'Horn, Andrew (*c.*1275–1328)', *ODNB,* vol. 28, pp. 114–15.

76 Sandys, 'Financial and Administrative Importance of the London Temple', pp. 147–62.; MS A, fol. 166v, 168r, 168v (Wilkins, pp. 390, 391).

77 MS A, fol. 166v (Wilkins, p. 390).

78 MS A, fol. 166v, quotation on 167v (Wilkins, pp. 390, 391).

79 MS A, fols 166v–167r (Wilkins omits).

80 MS A, fols 166v–167v (Wilkins, p. 390).

81 MS A, fols 167v–168r (Wilkins, p. 391).

82 J.S. Hamilton, 'Lords Ordainer (*act.* 1310–1313)', *ODNB*, vol. 34, pp. 443–5.

83 MS A, fol. 168r (Wilkins, p. 391).

84 MS A, fol. 168v (Wilkins, pp. 391–2).

85 MS A, fol. 169r–v (Wilkins, p. 392).

86 MS A, fols 168v–169v (Wilkins, p. 392); Forey, 'Ex-Templars', pp. 18–37.

87 MS A, fols 3v, 7r, 170r (Wilkins, pp. 331, 393).

88 MS A, fol. 170r (Wilkins, p. 393).

89 *Councils and Synods*, ed. Powicke and Cheney, vol. 2, pt 2, pp. 1319.

90 Ibid. pp. 1338–9; for the abjuration see also *Chronicle of Walter of Guisborough*, p. 395.

91 *CCR, 1307-1313*, pp. 373, 384; *Councils and Synods*, ed. Powicke and Cheney, vol. 2, pt 2, p. 1339.

92 Forey, 'Ex-Templars', p. 22; *Foedera*, ed. Rymer, vol. 2, pt 1, pp. 140, 141; MS A, fol. 91v (Wilkins, p. 358); and see above, chapter two.

93 Cheney, *Notaries Public*, p. 38; *Councils and Synods*, vol. 2, pt 1, ed. Powicke and Cheney, pp. 1324–8.

94 Callan, '"No such art"', p. 55, n. 133, citing Philomena Connolly's forthcoming edition of the justiciary roll for 6–7 Edward II.

95 Wood, pp. 357–9.

96 *CCR, 1307-1313*, pp. 365, 369, 370, 373, 375, 468, 473, 490, 497, 504, 509, 512, 521.

97 *Foedera*, ed. Rymer, vol. 2, pt 1, pp. 144, 148, 149, 150.

98 Ibid. pp. 155, 157, 166; *CPR, 1307-1313*, pp. 414, 440, 442, 453, 466; *CCR, 1307-1313*, pp. 410, 414, 426–7.

99 Maddicott, *Thomas of Lancaster*, p. 34.

100 *Foedera*, ed. Rymer, vol. 2, pt 1, p. 154; Prestwich, 'The Ordinances of 1311'; Hamilton, *Piers Gaveston*, pp. 79–89, 94, 164, n. 36.

101 Hamilton, *Piers Gaveston*, pp. 87–94.

102 Barber, *Trial of the Templars*, 2nd edn, pp. 267–9; *Foedera*, ed. Rymer, vol. 2, pt 1, pp. 167–9.

103 Hamilton, *Piers Gaveston*, pp. 95–9, 104–5.

104 *Foedera*, ed. Rymer, vol. 2, pt 1, pp. 169, 171, 172, 173, 180; *CPR, 1307-1313*, pp. 461, 465, 466, 467, 481, 484, 486, 501, 504, 511, etc.; *CCR, 1307-1313*, pp. 424, 467, 482.

105 *Foedera*, ed. Rymer, vol. 2, pt 1, p. 174; *CCR, 1307-1313*, p. 544.

106 Hamilton, *Piers Gaveston*, pp. 104–5.

107 *Foedera*, ed. Rymer, vol. 2, pt 1, pp. 182–4.

108 Ibid. pp. 209, 211, 214, 225, 235, 236–7; J.R.S. Phillips, *Aymer de Valence, Earl of Pembroke 1307–1324: Baronial Politics in the Reign of Edward II* (Oxford, 1972), pp. 71–2 and p. 72, n. 2. I am very grateful to Jochen Burgtorf for the information relating to the family background of Albert of Schwarzburg: see Jochen Burgtorf, *The Central Convent of Hospitallers and Templars: History, Organization, and Personnel (1099/1120–1310)* (Leiden, 2008).

Conclusion

The Council of Vienne
and the End of the Templars

The contemporary scholar Ptolemy of Lucca, a Dominican friar, described events at the Council of Vienne:

> Around the middle of October [1311] began the first session of the Council, which dealt with three matters: the Templars, the crusade to the Holy Land and the reform of the Church. The prelates and the cardinals were summoned to discuss the Templars. The prelates read proceedings of their trials, and those who had assembled were asked by the pope under seal whether he should give the Templars a hearing or defence. All the prelates of Italy except one, and all those of Spain, Germany, Denmark, England, Scotland and Ireland agreed that he should. So did the French, except for three archbishops, those of Reims, Sens and Rouen. This was done or transacted at the beginning of December.
>
> … In the same year, that is 1312, in the month of April, the Order of the Templars, both its persons and property, was condemned in the Council. The pope reserved the property for his own decision, in virtue of the Council and the college of cardinals.[1]

The Church Council at Vienne in France, which opened 1 October 1311, discussed the Templars' case alongside other heresies. The Council was a year late: back in early August 1308 when Pope Clement V had initially called the Council to discuss the Templars' affair, he had expected it to begin on 1 October 1310. But because the trial of the Templars had proceeded much more slowly than then foreseen, it was clear by early 1310 that the collection of evidence would not be completed in time, and so Pope Clement had postponed the opening of the Council for twelve months.[2]

No official list of delegates survives, but the records from the English bishoprics allow us to reconstruct the English contingent. There was Archbishop William Greenfield of York, who was acting not only for his own province but also representing King Edward II. Bishop Walter Reynolds of Worcester, who was royal chancellor, also represented the king. The bishops of London, Winchester and Carlisle also attended. Archbishop Robert Winchelsey of Canterbury and Bishop John Dalderby of Lincoln did not attend, but sent representatives. Master Walter of Wermington attended as representative of the bishop, dean and chapter of Lincoln cathedral. There were also representatives from the Benedictine monks and the Augustinian canons of the province of Canterbury.[3]

On 27 December 1311 Henry Fykeis, proctor at the papal court, wrote to Bishop John Salmon of Norwich about the progress of the Council, among other matters. He noted that the majority of the prelates wanted the Templars to be allowed to defend themselves, but five or six of the French prelates disagreed. The other delegates feared that the king of France would come to the Council with his army to force his wishes on them. Henry suggested that the pope might adjourn the Council and move it to a safer location (such as Avignon, outside the king of France's area of authority), in order to avoid the king of France's wrath.[4]

Although the Council made decisions about other heresies – condemning the freewheeling religious movement known as 'the heresy of the Free Spirit' and the radical concept of poverty held by the Spiritual Franciscans[5] – it remained divided over the Templars' affair. On 22 March 1312 Pope Clement V took the decision to dissolve the Order of the Temple, although he did not announce this publicly until two weeks later, on 3 April. He did not condemn the Order as guilty, but stated that no one should enter the Order, wear its habit or follow its Rule; anyone who did would be excommunicated. On 2 May he transferred the bulk of the Order's property to the Hospital of St John of Jerusalem, which would continue the Templars' vocation of defending Christendom.[6] On 6 May he declared by papal bull that the brothers of the Temple who had been acknowledged to be innocent, or who had confessed and been reconciled to the Church, would receive a pension and could live in the Order's former houses or in a monastery. As their monastic vows were still valid, they could not return to secular life.

Those Templars who were known to be guilty but who had not confessed, or those who had relapsed, would be tried.[7]

This last category included the grand master and three of the four provincial commanders of the Order in France: the grand commander of Normandy, Geoffrey de Charney; the grand commander of Aquitaine and Poitou, Geoffrey of Goneville; and the visitor and grand commander of the Île de la France, Hugh Peraud. In late December 1313 the pope set up a commission to judge them. Jacques de Molay tried to defend the Order, and was amazed to hear the final judgement on 18 March 1314: the four were condemned to eternal imprisonment as relapsed heretics. Jacques de Molay and Geoffrey de Charney protested loudly, and were condemned to burn as obdurate heretics that evening (plate 10).[8]

The trial of the Templars in the British Isles had ended in summer 1311 when the Templars in England were despatched to monasteries, but there were still some loose ends to tie up. In April and May 1312 a Provincial Church Council for the province of Canterbury met at St Paul's cathedral, London. A slip of parchment included in the manuscript of the *Annales Londonienses* records the proceedings of this Council so far as they affected the Templars.[9]

First, Brother Thomas of Lindsey appeared before the Council, explaining that he had fled to Ireland before the arrest of the Templars and he now wished to stand trial. He was sent away to a monastery to perform penance.

Then, some women appeared before the Council, alleging that some of the Templars of the Province of Canterbury were their husbands, and claiming them back. The council decided that they should do 'whatever right demands and requires'. As the men would have had to have obtained their wives' permission for a separation in order to join the Templars, and the dissolution of the Order had not changed this situation, the women would not have received their menfolk back.

Next, as the Templars had been doing their penance now for six months or more, the Council considered investigating whether they were performing it as they should. The decision was that no action was needed unless there were complaints.

Finally, although the pope had instructed that certain Templars should be referred to him for absolution or condemnation, nothing final had been done about this. The Council decided to proceed with the remaining Templars on the same lines as had been followed with the others.

Pope Clement had reserved judgement on the grand commander in England, William de la More, but in fact neither the grand commander nor his guest Himbert Blanc, grand commander of the Auvergne, ever received a final judgement. William de la More died in the Tower of London in December 1312. Himbert Blanc remained in prison; on 6 April 1313, the king instructed the sheriffs of London to hand him over to Archbishop Winchelsey of Canterbury, to be dealt with according to ecclesiastical law. The outcome is unclear, but Himbert was still alive on 8 February 1314, when Edward wrote to the prior of the Hospital of St John of Jerusalem in England about the former Templar's pension. When the archbishop of Canterbury and the Provincial Council (he wrote) had decided to send the Templars to monasteries to do penance, and that they should receive four pence per day, the grand commander of the Temple had been granted two shillings per day; as the grand commander was now dead, on the request of Lord Louis of Clermont, Edward had granted the two shillings to Himbert Blanc. He asked the prior to ensure that the Templars received the four pence per day from the revenues of their former properties, and that Himbert Blanc should receive two shillings per day.[10]

Alan Forey has traced the history of the Templars in England after 1311. By the end of September 1311 the Templars had all been dispersed to different monasteries. Various religious Orders were used: Benedictines, Cistercians and regular canons.[11] It would be pleasant to think that the Templars were sent back to their home counties, but there is no evidence of this. William of Pocklington or Pokelington, who to judge from his surname was from Pocklington in the East Riding of Yorkshire, had served the lord of Barmston in Holderness (East Riding) and joined the Templars at Ribston (West Riding), but was sent to the Cluniac priory of St Andrew in Northamptonshire.[12] Ralph of Evesham, who was received at Upleadon near Evesham, and so presumably came from the Herefordshire/Gloucestershire area, was assigned to a monastery further north and east, in the diocese of Coventry and Lichfield.[13] However, Templars who had been overseas could be sent back to their homeland after the dissolution of their Order: Richard of Grafton, who in 1309 was in Cyprus, was back in England in the diocese of Winchester in 1313.[14] Likewise, the Templar procurator-general Pietro da Bologna, whom many scholars have believed was murdered for his attempts to defend the Order in France, in fact returned to his home town of Bologna in Italy, where he died in 1329.[15]

The penances were not particularly severe – the Templars were not kept in chains. Yet, as Forey points out, modern readers may think it unjust that the Templars should have had to perform any sort of penance for sins they had always denied and of which they had not been found guilty by a court of law.[16] The harshest penance assigned to the Templars from the province of Canterbury was to be confined to their room at all times except when attending church. They were allowed out into the monastery enclosure for fresh air (but not outside the monastery) only once a week for four hours. Food included cheap meat twice a week, fish on four days and fasting on bread and water on Fridays. A large number of prayers had to be recited daily. John of Moun, John of Ecle or Eagle, Robert of Hameldon and John of Stoke, former treasurer of the New Temple, were among those who were given this severe punishment. Forey suggests that the main reason for the harsh penance for John of Stoke was of his long period of service: when first interrogated, he had been in the Order for seventeen years. In the same way, John of Moun had been in the Order for around thirty-eight years at the time he was first questioned, while John of Eagle and Robert of Hameldon had both been in the Order for around twenty years. At the other end of the scale, Templars with the least severe penance could take exercise in the monastery gardens twice a week, could eat meat three days a week and fish on three days a week, and had no additional prayers to say. This level of penance was given to Templars who had been in the Order for less than four years, such as Robert of Sautre, who had joined the Order just over a year before the arrests.[17] As Forey points out, while the restrictions on eating meat would have been familiar, the forced enclosure and lack of purpose would have been the most punishing part of the penance. The Templars were not used to being kept enclosed in one house; they had joined an active Order and expected to work.

Of course, we do not know how far the Templars actually followed their penitential regime. Some Templars lived quietly and caused no problems to anyone. The bishops' registers record that a few Templars caused trouble in the monasteries where they were housed. Henry Craven, who had been sent to Pontefract Abbey, was excommunicated for continuing to wear his Templar habit in violation of the pope's prohibition; in September 1312 the archbishop of York absolved him and sent him back to Pontefract with instructions to the prior and monks to keep him and look after him until the pope sent further instructions.[18] Roger of Sheffield escaped from Kirkstall Abbey and had to be tracked down and sent back, while Thomas of Staunford was accused of insulting the abbot and monks of Fountains Abbey. Some abbey communities simply did not want the responsibility of looking after these alleged heretics – even though the Templars had nearly all denied the charges and had abjured all heresy.[19] They also looked askance at the costs involved – the Templars' pensions did not always arrive promptly, and even when they did, some Templars refused to pay for their upkeep.[20]

In December 1318 Pope John XXII issued new instructions for the Templars. Concerned by reports that former Templars had gone back to living like secular knights and had married, he instructed that the bishops summon the Templars and assign them to approved religious houses. Only two could go to a single house, unless it was a house of the Hospitallers, which could take more than two former Templars.

The English Templars had not gone back to secular life, but were all living in their assigned monasteries. Still, those who were unhappy where they were could now move to another house. Some English Templars stayed put, but others moved, and a few moved to be with another former Templar: so Ralph of Ruston and William of Middleton were at Bridlington after 1319, and Thomas the Chamberlain and Simon Streche were at Spalding.[21]

By 1338, only thirteen of the Templars in Britain were still alive and receiving maintenance from the Hospitallers: one, Roger of Dalton, was custodian of the Hospitallers' house at Ashley in Cambridgeshire; the rest (including Thomas Totty and the priest Roger of Stowe) were receiving pensions.[22]

The Templars' Heirs: the Hospitallers

The fact that many of the Templars' former properties in England continued to be called 'Temple' long after the Order was dissolved, is a measure of the continuing respect for its memory at local level. At an international level matters were less clear. Pope Clement V had ordered that these lands should pass to the Hospitallers, but those who had seized the lands did not want to give them up. The preamble to the 'Statutum de Terris Templariorum' (statute regarding the Templars' lands) of 1324 explains how the English Parliament finally decided to hand the former Templar estates over to the Hospital of St John of Jerusalem. The Parliament at Westminster in February 1324 discussed whether the English lords could, by the law of the land and with safe conscience, retain these Templars lands. The king's council, including the justices, stated that they could. However, Parliament decided that because the lands had originally been given for religious purposes – to defend Christendom and the Holy Land – the lands should be held by religious persons. So Parliament ordained that no one should keep possession of any former Templar property.[23] This decision allowed the Hospitallers to gain most of the Templars' lands, yet it was not until the 1330s that the Hospitallers recovered the New Temple in London, and some of the Templars' property remained forever out of their reach, retained by the great nobles or the king's friends.[24]

Looking back over events, English writers differed in their views of the Templars and Hospitallers during the trial and its aftermath. In the late 1320s or 1330s, Adam of Murimuth, a cleric who acted as a diplomat for Archbishop Winchelsey and King Edward II among others, began to write a history of the years 1303–47. He referred to the 'lamentable crime of heresy' of which the Templars had been accused and said that the Templars admitted there were rumours of heresy but that no crimes had been committed, except by one or two troublemakers. At last, they had all admitted they could not purge themselves and were condemned by the Council to perpetual penance. Each was sent to a different monastery to carry this out, where they afterwards followed exemplary lives. The pope, Clement V, then held a council at Vienne, at which the Templars were condemned.

> The king of France, Philip called 'the Fair', was present and brought this about, because he hoped to make one of his sons king of Jerusalem and that all the Templars' lands would be given to this son. This proposal was justly thwarted, for the pope gave the Templars' possessions to the Hospitallers.

The pope sent his representatives to England to effect the transfer of lands, but all the nobles and counts of England resisted them, because their ancestors had given the lands and possessions to the Templars, and they had now taken them back.[25] Geoffrey Baker of Swinbrook in Oxfordshire, writing during the mid-fourteenth century, followed Adam of Murimuth but added some details:

> The king of France, Philip called 'the Fair' ... held the grand master of the Order in hatred because the master had been importuning him to repay the money which the head of the French Province [of the Order] had once lent the king for the marriage of his daughter Isabel, queen of England. Also,

the same King Philip hoped that one of his sons would be crowned as king of Jerusalem, and would be endowed with the plunder from the destroyed knights of God's Temple. And for this reason, he procured the burning of the aforesaid master and many others of that Order who were established in his kingdom, and that the [Church] Council should annihilate the whole Order. But his intended cruel greed was not satisfied, for the pope assigned the lands and possessions of the annulled brothers to the Hospitallers.

Geoffrey continued on the same lines as Adam, explaining that the pope's representatives came to England but 'the English nobles, whose ancestors had endowed the Templars with ample booty, resisted them, and when the Order had been condemned they occupied the possessions which had reverted to their hands'.[26]

At St Albans in the late fourteenth century, Thomas of Walsingham had a slightly different view of events:

Then Philip, king of France, planned to make one of his sons king of Jerusalem and get for him all the revenues and incomes of the Templars, and on these grounds he had earlier procured to have many Templars in his kingdom and especially the grand master of the Order and many others burned, and he procured and brought about the condemnation of the Order in the Council aforesaid. But, however, his intention for their revenues was not put into effect, because the pope assigned these to the Hospitallers; not without the intervention of a great deal of money.[27]

The Hospitallers were criticised for more than bribing the pope. The trial, it appeared, had changed the whole character of their Order. In the town of Sherborne, in Dorset, around 1399–1407, a scribe named John Whas produced a missal – a prayer book – which was illustrated by John Siferwas and others.[28] At the bottom of the pages showing the words and music for 'Prefaces of the Mass', to be used every Sunday from Holy Trinity to Advent Sunday, are a series of roundels containing the heads of men in religious dress. The roundels on page 371 show Templars and Hospitallers (plate 41). The accompanying text explains:

In the year of Our Lord 1180 the Order of the Templars began at Jerusalem in the portico of Solomon, from knights organised for the defence of Christendom.

> And in the year 1309 they are all arrested in one day and destroyed through-
> out the whole world on account of their idolatry, and their possessions given
> to the Hospitallers, who then began to be demanding.

What the producers of the Sherborne missal remembered about the
Templars was their beginnings in Jerusalem, their defence of Christendom,
and their dramatic fall. By the time the Sherborne missal was produced,
the Hospitallers were active in campaigns against the Ottoman Turks in the
Balkans and on the sea; but all that these men of Somerset knew of them
was that they had acquired the Templars' lands and caused trouble for their
neighbours in the process.

The Templars in the British Isles had denied all charges of heresy. In Ireland,
grand commander Henry Danet had accused Templars overseas of heretical practices; in England, three Templars finally confessed to some of the
charges, but only after they had been tortured. The Templars in the British
Isles agreed that new members were received in a private ceremony, but
insisted that nothing heretical occurred there. Some conceded that servants
who misbehaved were flogged by a lay official of the Order who spoke
words suggesting that the flogging was a religious ceremony, in which
case a priest should have performed it. All that could be proved against the
Templars was that some did not understand the crucial difference between
a sin against God, which could be absolved only by a priest, and a crime
against the Order, which could be punished or forgiven by a layman.
Apparently, the Templars in the British Isles believed that their institution
was so dedicated to God's service that breaking any of the Order's regulations was a sin.

Yet the summaries of the proceedings produced for the Church
Councils at London and at Vienne presented the evidence in such a way
that the Templars in the British Isles appeared guilty of all charges. By
quoting from the confessions of Templars from England who had been
interrogated under torture in France, the inquisitors could claim to have
firsthand evidence of misconduct in the British Isles. By repeating again
and again gossip reported by the likes of William of Jafford and Agnes
Cocacota, the summarisers built up a picture of the Templars in the British
Isles as idolators and sodomites. By emphasising the Templars' tight command structure, the inquisitors could claim that because Grand Master
Jacques de Molay had confessed to the charges, all the Templars must be

guilty; and because the French Templars had confessed, the Templars in the British Isles must be guilty too. So the inquisitors in the British Isles constructed their own version of the Templars which bore little resemblance to the actual Templars' own testimonies, and so justified the dissolution of the Order of the Temple, eight months before the pope formally dissolved it. Although the Templars in the British Isles were not declared guilty, because they had to reject all heresies before they were readmitted to the Church it appeared to outsiders that they were guilty – so the authors of the Sherborne missal, for example, believed that they had been guilty of idolatry. A determined king might have saved them, but King Edward II of England found that the dissolved Order's property was more useful to him than the Order itself. So the Templars in the British Isles passed into history, gone but not forgotten.

Notes

1 'Secunda Vita Clementis V auctore Ptolemao Lucensi, ordinis Praedicatorum, excerpta ex Historia ecclesiastica', in Étienne Baluze, *Vitae Paparum Avenionensium*, ed. G. Mollat, vol. 1 (Paris, 1914), pp. 42, 43.

2 *Councils and Synods*, ed. Powicke and Cheney, vol. 2, pt 2, pp. 1350–1.

3 Ibid., pp. 1351–2 and notes.

4 TNA:PRO SC1/58/16; printed by C.L. Langlois in *Revue historique*, 87 (1905), p. 73–6. For a discussion of the debates at the Council of Vienne, see William Chester Jordan, *Unceasing Strife, Unending Fear: Jacques de Thérines and the Freedom of the Church in the Age of the Last Capetians* (Princeton, 2005), pp. 40–55.

5 Malcolm Lambert, *Medieval Heresy: Popular Movements from the Gregorian Reform to the Reformation*, 3rd edn (Oxford, 2002), pp. 204–5, 212, 226; Robert E. Lerner, *The Heresy of the Free Spirit in the Later Middle Ages* (Berkeley, CA., 1972; repr. Notre Dame, Ind., 1993), pp. 78–84; Burr, *Spiritual Franciscans*, pp. 111–58.

6 These proceedings are described more fully by Barber, *Trial of the Templars*, 2nd edn, pp. 267–71; Menache, *Clement V*, pp. 235–9.

7 *Considerantes dudum*, 6 May 1312: see Barber, *Trial of the Templars*, 2nd edn, pp. 278–9.

8 Barber, *Trial of the Templars*, 2nd edn, pp. 281–2.

9 *Councils and Synods*, ed. Powicke and Cheney, vol. 2, pt 2, pp. 1369–70; *Annales Londonienses*, ed. Stubbs, pp. 176–9; British Library Cotton MS Otho B iii, fol. 28r.

10 *Foedera*, ed. Rymer, vol. 2, pt 1, pp. 198, 243; *CCR, 1307-1313*, pp. 508, 523, 533; on the death of William de la More, see Perkins, 'Trial of the Knights Templars in England', p. 443; Forey, 'Ex-Templars', p. 20.

11 Forey, 'Ex-Templars', p. 22.

12 Ibid., p. 23; MS A, fols 43v, 99r (Wilkins, pp. 344, 362; misreads 'Wermeston' for 'Berneston'); Dr John Walker of Hull University informed me that Berneston is an old spelling of Barmston. I am very grateful to Dr Walker for his help with this point.

13 MS A, fol. 111r (Wilkins, p. 366); Gooder, p. 148.

14 Forey, 'Ex-Templars', p. 36, note 101.

15 Elena Bellomo, *The Templar Order in North-west Italy (1142–c. 1330)* (Leiden, 2008), pp. 206–7.

16 Forey, 'Ex-Templars', p. 27.

17 Ibid., pp. 24-6; *Registrum Simonis de Gandavo*, vol. 1, p. 404; MS A, fols 33v, 40r, 104r, 105v, MS B fol. 73r (Wilkins, pp. 342, 343, 365).

18 *Register of William Greenfield*, part 5, p. 8.

19 Forey, 'Ex-Templars', pp. 23–24, 27, 28.

20 Ibid., pp. 28–30.

21 Ibid., pp. 31–33 and note 84.

22 L&K, pp. 121, 209.

23 James Davies, *The Baronial Opposition to Edward II: its Character and Policy. A Study in Administrative History* (London, 1918 repr. 1967), p. 290.

24 For further discussion, see Helen Nicholson, 'The Hospitallers in England, the Kings of England and Relations with Rhodes in the Fourteenth Century', *Sacra Militia: Rivista di Storia Degli Ordini Militari*, 2 (2002), pp. 25–45; Perkins, 'Wealth of the Knights Templars', pp. 259–63.

25 Adæ Murimuth, *Continuatio Chronicarum*, ed. Edward Maunde Thompson, Rolls Series 93 (London, 1889), pp. 13, 14–15, 16; C.L. Kingsford, 'Murimuth, Adam (1274/5–1347)', rev. Wendy R. Childs, *ODNB*, vol. 39, pp. 825–6.

26 *Chronicon Galfridi Le Baker de Swynebroke*, ed. Edward Maunde Thompson (Oxford, 1889), pp. 5–6, 185.

27 *Chronica monasterii S. Albanii Thomae Walsingham*, ed. Henry T. Riley, 2 vols, Rolls Series 28 (London, 1863–4), vol. 1, p. 127.

28 London, British Library, Add. MS 74236, p. 371; details from the online catalogue at British Library Images Online, http://www.imagesonline.bl.uk/; see also Janet Backhouse, *The Sherborne Missal* (London, 1999), pp. 13, 37, 44 (fig. 39).

Appendix 1

Templar brothers in the British Isles in 1308–1311

Templars whose names are in italics were not interrogated. For abbreviations, see p. 6.

	Name	Office, location and source	Sent to diocese and/or assigned to monastery for penance (P); death
1	*Adam of Crayk or Creyke*	Formerly *claviger* (keyholder) at Temple Hirst: TNO:PRO E 142/18 mem. 1 dorse	Died before interrogation
2	Adam of Langeport	Kilcloggan in Ireland: MacNiocaill, p.200	
3	*Adam the Mazun*	New Temple, London: Gooder, p. 147	Died 16 February 1308: TNA: PRO E358/18 rot. 7(1), under 'Exp'
4	Alan of Newesom (Newsam)	Shipley: MS A, fol. 58v	P: Revesby Abbey, Lincoln diocese: *CCR, 1307–1313*, p. 365; Forey, 'Ex-Templars', p. 32 n. 77. Still alive in 1338: L&K, p. 209
5	Alexander of Althon (Halton)	Bruer: Gooder, pp. 148–9	Died during trial? Not in London in April 1311, not absolved in July 1311
6	Alexander of Bulbeke	Denney: MS A, fol. 58r	Died during trial? Not in London in April 1311, not absolved in July 1311
7	*Edm Latimer, called 'Barvill'*	Fugitive: *Register of William Greenfield*, part 4, p. 337	

	Name	Office, location and source	Sent to diocese and/or assigned to monastery for penance (P); death
8	*Geoffrey Joliffe*	Eagle: Gooder, p. 149	Died in Lincoln Castle 25 Jan. 1308: TNA:PRO E358/18 rot. 18 dorse
9	Geoffrey of Welton/ Winton/ Wilton	Thornton: TNA:PRO E142/11 mem. 1 dorse	P: York diocese: *CCR, 1307–13*, p. 373; possibly Whitby Abbey: *Register of William Greenfield*, part 5, p. 8, n. 1
10	Godfrey de Archis (of Bowes)	Commander of Newsam	P: York diocese: *CCR, 1307–1313*, p. 373
11	Henry of Aslackby (Haselakeby)	Ireland	
12	Henry of Cravene	Ribston: TNA:PRO E142/18 mem 1 dorse	P: Pontefract Abbey, York diocese: *CCR, 1307–1313*, p. 373; *Register of William Greenfield*, part 5, p. 8
13	Henry Danet /Hanet	Grand commander of Ireland; his bed was at Cooley (aka Templetown) in Louth: MacNiocaill, p. 191	
14	Henry of the Ford	Ireland: MacNiocaill, p. 220	
15	Henry of Halthon/ Althon	Lieutenant-commander of Lydley: Gooder, p. 149	P: Coventry and Lichfield diocese: *CCR, 1307–1313*, p. 375
16	Henry of Kerby	Keyholder at Cowton: TN: PRO E142/18 mem. 1 dorse	P: Rievaulx Abbey, York diocese, later moved to Selby Abbey: *CCR, 1307–1313*, p. 373; Forey, 'Ex-Templars', pp. 24, 33
17	*Henry the Marshal*	Willoughton: Gooder, p. 148; TNA:PRO E358/18 rot. 15	Died before interrogation
18	Henry Mautravers	Ireland	
19	Henry Paul/ Pawel	Dinsley: MS A, fol. 58v	P: Chichester diocese: *CCR, 1307–1313*, p. 365
20	Henry of Rouclifis/ Rouchecliff/ Routheclif/ Rawcliffe	Keyholder at Ribston: TNA: PRO E142/18 mem. 1 dorse; TNA:PRO E358/18 rot. 31 recto	P: York diocese: *CCR, 1307–1313*, p. 373. Still alive in 1338: L&K, p. 209

	Name	Office, location and source	Sent to diocese and/or assigned to monastery for penance (P); death
21	Henry of Wickala/ Wythcal	Based in Lincoln diocese, England	P: Worcester diocese: *CCR, 1307–1313*, p. 365
22	Henry de la Wole/Valey /la Valicia/ Wolde	Eagle: Gooder, p. 149	Described as old and decrepit; abjured and was absolved 13 July 1311: MS A, fol. 168v
23	Himbert Blanc/Imbert Blank	Grand commander of the Auvergne; knight	Died in prison, probably in 1314: Forey, 'Ex-Templars', p. 20 n. 14
24	Hugh of Broghem/ Brouthton	Custodian of Kilsaran, in Ireland: MacNiocaill, p. 196	
25	*Hugh of Kyrketon/ Kirketoft*	Strood: arrested in Kent in January 1308 and held at Rochester Castle	Died 1 Nov. 1308: TNA: PRO E358/18 mem. 7(1)
26	Hugh of Tadecaster	Denney: MS A, fol. 58r; keyholder before joining the Order	P: Lincoln diocese: *CCR, 1307–1313*, p. 365
	Imbert *see* Himbert		
27	Ivo of Hoghton/ Etton	Commander of Temple Hirst TNA: PRO E142/18 mem. 1 dorse	P: York diocese: *CCR, 1307–1313*, p. 373
28	John of Bela sala/Balsall	Aslackby: Gooder, p. 148	P: Worcester diocese: *CCR, 1307–1313*, p. 365.
29	John de Cannville/J de Kanvyle	England. Testimony not included in MS A, but referred to in MS C	Died before March 1310
30	John Coffin	Cressing: MS A, fol. 58v	P: Norwich diocese: *CCR, 1307–1313*, p. 365. Still alive in 1338: L&K, p. 209
31	John of Coningeston	Commander of Guiting: MS A, fol. 58v	P: Worcester diocese: *CCR, 1307–1313*, p. 365
32	John of Ebreston	Fugitive: MS A, fol. 156v; gave himself up before 4 May 1310: MS A, fol. 133r	P: Sawley Abbey, York diocese: *CCR, 1307–1313*, p. 373; *Register of William Greenfield*, part 5, p. 3.
33	John of Euleye/eule/ Yvleath/Uley/ Aley	Combe: TNA: PRO E142/111 mem. 2 dorse	Died after the first interrogations: MS A, fol. 84r

	Name	Office, location and source	Sent to diocese and/or assigned to monastery for penance (P); death
34	John of Eyglas/Eycle/ Aykle /Eagle	Bruer: Gooder, pp. 148–9	P: Reading Abbey: *Registrum Simonis de Gandavo*, vol. 1, p. 403
35	John of Faversham	Ireland	
36	John of Grafton	Willoughton: Gooder, p. 148	P: Coventry and Lichfield diocese: *CCR, 1307–1313*, p. 375
37	*John de Hauwile or Hamil*	Denney: fol. 58r, and see TNA: PRO E358/18 rot. 11	*Demens* (insane)
38	*John of Husflet/ Huseflet/Usflete*	English by birth; commander of Balantrodoch for 2 years before Walter de Clifton, i.e. before Nov. 1306: MS A, fol. 156v. Fugitive: *Register of William Greenfield*, part 4, p. 337	
39	John of Moune	Commander at Duxford: MS A, fol. 58r	P: Malmesbury Abbey: *Registrum Simonis de Gandavo*, vol. 1, p. 403
40	John of Newent	Denney: MS A, fol. 58r. In Ludgate 30 April 1311: MS A, fol. 102r	Died before abjurations and absolutions of July 1311
41	*John of Poynton*	Fugitive: *Register of William Greenfield*, part 4, p. 337	
42	John Romayn	Ireland	
43	*John of Saddlecombe*	Eagle: Gooder, p. 149	P: Swineshead Abbey; Lincoln diocese; died early September 1311, not absolved: *CCR, 1307–1313*, p. 365; Forey, 'Ex-Templars', pp. 21, 34–5
44	John of Stoke	Priest at New Temple, and treasurer of London: MS A, fol. 58r	P: Lincoln diocese: *CCR, 1307–1313*, p. 365
45	John of Stoke, called 'of Sutton'	Commander of Sutton in Essex: a cripple: MS A, fols 58v, 89v	Abjured heresy 12 July 1311: MS A, fol. 168r; no further information
46	*John de Vale or du Vaal*	Eagle: Gooder, p. 149	Died 15 July 1308: TNA:PRO E358/18 rots 14, 18 dorse

	Name	Office, location and source	Sent to diocese and/or assigned to monastery for penance (P); death
47	John of Waddona/ Waldona	Priest, at Eagle: Gooder, p. 149	P: Worcester diocese: *CCR, 1307–1313*, p. 365
48	John of Walpole	Commander of Cowton TNA:PRO E142/18 mem. 1 dorse	P: Byland Abbey, York diocese: *CCR, 1307–1313*, p. 373; *Register of William Greenfield*, part 5, p. 8
49	John Wergrave	Balsall: Gooder, p. 147	P: Worcester diocese: *CCR, 1307–1313*, p. 365
50	John of Wirkeleye/ Wakeley/ Wakerley	Balsall: Gooder, p. 147	P: St Davids diocese: *CCR, 1307–1313*, p. 365
51	Michael de Baskerville	Commander of New Temple, London: MS A, fol. 58r	P: St Augustine's, Canterbury: *CCR, 1307–1313*, p. 497
52	*Michael de Karvyle*	Lydley? See MS A, fols 115v, 144v	Died before interrogation
53	Michael of Sowerby	Commander of Sowerby, custodian of Thornton	P: York diocese: *CCR, 1307–1313*, p. 373
54	*Michael of Sutton*	Ireland: *IEP*, p. 204	
55	*Patrick of Ripon*	Keyholder at Newsam: TNA: PRO E142/18 mem. 1 dorse	Died 29 October 1308: Gooder, p. 151
56	*Peter of Malvern*	Commander of Kilcloggan, Ireland: MacNiocaill, p. 199, 202	
57	Peter of Ottringham	Sergeant at New Temple, London: MS A, fol. 58r	P: Lincoln diocese: *CCR, 1307-1313*, p. 365
58	Philip de Meux	Knight, commander of Garway in 1308	Abjured heresy 9 July 1311: MS A, fols 166v–167r. No further information
59	Ralph of Barton	Priest, prior of New Temple, London: MS A, fol. 58r	P: Coventry and Lichfield diocese: *CCR, 1307–1313*, p. 375
60	Ralph of Bradley	Crook in Ireland: MacNiocaill, p. 209	
61	*Ralph of Bulford*	Fugitive: *Register of William Greenfield*, part 4, p. 337	
62	Ralph of Malton	Commander at Ewell: MS A, fol. 58r	P: Norwich diocese: *CCR, 1307–1313*, p. 365

	Name	Office, location and source	Sent to diocese and/or assigned to monastery for penance (P); death
63	Ralph of Ruston	Priest, at Faxfleet: TNA:PRO E142/18 mem. 1 dorse	P: York diocese; after 1319 moved to Bridlington Priory: *CCR, 1307–1313*, p. 373; Forey, 'Ex-Templars', p. 33
64	Ralph of Tanet/Chanet	Commander of Keele: Gooder, p. 149	P: Norwich diocese: *CCR, 1307–1313*, p. 365
65	Randulph of Evesham	Priest, at Bruer: Gooder, pp. 148–9	P: Coventry and Lichfield diocese: *CCR, 1307–1313*, p. 375
66	Richard of Brestsam/ Bistelesham	Bruer: Gooder, pp. 148–9	P: Coventry and Lichfield diocese: *CCR, 1307–1313*, p. 375
67	Richard of Burthesham/ Bustlesham	Ireland	
68	Richard of Casuyt/ Keselwik	Commander of Ribston: TNA:PRO E142/18 mem 1 dorse; also custodian of Wetherby: TNA: PRO E142/18 mem. 11	P: Kirkham Abbey, York diocese; later moved to Fountains Abbey: *CCR, 1307–1313*, p. 373; Forey, 'Ex-Templars', p. 33
69	Richard of Colingham	Sandford: MS A, fol. 58v	P: Bath and Wells diocese: *CCR, 1307-1313*, p. 391
70	*Richard Engayn*	Fugitive: *Register of William Greenfield*, part 4, p. 337	Arrested by end of 1311, sent to monastery in Bath and Wells diocese: Forey, 'Ex-Templars', p. 36, n. 101; *CCR, 1307–1313*, p. 391
71	*Richard of Hales*	Commander of Foulbridge: TNA:PRO E142/18 mem. 1 dorse	Died 23 June 1309: Gooder, p. 151
72	Richard of Herdwik	New Temple, London: MS A, fol. 58r	Died after 1st examination: MS A, fol. 84r
73	Richard of Newent	Aslackby: Gooder, p. 148	P: Wallingford Priory, Salisbury diocese: *CCR, 1307-1313*, p. 521; Forey, 'Ex-Templars', p. 21
74	Richard Poitevin	Dinsley: MS A, fol. 58v.	P: London diocese: *CCR, 1307–1313*, p. 369
75	Richard of Ripton/ Ripon	Foulbridge: TNA: PRO E142/18 mem. 1 dorse	P: York diocese: *CCR, 1307–1313*, p. 373; B. Abbey, possibly Bolton, or Burstall? *Register of William Greenfield*, part 5, p. 4

	Name	Office, location and source	Sent to diocese and/or assigned to monastery for penance (P); death
76	Richard of Upleadon	Ireland	
77	Robert of Amoldon (Hameldon)	Knight, at Balsall: Gooder, p. 147	P: Monkton Farleigh Priory: *Registrum Simonis de Gandavo*, vol. 1, p. 403; Forey, 'Ex-Templars', p. 21
78	*Robert of Bernewell*	Priest, at Eagle: Gooder, p. 149; TNA:PRO E358/18 rot. 18	Gooder, p. 149, states he did penance in Lincoln diocese. Same man as William de Barnwell?
79	Robert de Cavill (Cammvile)	Thornton: TNA:PRO E142/11, mem. 1, dorse	Died? Not sent to a monastery in Aug. 1311 to do penance: *Register of William Greenfield*, part 4, p. 336 n. 2
80	*Robert of Halton*	Eagle: Gooder, p. 149	Died 29 Dec. 1308: TNA:PRO E358/18 rot. 14
81	Robert of Langton	Commander of Whitley TNA:PRO E142/18 mem. 1 dorse	P: Bridlington Priory, York diocese: *CCR, 1307–1313*, p. 373; *Register of William Greenfield*, part 5, p. 8, n. 1.
82	Robert of Pourbrigge	Commander of Rathronan and Athkiltan in Ireland: MacNiocaill, pp. 212, 214	
83	Robert of Sautre	Ewell: MS A, fol. 58r	P: Abingdon Abbey: *Registrum Simonis de Gandavo*, vol. 1, p. 403; Forey, 'Ex-Templars', p. 25
84	Robert the Scot	Denney: MS A, fol. 58r; or Duxford: Gooder, p. 148	P: Ely diocese: *CCR, 1307–1313*, p. 365
85	Robert of Spanthon (Spaunton, Sprouton, Standon)	Willoughton: Gooder, p. 148	P: Norwich diocese: *CCR, 1307–1313*, p. 365
86	Robert of the Wolde	Listed under Essex in MS A, fol. 58v, but 'Essex' includes Dinsley in Hertfordshire	Old and decrepit. Abjured heresy and was absolved 13 July 1311: MS A, fol. 168v. No further information
87	Roger of Dalton	Denney: MS A, fol. 58r, or Duxford: Gooder, p. 148.	P: Ely diocese, possibly Barnwell Priory: *CCR, 1307-1313*, p. 365; Forey, 'Ex-Templars', p. 28, n. 51. Still alive in 1338: L&K, p. 121 (custodian of Ashley, Cambridgeshire)

	Name	Office, location and source	Sent to diocese and/or assigned to monastery for penance (P); death
88	Roger of Hogyndon or Hugande	Faxfleet: TNA:PRO E142/18 mem. 1 dorse	P: Guisborough Priory, York diocese; later went to a Hospitaller house: *CCR, 1307–1313*, p. 373; Forey, 'Ex-Templars', p. 33
89	*Roger of Lodelawe*	Denney: MS A, fol. 58r; mentioned fol. 54r; reported dead March 1310: ibid., fol. 84r; but in Ludgate April 1311: ibid., fol. 102r	Died before interrogation: MS A, fol. 84r
90	Roger the Norreis	Commander of Cressing in 1308: MS A, fol. 58v	P: Lincoln diocese: *CCR, 1307–1313*, p. 365
91	Roger of Sheffield or Thresk	Cowton in 1308: TN:PRO E 142/18 mem. 1 dorse	P: Kirkstall Abbey, York diocese: *CCR, 1307–1313*, p. 373; Forey, 'Ex-Templars', p. 24
92	Roger of Stowe	Priest; former Templar; left just before arrests with permission of William de la More: MS A, fol. 88r	P: Holy Trinity Priory, London: Forey, 'Ex-Templars', pp. 33–4. Still alive in 1338: L&K, p. 209
93	*Roger of Wyke*	Combe: TNA:PRO E 142/111 mem. 2 dorse	Died 15 April 1308: Gooder, p. 148
94	Simon of Streche	Knight, commander of Eagle: Gooder, p. 149	P: Spalding Priory, Lincoln diocese: *CCR, 1307–1313*, p. 365; Forey, 'Ex-Templars', p. 33 n. 84
95	Stephen of Radenhall (Redenay, Radeneth)	Commander of Westerdale TN:PRO E 142/18 mem. 1 dorse	P: Worksop Priory, York diocese: *CCR, 1307–1313*, p. 373; Forey, 'Ex-Templars', 22
96	Stephen of Stapelbrugge (Stalbridge)	Lydley: Gooder, p. 149; aide to William de Warenne in Ireland: *IEP*, pp. 204, 209	P: Winchester diocese: *CCR, 1307–1313*, p. 509
97	Thomas of Bolerby (Belleby)	Commander of Penhill TN:PRO E 142/18 mem. 1 dorse	P: York diocese: *CCR, 1307–1313*, p. 373
98	Thomas of Burton/ Barton	Priest, at New Temple, London: Gooder, p. 147; TNA: PRO E358/18 rot. 7(1); or Cressing: MS A, fol. 58r	P: Worcester diocese: *CCR, 1307–1313*, p. 521

	Name	Office, location and source	Sent to diocese and/or assigned to monastery for penance (P); death
99	Thomas the Chamberlain/ of the Chamber	Upleadon: MS A, fol. 58v	P: Spalding Priory, Lincoln diocese: *CCR, 1307–1313*, p. 365; Forey, 'Ex-Templars', p. 33
100	*Thomas of Frouby*	Fled before arrests: MS A, fol. 27r	
101	*Thomas of Hagworthingham*	Fugitive: MS A, fol. 120r	Returned after trial was over; in 1313 was doing penance in Winchester diocese: Forey, 'Ex-Templars', p. 36 n. 101
102	*Thomas of Lindsey*	Aide to Henry Danet in Ireland: *IEP*, p. 204; custodian at Kilsaran in Louth, 9 Feb–9 June 1309: MacNiocaill, pp. 196, 222	Fugitive. Returned to England 1312: MS D, fol. 171v
103	Thomas of Loudham	Sergeant. Received at Ewell 11 days before the arrests: MS A, fol. 44v. Listed in MS A, fol. 58r, as being at New Temple London, but arrested at Ewell: Gooder, p. 88; TNA:PRO E358/20 rot. 6 dorse	P: Lincoln diocese: *CCR, 1307–1313*, p. 365
104	*Thomas le Palmer*	Kilbarry, in Ireland; MacNiocaill, p. 207	
105	*Thomas of Rathenny*	Ireland: *IEP*, p. 204	
106	Thomas of Staundon	New Temple, London: MS A, fol. 58r	P: Chichester diocese: *CCR, 1307–1313*, p. 365; later moved to Burton Lazars: Forey, 'Ex-Templars', p. 33. Still alive in 1338: L&K, p. 209
107	Thomas of Staunford	Newsam: TNA:PRO E142/18 mem. 1 dorse	P: Fountains Abbey, York diocese: *CCR, 1307–1313*, p. 373; Forey, 'Ex-Templars', p. 27
108	Thomas of Strech or Trech	Keyholder at Faxfleet: TNA: PRO E142/18 mem. 1 dorse	P: York diocese: *CCR, 1307–1313*, p. 373. Still alive in 1338: L&K, p. 209
109	Thomas of Tholouse/ Toulouse	Knight, commander of Upleadon: MS A, fol. 58v	Died before 29 April 1311, as not mentioned in MS A, fols 101v–102r

	Name	Office, location and source	Sent to diocese and/or assigned to monastery for penance (P); death
110	Thomas of Thoraldeby (Totty)	Commander of Garway before Philip de Meux: *Flores Historiarum*, ed. H.R. Luard (London, 1890), vol. 3, p. 333; escaped after first interrogation; fugitive.	P: Winchester diocese: *CCR, 1307–1313*, p. 509. Still alive in 1338: L&K, p. 209
111	Thomas of Walkington	Commander of Balsall and Rothley	P: Coventry and Lichfield diocese: *CCR, 1307–1313*, p. 375
112	Thomas of Wothoppe/ Woop	Commander of Bisham: TNA: PRO, E142/13, mem. 2	P: Much Wenlock Abbey: *Registrum Ricardi de Swinfield*, p. 484; *CCR, 1307–1313*, p. 365
113	Walter of Clifton	Commander of Balantrodoch since Nov. 1306: MS A, fol. 156r; English born	P: Shelford priory, York diocese: *CCR, 1307–1313*, p. 373; Forey, 'Ex-Templars', p. 22 n. 26
114	Walter of Jonely/ Chonesby/ Domby; aka William of Cheveley	Kilcloggan in Ireland: MacNiocaill, 199	
115	Walter of Gadesby	Thornton: TNA:PRO E142/11, mem. 1 dorse	P: Jervaulx Abbey, York diocese: *CCR, 1307–1313*, p. 373; later moved to Leicester Abbey: Forey, 'Ex-Templars', pp. 21, 33. Still alive in 1338: L&K, p. 209
116	*Walter the Long*	Ireland: see *IEP*, p. 204	
117	*Walter the Rebel*	Fugitive: *Register of William Greenfield*, part 4, p. 337	
118	Walter of Rokeley	In Feb. 1310 in the custody of the constable of Marlborough: *CCR, 1307-1313*, p. 177; so probably at Rockley in Wiltshire	P: Winchester diocese: *CCR, 1307–1313*, p. 509. Still alive in 1338: L&K, p. 209
119	*William of Barnwell*		P: Warden Abbey, Lincoln diocese; died late August 1311, not absolved: *CCR, 1307–1313*, p. 365; Forey, 'Ex-Templars', pp. 21, 34–5

	Name	Office, location and source	Sent to diocese and/or assigned to monastery for penance (P); death
120	William of Burton/ Barton	Commander of Combe: TNA: PRO E142/111 mem. 2 dorse	P: Barlings Abbey, Lincoln diocese: *CCR, 1307–1313*, p. 365; Forey, 'Ex-Templars', p. 32 n. 77. Still alive in 1338: L&K, p. 209
121	William of Chalesey or Chelse ('Foliorum' in TNA:PRO E142/13 mem. 2)	Chelsing or Cowley: MS A, fol. 58r; arrested at Sandford: TNA: PRO, E 142/13 mem. 2	P: Kirkstead Abbey, Lincoln diocese: *CCR, 1307-1313*, p. 365; Forey, 'Ex-Templars', p. 32 n. 77. Still alive in 1338: L&K, p. 209
122	William of Chesterton	Denney: MS A, fol. 58r	P: Norwich diocese: *CCR, 1307–1313*, p. 365.
123	William of Craucombe	Guiting: MS A, fol. 58v	P: Muchelney Abbey, Bath and Wells diocese: *CCR, 1307–1313*, p. 391; Forey, 'Ex-Templars', p. 32. Still alive in 1338: L&K, p. 209
124	William of Egidon (Hedingdon)	Commander of Shipley: MS A, fol. 58v	P: Lincoln diocese: *CCR, 1307–1313*, p. 365.
125	William of the Fenne	Commander of Faxfleet in 1308; formerly commander of Westerdale: MS A, fol. 125v	P: Meaux Abbey, York diocese, later moved to Whitby: *CCR, 1307–1313*, p. 373; Forey, 'Ex-Templars', pp. 28, 34 n. 89
126	William of the Ford	Commander of Denney: MS A fol. 58r	P: Lincoln diocese: *CCR, 1307–1313*, p. 365
127	*William of Grafton junior*	Fugitive	Submitted before 1313: Forey, 'Ex-Templars', p. 36, n. 100. Possibly released from his religious vows in 1330: ibid., p. 36 n. 103
128	William of Grafton senior	Commander of Yorkshire TN:PRO E 142/18 mem. 1 dorse	P: Selby Abbey, York diocese: *CCR, 1307–1313*, p. 373; Forey, 'Ex-Templars', p. 24
129	William of Hereford/ Hertford	New Temple, London: MS A, fol. 58r; sergeant	Abjured heresy and absolved 9 July 1311: MS A, 166v. No further information

	Name	Office, location and source	Sent to diocese and/or assigned to monastery for penance (P); death
130	*William of Herewyk*	Yorkshire	Died? Listed in John le Gras's accounts (E358/18 rot. 31 recto) and by Eileen Gooder, p. 151, as having been arrested but not interrogated, but *not* listed by the sheriff of York in his list of arrests
131	William of Kilros/ Balygaueran/ the Chaplain	Priest, at Kilcloggan in Ireland: MacNiocaill, p. 200; *IEP*, p. 204	
132	*William de Marringe*	Denney: Gooder, p. 149; TNA: PRO E358/18 rot. 11	Died 6 Dec. 1308: TNA:PRO E358/20, rot. 8(2)
133	William of Middleton	Maryculter and Balantrodoch: MS A, fol. 157r; from Newcastle	P: Roche Abbey, York diocese, later moved to Bridlington Priory: *CCR, 1307–1313*, p. 373; Forey, 'Ex-Templars', pp. 22, 31–2
134	William de la More	Knight, grand commander of England	Died Dec. 1312: Perkins, 'Trial of the Knights Templars', p. 443
135	William of Pocklington	Garway: MS A, fol. 58v	P: St Andrew's priory, Northampton, in Lincoln diocese: *CCR, 1307–1313*, p. 365; Forey, 'Ex-Templars', p. 23
136	William Raven	Wilbraham, Cambs.: MS A, fol. 58r	P: Lincoln diocese: *CCR, 1307–1313*, p. 365
137	William of Sautre	Commander of Sandford: MS A, fol. 58v	P: Lincoln diocese: *CCR, 1307–1313*, p. 365
138	William Scotho	Denney: MS A, fol. 58r	P: Worcester diocese: *CCR, 1307–1313*, p. 365
139	*William Scurlagge*	Knight, at Balsall: Gooder, p. 147; his mantle was at New Temple, London: TNA:PRO E358/18 rot. 7 (1)	Died soon after arrest: Gooder, pp. 89, 147
140	William of Thorp	Wilbraham, Cambs: MS A, fol. 58r.	P: Thornton Abbey, Lincoln diocese: *CCR, 1307–1313*, p. 365; Forey, 'Ex-Templars', p. 32, n. 77
141	*William de Warenne*	Former commander of Ireland; at Clonoulty: MacNiocaill, p. 205	

	Name	Office, location and source	Sent to diocese and/or assigned to monastery for penance (P); death
142	William of Warwick	Priest, at Sandford: MS A, fol. 58v	P: Bath and Wells diocese: *CCR, 1307–1313*, p. 391
143	William of Welles	Denney: MS A, fol. 58r	P: London diocese: *CCR, 1307–1313*, p. 369
144	William of Winchester/ Winton	Priest, at Balsall: Gooder, p. 147	P: Norwich diocese: *CCR, 1307–1313*, p. 365

Appendix 2

Templar Properties in the British Isles that were Mentioned during the Trial

Name	Addington, Surrey
Location	To the S of London, 2.5 miles SE of Croydon in Surrey, next to a major route (now the A233).
Nearby religious houses	The Augustinian canons of St Mary Overie, Southwark, held a manor in Addington, with the advowson of the parish church; two hospices in Croydon; a house of Augustinian canons at Merton 5 miles NW; Templars' house at Saddlecombe some 35 miles to the south.
Background	Addington Temple may have been built on the land given by Walter de Merton and his wife to the Templars in 1241: *VCH, Surrey*, vol. 4, ed. H.E. Malden, p. 165; see also Daniel Lysons, *The Environs of London*, vol. 1: *County of Surrey* (London, 1792), pp. 1–10. Before January 1308 the Templars had leased Addington to John Blebury or Bloebury for life: TNA:PRO E358/18 rot. 13 dorse; BL Cotton MS Nero E vi, fol. 100r–v; see also L&K, p. 95.
After the trial	1324: Parliament assigned Addington with the Templars' other properties to the Hospital of St John, which recovered it from John Blebury and held it until the Dissolution in 1540.
Today	The former Addington Palace is a hotel and conference centre; the estate grounds are a golf course.

Name	Aslackby, Lincolnshire
Location	South Lincolnshire, on what is now the A15 (Peterborough to Lincoln), just off the old N–S Roman road. The town of Sleaford is 10 miles N; Bourne is 7 miles S.
Nearby religious houses	Sempringham, the main house of the Gilbertine Order, is 2 miles NE.
Background	Donated by Hubert of Rye in 1164: K&H, pp. 292–3; Pevsner and John Harris, *Lincolnshire* (1964), p. 441.
After the trial	The Hospitallers obtained nominal ownership, but Brother Thomas Larcher, prior of the Hospital, granted the house to John, son of Richard, son of Petronilla of Boston: *CPR, 1330–1334*, p. 414. In 1338 the house was on lease to Lord Henry de la Dale, secretary of the earl of Lancaster, for 60 marks per year: L&K, p. 160.
Today	Temple Farm stands on the site (on the S side of the main E–W street, E of the church and the Methodist chapel), incorporating a fifteenth-century window from the Hospitallers' rebuilding of the commandery: Pevsner and Harris, *Lincolnshire*, p. 441.

Name	Athkiltan (Takyltan), Co. Carlow, Ireland
Location	Precise location unknown.
Back-ground	Founder unknown: G&H, p. 339.
After the trial	Apparently passed to the Hospitallers, but no further information is available: G&H, p. 339.
Today	G&H, p. 339: at the time of writing the site of this house had not been identified.

Name	Balantrodoch (Temple), Midlothian, Scotland
Location	About 10 miles SE of Edinburgh, in the heartland of royal authority in the Scottish lowlands, on the modern B6372 road; W of what is now the main A7 road and E of the A6094.
Nearby religious houses	The Cistercian abbey of Newbattle, around 5 miles to the N.
Background	First mentioned in documents of 1175, but possibly founded by King David I of Scotland: Easson, pp. 131–2; *Knights of St John of Jerusalem in Scotland*, ed. Cowan, Mackay and Macquarrie, p. xviii.
After the trial	Obtained by the Hospitallers. In 1338 the Hospitallers reported that all their properties in Scotland had been destroyed: L&K, p. 201. At the Reformation in Scotland, in February 1563/4, the commander of Scotland resigned his property into the hands of Queen Mary: *Knights of St John of Jerusalem in Scotland*, ed. Cowan, Mackay and Macquarrie, p. liv.
Today	The ruins of the Templars' chapel are by 'the South Esk in the valley below the village': Lord, p. 243.

Name	Balsall (Temple Balsall), Warwickshire
Location	North Warwickshire, W of Coventry and SE of Birmingham; to S of the modern B4101, halfway between Knowle and Balsall.
Nearby religious houses	There were many other religious houses in the area, e.g. a house of Augustinian canons about 5 miles SE in Kenilworth, and houses of various Orders in Coventry to the NE.
Background	Founded by Roger Mowbray in around 1142: K&H, pp. 292–3; and see Gooder, *Temple Balsall*.
After the trial	See Eileen Gooder, *Temple Balsall: From Hospitallers to a Caring Community, 1322 to Modern Times* (Chichester, 1999); L&K, pp. 179–81.
Today	The commandery survives as a house called 'Old Hall' in the centre of the village.

Name	Bisham (Bristelesham), Berkshire
Location	Beside the River Thames near Marlow, midway between Windsor and Reading.
Nearby religious houses	A Benedictine house 2 miles to the SW at Hurley; a house of Benedictine nuns 3 miles to the NE at Little Marlow.
Background	Bisham was founded by Robert de Ferrers, earl of Derby, before 1139: Janet Burton, 'The Knights Templar in Yorkshire in the Twelfth Century: A Reassessment', *Northern History*, 27 (1991), pp. 26–40, here p. 31, n. 20; K&H, pp. 292–3.
After the trial	Occupied by the lord of the fief, Earl Thomas of Lancaster; escheated to the king after the earl's execution in 1322. The Hospitallers obtained only nominal ownership of Bisham. In 1325 Prior Thomas Larcher granted it to Edward II's favourite, Hugh le Despenser the younger: *CPR, 1340–1343*, p. 39; *CPR, 1345–1348*, p. 22; *VCH, Berkshire*, vol. 3, ed. P.H. Ditchfield and William Page, p. 146. After the fall of Hugh Despenser in Nov. 1326 Bisham returned to the king; he granted it to a succession of different persons. In 1335 Edward III granted Bisham to William Montacute (earl of Salisbury from 1337), who held it in 1338: L&K, p. 213. In 1337 William Montacute founded a house of Augustinian canons in the manor. At the Dissolution, King Henry VIII refounded the Augustinian priory as a Benedictine abbey: *VCH, Berkshire*, vol. 2, ed. Ditchfield and Page, pp. 82–3; but a few months later he abandoned this plan. After being used as a royal residence, in 1553 the abbey site and manor were granted to Sir Philip Hoby, who built a new house there.
Today	Bisham Abbey is now the headquarters of the National Sports Council. The Templars' hall, dating from around 1260, survives as part of the modern house. The abbey itself is not open to the public, but is used as a conference centre.

Name	Bruer (Temple Bruer), Lincolnshire
Location	On a ridge some 11 miles S of Lincoln, next to Ermine Street (important Roman road running from London to Lincoln and on to the N) and a few miles to the W of the modern A15.
Nearby religious houses	About 6 miles to the SE stood the Gilbertine house of Halverholme; the same distance to the ENE was the Gilbertine house of Catley.
Background	Granted to the Templars before 1169 by William of Ashby: Lees, pp. clxxxii–iii; Lord, pp. 44, 73–8; *VCH, Lincs.*, vol. 2, ed. William Page, pp. 211–12; W.H. St John Hope, 'The Round Church of the Knights Templars at Temple Bruer, Lincolnshire', *Archaeologia, Or Miscellaneous Tracts Relating to Antiquity*, 61 (1907–9), pp. 177–98; Pevsner and Harris, *Lincolnshire*, pp. 693–4.
After the trial	Thomas Tuscet of Scaleby in Cumberland took over Bruer, as it was originally granted to the Templars by his ancestors. In 1315–16 he enfeoffed Robert de Holland with Bruer (TNA:PRO DL 25/3332, 3333). As a close supporter of Earl Thomas of Lancaster, Robert de Holland's lands were forfeited to the king after the battle of Boroughbridge in March 1322. In Feb. 1325 King Edward II allowed Hugh le Despenser to keep Bruer and other lands, which he had acquired from Alicia, widow of Thomas of Lancaster: *CPR, 1324–1327*, p. 103. The Hospitallers obtained possession of Bruer after Hugh le Despenser's fall in Nov. 1326. In 1338 there was one commander (a knight) and a brother-sergeant there, and the house was lodging many travellers 'as the founders of the house ordained': L&K, pp. 155–6. The Hospitallers built a chapel on the S side of the chancel of Temple Bruer church, and may have enlarged the tower: Pevsner and Harris, *Lincolnshire*, pp. 62, 694.
Today	Temple Farm now stands on the site, incorporating some Templar stonework, and the S church tower still stands: see Pevsner and Harris, *Lincolnshire*, pp. 693–4. The farm is private property, but a public footpath runs through the site.

Name	Clonoulty, South Riding of Co. Tipperary, Ireland
Location	23 miles NE of Tipperary, on the R661, where this crosses the road between Cashel and Drumbane.
Nearby religious houses	Clonoulty lies about 6 miles NW of Cashel, which had many religious houses, and 5 miles SW of Holy Cross, which had a house of Cistercian monks.
Background	Founder unknown: G&H, p. 329.
After the trial	Clonoulty passed to the Hospitallers after the dissolution of the Templars; 'the annual value of its lands and churches was over £87 in 1327': G&H, p. 335. In 1541, at the dissolution of the monasteries in Ireland, it was leased to the earl of Ormond: G&H, p. 335. [*cont.*]

Today	At the time of writing, the full archaeological inventory for South Tipperary had not yet been published.

Name	Clontarf, Dublin, Ireland
Location	Clontarf lies a few miles NE of Dublin (or Baile átha Cliath), just off the R105 to Howth, on the coast overlooking Dublin Bay.
Nearby religious houses	The city of Dublin had many religious houses in the Middle Ages, as well as being a thriving port and centre of commerce.
Background	Clontarf was originally granted to the Templars by Henry II: Wood, p. 365; see also G&H, p. 329.
After the trial	In 1310 the manor of Clontarf was granted to Richard de Burgh, earl of Ulster, but as he did not hold it on his death he presumably gave it up. The Hospitallers still held it at the dissolution of the monasteries: Wood, p. 365; but from the fifteenth century they had leased it out to tenants. At the dissolution the king granted Clontarf to Prior Rawson, last prior of the Hospital in Ireland, who was created viscount of Clontarf: G&H, p. 335.
Today	The house now on the site was built in the nineteenth century. Nothing survives of the Templars' commandery here.

Name	Combe (Templecombe), Somerset
Location	About 5 miles NE of Sherborne (Dorset); and a mile to N of Yenston. The commandery stood at the junction of two locally important routes, now where the modern A357 road crosses the cross-country road from Gillingham to Sherborne.
Nearby religious houses	Sherborne had two hospitals and a Benedictine abbey; Yenston had a Benedictine cell.
Background	K&H, p. 295, state that the house was founded by Serlo fitz Odo before 1185, but the jurors drawing up an 'extent' of the Templars' lands at Combe in February 1309 stated that property worth £26 12s. per year was given from the fee of William Marshal, while the Templars at Combe also had a messuage and carucate at La Lode by the gift of Pharamus de Boulogne. Also lands at Lopene, Templefiret, Hydon, Worle and Wyshupworch (TNA:PRO E142/111 mem. 1) as well as Wylton (ibid, mem. 3). See also Lord, pp. 117–18.
After the trial	In 1332 King Edward III instructed that the sheriff of Somerset hand over to the Hospital the manor of Templecombe, which was occupied by Geoffrey de Stawell (a Somerset landowner) and was worth £30 per year: *CCRI, 1330–1333*, p. 514. The house was still a commandery in 1338, with a commander, a brother knight and another brother in residence: L&K, p. 186; see also Lord, pp. 117–18; *VCH Somerset*, vol. 2, ed. William Page, pp. 146–7. In 1338 the cost of lodging travellers' horses was a considerable expense: L&K, p. 186.

Today	Dendrology evidence taken in 1996 indicates that the house now on the site was constructed in the early seventeenth century. The site of the commandery buildings lay to the N of the modern house: Tim Taylor, *Time Team 96: The Site Reports* (London, 1996), pp. 20, 21.

Name	Cooley (Templetown), Co. Louth, Ireland
Location	Cooley was the most northerly of the Templars' houses in eastern Ireland. It stood at the southern end of Ballaghan Point, at the mouth of Carlingford Lough.
Nearby religious houses	The Templars' commandery of Kilsaran stood some 12 miles away as the crow flies, on the other side of Dundalk Bay. Dominican friary 3 miles NW in Carlingford.
Background	Cooley was originally granted to the Templars with Carlingford church by Matilda de Lacy: Wood, pp. 367, 275; see also G&H, p. 331.
After the trial	The property (around 200 acres with two castles and a mill) passed to the Hospitallers. It was administered by the commander of Kilsaran. In 1541 the Hospitallers held a ruined castle and 120 acres here, which all lay waste: G&H, pp. 331, 342.
Today	A small ruined church remains, which includes some late medieval (therefore, post-Templar) stonework: Christine Casey and Alistair Rowan, *The Buildings of Ireland: North Leinster* (Harmondsworth, 1993), p. 310; Victor M. Buckley, *Archaeological Inventory of County Louth* (Dublin, 1986), pp. 79–80.

Name	Cowton (East Cowton), Yorkshire (North Riding)
Location	On the watershed between the valleys of the River Tees and the River Swale, some 6 miles ESE of Dere Street (a Roman road which ran from Lincoln to Corbridge and then to N of Hadrian's Wall) – the modern A1 – at its junction ('Scotch Corner') with the cross-Pennine Roman road from Penrith, the modern A66.
Nearby religious houses	5 miles to the NE: house of Benedictine nuns at Neasham; 9 miles E of Richmond, with a Benedictine monastery, a house of Franciscans and a hospital or hospice. The Templars' commandery of Westerdale was around 26 miles to the E.
Background	Given by Roger Mowbray: K&H, p. 293, date uncertain: Burton, 'The Knights Templar in Yorkshire', p. 31, and see also pp. 29–30, 35, 37. See also *VCH York*, vol. 3, ed. William Page, p. 259; *Survey of the County of York taken by John de Kirkby, commonly called Kirkby's Inquest*, Surtees Society 49 (1866), p. 177 and note; E.J. Martin, 'The Templars in Yorkshire', *Yorkshire Archaeological Journal*, 29 (1927–9), pp. 366–85, here pp. 368, 370, 371, 375, 376, 378–9; Lord, pp. 82–3, 86.
After the trial	Cowton passed to the Hospitallers on the dissolution of the Templars. For the property in 1338, see L&K, p. 135.
Today	The site of the commandery is now marked by Temple House Farm, on the west side of East Cowton in North Yorkshire.

Name	Cressing (Temple Cressing), Essex
Location	In central Essex 5 miles SW of Coggeshall, 3 miles SE of the town of Braintree and situated between two Roman roads: Staine Street, which runs E–W across the county, and the N–S road from Chelmsford to Colchester.
Nearby religious houses	An important Cistercian abbey at Coggeshall.
Background	Cressing was part of the lands of the counts of Boulogne and was given to the Templars by the heiress to the county, Matilda of Boulogne, in 1136/7: *Cressing Temple: A Templar and Hospitaller Manor in Essex*, ed. D.D. Andrews (Chelmsford, 1993); Michael Gervers, '*Pro defensione Terre Sancte*: the Development and Exploitation of the Hospitallers' Landed Estate in Essex', in *The Military Orders: Fighting for the Faith and Caring for the Sick*, ed. Malcolm Barber (Aldershot, 1994), pp. 3–20; Gervers, *Cartulary of the Knights of St John of Jerusalem in England: Secunda Camera*, pp. xli, 1–3, and *passim*; *VCH, Essex*, vol. 2, ed. William Page and J. Horace Round, pp. 177–8; see also Lord, pp. 48–53.
After the trial	By 1321 the Hospitallers had obtained tenure of the Essex properties of Cressing, Witham (on the modern A12 road) and Haningfield, but had to pay Aymer of Valence, earl of Pembroke, £50 per year rent: *CCR, 1318–1323*, p. 485. In 1338 there were two brothers of the Hospital in residence: L&K, p. 169. In 1381 the house was sacked by the rebels during the 'Peasants' Revolt': Herbert Eiden, 'Joint Action against "Bad" Lordship: The Peasants' Revolt in Essex and Norfolk', *History*, 83 (1998), pp. 5–30: here p. 13.
Today	Cressing is now most famous for its enormous thirteenth-century barns. There is still a farm on the commandery site; the Templars' commandery buildings and chapel no longer exist, although some foundations have been excavated. The barns are in the care of Essex County Council and are open to the public.

Name	Denney, Cambridgeshire
Location	8 miles to N of Cambridge, on the Roman road to Ely (now the A10).
Nearby religious houses	A Benedictine monastery 8 miles N at Ely; before the site at Denney was given to the Templars in around 1170 it was occupied by a cell of Benedictine monks from Ely: K&H, p. 293. 7 miles N of Denney was the Augustinian priory at Barnwell, while there were many religious houses in Cambridge. The Templars' house of Wilbraham was 7 miles to the SE.
Background	The Templars had a hospital at Denney for elderly and sick brothers: Eileen Gooder, 'South Witham and the Templars', in *Excavations at a Templar Preceptory: South Witham, Lincolnshire, 1965–67*, ed. Philip Mayes (Leeds, 2002), p. 90: quoting *VCH, Cambridge*, vol. 2, ed. L.F. Salzman, pp. 259–60. See also *VCH, Cambridge*, vol. 9, ed. A.P.M. Wright and C.P. Lewis, pp. 244–5, 251, 256. [*cont.*]

After the trial	In 1315 held by Humphrey de Bohun, earl of Hereford, but after he joined Earl Thomas of Lancaster and was killed at Boroughbridge in 1322, Denney returned to the king. In August 1325, Prior Thomas Larcher of the Hospital in England granted to King Edward II 'in fee simple' the manors of Temple Hirst, Temple Newsam, Faxfleet, Denny and Strood, although the Hospitallers kept the churches in those manors appropriated to the Templars: *CPR, 1377–1381*, p. 444. It was one of the king's 'chamber manors', with its income going directly to the king's personal accounts, until in March 1327 King Edward III granted Denney, Temple Hirst, Temple Newsam and Strood, as well as other properties, to his kinswoman Mary of St Pol, widow of Aymer de Valence, earl of Pembroke: *CPR, 1327–1330*, p. 37; L&K, p. 212. Mary of St Pol gave Denney to the nearby abbey of Waterbeach, which was a house of Minoresses or 'Poor Clares' that she had founded in 1294 but which badly needed a new building for the nuns to live in. She also endowed the house with the former Temple Strood.
Today	Denney Abbey is now in the care of English Heritage.

Name	Dinsley (Temple Dinsley), Hertfordshire
Location	Just E of the village of Preston, about 4 miles S of Hitchin in Herts., and 30 miles NE of the city of London.
Nearby religious houses	At Hitchin there was a house of Gilbertines and a house of Carmelite friars; at Wymondley, 4 miles NE of Dinsley, there was a house of Augustinian canons and a hospital or hospice; at Dunstable, 6 miles to the W, was a house of Augustinian canons and a house of Dominican friars. Stevenage, 3 miles to the E, had a hospital or hospice, while the house of Benedictine nuns at Markyate lay 10 miles to the SW.
Background	Given to the Templars by Bernard de Balliol in 1147: K&H, p. 295; see also *VCH, Hertford*, vol. 4, ed. William Page, pp. 445–6; Lord, pp. 56–60. By 1266, the English provincial chapters were being held here: *CPR, 1258–66*, pp. 586–7.
After the trial	The Hospitallers obtained nominal possession, but could not obtain actual possession. Brother Thomas Larcher, prior of the Hospital in England, leased the house out for life at an annual rent of 22s. to William de Langford, who had rented it from the lord who had usurped it after the Templars' dissolution: *CPR, 1327–1330*, p. 351; L&K, p. 172. By the end of the fourteenth century Dinsley was in the Hospitallers' possession, but by the early sixteenth century it was leased out and does not appear in the *Valor Ecclesiasticus* at the time of the dissolution of the monasteries: *VCH, Hertford.*, vol. 2, p. 446.
Today	There is a girls school on the site, Princess Helena College. Originally founded in Ealing, London, in 1820, the school moved to Temple Dinsley in 1935.

Name	Dokesworth, Ducksworth or Duxford, Cambridgeshire
Location	10 miles SSE from Cambridge just W of the road to Saffron Walden (now the A1301; the modern M11 runs just to the W). [*cont.*]

Nearby religious houses	A hospice a little to the N at Whittlesford, and a Benedictine nunnery to the S at Ickleton. The Templar house at Wilbraham is 9 miles to the NE.
Background	See Lord, p. 67, and *VCH Cambs.*, vol. 2, p. 262.
After the trial	The house passed to the Hospitallers. In 1338 there were no brothers at Dokesworth: L&K, p. 165. The house was attacked by the rebels during the 'Peasants' Revolt' of June 1381: TNA: PRO JUST 1/103 mem. 3r.
Today	Temple farmhouse, dating from the sixteenth century, stands between Mill Lane and Temple Close on the west bank of the River Cam, on the site of the Templars' former house. There are traces of a moat between the farm and the river: *VCH, Cambridge*, vol. 6, p. 204.

Name	Eagle, Lincolnshire
Location	Approx. 11 miles SW of the city of Lincoln, 1 mile SW of the village of Eagle, at Eagle Hall Farm; situated to the NW of the modern railway line, around 3 miles WNW of the village of Thorpe on the Hill and 4 miles NW of the Fosse Way (a Roman road which runs from Exeter to Lincoln).
Nearby religious houses	A house of Premonstratensian nuns about 4 miles NNE at Broadholme; the Hospitallers had a commandery at Ossington, about 10 miles WSW, over the border in Nottinghamshire. There were also many religious houses at Lincoln.
Background	Given to the Templars by King Henry II of England: see Lees, pp. clxxx–xxxi. Like Denney, the house also housed sick brothers.
After the trial	King Edward II claimed it, as a donation by his ancestors, and in 1320 it was granted to Thomas, earl of Norfolk and marshal of England, the king's half-brother: *CPR, 1317–1321*, p. 410. The Hospitallers recovered Eagle by 1335, and in 1338 they had a commander, a chaplain-brother and four corrodary holders there, and expenses for caring for guests' horses: L&K, pp. 158–9. In 1345 the prior of the Hospital won permission from King Edward III to found a settlement on Swinderby Moor and bring in settlers 'for the greater safety of travellers there and the repressing of ill-doing', and to build a chapel at nearby Eagle to serve the settlement: *Calendar of the Charter Rolls, Edward III*, vol. 5, *1341–1417*, p. 40. In the mid-fifteenth century the Hospitallers' *baili* (sometimes called Bailiff) of Eagle became an important official within the Order, one of the capitular *bailis*, who were the highest office-holders in the Order appointed by the General Chapter on Rhodes: Jürgen Sarnowsky, *Macht und Herrschaft im Johanniterorden des 15. Jahrhunderts: Verfassung und Verwaltung der Johanniter auf Rhodos (1421–1522)* (Münster and Hamburg, 2001), pp. 18, 52–4, 140, 216, note 28, 288, 584–5, 693. [*cont.*]

Today	Eagle Hall Farm now stands on the site of the former commandery: Lord, p. 79. Eagle Hall is 'a modest early C18 house altered in the C19. Some of the rubble walls may be medieval': Pevsner and Harris, revised by Nicholas Antram, *Lincolnshire* (2002), p. 262.

Name	Ewell (Temple Ewell), Kent
Location	3 miles inland from the major port of Dover, just E of the Roman road from Dover to London, now the A2. The Templars also owned Temple Ewell village church.
Nearby religious houses	Several other religious houses at Dover, and the Hospitallers had a house at Swingfield (or Swenefield), about 4 miles WSW, which lodged travellers: L&K, p. 91.
Background	Given to the Order before 1185: K&H, p. 295. On Ewell, see the very brief notice in *VCH Kent*, vol. 2, ed. William Page, p. 175; and Lord, pp. 126–8. The church was also appropriated to the Templars: L&K, p. 173.
After the trial	1325: Brother Thomas Larcher, then prior of the Hospital, leased Ewell to Hamo Godechepe of London and Isabella his wife, for their lifetimes and for one year after their deaths, at a rent of £20 per year. This grant was confirmed by the king in 1335: *CPR, 1334–1338*, p. 150. Hamo and Isabella were still leasing Ewell in 1338: L&K, p. 173.
Today	The site of the commandery was in a field next to Temple farmhouse, Singledge Lane, to the E of the modern A2. The present parish church at Ewell, dedicated to Saints Peter and Paul, dates largely from the time of the Templars' ownership in the twelfth century, and the earliest recorded priest there, John *sacerdos*, was appointed by the master of the Temple in England in 1185.

Name	Faxfleet, Yorkshire (East Riding)
Location	Built on low-lying, marshy ground at the western extreme of the north bank of the Humber estuary at the confluence of the Rivers Ouse and Trent. These rivers were important communications links until modern times.
Nearby religious houses	When the Templars arrived, there were few other religious houses in the area; the nearest were a Benedictine cell at Alkborough, about 2 miles SE on the other side of the Humber, and a house of secular canons at Howden, about 10 miles to the NW. The Templars' house at Etton was 14 miles NE; Temple Hirst was 16 miles W up the River Aire, with Whitley 4 miles further on; while Temple Belwood was 11 miles SSW, on the other side of the Humber. [*cont.*]

Back-ground	The Templars held property here by 1185, given by Roger de Mowbray: Lees, pp. ccxi, 125; Lord, p. 82; *VCH, York: East Riding*, vol. 4, ed. K.J.Allison (1979), pp. 45–6; see also *VCH, York*, vol. 3, ed. William Page (1913), p. 257; *Kirkby's Inquest*, p. 177 and note; Martin, 'The Templars in Yorkshire', pp. 367, 368, 371, 372, 376, 381. The commandery at Faxfleet was founded in the thirteenth century: Burton, 'Knights Templar in Yorkshire', pp. 37, 38. Faxfleet commandery was moated by 1322, but did not have a moat while the Templars held it: H.E. Jean le Patourel, *The Moated Sites of Yorkshire* (London, 1973), pp. 18, 111. An inquest of 1323 into the rights of the Templars' manor here (TNA:PRO E142/30 mem.1) identified a right to a 'water passage of the Humber' worth 18*d*. per year.
After the trial	Flaxfleet did not pass to the Hospital. After the Templars were dissolved, it returned to the hands of the lord of Mowbray: *CPR, 1354–1358*, p. 15. John, second baron Mowbray, a supporter of Earl Thomas of Lancaster, was captured at the battle of Boroughbridge in 1322 and executed. His lands reverted to the Crown. For the Hospital's grant of Faxfleet to Edward II, see under Denney, above. The Crown granted the Templars' manor at Faxfleet to a succession of landowners for their lifetimes: L&K, p. 212; *VCH, York. East Riding*, vol. 4, pp. 45–6. The modern Faxfleet Hall was built in the eighteenth and nineteenth centuries: *VCH, York: East Riding*, vol. 4, p. 46.
Today	The manor house of Faxfleet was noted in 1323; a moated site remains near Faxfleet Hall (N of the seawall), presumably the site of the Templar commandery. The shoreline is now a Site of Special Scientific Interest (SSSI).

Name	Foulbridge, Yorkshire (North Riding)
Location	In the valley of the River Derwent, S of the North Yorkshire moors. The commandery was built on flat, marshy land, next to the River Derwent. The pattern of lanes and bridle paths converging on Foulbridge suggest that it was more important as a crossing point over the river in the past than it is today. The modern road crosses the Derwent 2 miles downstream at Yedingham, over a bridge built in the eighteenth century.
Nearby religious houses	The Benedictine nuns at Yedingham, 2 miles WNW and the Cistercian nuns of Wykeham, 5 miles NE; both of these were also next to the River Derwent and were direct neighbours of Foulbridge.
Back-ground	Not in the 1185 inquest, but held by the Order before 1226: K&H, p. 292; Burton, 'Knights Templar in Yorkshire', p. 38. See also *Kirkby's Inquest*, p. 141; Martin, 'The Templars in Yorkshire', pp. 370, 372, 383; Lord, pp. 87–8. [*cont.*]

After the trial	In 1338 'Foukebrigg' was held by the Hospitallers; it was in ruins and there were no brothers resident, but it produced some revenue and the prior visited it each year: L&K, p. 140. It had probably been sacked by the Scots during the Anglo-Scottish war: in summer 1322 the Scots under King Robert Bruce had burnt Ripon, occupied nearby Malton and ravaged the surrounding land: Laurence Butler, *Pickering Castle: North Yorkshire* (London, 1993), p. 27.
Today	Part of a three-bay aisled hall survives, built in 1288: Royal Commission on the Historical Monuments of England, *Houses of the North Yorkshire Moors* (London, 1987), pp. 15–17; see also John Walker, 'Late Twelfth and Early Thirteenth Century Aisled Buildings: A Comparison', *Vernacular Architecture*, 30 (1991), pp. 21–53; Burton, 'Knights Templar in Yorkshire', p. 39.

Name	Garway, Herefordshire
Location	SW Herefordshire, near to Skenfrith and Grosmont Castles, standing on the E (i.e. English) bank of the River Monnow, on a low ridge that runs NW–SE along the border with Wales. The village of Garway lies on the ridgeway road.
Nearby religious houses	Midway between the Cistercian Abbey Dore, 7 miles NW, and the Benedictine abbey at Monmouth, 7 miles SE. At the S end of the ridge, 4 miles SE, lies St Wolstans, which was also held by the Templars.
Background	The original donation charters do not survive. Professor William Rees considered that King Henry II was the donor, calculating that the donation had taken place between 1185 and 1188: William Rees, *A History of the Order of St John of Jerusalem in Wales and on the Welsh Border, including an Account of the Templars* (Cardiff, 1947), p. 51. Much of the interior decoration of Garway church dates from the twelfth century, produced in the famous and distinctive Herefordshire style: Malcolm Thurlby, *The Herefordshire School of Romanesque Architecture* (Almeley, 2001).
After the trial	The house passed to the Hospitallers after the dissolution of the Templars, and in 1338 there was one brother, a chaplain-custodian: L&K, p. 198. The Hospitallers' report of 1338 also mentioned many people 'coming over' to Garway, especially from Wales: L&K, pp. 195, 198. These visitors caused the Hospitallers considerable expense, but there is no mention of a guest-house.
Today	Only the church at Garway survives from the period of the Templars. The farm and dovecote now standing were built later (although there was a dovecote in Templar times: see TNA: PRO E358/19 rot. 2), and even the church tower was rebuilt by the Hospitallers.

Name	Guiting (Temple Guiting), Gloucestershire
Location	In the Cotswolds, 5 miles E of Winchcombe, and about 4 miles SE of Hailes.
Nearby religious houses	A Benedictine abbey at Winchcombe and an important Cistercian abbey at Hailes, which was a major pilgrim centre.
Background	Given by Gilbert de Lacy, earl of Gloucester, who later joined the Order; see Lord, pp. 117–18.
After the trial	The Hospitallers obtained nominal possession, but around 1325 Prior Thomas Larcher granted Temple Guiting to Hugh Despenser: *CPR, 1340–1343*, p. 39; *CPR, 1345–1348*, p. 22. On the execution of Hugh Despenser in Nov. 1326 his lands fell into the hands of King Edward III. In March 1328 Edward granted Temple Guiting to his doctor Pancius de Controne: *CCR, 1327–1330*, p. 290; *CCR, 1330–1333*, p. 47; see also *CPR, 1327–1330*, pp. 243, 321, 488. In 1340 Pancius granted Temple Guiting to Sir William de Clinton, earl of Huntingdon, and his wife Juliana: *CCR, 1339–1341*, p. 623. The manor never returned to the Hospitallers, although they did obtain possession of the church: 'House of Knights Hospitallers: The preceptory of Quenington', *VCH Gloucester, vol.* 2, ed. William Page, p. 113.
Today	A post-medieval house stands on the site of the commandery: Pevsner and David Verey, *Gloucestershire 1, The Cotswolds* (1970), p. 448. The village church, dedicated to St Mary, incorporates stonework and carvings from the twelfth–early-fourteenth centuries.

Name	Hirst (Temple Hirst), Yorkshire (West Riding)
Location	Situated on the N bank of the River Aire, on the direct route between Selby and Doncaster, 2 miles E of the modern Selby-Doncaster road (now the A19).
Nearby religious houses	Pontefract is 10 miles W, with many religious houses, Selby is 5 miles N, with an important Benedictine abbey. The Templars' house at Whitley was 4 miles SW; Faxfleet commandery is 16 miles E and could be reached by travelling down the Rivers Aire and Ouse; Temple Newsam was 16 miles NW, up the River Aire.
Back-ground	Founded by Ralph Hastings in 1152: K&H, p. 296; Burton, 'Knights Templar in Yorkshire', p. 28, notes that the details were recorded by the Hospitaller historian John Stillingflete, writing in around 1434. Ralph Hastings was a tenant of the Yorkshire Lacy family of Pontefract: ibid., p. 34. See also *VCH, York*, vol. 3, ed. William Page, p. 259; Burton, 'Knights Templar in Yorkshire', p. 36; Martin, 'The Templars in Yorkshire', pp. 367, 368, 370, 371, 373, 376, 377, 381; Lord, pp. 82–3, 89.

After the trial	The Hospitallers obtained only nominal ownership of Temple Hirst, which was taken over by Lord Robert de Holland. On his fall in 1322 (see under Bruer, above), an inventory was taken for the king: TNA:PRO E142/30 mem. 2. For its grant to Edward II and then to Mary of St Pol, see under Denney, above. After her death it reverted to the king. By January 1344 Temple Hirst and Temple Newsam were held by John Darcy senior: *CPR, 1343–1345*, p. 382. In 1379 Prior Robert Hales claimed Temple Hirst and Temple Newsam from Philip Darcy, knight, who in 1380 successfully defended his claim to hold the properties, by virtue of Prior Thomas Larcher's grant of 1325: *CCR, 1377–1381*, p. 187; *CPR, 1377–1381*, p. 444. According to A. Chetwynd-Staplyton, 'The Templars at Temple Hurst', *Yorkshire Archaeological and Topographical Journal*, 10 (1887–89), pp. 276–96, in the nineteenth century there were some remains of the Templars' buildings at Temple Hirst, which then formed part of Temple Farm.
Today	A nineteenth-century brick house with a staircase tower at the E end now stands on the site at Temple Hirst, named 'Temple Manor', which at the time of writing is a residential nursing home.

Name	Keele, Staffordshire
Location	Approx. 5 miles W of Newcastle-under-Lyme and 8 miles SE of Wybunbury.
Nearby religious houses	A house of Dominican friars and a hospice at Newcastle-under-Lyme, a hospice at Wybunbury and a house of Augustinian canons at Trentham, 8 miles SE.
Background	The land was given to the Order by King Henry II, but was initially leased out. Lord points out that Keele was on a major road (now the A525) and adds that the Templars charged tolls on packhorses passing through: Lord, pp. 99–100, quoting C. Harrison, *Essays on the History of Keele* (Keele, 1986), pp. 6–14, and TNA: PRO E358/19 rot. 36. There was no mention of this toll in the Hospitallers' report of 1338.
After the trial	Earl Thomas of Lancaster, lord of Newcastle under Lyme, took the property on the dissolution of the Templars, but after his execution in 1322 it was given to the Hospitallers: *VCH, Staffordshire*, vol. 3, ed. M.W. Greenslade, pp. 267–8. In 1338 the Hospitallers held there land worth 20 marks per year, which had been taken by Sir Thomas of Leicester, cleric, since the time of Brother Thomas Larcher, former prior of the Hospital in England: L&K, p. 200. There was one sergeant-brother there, Richard de Hulles.
Today	Nothing remains of the Templars' property at Keele.

Name	Kilbarry, Co. Waterford, Ireland
Location	Some 4 miles S of Waterford on the main road to Tramore: G&H, pp. 329–30.
Nearby religious houses	The Hospitallers' house of Killure lay 2 miles E. The Templars' house of Crooke was 4 miles E. The city of Waterford (Port Láirge), with its important port and its many religious houses, is around 4 miles N.
Background	The Templars' property at Kilbarry was given to them by King Henry II of England before 1180: G&H, pp. 329–30.
After the trial	In 1348 the Hospitaller brother William de Fyncham was commander of both Crooke and Kilbarry; in 1368 Richard Walsh, Hospitaller commander of Kilbarry, was killed in battle fighting for the king against the Poers and O'Hedriscols; after this no more Hospitaller commanders appear in the records for these properties and apparently the Hospitallers leased both estates out to tenants. In 1541, at the dissolution, both were being rented by one William Wyse (G&H, p. 336).
Today	There is a ruined church and attached buildings: Michael Moore, *Archaeological Inventory of County Waterford* (Dublin, 1999), pp. 176–7, no. 1365.

Name	Kilcloggan (Templetown), Co. Wexford, Ireland
Location	On Hook Head, overlooking Waterford Harbour from the E. Fethard is 2 miles E; Duncannon is 3 miles N.
Nearby religious houses	Tintern Abbey (founded by William Marshal in 1200, in commemoration of the original Tintern Abbey in the Wye Valley in Wales), a Cistercian house, lies 4 miles NW: G&H, p. 142. The Cistercian house of Dunbrody is 7 miles N: ibid., pp. 131–2. The Hospitallers' house of Ballyhack is 5 miles NW; the Templars' house of Crooke is 4 miles NW, on the other side of Waterford Harbour. The city of Waterford (Port Láirge), with its important port and its many religious houses, is around 12 miles distant by land, less by water.
Background	According to Herbert Wood, Kilcloggan was originally granted to the Templars by the O'Morras: Wood, p. 371; G&H, p. 330, give Connor O'More as the founder, 1183–1200.
After the trial	Kilcloggan passed to the Hospitallers after the dissolution of the Templars, and it continued to be a commandery until the Dissolution of the Monasteries. In 1541, at the Dissolution, the jurors reported that the site contained a castle that was in good repair and that it was very useful for defence against the rebellious Irish, but much of the estate was not in cultivation. After the Dissolution, Kilcloggan and the Hospitallers' house at Wexford were leased to James Sherlock of Waterford: G&H, p. 336. [*cont.*]

Today	Nothing remains of the Templars' property here. The tower house at Kilcloggan that has traditionally been associated with the Templars probably belonged to the Cistercians (Michael J. Moore, *Archaeological Inventory of County Wexford* (Dublin, 1996), p. 173, no. 1528, p. 174, fig. 35; private communication from Conleth Manning of Dúchas, The Heritage Service, National Monuments and Historic Properties of Ireland, 5 July 2000).

Name	Kilcork in Co. Kildare, Ireland
Location	In the parish of Kilrush, around 32 miles SW of Dublin and 6 miles S of the town of Kildare. The site of Kilcork was 1 mile NW of the modern N78 road to Dublin; the village of Nurney is 3 miles NW and Kilcullen is 7 miles NE.
Nearby religious houses	At Kildare was an ancient convent of nuns, originally founded as a house for women and later as a house for women and men by St Brigid (patroness of Ireland) in the fifth century AD; after the Anglo-Normans arrived in 1171 it may have become a house of Augustinian canonesses. There was also a house of Carmelite friars and of Franciscan friars: G&H, pp. 38, 241, 252, 286, 290, 311, 320. The Hospitaller house of Tully is 4 miles N.
Background	Founder unknown.
After the trial	Kilcork passed to the Hospitallers after the dissolution of the Templars and was incorporated into the manor of Tully: Wood, p. 365. In 1318 the Hospitallers of Ireland exchanged the manors of Kilcork and Tully with Thomas fitz John, earl of Kildare, but kept the rectories: G&H, p. 330. The Hospitallers farmed out the manor of Tully in the 1520s. In 1549 the jurors who examined the site after the Dissolution of the Monasteries found a fortification there and that much of the land was waste: ibid., pp. 338–9.
Today	Apparently nothing remains of this house. The site was in doubt until it was identified by Professor J. Otway-Ruthven: G&H, p. 330.

Name	Kilsaran, Co. Louth, Ireland
Location	On the S bank of the River Glyde, about 2 miles from the river mouth, and less than 1 mile SW of the village of Castlebellingham, which stands on what used to be the main road to Dublin. Dundalk is 7 miles N and Drogheda 11 miles S. The village of Kilsaran lies 1 mile SE.
Nearby religious houses	A reputed early Christian monastic site lies 2 miles to the SE, on the north bank of the River Glyde at Linns, and another just over 2 miles to the S on the S bank of the River Dee, at Drumcar; 4 miles N stood the ancient Irish monastery of Dromiskin, reputed to have been founded by St Patrick's companions; 6 miles SW at Ardee was a house of *fratres cruciferi* and of Carmelite friars, and 9 miles WNW and NW respectively were Augustinian priories at Knock and at Louth: see Victor M. Buckley, *Archaeological Inventory of County Louth* (Dublin, 1986), p. 123, map 6; G&H, pp. 34, 155, 210, 286. [*cont.*]

Background	Originally granted to the Templars in the late twelth century by Matilda de Lacy: Wood, p. 367; G&H, p. 330.
After the trial	Kilsaran passed to the Hospitallers after the dissolution of the Templars, and became one of the grand master's 'chambers', which meant that it was under his jurisdiction and its revenues went directly to him. After the Dissolution of the Monasteries the house eventually passed into the hands of the Bellew family: G&H, p. 338.
Today	All that remains is a 'slight hollow': Buckley, *Archaeological Inventory of County Louth*, p. 75, no. 939.

Name	Lydley, Shropshire
Location	Lydley Heys was on the site of the modern Penkridge Hall, in the parish of Cardington in the Welsh March, about 10 miles S of Shrewsbury, 2 miles E of the modern A49. It lay 3½ miles NE of Church Stretton, which lies on the old Roman road running N to Wroxeter, and was sited at the base of the Lawley ridge, next to the public track that runs alongside the ridge. It is about 1 mile E of the Roman road to Wroxeter.
Nearby religious houses	There was a Cistercian abbey 10 miles NE at Buildwas, a Cluniac house 8 miles ENE at Much Wenlock with a dependent cell at Church Preen, 2 miles E; and a house of Augustinian canons at Ratlinghope, 6 miles W.
Background	Founded probably in 1155–60: K&H, p. 294; on Lydley, see also Rees, *A History of the Order of St John of Jerusalem in Wales*, pp. 46–51.
After the trial	In 1338 Lydley was occupied by Earl Edmund of Arundel, who was descended from one of the original donors who gave Lydley to the Templars, and it was estimated to be worth 100 marks per year: L&K, p. 213. Until 1560 Lydley belonged to the same family as Cardington and Sutton-en-le-Dale: *VCH, Shropshire*, vol. 10, pp. 27, 89.
Today	On the site today is Penkridge Hall, built in the sixteenth century: *VCH, Shropshire*, vol. 2, ed. A. Gaydon (Oxford, 1973), pp. 85–6.

Name	Maryculter, Aberdeenshire, Scotland.
Location	6 miles SSE of Aberdeen on the south bank of the River Dee, roughly equidistant from Peterculter (NW on the A93) and Kirkton of Maryculter (SE on the B9077). The site of a Roman camp lay nearby to the W, on the N bank of the river.
Nearby religious houses	Several religious houses in Aberdeen, but no others outside the city for many miles, although Kelso Abbey had land in the area: *Knights of St John in Scotland*, ed. Cowan, Mackay and Macquarrie, p. xix. [*cont.*]

Background	Given to Templars by Walter Byset between 1221 and 1236: *Knights of St John in Scotland*, ed. Cowan, Mackay and Macquarrie, p. xix; Easson, p. 131; Lord, p. 148. In the area, attached to Maryculter commandery, the Templars also had churches at Aboyne and at Tullich: *Knights of St John in Scotland*, ed. Cowan, Mackay and Macquarrie, p. 13; Easson, p. 132.
After the trial	Passed to the Hospitallers, but in 1338 it was ruined and the Order received no income from it: L&K, p. 201.
Today	The buildings of the Templars' former commandery are incorporated into the modern Maryculter House, now a hotel. An area of parkland known as Templars Park adjoins it, and nearby is the ruined chapel.

Name	Newsam (Temple Newsam), Yorkshire (West Riding)
Location	On low-lying land to the N of the River Aire in Yorkshire, E of the modern city of Leeds. The Templars' commandery lay within the former Temple Thorpe Farm at Skelton. It stood approx. ⅛ mile SW of the modern junction 45 on the M1 motorway, and 2 miles W of the village of Newsam Green.
Nearby religious houses	The great Cistercian house of Kirkstall was 5 miles NW. The Templars' houses of Whitley (12 miles SE) and Hirst (16 miles SE) could be reached by travelling down the River Aire.
Background	The house was given or sold to the Order by William de Villiers (d. 1181): K&H, p. 296; Burton, 'Knights Templar in Yorkshire', pp. 28, 29: William de Villiers was a tenant of the Lacy family of Pontefract. See *VCH, York*, vol. 3, ed. Page (1913), pp. 259–60; Burton, 'Knights Templar in Yorkshire', p. 36; Lord, pp. 85–6, 89; *Kirkby's Inquest*, p. 38; Martin, 'The Templars in Yorkshire', pp. 366, 367, 368, 370, 371, 373–4, 376, 382.
After the trial	The Hospitallers obtained only nominal ownership of Temple Newsam. The house was taken over by a supporter of Earl Thomas of Lancaster, and on his defeat and execution in 1322 it came back into the king's hands. For its incomes at that time, see TN:PRO E142/30 mem. 1. For its grant to King Edward II in August 1325, see under Denney and Hirst: from this time the history of Newsam was the same as that of Hirst. By 1347 the commandery buildings themselves were derelict: 'Medieval Britain and Ireland in 1989', ed. David R.M. Gaimster, Sue Margeson and Maurice Hurley, *Medieval Archaeology*, 34 (1990), p. 224. The modern Temple Newsam House was built in the 17th century within the commandery's estate but some 2 miles N of the original commandery, on higher ground away from the risk of flooding. The house was developed in the eighteenth and nineteenth centuries. [*cont.*]

| Today | The site of the commandery was excavated in 1989–91: Graham Eyre-Morgan, 'Temple Newsam preceptory excavations, 1989–1991', *Medieval Yorkshire*, 21 (1992), pp. 11–14. The site was completely destroyed during the 1990s by an open-cast coal mine worked by British Coal. The open-cast workings have now been completed and the area has been landscaped with grass and trees, forming part of Rothwell Colliery Country Park. |

Name	New Temple, Middlesex
Location	Just outside Ludgate (the west gate of the city of London), on land W of the River Fleet, between Fleet Street (the main road to Westminster) and the N bank of the River Thames.
Nearby religious houses	There were many other religious Orders and churches nearby.
Background	Founded as the headquarters of the Order in England in 1161: K&H, p. 294; Lord, pp. 26–30; T. Henry Baylis, *The Temple Church and Chapel of St Ann, an Historical Record and Guide* (London, 1893).
After the trial	Aymer de Valence, earl of Pembroke, and Thomas, earl of Lancaster, claimed the New Temple; on 1 Oct. 1314 Aymer abandoned his claims in favour of Earl Thomas of Lancaster, but the day after the earl's execution on 22 March 1322 Edward II granted it to Aymer: *CPR, 1313–1317*, p. 184; *Foedera*, ed. Rymer, vol. 2, pt 1, p. 480. In 1324 Thomas Larcher, prior of the Hospital in England, granted New Temple to Hugh le Despenser: TNA:PRO E40/1469; but it escheated to the king on Hugh's execution in Nov. 1326. In 1336 Prior Philip de Thame claimed it, stating that Hugh Despenser had acquired the New Temple by force. King Edward III ordered an investigation, and the Parliament of June 1338 agreed to hand over the spiritualities of the New Temple to the Hospital, while William de Langford remained as 'custodian'. William was clerk to the prior of the Hospital and had assisted the Hospital in recovering the New Temple: *CPR, 1330–1334*, p. 373; *CPR, 1334–1338*, pp. 314, 352; *CPR, 1338–1340*, pp. 99, 125, 303–4. New Temple continued to be a depository for legal records, and in June 1381 was sacked by the rebels during the 'Peasants' Revolt': *CPR, 1381–1385*, p. 394.
Today	The Templars' church still stands, although the interior was restored in the eighteenth and nineteenth centuries and again after it was bombed during the Second World War. It is now the chapel for the Temple Inn of Court, and is open to the public at certain times.

Name	Penhill, Yorkshire (North Riding)
Location	At OS ref. SE 0388, on the S side of Wensleydale, between Aysgarth and the village of West Witton. The dale forms an E–W route across the Pennine Hills from Yorkshire to Lancashire. [*cont.*]

Nearby religious houses	The Cistercian house of Fors was 4 miles W, while the Premonstratensian house of Coverham was 5 miles ESE, with the Cistercian house of Jervaulx 6 miles beyond. There was a house of Benedictine nuns at Marrick, 7 miles N.
Background	According to the inquest of 1185, the Templars received their land at Penhill from William son of Hervey; the donation was confirmed by his lord, Roger de Mowbray: Burton, 'Knights Templar in Yorkshire', pp. 29–30. But the origins of the commandery are complex and unclear: see also *VCH, York*, vol. 3, p. 258; K&H, pp. 292–4; Martin, 'The Templars in Yorkshire', pp. 367, 368, 370, 371, 374–5, 378; Lord, p. 87. Burton (p. 31) found 'no support' for the date of foundation of 1142 given by K&H.
After the trial	The Hospitallers obtained the legal ownership after the dissolution of the Templars, but in 1338 the house was ruinous and let to Lord Geoffrey de Scrop, chief justiciar of England, rent free for life: L&K, p. 134.
Today	The foundations of the chapel were excavated in about 1840: Martin and Lord cite E. Bogg, *Richmondshire* (Leeds, 1908), pp. 641–2; see also W.S.B. Jones Barker, *Historical and Topographical Account of Wensleydale* (1853), cited by *VCH, Yorks*, vol. 3, p. 258. The excavated ruins of a chapel can still be seen: Burton, 'Knights Templar in Yorkshire', p. 39; Lord, p. 243. 'Temple farm' lies just down the hill.

Name	Rathronan, Co. Tipperary or Carlow, Ireland
Location	The location of this house has been disputed; Wood, p. 364, claimed it was in Co. Carlow; C. McNeill in the *Registrum de Kilmainham* (Dublin, 1932) identified it as being Rathronan, 2 miles NW of Clonmel, in Co. Tipperary, on the road between Clonmel and Cashal: G&H, pp. 330, 451 (for map reference).
Background	Founder unknown: G&H, p. 330.
After the trial	Apparently this house did not pass to the Hospitallers: G&H, p. 330.
Today	At the time of writing, the archaeological inventory for South Tipperary has not yet been published.

Name	Ribston, Yorkshire (West Riding)
Location	At OS ref. SE 3954, now the site of Ribston Hall at Little Ribston. The Templars' commandery here stood on the bank of the River Nidd, 3 miles SE from Knaresborough and 5 miles ESE of Harrogate.
Nearby religious houses	There was a Cluniac house at Knaresborough. The Templar house of Wetherby was 4 miles to the SE: for other neighbouring religious houses see the entry for Wetherby. [*cont.*]

Background	Founded by Robert de Ros II in around 1217. See R.V. Taylor, 'Ribston and the Knights Templars', *Yorkshire Archaeological and Topographical Journal*, 7 (1882), pp. 429–52 (here p. 431); Burton, 'Knights Templar in Yorkshire', pp. 38–9. Taylor's article published a collection of charters which has survived from Ribston. See also R.V. Taylor, 'Ribston and the Knights Templars', *Yorkshire Archaeological and Topographical Journal*, 8 (1883), pp. 259–99; 9 (1884), pp. 71–98; Martin, 'The Templars in Yorkshire', pp. 367, 368, 369, 371, 372–3, 376, 381; *Kirkby's Inquest*, p. 205 ('Magna Rybstan').
After the trial	Ribston passed to the Hospitallers and in 1338 there were three brothers resident: L&K, pp. 136–8. After the Dissolution of the Monasteries the house was granted to Charles Brandon, duke of Suffolk, who sold it in 1542 to Henry Goodricke: Taylor, 'Ribston and the Knights Templars', *Yorkshire Archaeological and Topographical Journal*, 7 (1882), p. 431.
Today	Ribston Hall, constructed in 1674, stands on the site of the commandery. The chapel of St Andrew, which is attached to the house, dates from the thirteenth century and still has two thirteenth-century doorways, but was rebuilt in 1700: Pevsner and Radcliffe, *Yorkshire: The West Riding* (1967), pp. 399–400; Burton, 'Knights Templar in Yorkshire', p. 39. Taylor ('Ribston and the Knights Templars' (1882), p. 431) noted that 'on each side of the altar-table is a great tomb, supposed to cover the remains of two Knights Templars', but Pevsner's interpretation of these tombs is rather different, noting among the monuments in the chapel (p. 400): 'slabs of blue marble with indents of brasses, probably two ladies on one, one on the other. L. and r. of the altar.'

Name	Rockley, Wiltshire
Location	Around 3 miles NW of Marlborough, on the Marlborough downs.
Nearby religious houses	At Marlborough there was a late twelfth-century Gilbertine house and two thirteenth-century hospitals. Around 3 miles S there was a Benedictine cell at Clatford; there was another 4 miles SW at Avebury and a cell of the Benedictine abbey of Bec at Ogbourne St George, 3 miles NE.
Background	Given to the Templars in 1155 by John Marshal, ancestor of the earls of Pembroke: K&H, p. 295; Lord, pp. 117–18.
After the trial	Rockley passed to the Hospitallers. In 1338 no Hospitallers were resident, but a chaplain, a bailiff and a harvest overseer were employed there: L&K, p. 187.
Today	The site of the Templars' house was at Temple Farm, about a mile WNW of Rockley Village.

Name	Rothley, Leicestershire
Location	On the main road from Leicester to Derby (now the A6), halfway between Leicester and Loughborough.
Nearby religious houses	6 miles W was the Augustinian house of Ulverscroft, and 6 miles S up the River Soar was the city of Leicester, with houses belonging to the Augustinian Order and the friars as well as hospices.
Background	The Templars received land here before 1203, and Henry III granted the manor in 1231: K&H, p. 295; see also Lord, pp. 93–6, and Gooder, pp. 26–7, 34–5, 41, 86, 137. The Templars at Rothley held the advowson of the village church as well as having their own chapel in the commandery: *Rotuli Ricardi Gravesend diocesis Lincolnensis*, ed. E.N. Davis with C.W. Foster and A. Hamilton Thompson, Canterbury and York Society 31 (Oxford, 1925), pp. 162–3, 163–4. In 1308 the house was apparently being run with Balsall, as Thomas of Walkington was commander of both: Gooder, pp. 26, 92, 102; a similar arrangement was in operation at Ribston and Wetherby. See also George Thomas Clark, 'The Custumary of the Manor and Soke of Rothley in the County of Leicester', *Archaeologia, Or Miscellaneous Tracts Relating to Antiquity*, 47.1 (1883), pp. 89–130; T.H. Forbrooke, 'Rothley: I. The Preceptory', in *Transactions of the Leicestershire Archaeological Society*, 12, pp. 32–34.
After the trial	The house passed to the Hospital, and was leased out by Brother Richard de Pavely, prior of the Hospital in England, to one Roger Beler: *CPR, 1317–1321*, p. 80. In *1328–29* King Edward III confirmed the Hospitallers' right to hold Rothley: *CPR, 1327–1330*, pp. 340, 387. The Hospitallers' report of 1338 recorded that Rothley had been lost in the time of Brother Thomas Larcher, prior of the Hospital in England, and recovered at great expense at the time of Philip de Thame, prior in 1338. There were no brothers resident in 1338: L&K, p. 177.
Today	The commandery chapel still stands; a hotel now stands on the site of the main commandery buildings.

Name	Sandford, Oxfordshire
Location	On the E bank of the River Thames (a major thoroughfare in the Middle Ages), a few miles S of the city of Oxford.
Nearby religious houses	There were many religious establishments in Oxford.
Background	The land was given to the Templars in around 1240, and the Templars moved their Cowley commandery here: *VCH Oxon*, vol. 5, ed. Mary D. Lobel, p. 269; Lord, p. 105. The cartulary of Sandford has survived: *The Sandford Cartulary*, ed. Agnes Leys, 2 vols, Oxfordshire Record Society 19, 22 (Oxford, 1938–1941). [*cont.*]

After the trial	The house at Sandford passed to the Hospitallers. In 1338 there were only two brothers in residence at Sandford, and a major expense was the cost of looking after the horses of travellers. Stephen de Sautre, a corrodarian from the time of the Templars, was still in residence in 1338: see L&K, p. 192.
Today	Oxford Thames Four Pillars Hotel stands on the site and incorporates the surviving medieval buildings.

Name	Shipley, Sussex
Location	1½ miles W of the modern A24 (the road N from Worthing to Horsham, and on to London), 2 miles NW of West Grinstead. Shipley lies on the upper reaches of the River Adur, which in the Middle Ages was navigable to this point.
Nearby religious houses	The area is almost empty of religious houses. The nearest house of size was the Augustinian house of Hardham, 7 miles SW.
Background	Lord, p. 122, notes that the Templars were given Shipley 'by Philip de Harcourt when he became Dean of Lincoln in around 1139'. On the Templars' church at Shipley (dedicated to the Blessed Virgin Mary), see Richard Gem, 'An Early Church of the Knights Templar at Shipley, Sussex', *Anglo-Norman Studies VI: Proceedings of the Battle Conference 1983*, ed. R. Allen Brown (Woodbridge, 1990), 238–46; W.H. Blaauw, 'Sadelescombe and Shipley, the Preceptories of the Knights Templars in Sussex', *Sussex Archaeological Collections relating to the History and Antiquities of the County*, 9 (1857), pp. 227–74; *VCH, Sussex*, vol. 2, ed. William Page (1907), p. 92.
After the trial	In 1338 Shipley was officially held by the Hospitallers but leased out to William de Langeford: L&K, p. 175. The Hospitallers did not gain physical possession of the house itself until the end of the fourteenth century.
Today	The church at Shipley survives, but nothing remains of the commandery. Possibly the commandery buildings lay to the S of the church. For the archaeological finds at the church, see: W.H. Godfrey, 'Sussex church plans: St Mary, Shipley', *Sussex Notes and Queries*, 8 (1940), pp. 50–1, cited by Gem, 'Early Church of the Knights Templars', p. 240, n. 22.

Name	Sligo (Loghnehely, Teach Temple, Templehouse), Co. Sligo, Ireland
Location	3 miles NW of Ballymote, on the road between Collooney and Tobercurry.
Nearby religious houses	There was a house of Franciscan tertiaries at Ballymote, 3 miles to the SE and another at Court, 3 miles W; and a Dominican friary 5 miles S at Cloonameehan. [*cont.*]

Background	The Templars apparently acquired their property here in the third quarter of the thirteenth century: Wood, p. 368; G&H, p. 330.
After the trial	Apparently this house did not pass to the Hospitallers: G&H, pp. 330–1. Sligo passed to the *fratres Cruciferi* (Augustinian Hospitallers who wore a cross on their habits) of Rindown: see G&H, pp. 215–16.
Today	The medieval commandery is now a ruin in the grounds of a modern hotel.

Name	South Witham, Lincolnshire
Location	In south Lincolnshire near the NE Leicestershire border, this house was built on marginal land 1 mile to the W of the Roman road of Ermine Street (the modern A1).
Nearby religious houses	South Witham stood 11 miles ENE of the house of the Order of St Lazarus at Burton Lazars, and 9 miles S of the important market town of Grantham which had two hospices, a house of Franciscans and a college of secular canons.
Background	Granted by King Stephen, Matilda and their son Eustace: K&H, p. 296; see also *VCH, Lincs.*, vol. 2, p. 212 and Philip Mayes, *Excavations at a Templar Preceptory: South Witham, Lincolnshire 1965–67* (Leeds, 2002).
After the trial	In 1338 it was wasteland, leased out to Lord Richard de Ty for his lifetime at a rent of 40 marks per year: L&K, p. 160. The name of the site is given as 'Suth Wyme'.
Today	There are no visible remains. The site was excavated in 1965–7 and the excavation published in Mayes, *Excavations*, in 2002.

Name	Sowerby (Temple Sowerby), Cumbria
Location	In the parish of Kirkby Thore, formerly in Westmorland. Sited just E of the Roman road that ran from Carlisle to Penrith, Brough and across the Pennine Hills to meet Dere Street at a junction now called Scotch Corner. In the medieval period this was a major route between Scotland and England; it is now the main A66 trunk road.
Nearby religious houses	Temple Sowerby stood approx. 6 miles ESE from the town of Penrith, where there was a house of Augustinian friars, and 7 miles NW from Appleby, where there was a house of Carmelite friars and a hospice.
Background	The commandery was not held in 1185 and so is not in the 1185 list of Templar holdings in England edited by Lees, and hence is overlooked by Gooder and Lord. According to the National Trust, the first record of Templar ownership dates from 1228. [*cont.*]

After the trial	Robert de Clifford held the house after the dissolution of the Templars. On his death in 1314 Temple Sowerby was his possession, 'held as escheat': *Calendar of Inquisitions post Mortem preserved in the Public Record Office, prepared under the superintendence of the Deputy Keeper of the Rolls*, vol. 5, *Edward II* (London, 1908), p. 301. In 1323 the Hospitallers were given formal ownership. Sowerby does not appear in the 1338 return to Rhodes, perhaps because it had been destroyed in the Scottish Wars, but possibly because it was still actually under the control of Robert de Clifford, who in 1344 was granting land at Temple Sowerby to three men: *CPR, 1343–1345*, p. 189. According to the National Trust, the Hospital held the house at the Dissolution.
Today	The modern Acorn Bank house, owned by the National Trust, incorporates some sixteenth-century Hospitaller buildings, but nothing remains of the Templar commandery.

Name	Strood (Temple Strood), Kent
Location	Approx. 2 miles NW of the cathedral city of Rochester. Strood lies on the Roman road from Dover to London (now the A2 trunk road).
Nearby religious houses	There were also at least two hospices in Strood.
Background	See S.E. Rigold, *Temple Manor: Strood, Rochester, Kent* (London, 1990). It may have acted as lodging for Templars travelling between London and Dover: ibid., p. 11; it may also have lodged other travellers.
After the trial	See under Denney. In Jan. 1338 the king confirmed that Brother Philip de Thame, prior of the Hospital in England, had leased Temple Strood to the countess of Pembroke for her lifetime only, at an annual rent of £45: *CPR, 1334–1338*, p. 571. In April 1339 the king made this a formal grant of the manor in fee with various rights and liberties, in compensation for the countess having looked after his daughter, Joan of Woodstock: *CPR, 1340–1343*, p. 461. After various disputes over the terms of the grant, the king allowed her to give Strood to any religious house she pleased: Rigold, *Temple Manor*, p. 13. Mary of St Pol donated Strood to the nunnery she had founded in the former Templar house of Denney in Cambridgeshire.
Today	The surviving hall belongs to English Heritage.

Name	Sutton, Essex
Location	Sutton is a village in SE Essex, a mile SSE of Rochford, next to the estuary of the River Roach. It lies a short distance N of Southend on Sea, to the E of the modern London Southend airport.
Nearby religious houses	The Cluniac house at Prittlewell lay around ½ mile SSE of Temple Farm at Sutton. [*cont.*]

Background	18½ acres were given to the Templars at Sutton by Constance Partridge in around 1245; the Templars went on to buy further land in this area: Gervers, *Cartulary of the Knights of St John of Jerusalem in England: Prima Camera*, pp. xliv–xlvi. See also Lord, p. 55.
After the trial	Little Sutton manor was leased out to William of Langford by the royal custodians: Gervers, *Cartulary: Prima Camera*, p. xlvi and note 69. After 1312 legal title to the lands passed to the Hospitallers, but in 1331 the Hospitallers confirmed William's tenure (ibid.), and in 1338 Sutton was still leased out to him, now rent free: L&K, p. 170. In 1338 the Hospitallers had a small chapel here: L&K, p. 170. After the dissolution, the estate was sold to one George Harper: Gervers, *Cartulary: Secunda Camera*, pp. xxv, xxviii note 19; idem, *Cartulary: Prima Camera*, p. xlvi and notes 69, 70.
Today	Apparently nothing remains of the medieval buildings. Sutton Hall on Sutton Road dates from the fourteenth century; the church of All Saints dates from the early seventeenth but includes some twelfth, thirteenth and fourteenth to sixteenth century material: see Pevsner, *Essex*, 2nd edn, revised by Enid Radcliffe (1965), p. 377. To the S of these, Temple Farm is a group of modern buildings, now forming a small industrial estate.

Name	Thornton (Middle Thornton, Temple Thornton), Northumberland
Location	In the Wansbeck valley, W of Morpeth on the S side of the modern B6343, 1 mile E of the village of Hartburn, on the W side of Meldon Park. A Roman road now called the 'Devil's Causeway' passes a little to the W of Hartburn, a mile W of Temple Thornton. See John Hodgson, *A History of Northumberland in Three Parts* (Newcastle upon Tyne, 1827), part 2, vol. 1, p. 311.
Nearby religious houses	There was a Cistercian house about 6 miles E at Newminster. The Templars had no other commanderies in Northumberland, while the Hospitallers had only Chibburn, at Widdrington village 13 miles ENE.
Back-ground	Thornton was given to the Order by William de Lisle before 1205: Hodgson, *History of Northumberland*, part 2, vol. 1, p. 311; K&H, p. 296; see also Lord, pp. 89–92, who emphasizes its vulnerability to Scottish attack.
After the trial	Hodgson, *History of Northumberland*, part 2, vol. 1, p. 311, noted that Temple Thornton was granted to John de Kingston in 1312. In 1338 it was reported that the house was pulled down after the dissolution of the Templars and the goods carried away by the lords of the fees where it stood, but Brother Leonard of Tibertis, late prior, had rebuilt it. The land used to be worth 6*d.* an acre, but because of the war it was now worth scarcely 3*d.*, and currently there was no revenue because of the Scottish war: L&K, pp. 133–4.
Today	A new house was built at Temple Thornton in 1694, and rebuilt in the ninteenth century: Pevsner, with John Grundy, Grace McCombie *et al.*, *Northumberland* (1992), p. 305. It is still a working farm.

Name	Upleadon (Bosbury), Herefordshire
Location	Now Temple Court, on the W bank of the River Leadon just outside the village of Bosbury in E Herefordshire; on the road N from Ledbury (now the B4220).
Nearby religious houses	A house of the bishop of Hereford is in Bosbury, just across the River Leadon, which at this point is little more than a stream. Nearby Ledbury Minster was an important religious site; there was also a hospice in the town.
Background	Founded by William Marshal, earl of Pembroke, in 1217–19: K&H, pp. 292–3. See also Rees, *A History of the Order of St John of Jerusalem in Wales*, pp. 55–6.
After the trial	The house passed to the Hospital on the dissolution of the Templars. One Hospitaller brother, the commander, lived there in 1338: L&K, p. 196. The original donor of the house apparently stipulated that certain charitable services were to be offered by the Templars, which were not maintained by the Hospitallers. Simon Phillips has noted that in the 1420s this led to the property being taken into the king's hands while the Order's obligations were investigated: Simon Phillips, 'The Role of the Prior of St John in Late Medieval England, c. 1300–1540', unpublished Ph.D thesis, University College Winchester, April 2005, pp. 13, 37, citing *CCR, 1422–1429*, p. 244.
Today	The modern house at Temple Court has an eighteenth-century frontage: Pevsner, *Herefordshire* (1963), p. 80. The stone north wing may be medieval, but there is no definite evidence of this; the rest was rebuilt in the eighteenth century, although it may preserve some seventeenth-century work: *Royal Commission on Historical Monuments (England): an Inventory of Historical Monuments in Herefordshire*, vol. 2, *East* (London, 1932; repr. 1977), p. 19. Temple Court is private property, but a public footpath runs through the site.

Name	Waterford, Co. Waterford, Ireland
Location	According to Wood, p. 370, the Templars possessed mills in the city of Waterford, a small marsh, an island and a house. In the county of Waterford they had small houses at Bewley, on the floodplain on the E bank of the Finisk River, and at Rincrew at the east end of a ridge overlooking the Blackwater river. They also had larger houses at Crooke and at Kilbarry: G&H, pp. 329–30.
Nearby religious houses	All the major religious Orders had houses in the city of Waterford: see the entry under Kilcloggan.
Background	The Templars' property at Crooke and Kilbarry was given to them by King Henry II of England before 1180: G&H, pp. 329–30. The dates of the other acquisitions are uncertain. [*cont.*]

After the trial	Apparently, neither Bewley nor Rincrew passed to the Hospitallers: G&H, pp. 329, 330. In 1348 the Hospitaller brother William de Fyncham was commander of both Crooke and Kilbarry; in 1368 Richard Walsh, Hospitaller commander of Kilbarry, was killed in battle fighting for the king against the Poers and O'Hedriscols; after this no more Hospitaller commanders appear in the records for these properties and apparently the Hospitallers leased both estates out to tenants. In 1541, at the Dissolution, both were being rented by William Wyse: ibid., p. 336.
Today	For the archaeological remains at Bewley, see Michael Moore, *Archaeological Inventory of County Waterford* (Dublin, 1999), p. 168, no. 1329 (enclosure and east gable of church); for Rincrew, see ibid., p. 188, no. 1425; for Crooke, see ibid., p. 171, nos 1341 and 1605 (ruined medieval church with tower house built in seventeenth century); for Kilbarry, see ibid., pp. 176–7, no. 1365 (ruined church and attached buildings).

Name	Westerdale, Yorkshire (North Riding)
Location	At the top of the Esk valley on the northern side of the North Yorkshire Moors.
Nearby religious houses	A house of Cistercian nuns 3 miles NW at Baysdale; the Augustinian house at Guisborough was 10 miles N across the hills. To the S, on the other side of the moors, there was a house of Cistercian nuns in Rosedale. It was a journey of 23 miles SW across the moors to the nearest Templar house at Foulbridge, and 26 miles to Cowton, N into the Tees valley and then W up the valley.
Background	Given to the Order by Guy de Bovingcourt and confirmed by King John in 1203: K&H, p. 296. There is a brief notice of this commandery in *VCH, Yorks*, vol. 3, ed. Page, p. 260, and in Burton, 'Knights Templar in Yorkshire', p. 38. See also Martin, 'The Templars in Yorkshire', pp. 367, 368, 374, 375, 383; *Kirkby's Inquest*, p. 125.
After the trial	Guy Beauchamp, earl of Warwick, took possession of the house (TNA:PRO SC1/36/117); on his death in August 1315 it was recorded as being in his possession, held in chief from the king. John of Eure, former sheriff of York, gave evidence that in fact it had belonged to the Templars, who held it from him as part of his barony of Stokesley: *Calendar of Inquisitions post Mortem preserved in the Public Record Office*, vol. 5, *Edward II* (London, 1908), pp. 406, 411, 412. After the king's order in 1323 to restore all the former Templar lands to the Hospitallers, the constable of Barnard's Castle wrote to the chancellor that Westerdale was held by the dowager countess of Warwick (Alice, who had since married William de la Zouch), and that he could therefore not hand it over: TNA:PRO SC1/36/117. The manor of Westerdale did eventually pass to the Hospitallers, and was recorded in their 1338 report as a messuage in the care of a bailiff with revenues from 'Beford, Cysterfield and Dancaster', supporting a chaplain: L&K, p. 142. [*cont.*]

Today	The commandery may have been on the site of Town Farm in the centre of the village; this farm is set back from the main north–south road and not actually visible from the street. Apparently no medieval Templar buildings survive. The village church, dedicated to Christ, was fully restored in 1838 and again in 1875: Pevsner, *Yorkshire: the North Riding*, pp. 383–4. It is now usually kept locked. Hunter's Bridge was built in the Middle Ages over the River Esk at Westerdale to carry the heavy north–south traffic that crossed the moors, and restored in 1874: *Old Pannier Tracks and Other Moorland Features* (Helmsley: North Yorkshire Moors National Park, no date), p. 20. Nikolaus Pevsner notes a suggestion that the original bridge was built in the thirteenth century: Pevsner, *Yorkshire: the North Riding*, p. 384. The bridge is no longer used; modern traffic has to cross a ford.

Name	Wetherby, Yorkshire (West Riding)
Location	A town at the mouth of Wharfedale, 13 miles WSW of York, on the Roman road Dere Street (now the route of the A1). A bridge was built across the River Wharfe here in the thirteenth century. The exact position of the Templars' house here is apparently uncertain.
Nearby religious houses	The Cistercian nuns at Sithingthwaite, 5 miles ENE, the Templars' house at Ribston, 5 miles NNW, and the Augustinian canons at Healaugh, 6 miles ESE.
Background	Wetherby was given to the Templars by Robert de Ros, who also gave them Ribston: Lord, p. 86. Martin, 'The Templars in Yorkshire', p. 370, states that it was given by William de Denby. See also ibid., pp. 368, 371, 376, 381; *Kirkby's Inquest*, p. 204 and note e; Burton, 'Knights Templar in Yorkshire', p. 38.
After the trial	Wetherby passed to the Hospitallers. In 1338 this house was still being administered with Ribston, with which it shared three brothers, and was recorded giving hospitality to travellers: L&K 1388, p. 137.
Today	Apparently nothing remains of the former Templar and Hospitaller property here.

Name	Whitley, Yorkshire (West Riding)
Location	S of the River Aire, on the Selby–Doncaster road (now the A19). The site of the Templar house was probably the moated site at Whitley Thorpe, 1 mile S of the modern M62.
Nearby religious houses	The Templars' commandery of Temple Hirst is 4 miles NE, and Faxfleet lies 20 miles to the ENE; these could easily be reached by water down the River Aire. The Templars' land at Kellington, which was associated with Temple Hirst, lay just N of Whitley. See Hirst for other religious houses in the vicinity. [*cont.*]

Background	Whitley was held by the Templars by 1248: *VCH, York*, vol. 3, p. 260; K&H, p. 296; see also Burton, 'Knights Templar in Yorkshire', p. 38. Martin, 'The Templars in Yorkshire', pp. 369, 380, stated that it was originally given by Roger de Mowbray, but later historians disagree. See also on this house, ibid., pp. 367, 372, 373, 377. The fact that it was taken over by John de Mowbray on the dissolution of the Templars indicates that Robert de Mowbray was the original donor.
After the trial	John de Mowbray took over Whitley. After his execution in 1322 because of his support for Earl Thomas of Lancaster, the king granted Whitley to one Thomas Brown. When it was realised that Whitley was in fact a former Templar property the estate was given up to the Hospitallers, who had received it by 1 July 1325: *CPR, Edward II, A.D. 1324–1327*, p. 134. In 1338 there were no Hospitaller brothers at 'Wythelee' and the farm was let out to tenants-at-will for 20 marks per year: L&K, p. 139.
Today	Nothing remains of the commandery. There is a road named Templar Close just south of the Aire and Calder Canal where it passes below the modern A19 road, opposite Whitley Bridge station, but the most probable site of the Templars' house is the moated site at Whitley Thorpe: Le Patourel, *The Moated Sites of Yorkshire*, p. 129.

Name	Wilbraham, Cambridgeshire
Location	At Great Wilbraham, which lies 6 miles E of Cambridge; Temple Wilbraham stands a little to the NE of the village.
Nearby religious houses	Augustinian houses at Barnwell to the W and Anglesey to the N; the Templar house of Denney was 8 miles NNE and Duxford 9 miles SSW.
Background	Given to the Templars with Denney in around 1170: K&H, p. 296; *VCH, Cambridge*, vol. 2, ed. L.F. Salzman (1948), p. 263; *VCH, Cambridge*, vol. 10, ed. A.F. Wareham and A.P.M. Wright (London, 2002), pp. 306–8, 311–15; Lord, p. 67.
After the trial	The house was transferred directly to the Hospital of St John on the dissolution of the Templars. In 1338 Wilbraham was catering for a large number of horses for travellers, and there were two brothers in residence – a 'custodian' chaplain and a sergeant: L&K, p. 164.
Today	The site of the commandery lies to the NE of the village in an area called Wilbraham Temple. Although one of the outbuildings includes the solar wing of a fifteenth-century manor house built by the Hospitallers, the bulk of the buildings are late eighteenth century or early nineteenth century. The church (dedicated to St Nicholas) was appropriated to the Templars and passed to the Hospitallers: L&K, p. 163; Pevsner, *Cambridgeshire*, p. 319; *VCH, Cambridge*, vol. 10, pp. 306–8.

Name	Willoughton, Lincolnshire
Location	North Lincolnshire, 2 miles W of the Roman road Ermine Street (see Lord, p. 79), and 2 miles N of the modern A631 (the road from Gainsborough to Market Rasen). The village is 7 miles ENE of Gainsborough and 18 miles S of Scunthorpe. The commandery was on the west side of the village.
Nearby religious houses	The Cistercian house of Axholme lay 10 miles NW; the Gilbertine house of Tunstall was 10 miles NE; the Cistercian nuns of Heynings lived 10 miles SW. There was a hospice at 'Spital in the Street' 5 miles SE on Ermine Street. Temple Belwood lay 13 miles NE; Faxfleet 21 miles NNE.
Background	Founded by Roger de Builli or Buslei in the reign of King Stephen: K&H, p. 296; see also VCH Lincs., vol. 2, pp. 210–11. Willoughton lies in the Lincolnshire Wolds, which was a relatively uninhabited and underdeveloped area in the twelfth century. Local landowners gave the Cistercians and Templars property here because it was cheap to give and these orders could help to develop the area. They could also provide lodging – in 1338 the Hospitallers stated that Willoughton gave hospitality to travellers: L&K, p. 149.
After the trial	John de Mowbray took over Willoughton after the dissolution of the Templars. After his execution in 1322 because of his involvement in the earl of Lancaster's rebellion, the king handed Willoughton to the Hospitallers: CCR, 1323–1327, pp. 108–9. In 1338 there were two brothers in residence at Willoughton and three corrodarians: L&K, p. 151.
Today	The site of the commandery lies to the W of the village, between Templefield road and Northfield lane, and S of the moat on the S side of Northfield Lane. On the OS map of 1891 it was labelled 'Temple Garth'. Nothing remains of the Templars' buildings, but there are the remains of fishponds in the fields S of the modern house.

Name	York, Yorkshire
Location	The mills on the River Foss, S of Clifford's tower in the centre of York.
Nearby religious houses	There were many religious houses of various Orders in York: see K&H, p. 565.
Back-ground	The Templars owned the castle mills at York (given by Roger de Mowbray: Lees, p. 132; Martin, 'The Templars in Yorkshire', p. 369; Lord, p. 81). The establishment formed a complete house, with a chapel, a hall (aula) and a kitchen (coquina): TNA:PRO E142/18 mem. 6; see also Martin, 'The Templars in Yorkshire', pp. 368, 382, and E.J. Martin, 'The Templars in Yorkshire', Yorkshire Archaeological Journal, 30 (1930–31), p. 155. By 1292 the commander of nearby Copmanthorpe was also custodian of the mills at York: 'Houses of Knights Templar', VCH, York, vol. 3, ed. William Page, pp. 256–60, section 68. [cont.]

After the trial	In 1314 the king noted that the chapel was still in his possession: *CPR, 1313–1317*, p. 173. In 1338 the Hospitallers recorded that the mills were worth 20 marks per year and were still in the king's hands: L&K, p. 212
Today	The Templars' mill no longer exists. A mill building which now stands near to the site of the medieval castle mills is the former Raindale mill, which used to stand 6 miles N of the town of Pickering on the North Yorkshire Moors, near to the modern Levisham railway station. It was reconstructed on its present site in the mid-1960s. This forms part of the York Castle museum and is accessible only through the museum.

Further Reading

This is a selection of published work relating to the subject. A complete list of references can be found in the notes.

Primary Sources

W.H. Blaauw, 'Sadelescombe and Shipley, the Preceptories of the Knights Templars in Sussex', *Sussex Archaeological Collections relating to the History and Antiquities of the County*, 9 (1857), pp. 227–74

Calendar of the Close Rolls preserved in the Public Record Office, prepared under the Superintendence of the Deputy Keeper of the Records, Edward II. AD 1307–1313 (London, 1892)

Calendar of the Patent Rolls preserved in the Public Record Office, prepared under the Superintendence of the Deputy Keeper of the Records, Edward III. AD 1307–1313 (London, 1894)

The Cartulary of the Knights of St. John of Jerusalem in England. Secunda Camera: Essex, ed. Michael Gervers (Oxford, 1982)

The Cartulary of the Knights of St. John of Jerusalem in England, part 2. Prima Camera: Essex, ed. Michael Gervers (Oxford, 1996)

The Chronicle of Walter of Guisborough, previously edited as the Chronicle of Walter of Hemingford or Hemingburgh, ed. H. Rothwell, Camden Society 3rd series, 89 (London, 1957)

Continuatio Chronicarum Adæ Murimuth, ed. Edward Maunde Thompson, Rolls Series 93 (London, 1889)

Chronicon Galfridi le Baker de Swynebroke, ed. Edward Maunde Thompson (Oxford, 1889)

'Documents Relating to the Suppression of the Templars in Ireland', ed. G. MacNiocaill, *Analecta hibernica*, 24 (1967), pp. 183–226

Flores Historiarum, ed. Henry Richards Luard, Rolls Series 95 (London, 1890), vol. 3

Foedera, conventiones, literæ, et cujuscunque generis acta publica, ed. Thomas Rymer, revised
by Robert Sanderson, Adam Clarke and Frederic Holbrooke, 4 vols in 7 (London,
1816–69), vol. 2, part 1 (1307–27)
The Trial of the Templars in the British Isles, 1308–1311, ed. Helen J. Nicholson, 2 vols
(Aldershot, forthcoming)
Vita Edwardi Secundi, re-edited text with new introduction, new historical notes, and
revised translation based on that of N. Denholm-Young by Wendy R. Childs
(Oxford, 2005)

Secondary Sources

Malcolm Barber, *The Trial of the Templars*, 2nd edn (Cambridge, 2006)
Ian B. Cowan, P.H.R. Mackay and Alan Macquarrie, eds, *The Knights of St John of Jerusalem
in Scotland*, Scottish History Society, 4th ser. 19 (Edinburgh, 1983)
Alan J. Forey, 'Ex-Templars in England', *Journal of Ecclesiastical History*, 53 (2002), pp. 18–37.
Alan J. Forey, 'Desertions and Transfers from Military Orders (Twelfth to early-Fourteenth
Centuries)', *Traditio*, 60 (2005), pp. 143–200
Anne Gilmour-Bryson, 'The London Templar Trial Testimony: "Truth", Myth or Fable?'
in *A World Explored: Essays in Honour of Laurie Gardiner*, ed. Anne Gilmour-Bryson
(Melbourne Australia, 1993), pp. 44–61
Eileen Gooder, 'South Witham and the Templars. The Documentary Evidence', in
Excavations at a Templar Preceptory: South Witham, Lincolnshire, 1965–67, ed. Philip Mayes
(Leeds, 2002), pp. 80–95
Eileen Gooder, *Temple Balsall: The Warwickshire Preceptory of the Templars and their Fate*
(Chichester, 1995)
J.S. Hamilton, 'Apocalypse Not: Edward II and the Suppression of the Templars', *Medieval
Perspectives*, 12 (1997), pp. 90–100
Rosalind Hill, 'Fourpenny Retirement: The Yorkshire Templars in the Fourteenth
Century', in *The Church and Wealth: Papers read at the 1986 Summer Meeting and the 1987
Winter Meeting of the Ecclesiastical History Society*, ed. W.J. Sheils and Diana Wood, Studies
in Church History, 24 (Oxford, 1987), pp. 123–8
Agnes M. Leys, 'The Forfeiture of the Lands of the Templars in England', in *Oxford Essays
in Medieval History presented to Herbert Edward Salter* (Oxford, 1934), pp. 155–63
Evelyn Lord, *The Knights Templar in Britain* (Harlow, 2002)
Thomas W. Parker, *The Knights Templars in England* (Tucson, 1963)
Clarence Perkins, 'The Trial of the Knights Templars in England', *English Historical Review*,
24 (1909), pp. 432–47
P.M. Ryan, 'Cressing Temple: its History from Documentary Sources', in *Cressing
Temple: A Templar and Hospitaller Manor in Essex*, ed. D.D. Andrews (Chelmsford, 1993),
pp. 11–24
Herbert Wood, 'The Templars in Ireland', *Proceedings of the Royal Irish Academy*, section C,
25 (1906), pp. 363–75

Index

Persons with the same Christian name are listed in alphabetical order of surname. As the spelling of names varies widely in the manuscripts, I have included variants here. Templars who appear only in Appendix 1 are not listed here. The following abbreviations are used:

c   commander
cy commandery
gc grand commander
T   Templar